Appropriate development for basic needs

Appropriate development for basic needs

Proceedings of the conference on Appropriate development for survival - the contribution of technology, organized by the Institution of Civil Engineers and held in London on 9-11 October 1990

Edited by D. P. Maguire

Thomas Telford, London

Conference organized by the Institution of Civil Engineers and co-sponsored by the British Council, International Labour Organisation and Overseas Development Administration

Organizing Committee

D. P. Maguire, Consultant, *Chairman*

A. D. Austen, Chief Executive, Construction and Advisory Training Services Ltd

R. D. Bell, Consultant

H. Byrne, Social Planning Consultant, WS Atkins Group Consultants

Brigadier J. N. S. Drake

Dr G. Edmonds, Head, Infrastructure Programmes and Engineering, International Labour Office

F. Grover, Principal, Frederick Grover & Associates

P. M. Guthrie, Partner, Scott Wilson & Kirkpatrick

C. E. Hood

T. Pike, Chief Engineering Advisor, Overseas Development Administration

Dr R. E. Sowden, Deputy Head, Department of Science and Technology, The British Council

First published 1991

British Library Cataloguing in Publication Data
   Appropriate development for basic needs
     I. Maguire, D. P.
     338.9172

ISBN 0 7277 1618 2

© The Institution of Civil Engineers, 1990, 1991, unless otherwise stated.

All rights, including translation, reserved. Except for fair copying, no part of this publication may be reproduced, stored in a retrieval system or transmitted in any form or by any means electronic, mechanical, photocopying, recording or otherwise, without the prior written permission of the Publications Manager, Publications Division, Thomas Telford Ltd, Thomas Telford House, 1 Heron Quay, London E14 9XF.

Papers or other contributions and the statements made or the opinions expressed therein are published on the understanding that the author of the contribution is solely responsible for the opinions expressed in it and that its publication does not necessarily imply that such statements and/or opinions are or reflect the views or opinions of the ICE Council or ICE Committees.

Published on behalf of the Institution of Civil Engineers by Thomas Telford Ltd, Thomas Telford House, 1 Heron Quay, London E14 9XF.

Printed in England by Redwood Press Limited, Melksham, Wiltshire

Contents

Welcoming address. SIR ALAN MUIR WOOD   1

Keynote address. SIR CRISPIN TICKELL   3

How appropriate is development?

1. Appropriate development: a change in approach. M. W. THRING   9
2. How appropriate is development? J. B. WILMSHURST   21
3. Development and implementation of innovation in irrigation.
   R. LENTON   29
4. Practical implementation - value for money. A. C. REED   43

Discussion   57

Constraints and opportunities

5. Appropriate technological development for sustainable
   conservation and exploitation of natural resources in the
   SADCC region of Africa. M. L. KYOMO and C. L. KESWANI   65
6. The social appropriation of technology. A. REW   85
7. The engineer's contribution. P. A. GREEN   95
8. Education and training - communication. J. C. BLACKWELL   111

Discussion   119

Implementation

9. Food: survival and appropriate development. S. MAXWELL   123
10. Energy consumption and generation. J. D. L. HARRISON   139
11. Water and sanitation. J. PICKFORD   145
12. Infrastructure. MARGARET J. HERATY   161
13. Management and planning. J. HENNESSY   173
14. Technology choice. G. A. EDMONDS   185

15. Maintenance. R. ROBINSON	203
16. Education and training - issues and roles. J. E. THEAKER	219
Discussion	223

Workshop on energy

Fossil fuel energy and the survival of mankind. P. GARRATT	229
Low-wattage electric cookers - making the most of micro-hydro power. L. J. MacKAY	233
Fossil fuels, air pollution and sustainable development issues and priorities. P. J. G. PEARSON	237
Energy in the developing world. D. D. A. PIESOLD	241
Small hydro systems using pump impellers as turbines and local materials for casings and bearings. T. SANCHEZ	245
Rehabilitation of estate hydro schemes in Sri Lanka. R. M. YOUNG	249
Summary of discussion. R. E. HOLLAND	253

Workshop on water, sanitation and food

Observations on the plight of urban water supply in Nigeria. J. T. ARMSTRONG	257
Environmental monitoring and institutional roles in post-disaster development. J. BARTRAM, M. SUAREZ, E. QUIROGA and G. GALVIS	265
Appropriate vehicles for municipal services in developing countries. M. COFFEY	269
Appropriate development: the contribution of rainwater catchment systems technology. J. E. GOULD	273
Participation in health for survival. D. M. B. JAGNE	277
Rural water supply borehole construction programmes in Africa. M. J. JONES	281
Community wastewater treatment systems using indigenous aquatic/marginal plants. P. C. LAWRENCE, J. BUTLER and U. BURKA	287
Use of seeds of *Moringa oleifera* and solar radiation for drinking water purification in West Africa. O. ODEYEMI	291
Importance of software aspects involved in technology transfer. O. PRAKASH	295
Rural water supply: infrastructure development. S. E. SUTTON and J. S. SUTTON	299
Financial principles and methods - the WHO handbook. C. TIMBRELL	303

The role of education and training in developing countries self-help water supply and sanitation, with particular reference to Sierra Leone. G. WHITESIDE	307
Water quality: the Paqualab concept. N. WORRILL	311
Summary of discussion. I. A. RICHARDSON and H. M. BYRNE	315

Workshop on infrastructure

Technology, development and investment appraisal methods. G. K. BAMBRAH	319
Services for shelter. R. FRANCEYS and A. COTTON	323
Low density foundation systems for human resettlement programmes. T. H. HANNA	327
Economic transportation influenced by development and environmental issues. A. G. H. McCLINTOCK	331
The apparent duality of infrastructure design strategies. K. G. SMITH	335
The human infrastructure requirements of technicians. E. G. SNAPE	339
The application of appropriate technology for rural development in Thailand. M. SRINARAWAT and K. J. MILLBAND	343
Summary of discussion. G. A. EDMONDS	347
Discussion on workshop summaries	351
Open forum	355
Closing address. R. SEVERN	359

Welcoming address

SIR ALAN MUIR WOOD, Consultant, Sir William Halcrow & Partners

My interest in appropriate development and the concept of sustainability extends over many years. My Presidential Address to the Institution of Civil Engineers in 1977 touched on this theme and subsequently I suggested the formation of the Appropriate Development Forum to bring together all those involved in development: engineers, scientists, economists, social scientists and those working in firms, universities, government and agencies. My main message is to encourage each person to appreciate what others have to contribute. Development requires the successful crossing of many disciplines and it is far too easy to dismiss those aspects one does not understand as unimportant. Francis Bacon expressed this failing more elegantly: 'Some, whatsoever is beyond their reach, will seem to despise or make light of it as impertinent or curious; and so would have their ignorance seem judgment'.

Apart from the direct benefit of participating in such a conference, equally important is the demonstration that issues of survival and sustainability are perceived as important to our professions. Politicians respond only to cataclysmic events, such as may be presented by the greenhouse effect, in environmental and social issues, but the greater the lead by those in positions of influence the lesser the degree of crisis required to provoke action.

The Gulf War released much frustration caused primarily by social and economic inequality. This event should be taken as a warning signal and, in order to leave a world safe for posterity, the fundamental issues must be addressed as the highest priority. I hope our motivation combines enlightened self-interest with the philanthropy of John Donne: 'No man is an island, entire of itself. Any man's death diminishes me because I am involved in mankind. And therefore never send to know for whom the bell tolls; it tolls for thee'. A hedonistic society dominated by market forces lacks the necessary vision to tackle such problems; we need to find mechanisms and means to enhance perceptions. As ever, example is worth so much more than precept.

Keynote address

SIR CRISPIN TICKELL, Warden, Green College, Oxford

The French physicist Lavoisier, who lost his head in the French Revolution, once said 'Man's mind is creased into a way of looking at things.' We are now at one of those moments in politics, thinking and conduct when we have to iron out previous creases and maybe put in some new ones. In short we have to think differently from the way we did before. Let me start with the title of this conference 'Appropriate development for survival'.

DEVELOPMENT
I had a friend who was a director of a property company in Spain. She was once asked by a new director, 'What is the purpose of this company?' She replied with excessive honesty, 'To muck up the coastline'. Unfortunately the new director's command of English and English hypocrisy was imperfect. When asked the same question at a press conference later that day, he replied, 'Our purpose is to muck up the coastline.' That is what a lot of people understood by development: putting up bricks and mortar and destroying natural beauty to get a good short-term market result.

I want to suggest what development should mean and what it should not mean. What it should mean is beneficent change by which people use the resources which are available to them to improve their circumstances. They should act in such a fashion that they preserve and even enlarge the capital stock which they can pass down to future generations. It is important that in doing so they preserve cultural continuity so that the future grows out of the past, and is not a shallow seedling without roots.

What development should not mean is indiscriminate industrialization where indigenous resources do not permit it on a sustainable basis. When I was Permanent Secretary of the Overseas Development Administration I saw many examples of projects which sounded good until one looked for the resources necessary to sustain them. People wanted industrialization because they rightly saw it as a source of wealth; but industrialization or any kind of development needs raw materials, and if such materials or special skills

KEYNOTE ADDRESS

are not available, they have to come from somewhere else, thereby creating dependence on outside suppliers. An example is a recent huge development project in Ethiopia. The idea was to move people down from the overpopulated mountains and plant them in the plains. Unfortunately agriculture in the lowland plains turned out to be dependent on imported fertilizer. The project was disappointing for other reasons. But even if it had been successful, it would have condemned those concerned to permanent dependence on high-cost imports which would have made the project uncompetitive and unsustainable.

Projects of this or any other kind should aim for maximum exploitation of natural resources: they should go for the optimum exploitation of such resources, particularly when they are non-renewable. Exploitation should not mean destruction of the natural resource base. This often happens if dams are built in the wrong places or if forest is levelled for cattle ranching. Often the price is paid by the next generation rather than the one that derives the short-term benefit.

I am dubious about the value of the distinction some people make between developed countries and developing countries, or between north and south, or between the First and Third Worlds. The important difference is between those who have learnt the tricks of industrialization and have the resources to maintain it, and those who have not. It is no coincidence that the industrial countries are the ones which usually have the resources: they have the water and the resources, and they have acquired the skills with which to make the most of them. The first requirement for development is to make creative use of what is available. Successful agriculture is the indispensable base. We sometimes forget that the industrial revolution which began in the UK about 250 years ago was preceded by an agricultural revolution which sustained the greatly increasing population and made possible what followed.

APPROPRIATE

Appropriate means the right kind of development. I cannot exaggerate the importance of agriculture. That means not just food production but also sensible land use. Engineers know this better than most. I often think that ministries of agriculture and forestry commissions should be abolished and that each country should have a single ministry of land use to work out land policy as a whole.

Appropriate development is particularly important in the field of engineering. There again people have to make the most of what they already have and minimize their dependence on imported supplies, especially of fossil fuel. The most unused - and wasted - resource is sunlight. All energy comes from the sun, whether it be fossil fuel which is stored sunlight, or nuclear fuel which derives from and is similar to the energy which pours out of the sun. The sun is no more than a sustained hydrogen bomb explosion. Yet little of this sunlight is used by those who have most of it.

I was in Jordan recently. Some people there talked about building a nuclear power station in the Gulf of Aqaba. I said I thought they were crazy. They had the biggest resource ever above them. Its exploitation did not require cripplingly expensive imports, and they had space enough for any of the new solar technologies. Solar power stations are coming on stream in several parts of the world. There will soon be up to 1000 MW generated in the USA by these means, and there is already a solar power station in the Pyrenees feeding energy into the French national grid.

Poor countries should also think about small-scale energy generation. Micro-hydro projects make use of limited water supplies with simple turbines, sometimes made of wood. The Intermediate Technology Development Group has done a lot of work on the problem. For many such countries distribution of energy is more of a problem than generation. Help from outside can help countries make best use of what they have got.

Likewise in industry. Industrial development among other forms of economic activity should follow the same principles. A major difficulty is that countries with limited resources and knowledge of technology are often capable of producing only the same relatively unsophisticated goods. So joining together, as in the Andean or Central American common markets, does not necessarily help. What is important is that industrial countries should offer markets for such goods, untrammelled by tariffs or quotas, to enable other countries to earn the foreign exchange they need to trade with the rest of the world. This is very much in the interest of the industrial countries themselves. Access to industrial country markets is usually more important than aid programmes. Too often aid has gone to waste in lining the pockets of the local rich or in financing the white elephants whose fly-blown relics in funny places are a monument to misapplied good intentions.

Of what then should aid consist? When in charge of the aid programme, I used to travel round the world finding not only misapplication of good intentions but also failure to communicate. Aid can have marvellously catalytic effects for good. But aid which supplies machinery without proper technical support, or technical support without fundamental training in the wider aspects of science and technology, cannot be of more than short-term value, and is often a major disappointment to donor and recipient alike. For example, recipients must be enabled to invent their own solutions to things and given the means to develop responses to local problems.

Of course good advice has been given. But bad advice has also been given. Efforts to turn nomads into pastoralists have usually failed, often for environmental reasons. We are also guilty from time to time of wanton interference in local

KEYNOTE ADDRESS

traditions. For example, experts went to Ethiopia and told people that they should switch from the local cereal teff to maize or wheat. Teff may be less nutritious, but it is widely available, its cultivation is appropriate to the environment of the highlands, and its consumption forms part of a culture which goes back thousands of years. The advice to go for plants of quite different character and requirements (in particular for water) was rightly rejected.

Then there has been the problem of ideology. I suppose that at least in the early days we remained the inheritors of colonial attitudes. But these were overtaken by market economics which is usually closer to indigenous traditions than the ideology labelled Communism. The failure of Communism is one of the most spectacular happenings of the past few years, and those countries which sought to apply it in the conditions of Africa, Asia and Latin America have nearly all rued the day. Meanwhile, immense damage has been done which will take a long time to repair.

Appropriate development is what is best adapted to the needs and resources of each place. Inappropriate development is wrong ideology, wrong technology, a wrong industrial base, wrong agriculture, and wrong - usually alien - thinking.

SURVIVAL

Our species is a part of life as a whole. It is one among myriads. There are about 20 million species of insect, and only about three thousand mammals. We are no more than one among the mammals. We see ourselves as the top species. We are certainly the top predators. But even we are an assemblage of species. For example, the mitochondria in every human cell began life as a parasite from outside. Just as our bodies are a meeting place of species, so we are at the meeting place of countless other forms of life on which we depend.

We have also an almost unique capacity for destruction. In Permian times over 200 million years ago, almost 90% of all living species were extinguished. At the end of Cretaceous times, when the dinosaurs went 65 million years ago, there was another extinction of species. In our own epoch, labelled Holocene, there have been extinctions on a comparable scale. They are continuing at an incredible rate, and we are unwittingly responsible. We are thereby doing damage to ourselves and subsequent generations for whom the natural world we know in its present form may not exist. Diminishing genetic resources are matched by the rise of new predators such as viruses and bacteria with which we are sometimes ill-equipped to cope. I hope that the world conference on environment and development in 1992 will take practical steps to protect the riches of our natural environment of and put the result into an international framework of agreement.

So far our species has celebrated its success by multiplying its numbers. When I was born in 1930 there were two billion human beings. Now there are about five billion. By 2020 there will probably be eight billion. This rise in the human population gravely affects the 30% of the world's surface which is land. Of that 30% only a relatively small proportion can be cultivated for crops; and of the cropland about one third is already subject to one degree or another of desertification. Land, sea and air are all registering the relentless pressures of human numbers. Engineers know there are limits to any tolerance. We do not know where those limits are, and we can scarcely experiment to find out.

OUR RESPONSIBILITIES

It is encouraging that the problems of the environment are more widely understood than ever before. The document produced by the Club of Rome in 1970 can be faulted in many respects, but it contributed positively to the work of the first United Nations conference on the environment in 1972 and the results which came from it. The conversion of informed opinion in industrial countries has steadily become more apparent. But for the rest of the world, struggling with poverty, concern about the environment was often seen as a luxury of the rich. Perhaps the turning point was the publication of the Brundtland Commission Report in 1987. In this report, compiled by people from all parts of the world, the main environmental problems were faced. In 1989 such organizations as the non-aligned Heads of State and Government and the Commonwealth Prime Ministers were as forthright in their pronouncements on the environment as were the participants in the Economics Summit of the main industrial countries. Even if some felt that as the industrial countries were responsible for the mess they should clear it up, nearly all recognized that a global problem needed global treatment. The test will come with the world conference on environment and development in 1992. Preparations for it have already brought out the difficulties. They can be overcome.

Management of environmental issues at the international level must be matched at the national level. If the industrial countries are to exert leadership in the world, they will have to give the example at home. In some public opinion is ahead of governments and in others government are ahead of public opinion. In Britain the 1989 White Paper on the environment is an important step forward: most important, it establishes the environmental dimension in each aspect of government and provides the means for co-ordinated action. Too often one ministry works to enlarge the road network with cars to drive on it, while another tries to conserve the countryside and sets targets for the reduction of carbon emissions. Somewhere priorities have to be chosen and maintained.

Nowhere is the need for co-ordination greater than in the USA where I have been living for the past few years. There the battle has just begun. However great the contribution of

KEYNOTE ADDRESS

American scientists to understanding of the problem, their work will continue to be frustrated if the administration continues to look the other way and to preside over a society which wastes more energy than any other country in the world.

Engineers have a vital role to play in putting together a national as well as international consensus. They understand better than anyone not just what should be done, but how it should be done. On them rest major responsibilities. As knowledge is the beginning of wisdom, this conference is a sign of the new thinking to which I drew attention at the beginning of this address.

1. Appropriate development: a change in approach

PROFESSOR M. W. THRING, ScD, FEng, FIMechE, FIEE, FInstP, FIChemE, FInstE, Chairman, Working Party on Engineering for the Developing Countries

---

Development is appropriate if it will enable our remote descendents to live in stable equilibrium with the environment. It must lead to Equilibrium Engineering which would enable all humanity permanently to live full lives.
High Technology is having many potentially disastrous consequences: pollution, genocidal weapons, exhaustion of scarce resources, traffic jams, accidents, unemployment and human stress. However it overlaps Equilibrium Engineering: for example in the provision of electric light from renewable energy sources.
In those parts of the world where there is still Primitive Engineering, population growth is likewise potentially disastrous, as deserts grow, forests disappear and people starve. Such areas could go straight to Equilibrium Engineering if the First World can unselfishly cooperate with development via Pilot Plants and with loans at the same rate of interest that served the development of the Industrial Revolution in Britain.

I. What Development is Appropriate?

If we want our descendents for many generations to have a satisfying life, then development is only appropriate if it takes us towards a situation in which all mankind lives in stable equilibrium with the environment. Engineering has already so shrunk the world that no country can hope to survive in isolation.

Stable equilibrium implies that all humans will have the opportunity to earn a living which gives themselves and their children the full possibility of finding self-fulfilment by their own efforts. Otherwise the problems of war, overpopulation and environmental destruction will leave nothing for our descendents.

Almost all development at present is towards High Technology which is taking us in the direction opposite to that of stable equilibrium: complex weapons, high speeds,

HOW APPROPRIATE IS DEVELOPMENT?

unemployment, exploitation, disappearance of crafts, pollution and reckless consumption of scarce raw materials.

I suggest that it is useful to give the name Equilibrium Engineering (EE) to the engineering developments that would enable mankind to live in this state of permanent equilibrium with the environment. In #4 I shall try to outline some of its characteristics.

It will be said that this is an impossible Utopia, and indeed it is. However it is certain that unless we face squarely the problem of the survival of our descendents we shall continue to go in the wrong direction. We shall continue to allow short term, local or national expediency to destroy the world.

The gut feeling of an individual that their life is worthwhile can be regarded as a measure of their Quality of Life. I have shown in 'The Engineer's Conscience' (1), how this is definitely related to their consumption of raw materials or standard of living by the curve of fig1. Too little consumption (starvation) or too much (extravagance) both reduce the Quality of Life below the maximum. There is an optimum consumption which is the best for life Quality

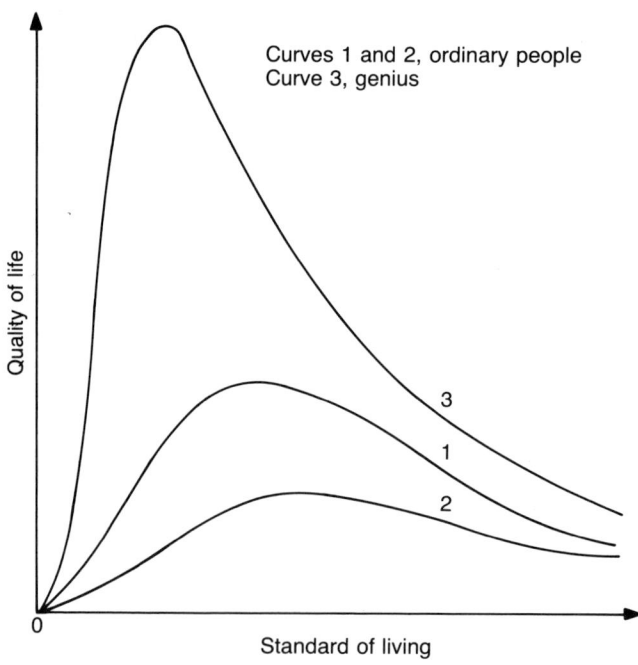

Fig. 1. The relationship between quality of life and standard of living for different people

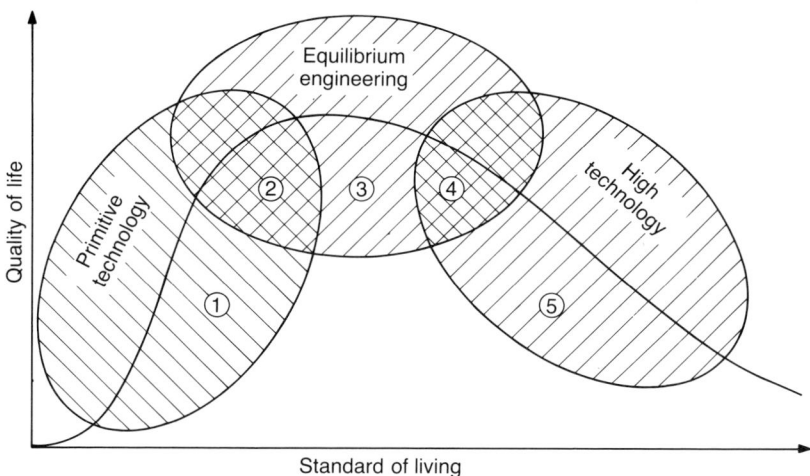

Fig. 2. Three kinds of engineering

just as there is of food for health Quality. Earning this optimum consumption and no more leaves us with enough energy to seek creative self-fulfilment.

EE corresponds to making this optimum consumption earnable by all; primitive engineering does not give such necessary things as good lighting, hygiene, sanitation, and does not enable enough food to be grown to provide a healthy diet to all in a crowded world. It also demands excessive labour. High technology leads to all the problems mentioned above. As shown in fig 2, EE overlaps primitive technology, for example in the skilled use of hand tools; it overlaps High Technology, for example in the provision of efficient electric lighting from renewable energy, robot brain surgery or high efficiency solid fuel locomotives.

II. High Technology.

High Technology is based on the clearly impossible idea of a perpetually rising standard of living, energy consumption, speed of movement, number of cars per person, kitchen gadgets and even executive toys!

This is having many disastrous consequences, some of which are described below.

Vast resources are spent on the branch of Engineering which is most repugnant to the human Conscience: the production of machines for killing people and destroying their homes.

HOW APPROPRIATE IS DEVELOPMENT?

As fast as new roads are built in Britain traffic expands and there are endless delays with enormous petrol consumption. In almost all the big towns of the world traffic grinds to a halt twice a day. Buses are useless as they are blocked totally in the traffic. If the shops move out to the perimeter with giant car parks, the centre of the town decays. In 1969 King-Hubbert (2) pointed out that petroleum production would peak early in the XXIst Century and taper off for another century. Vegetable oils cannot be grown in quantities which will allow our descendents to use liquid fuels on the scale used now in the First World.

While we can develop cars which give far more mpg, there will remain the problems of traffic jams and of pollution by noise, CO and unburnt hydrocarbons, CO_2, carcinogens and, until recently, lead. EE will certainly imply mainly public transport unimpeded by cars, with all long distance goods transport by efficient rail.

In the society of perpetual growth pollutants are regarded as innocent even long after there is clear evidence that they are damaging to health on a short or long term. This applies to artificially radioactive materials emitted or stored, and to many chemical poisons put into the air, land or water.

At last the public is becoming aware of three especially widespread pollutants, although in each case governments and vested interests are using delaying tactics: saying that more proof is necessary.

1). The Greenhouse Effect: the rising level of certain gases, especially CO_2 and CH_4, is causing the temperature of the air to rise and this in turn will cause a rise in sea-level, flooding many cities and low lying areas eg Bangladesh. In my view the total world consumption of fossil carbon must be reduced to less than 1/2 of the present figure, which is about 7000MTOE/a (Tons Oil Equivalent per annum) to reduce this effect. However in China the 1000M people use about 1 TC/ca (1.5 TC=1TOE) and they wish to double this figure, with considerable justification considering the use per capita in the first world. The need for EE which would give them all the benefits of the Industrial Revolution with 1/3 TOE/ca is therefore urgent!

In the first world we have been spoilt by cheap fuel and waste it in our homes, factories, offices as well as our cars. We use electricity for space and water heating -a crime against the Second Law of Thermodynamics!

2). The hole in the ozone layer, caused largely by the use of CFCs is becoming serious and is already causing skin cancers in Australia and USA. We have to develop alternative refrigeration cycles and avoid all emissions which destroy this protective layer.

3). Acid rain, caused by SOx and NOx from combustion, is killing whole forests. Here the cause is primarily our over-expanded use of electricity, produced in Gigawatt power stations. In England we use about 400 W/c and have installed capacity for about 1000W/c. (1 W/c equals 8.8 kWh/ca) In the USA they use 360 W/c of electricity in their homes alone, together with 1140 W/c as fuel. We know how to eliminate SOx and NOx but only on plants of 100MW scale.

High technology leads to terrible accidents: Chernobyl, Serveso, Bhopal, Flixborough, Sinking of car ferries, enormous oil spills and hundreds killed on roads every year.

Farming produces more than we need in the West by 'mining the soil´, mono-cropping of high yield varieties which are delicate and require much fertiliser (especially N fixed by burning fuel) and pesticides. Big tractors and combine harvesters are very heavy and expensive and 'pan the soil´. We spend more energy on, largely unnecessary, processing of foodstuffs than on growing them (3).

Where large dams have been installed to generate electricity they require costly distribution systems so that people must consume larger quantities of electricity than they can afford if the debt is to be repaid. In Egypt the flow of silt which fertilised the land for 5000 years is now filling up the reservoir. Dams often displace people and upset the whole hydrology of the region. They can also upset the whole economy of a country downstream.

On the perpetual growth economy if a machine is cheaper than a man, you sack the man. Much work is now going on to replace men in skilled assembly by robots. Thus as well as destroying craft skills High technology leads to rising unemployment.

III. Development in the Third World.

In the Third World some Governments have attempted to copy the High Technology of the First World: this leads not only to the disastrous results described above but also lands them with unpayable debts. When money was required for the development of the machines and power sources of the Industrial Revolution in Britain it could be borrowed at 2 1/2% interest. If we had had to borrow it at 15% we should never have had the Industrial Revolution and even at those low rates of interest several railway companies went bankrupt and had to sell their lines below cost.

HOW APPROPRIATE IS DEVELOPMENT?

Building skyscrapers with air conditioning, making their own steel when the world has manyfold excess capacity, setting up airlines, destroying forests, taking land from traditional family farming for large scale production of export crops (even drugs) are all actions for which their and our descendants will pay dearly.

Many of the problems of the Third World come from their population growth rate. Fortunately, it is an observed fact that when people can earn a decent standard of living, even after retirement, and can give their children an education which gives them the opportunity to develop their talents, they have smaller families. Thus an essential condition for the successful future of humanity is that during the XXIst Century these benefits come to all mankind.

The steady growth of deserts is largely due to the need of families for fuelwood, and this need must be filled on a renewable basis. Work on planting trees in the desert has started in many places eg Nigeria, this and other methods will have to restore the deserts to greenery.

Another major problem is that the young leave the rural areas to go into towns, where they live in far worse conditions than those they left, and rarely find paid work. They do this partly because they are attracted to the sophistication of the town and partly because they hope to earn a better standard of living. Only by providing these benefits in the rural areas will this problem be solved. Thus, for example, one electric light in each home, a TV in the communal hut and a refrigerator locker for every family must form part of EE.

The last major problem is that of nomads whose traditional way of life is becoming almost unsustainable, largely because of insufficient water to support increased numbers. Many organisations have done splendid work in installing wind pumps to irrigate oases, but these lead to problems which are not yet solved.

There are at least a dozen charitable organisations and University Depts in Britain and many more in other countries who have done sterling work on the development and installation of small scale equipment in particular areas. They are genuinely doing it to help the local people and not for the economic benefit of their own country: this is an essential prerequisite of success. They also study the needs, both known and unknown, of the people before installing the equipment, and try to interfere as little as possible with the traditions of the local people.

In some cases, however, it is clearly necessary gradually to educate them to see that these traditions are incompatible with a stable world: the tradition of treating women as inferior beings is an example.

In the work of the IMechE CEDC in a village in Tanzania it was found that three diesels which had been donated for pumping water and grinding maize were not working because there was no local maintenance system, and not a trace of technical understanding.

This work has convinced me that high level engineering coordination could help these organisations to spread their work much wider and follow it up with maintenance and education much more, and have closer relations with the local governments. A proposal to this end is given in App I.

IV. Equilibrium Engineering.

Let us make the hopeful assumption that the growth in the world's population finally levels off at 10,000M in the second half of the XXIst Century, because all people have an adequate standard of living (including old age pensions!) and of education. What machines and energy supply will be necessary to stabilize this condition?

Table I (4) is a calculation of the Minimum Energy Required for Decent Life.
Units kCE/ca (kg of coal equiv./person-year)
1 kCE(p)= 2.8×10^7 J or 7.8 kWh.
10 kCE(p)/a = 78 kWh/a = 8.9 W cts.
Assumed conversion heat->power 10% (+50% avail.as hot water)

Requirement.	Direct Power kCE(p)/ca	Heat Equiv. kCE(h)/ca	Fuel kCE(h)/ca.
1. Food Production			52.
2. Leaf fractionation.	0.67	6.7	--
3. Irrigation.	0.06	0.6	--
4. Refrigeration.	4.2	42	--
5. Cooking+hot/boiled water.	--	--	60.
6. Light.	1.2	12	--
7a. Clothes and Houses	1.0	10	2
7b. Village imports.	--	--	10
8. Local Industry.	5.0	50	20
9. Industrial Imports	--	--	20
10. Personal Transport.	--	--	7.5
11. Goods Transport.	--	--	7.5
12. Communication.	0.7	7.0	--

Total Required as power   12.8 kCE(p)or128 kCE(h)
Total Required as heat   179 kCE(h).

HOW APPROPRIATE IS DEVELOPMENT?

Since world peace is impossible so long as the gap between the standards of living and use of energy in rich countries and poor ones is large, we must assume that roughly equal resources are available to all people.

EE must not produce any cumulative pollution of land, sea or air. To avoid the greenhouse effect the total annual world use of fossil carbon must be less than 1/2 the present total: let us assume 1/3. This means that there would be 2-3 bbl oil (0.25-0.4 TOE) or 0.4-0.6 TCE/ca (per person-year). There is no rigid limit to renewable energy, even biofuels since these take as much CO_2 from the air as they put back.

As much of the earth's surface as possible will be covered with green leaves, and any timber will be grown on a renewable basis. Coppicing will be used widely as a source of fuel, and as a source of shade, leaf fertiliser and to bring trace elements and water up when grown among crops. (4)

Fossil fuels must be regarded as a capital resource, ie a substantial fraction of them must be spent on installing equipment for renewable energy supply. Electricity will only be used for those purposes for which it is uniquely suitable namely efficient lighting, power and very high temperature heating. There will be no Gigawatt power stations with the grid distribution which requires a very large consumption to pay for it. Village stations of a few KW and town ones of a few hundred KW will suffice to give the 20 W/c which will be needed.

This is based on the assumptions that every household has a compartment in a communal refrigerator, one room lit with a high efficiency electric light for the whole evening, and everyone has one trip by bus to the nearest town once a month. All the chores like grinding meal and fetching water or fuel are done by mechanical power and power is available to run village workshops during the day. Low power tractors (eg 10kW) are shared between families, and mixed farming and tree coppicing are used. Some irrigation is assumed and Pirie's leaf fractionation process provides supplementary protein. (5).

It follows that if each person only uses less than 20 W on average then central power stations and grid distribution do not have any place in the Equilibrium World. A village of 1000 people would be responsible for its own local generation system of 20 kW.
All the necessary energy for this engineering can ultimately be supplied by renewables:
i. Solar steam or solar cells (the former can also supply boiling and boiled water). ii. Wind. iii. Micro-hydro. iv. Coppiced wood, charcoal and agricultural by-products such as straw. v. Biogas.

Liquid fuel for transport will be made on an area basis from specially grown crops. Public transport and goods transport by rail, bus and air will have to come within this figure of 2-3 bbl oil/ca.

V. Steps towards EE.

The problems of bringing the rich down to a sustainable level and of bringing the poor up to this level are quite different. In Britain in 1939-46 the overriding fear of defeat made us accept rationing of many luxuries although we never went without necessities. EE requires similar sacrifices by the First World and the wealthy in the Third World; many of them are things we hardly dreamt of in my boyhood! I have tried to show in #I that a shift from measuring ones success in life by possessions to measuring it by Quality of Life based on Creative self-fulfilment could turn this apparent sacrifice into a blessing. However we all have in us the Hawk of Egoism which outshouts the Dove of Conscience, so we will not give up our luxuries lightly. Perhaps when the public sees how imminent are the dangers of our present path they will listen to the voice of the Dove.

This voice is expressed in the Hippocratic Oath published by the Institute for Social Inventions (6):
I vow to practise my profession with conscience and dignity;
I will strive to apply my skills only with the utmost respect for the well-being of humanity, the earth and all its species;
I will not permit considerations of nationality, politics, prejudice or material advancement to intervene between my work and this duty to present and future generations.

The rural poor of the world can go straight to the condition of Equilibrium without following our disastrous path and so reach the stable condition before us.

In addition to the principle of sustainability two other principles are essential in helping the rural Third World to come to Equilibrium Engineering.
i. Responsibility. The local people must want the development enough to be prepared ultimately to pay for it and to maintain it when it is successful. Payment must be based on the kind of interest rates that we had in the XIXth Century.
   This implies that the essential first step in any project is to spend time living with the local people to relate their known wishes and needs, their customs and traditions to the equipment necessary for Equilibrium Engineering.

ii. The Pilot Plant Principle of Development. All developments require adaptations which cannot be foreseen and hence it is essential to try out any idea under conditions where it can be modified over a period without ´loss of face´. In the work of the IMechE CEDC we chose a village in Tanzania as our pilot plant.

This CEDC was set up in 1984 under the Chairmanship of Dr J.West and in 1985 M.Carey spent a fortnight in the village chosen. Results so far: 2 grain milling diesels have been repaired, a third diesel donated, and a diesel maintenance system for the whole area set up; machine operators and village technicians trained; clean water pump installed; school equipped and extended; several visits by family planning trainers.

VI Conclusion.

The rural areas of the Third World constitute the best place for the start of development towards Equilibrium Engineering.

Appendix I.
Proposal for project "Energy for Rural Africa".

Thus the first step towards EE is to develop for the ´have-nots´ the necessary equipment and processes. Rural Africa could be one of the best places in the world for this step.

I therefore propose that one or more of the British Engineering Bodies should act as organisers of some dozen Pilot plant projects in African villages on developments towards EE. A list of possible projects is given below.

When the projects have been specified the organisers would choose an Executive organisation for each project, who are already experienced in the area, eg ITDG, or a University Dept, and get them to cost 5-years pilot plant work, aimed at reaching a condition in which the villagers would be glad and able to look after the equipment at the end of the 5-years. A suitable village would be selected for each project.

At the same time the organisers would approach various bodies having the necessary funds to set up a single Trust to fund the 5-years work of all the projects.

Some possible pilot plant projects.
1. Windmills for electricity generation: 20w/person.
2. Micro-hydro electricity possibly combined with village irrigation scheme.
3. Solar concentrator with cheap mirrors raising steam for electricity generation + boiling water. ´Steam accumulator´ for storage.
4. Solar cells, with battery storage.
5. Village ice-house with multi-compartment refrigerator, solar/thermal: no moving parts.
6. Village washing machine: electric drive, solar heated water.

7. Village electricity distribution system for grinding, workshop, sawmill, water pumping and house lighting.
8. Biogas generation from sewage, compost, cowdung, with solar heat acceleration.
9. Leaf fractionation system powered by steam (solar or biofuels) which also provides evaporation heat.
10. Simple 15 HP tractor, locally maintainable.
11. Tree coppicing for direct fuel (eg trains) and for charcoal production for lorries.
12. 500 kW electricity for 25000 in a town with boiling water supply to industry and homes. Diesel, or turbine (steam or gas). Use of sewage gas and refuse as partial fuels.
13. Small Nitrogen fixation plant: straw as fuel.
14. Desert restoration by: i. Solar distillation of salt water. ii. Dew collection. iii. Gradual tree planting.
15. Development of high efficiency solid fuel locomotive with minimum pollution.
16. Improved solar dryers for crops.
17. Biofuels for buses.

2. How appropriate is development?

J. B. WILMSHURST, BA(Econ), Head, Aid and Social Policy Group, Overseas Development Administration

INTRODUCTION
An attempt to answer the question, "How appropriate is development", needs to be preceded by a statement on criteria. From the point of view of a development economist, there are several aspects:

Efficiency
 The end-product of development is consumption, so a necessary test is whether development is providing an expanding provision of goods and services people want, at least cost. This term (cost) should be interpreted widely; it is not always measured by the amount of cash which changes hands.

Equity
 Development should have a wider meaning than growth in Gross Domestic Product. Wide participation in the fruits of material advance is a minimum requirement, with social advance, equality before the law and pluralism as other necessary elements.

Environmental soundness
 This is a topical issue where concepts are changing. But a fundamental point is inter-generational equity: each generation should bequeath to the next a stock of natural capital no less valuable than that which it inherited. The balance should be struck after netting out gains (coastal defences, cleaner water, better sewers) and losses (disappearing forests, polluted atmosphere, etc).

Human resource development
 Better health and education are goals in themselves as well as contributory ingredients to economic growth and equity.

HOW APPROPRIATE IS DEVELOPMENT?

<u>Low risk</u>

Low income countries, and poor families, have no margin for error. Development strategies which carry high risks are unlikely to be appropriate.

2. Many of these aspects can be captured in the concept of sustainability. Apart from the obvious characteristic of environmental sustainability, the concept should cover aspects such as prudent foreign exchange management (no debt mountains), responsible fiscal policies, avoidance of policies which result in civil breakdowns (i.e. wide political and social participation is needed), delivery of the economic growth needed to meet reasonable material aspirations and the development of institutions which can manage and promote change.

3. The qualification which is immediately needed to this outline is that in all cases the criteria must be set in the national context (i.e. about 150 national contexts). Every developing country is unique. The assessment of what is appropriate must always take into account national resource endowments, geographical locations, political and cultural traditions, the history of development strategies adopted, foreign obligations (including debt), national structures and a hundred other considerations. This suggests that attempts at global generalisation - as in this paper - are foolhardy!

4. Even so it does not seem too provocative to suggest that much development has not been appropriate. The signs are everywhere: capital assets which are under-employed or under-maintained; new investments which are draining resources from other sectors and neighbouring regions; huge disparities between haves and have-nots in individual countries and cities; military and civil disorders; unstable and ineffective governments; environmental degradation; whole countries sinking under the burden of failed economic policies and debt. This is not universal experience: many countries, particularly in Asia, have made steady progress against the criteria outlined above. But the experience suggests a need for questioning fundamental strategies as well as individual development projects in some countries. These issues are examined from the points of view of both development countries and donor agencies in the rest of this paper.

OBSTACLES TO APPROPRIATE DEVELOPMENT

5. The major causes of inappropriate development have been inappropriate development strategies and macro-economic policies, which fed through to micro policies and choice of technology. Developing country governments, sometimes encouraged by Western economists and other experts, often adopted over-centralised planning procedures and strategies aimed at rapid industrialisation, import-substitution and public ownership. These policies were usually well-intentioned initially, but when their deficiencies were exposed the reforms necessary - liberalisation and

decentralisation - were often opposed by the vested interests which profited from the old system.

6. The most serious shortcoming has been unwillingness to let the price mechanism operate freely to balance supply and demand in the market place. Overvalued exchange rates, arbitrary and complex import tariffs, negative real interest rates, subsidised prices for energy and some foodstuffs, have been common in many developing countries. Problems were often compounded by failure to control budget deficits, leading to inflation and uncertainty about future relative prices and the availability of goods. The resulting prices, often associated with shortages and with corrupt or inefficient systems of rationing, do not encourage development of competitive industries using appropriate technology. Typical biases include excessive demand for imported consumer and producer goods, the latter often including inappropriately capital-intensive technology which is economically undesirable (but privately profitable) at the ruling heavily distorted prices. Exports are discouraged under these arrangements while low value-added assembly of luxuries for the domestic market is often encouraged by the tariff structure.

7. The key prices at this macro-economic level are the prices of capital (i.e. interest rates), foreign exchange (i.e. the exchange rate) and labour (i.e. wages). Liberalisation should lead to prices which balance supply and demand in each of these markets, but this does not mean complete abdication by the government. Some supervision is needed to keep the markets free, to prevent market-rigging by major participants such as banks and other financial institutions, trade unions or import/export companies.

8. These macro obstacles have often been exacerbated by institutional weaknesses, failures of governance and local customs. Examples include inappropriate laws and administrative regulations and weak parastatal structures; political arrangements which leave much of the population uninvolved; and traditions which exclude women from economic activity (or place the main farming burdens on them while directing training and advice at men).

9. Removal of macro obstacles does not amount simply to "getting prices right", however. Apart from the need to prevent market-rigging, noted above, it is necessary to recognise that market failure is not unknown. This is particularly relevant to environmental issues where many of the problems arise from the failure of markets to take into account externalities, "public goods" and qualities which cannot be valued in any conventional way.

10. Problems often result from the fact that no one "owns" the natural environment, and therefore everyone treats it as if it were effectively free. Government intervention is needed in some form if the environment is not to be damaged by over-use. Examples are:-

HOW APPROPRIATE IS DEVELOPMENT?

(a) Groundwater extraction for irrigation typically costs the farmer only his costs for pumping. In many parts of the world, investment by farmers in irrigation equipment exceeds the recharge capacity of the aquifer, leading to dropping water tables, and increased pumping costs for existing users. The poor and vulnerable, who depend on cheaper, shallower wells, often suffer most. Public sector intervention is needed to regulate in some way the proliferation of pump sets. Effective control is not easy, however, and cases where governments have succeeded in enforcing legislation which limits sinking of wells are scarce.

(b) Manufacturers pay nothing for the freedom to pollute the air of the oceans and rivers, and consequently pay little attention to the environmental costs they impose on others. Government intervention is needed to enforce the polluter pays principle. Ways to do this include taxes, marketable licences and direct controls. Market-based controls have the advantage of concentrating the reduction in pollution on those enterprises who can reduce emissions at least cost.

(c) Communal grazing land will tend to be overused leading to potential desertification, because the benefits of grazing animals go to the owner of the animals, while the costs of deterioration in the quality of grazing are shared among all users. This example illustrates the link between the environment, population and economic growth. Land will tend to be free in situations where it is not scarce - hence the contrast between communal land-holdings in many parts of Africa and individual tenure arrangements in high population-density Asia. Land holding systems which work well when human and livestock population density is low become inappropriate when population growth begins to put pressure on the finite land resource. Similar arguments apply to the use of forest resources for fuel. As the resource shrinks relative to population, it is essential to move towards a system of ownership which encourages the population to use the resource sustainably. Traditional user rights may go back many generations, however, and are difficult to change over the much shorter time frame needed if soil erosion and deforestation is to be effectively controlled before it goes too far to be reversible. Moreover, much of the pressure on the land may come not from the original users, but from outside: arable farmers forced by population growth to encroach on grazing lands, loggers and other commercial users of forests.

11. Other obstacles to appropriate development are apparent at the project level. Assuming that demand has been correctly assessed in an undistorted economic context, inappropriate designs can result from:

- Failure to consider the full range of options for meeting demand.
- Inadequate assessment of local capacities and weaknesses, sometimes because these are not properly reflected in prices and sometimes following from the use of "off-the-shelf" designs and standards which were proved in the different conditions of developed countries.
- <u>Interventions by foreign donors with aid-tying rules.</u>

12. On the last of these, there is a sound argument for procurement-tying which includes the justification for large aid programmes in donor countries and the procedures which exist for ensuring that no distortions are created by such tying. But it would be absurd to deny that aid-tying has resulted in cases of inappropriate development. Examples range from the stunting of local agriculture as a result of food aid, installation of high technology machinery which is beyond local capacity to maintain, creation of new capacity rather than lower-cost rehabilitation of existing assets and supply of machinery distinguished by its labour-saving characteristics when local labour is cheap and has no alternative employment. Cases such as these will continue to occur. But the ODA and other aid agencies have adopted a range of procedures such as shadow-pricing in appraisal methodologies and value-for-money rules which should make them exceptions rather than familiar experience in the future.

HOW TO MAKE DEVELOPMENT MORE APPROPRIATE

13. The framework for appropriate development is provided by liberal economic policies and good government. Both are largely the responsibility of developing country governments and touch on sensitive issues, including pluralism, accountability, human rights and the rule of law. Donors can make useful contributions, however.

14. The ODA is increasingly concentrating aid resources on those countries which are adopting sound economic policies and moving away from the distortions which make it difficult or impossible for any aid activity to be effective. General balance of payments support has been increasingly used to support policy reform, in situations where the economy needs foreign exchange more to keep existing capital functioning than to implement new investment.

15. In addition to an appropriate macro-economic framework, ODA pays close attention to the sectoral and institutional setting within which aid activities must operate. Are sectoral policies appropriate? Are resources adequate and priorities sensible? Are the institutions which will implement and operate the project effective? Are weaknesses being addressed through training and technical assistance?

16. The impact of ODA projects on the environment is carefully assessed, and every effort made to ensure that the

principles of sustainability are respected. This kind of assessment complements the usual technical, financial, economic and social assessments.

17. The choice between large-scale, modern technology and smaller-scale, intermediate technology is not a controversial issue in ODA. Both are appropriate, but in different circumstances. ODA is the main support of the Intermediate Technology Development Group and it appointed a full-time, Senior Adviser on small-scale enterprise earlier this year. These arrangements have allowed ODA to expand its intermediate technology activities significantly in recent years.

18. Such activities cannot be expected to absorb a large part of an aid programme which is now running at over 1.6 billion per year, however. In many sectors, modern large-scale technology is more efficient in absolute terms at almost any set of relative factor prices, though there is often a role for intermediate technology to complement it. The creation of modern economic and social infrastructure in power, energy, transport and communications, education and health services cannot depend entirely on small-scale or labour-intensive methods.

19. The "process" approach to development projects is a useful instrument in this context. This approach recognises that present knowledge is often inadequate to fully design a project, and substitutes an approach whereby the project proceeds by a process of action research which involves the beneficiaries in identifying needs, testing innovation, and feeding back the results through careful monitoring. The approach may be especially appropriate in the context of rainfed agriculture, where agro-ecological conditions can differ markedly over quite small areas and the blueprint approach cannot easily work. Success will depend heavily on the management and organisational skills of the institutions responsible for implementation, but the principle of delegating more decision-making to project managers seems essential if ODA is to directly participate in activities aimed at reaching poor people directly.

20. My last point on the strategy for appropriate development relates to the interaction between engineers and economists. This has come a long way in ODA since the organisation was set up in 1964. Economists have probably learned the most, because they had most to learn. They now understand the basis for engineering standards, for reliance on tried and tested technologies, for conceding theoretical niceties to management realities. ODA engineers in turn have come to appreciate the need to adapt designs to fit local conditions, particularly labour surplus, the value of cost-benefit and cost-effectiveness analysis and the failure of market prices to properly reflect true resource costs in many developing countries.

21. Challenges for both disciplines in the future include the need for institutional strengthening, how to provide for

much greater maintenance and rehabilitation needs in development programmes and training requirements. The limitations on turnkey projects in the future, the need to mix UK, local and third country procurement in even more exotic cocktails and the greater role of the private sector in developing countries will also call for imagination and experience. All of these should contribute to more appropriate development.

3. Development and implementation of innovation in irrigation

R. LENTON, Director General, International Irrigation Management Institute

SYNOPSIS. This paper analyzes the process of implementation of technological and managerial innovation in developing countries. The focus is on irrigation, although the conclusions are intended to apply to such other vital sectors as energy, transport, housing, and water supply. After briefly describing aspects of irrigation and its management, two case studies on the development and practical implementation of innovations are presented. The paper ends with some conclusions on what works (and doesn't work) in technology development and transfer in developing countries.

1. This paper is written to shed light on how technological and managerial innovation is implemented in developing countries, and to help define the characteristics of effective technology development and transfer. The focus is on irrigation, a sector that is critical to the survival of millions of rural people in the developing world whose livelihoods depend on irrigated agriculture. However, the conclusions of the paper are relevant to such other vital sectors as energy, housing, transport, and water and sanitation.

2. The paper has three parts. The first briefly describes aspects of irrigation and its management to provide the context for later discussion. The second part presents two case studies on the development and practical implementation of innovations that have involved the International Irrigation Management Institute (IIMI) and its collaborators in Indonesia and Sri Lanka. Part three presents the generic lessons learned from these case studies and IIMI's experience elsewhere. The paper concludes that successful implementation of innovations requires a process of technology development and implementation that is both interactive and long-term; that innovations cannot be effectively implemented without strong policy commitment at the highest governmental levels; and that strong and effective national research and development systems in

developing countries ultimately hold the key to successful technology development and implementation.

3. Technology is used in this paper in a broad sense that embraces the full array of means, processes, and ideas required to fulfil human needs in such areas as energy, housing, transport, or water supply. Technology development and implementation thus encompasses not only physical infrastructure issues but also a broad set of policy, institutional, and management questions. Innovation is used equally broadly to denote any significant planned change toward new policies, institutional arrangements, management practices, or physical infrastructure.

4. This paper uses the management of irrigation systems in developing countries as its framework. The topic is important and appropriate to the discussion; improving the management of irrigation systems in developing countries is a critical component of those countries' programmes to address food security and sustainability in the decades to come, while efforts to improve irrigation management require the successful implementation of technological change.

IRRIGATION IN DEVELOPING COUNTRIES
5. There are now close to 185 million hectares of irrigated land in the developing countries of this world, which constitute some 20% of the total cultivated area of those countries (ref. 1). The impact of irrigation on food security and rural incomes is, however, significantly greater than these figures suggest. For example, more than half of the total food production in South Asia comes from irrigated lands. Two thirds of the growth of cereal output in South Asia in the 1960s and 1970s has been attributed to irrigation. Irrigator developing countries frequently devote over three-fourths of their public spending for agriculture to irrigation. World-wide, as much as US $10 billion are currently invested each year to develop some 2 million hectares of new irrigation (ref. 2).

6. Despite these statistics, the performance of irrigation systems in developing countries is far below their potential in terms of productivity, equity, sustainability, and positive social and environmental effects. In many systems, total area irrigated is much less than is possible; water is distributed inequitably among farmers; water deliveries do not correspond to the true requirements of farmers' crops; net incomes (both for farmers and landless laborers) are low; and waterlogging, salinity and water-borne diseases are widespread. Clearly, if global food security and sustainability goals are to be attained, the performance of irrigation in developing countries needs to be substantially improved.

7. But improvements in performance require substantial changes in irrigation policy, in irrigation management, and in irrigation infrastructure - in other words, they require a spirit of innovation on the part of both irrigation agencies and farmers. A key feature of innovation in the irrigation sector - as in many other areas of economic and rural development -- is that it must inherently be both "managerial" and "technological" in character. For example, achieving more efficient use of available water supplies in irrigation systems frequently requires both physical modernization and improved operation and management; and effective rehabilitation and modernization of irrigation systems often requires changes in management as well as changes in infrastructure. Although improvements in one dimension without the other can achieve modest gains, changes in both dimensions are needed to substantially improve and sustain irrigation performance (ref. 3).

8. A second key feature of innovation in the irrigation sector is that implementation as well as development issues require significant research and experimentation. It is not enough for researchers to design new monitoring techniques, or recommend changes in organizational structure, or propose policy changes. If changes in current practices are to be fully accepted, utilized, and institutionalized, a significant number of implementation problems will need to be addressed by researchers and practitioners as they arise. For example, many countries have recently introduced policy changes that transfer responsibility and authority for irrigation operations and maintenance from government to water users' associations. The effective implementation of these policy changes will require research and experimentation on such crucial issues as how to prepare and motivate water user associations and re-orient operating agencies to a new role as support services providers.

9. Technology transfer and practical implementation in irrigation thus involves much more than developing physical innovations and offering them to client users. It also involves more than adaptive research by scientists in developing countries to pick-up ideas from western universities or research institutes (ref. 4). It is not primarily a question of regional transfer between West and East or North and South, in whatever direction. Effective technology transfer and implementation in irrigation must include simultaneous consideration of the wide range of policies, institutional arrangements, management practices and physical hardware required to achieve high levels of performance. It must include the sharing of ideas and experience between researchers and practitioners. It therefore requires a range of activities of a multiplicity of different groups involved in the evaluation, adoption, full acceptance and institutionalization of innovations.

HOW APPROPRIATE IS DEVELOPMENT?

CASE STUDIES

10. The complex processes of technology development and adoption are best described by reference to specific examples. This paper therefore presents two case studies, in Indonesia and Sri Lanka, in which IIMI was involved. The first describes the development and testing of a set of low-cost operational changes in the management of irrigation systems in Indonesia designed to use the country's existing irrigation infrastructure more efficiently. The second case study describes the development and initial implementation of a recommended organizational change in an irrigation scheme in Southern Sri Lanka that holds promise for significantly improving the performance of that scheme and perhaps other similar schemes elsewhere.

Case Study 1: Operational Planning and Practices in Indonesia

11. This case study summarizes one component of a collaborative research and development project undertaken by IIMI and partner institutions in Indonesia between 1986 and 1989, financed by the Asian Development Bank, the Ford Foundation, IIMI, and the Government of Indonesia (GOI). The project was one of many efforts to improve irrigation management to maintain Indonesia's transformation from the world's largest importer of rice to a country that enjoys rice self-sufficiency. This transformation has moved government priorities towards a more sustained, self-financing irrigation sector serving a more diversified cropping base. In recent years the GOI has placed increasing emphasis on revenue generation, cost reduction, and more efficient use of existing irrigation infrastructure. A full description of the project, which was carried out by IIMI, the Ministry of Public Works of Indonesia, and several Provincial Irrigation Services, is available in ref. 5.

12. This case study covers the project component concerned with developing cost effective procedures for irrigation operations that would help stabilize financial requirements. Specifically, the component involved examining current management practices and developing alternatives for testing and adoption by Indonesia's Provincial Irrigation Services, to help the Services use existing resources more effectively.

13. The activity was carried out in several stages (ref. 6). The first included data collection and observation of current formal and informal irrigation practices, as well as the development of open and trustful relationships between staff of IIMI and the Public Works Department. Several Public Works Department staff, especially at the field operations level, were assigned full time to the project team. The second stage entailed problem diagnosis, in which initial results and experiences were translated into problem identification statements and initial discussions of ways to

improve performance. The third stage involved pilot testing of selected operational procedures to improve irrigation performance. A fourth implementation stage is still needed, both to help in the adoption of improved procedures outside the pilot areas and to help develop the required operating policy reforms. It should be noted that these stages were all shaped by a mutual understanding that the programme should first explore the potential for improving performance within the current management system before moving towards other changes.

14. As part of the second stage and on the basis of detailed field research in several irrigation systems, the project team came to several conclusions about current irrigation practices in Indonesia. Such practices are characterized by (1) the "Factor-K" system based on the earlier "pasten" system of irrigation planning that aims at calculating overall water supply and demand every 10 or 15 days; (2) sophisticated standards for irrigation infrastructure designed to provide full control of water; and (3) annual and seasonal planning procedures down to the tertiary level that entail elicitation of farmer group intentions and reconciliation with provincial and national objectives.

15. The team determined that proper implementation of the "Factor-K" system is inhibited by the inaccuracy of the database available to system managers, the inadequate condition of the irrigation infrastructure, insufficient management control, and problematic monitoring of water distribution and allocation. For example, while field reports of actual water conditions generally indicated that allocation had been implemented as planned, field data showed frequent large discrepancies between planned and actual discharges, particularly in the dry season when water was scarce.

16. As a result of these findings, the team made six recommendations aimed at both the system level (for implementation of improved operational procedures) and at the provincial or national level (for the institutional framework required to support effective operation and maintenance). These recommendations were based on two important assumptions: that the operational performance of irrigation systems in Indonesia can be improved without significant additional expenditure through the adoption of simplified operational procedures, and that rehabilitation should be preceded by operational improvements and development of operationally-oriented priorities for investment in improved infrastructure. Physical improvements can be justified only after first demonstrating that the potential for improving performance through better management has already been achieved within current infrastructural parameters. Wherever possible, the recommendations were accompanied by detailed implementation instructions and materials.

HOW APPROPRIATE IS DEVELOPMENT?

17. Recommendations addressed to system managers focussed on simple, low-cost methods for improving the data-base for irrigation management (refs. 7 and 8). These methods included mapping landholdings and water inlets and outlets for tertiary blocks (using roll meters and diagonal, triangulation measurement to compute areas), calibration of gates and measuring structures (usually with portable flumes), measurement of conveyance losses (using floats and existing measurement devices), and inclusion of the "delivery performance ratio" (DPR -- the ratio of actual to target deliveries) in standard operational forms to enable quick evaluation of water distribution performance. Annual costs per hectare ranged from about US$ 0.25 for calibration to about US$ 1.50 for mapping -- only a fraction of average annualized costs of infrastructure rehabilitation. The study team also developed and tested a simplified rotational irrigation delivery schedule that reduced management inputs (gate operations and monitoring) of agency staff by 15%, yet resulted in a more equitable and better implemented plan.

18. Many recommendations were adopted on a pilot basis in a number of the systems in the study area. In particular, a major testing programme was undertaken in four irrigation systems in West Java with a total command area of about 16,000 hectares, which involved the mapping of tertiary blocks, the identification of additional water sources, the calibration of measuring devices and gates, and the undertaking of a complete inventory of control structures. The pilot testing showed that field level mapping and calibration and conveyance loss measurements can be highly cost-effective and that improvements are within the constraints of staff levels and skills, if staff are given a modest amount of mostly on-site training. A major revision of rotational irrigation practices was also pilot-tested in a 4,000 hectare system in West Java. The pilot project, which revolved around assuring uniformity in the time each tertiary block received water, resulted in significant improvements in performance at a low cost.

19. Overall, the pilot tests demonstrated that significantly improving irrigation management practices within existing staff and resources is feasible; that normal procedures can be adapted without changes in overall rules to accommodate changed operational practices; and that improved cooperation between farmers and irrigation staff can be obtained without major special programmes. However, the pilot project also identified several constraints that need to be overcome to achieve wider adoption and dissemination of improved operational practices. Pre-requisites for successful adoption include the need for a programme rather than a project mentality, a willingness to change standard procedures, and a willingness to re-allocate budgets to meet changed priorities for operation and management. Pre-requisites for sustained implementation include supportive

institutional incentives and effective monitoring and supervision.

20. Provincial and national level recommendations included the redefinition of operational responsibilities of irrigation agencies, the participation of farmers in system operation and maintenance, and need-based budget allocation procedures. These changes, however, cannot normally be adopted without accompanying changes in operational policies and practices. Proposals for bringing these changes about within Indonesia have not yet been fully developed.

Case Study 2: Project Management Structures in Sri Lanka

21. This case study summarizes the results to date of an on-going research and development project on irrigation management and crop diversification conducted by IIMI and several partner institutions in Sri Lanka since early 1988. The project is being financed by ADB, the Government of Sri Lanka, and IIMI. The project team includes staff from IIMI, the Irrigation Department, the Irrigation Management Division, the Mahaweli Economic Agency, and the Department of Agriculture of the Government of Sri Lanka. Although the overall project addresses a number of priority issues related to irrigation system management in two schemes in Southern Sri Lanka - Kirindi Oya and Uda Walawe - this case study will focus only on the first of these two schemes. A full description of the overall project and its results can be found in refs. 9 and 10.

22. The Kirindi Oya scheme, developed in two phases beginning in 1986 with financial assistance from ADB, Kreditanstalt Fuer Wiederanfbam (KFW), and the International Fund for Agricultural Development (IFAD), is a new settlement scheme located in the dry zone of Sri Lanka about 260 km south-east of Colombo. The scheme includes the augmentation of irrigation water supplies for existing irrigation systems covering some 4,500 hectares, the construction of new irrigation infrastructure to permit an additional 8,500 hectares of irrigation, and the settlement of some 8,000 families on newly-irrigated land. The scheme was justified economically from the beginning on the assumption that farmers would grow crops other than rice in a significant proportion of the command area. Important objectives included increasing agricultural production through crop diversification and settlement of landless people.

23. Experience with the Kirindi Oya scheme to date has not proved satisfactory, and there is widespread agreement that the scheme's original objectives have not been achieved to any significant degree. In particular, water delivery performance in terms of both adequacy and predictability of water supply has been poor; deficiencies in design and maintenance have affected the long-term capability of the system's water delivery system to perform at expected levels;

there is a serious conflict over water allocation between old and new areas; actual water usage has not corresponded with design assumptions; and settler farmers have had inadequate incentives to carry-out efficient farming operations. A major difficulty with the Kirindi Oya scheme to date is that, despite its original objectives, it continues to be operated as a rice-based system.

24. The objective of the case study was to analyze in detail the major causes of inefficiency in the operation of the Kirindi Oya scheme (particularly the difficulty in implementing crop diversification), and to help develop innovations for improved irrigation system management and diversification. Following extensive field research, the study team concluded that a major factor lay in the project's fragmented management structure. Responsibility for the operation and maintenance (O & M) of the Kirindi Oya scheme was divided between the Irrigation Department and the Irrigation Management Division; the former was responsible for system O & M up to the field channel level, while farmers' groups organized by the latter were intended to be responsible for O & M below this level. The Agriculture Department was responsible for providing agricultural advice and assistance, but had no direct responsibility for irrigation management. Significantly, no agency alone was responsible for achieving the long-term objectives of the project. The Irrigation Department, for example, had responsibility neither for achieving overall project objectives nor for implementing a long-term agricultural production plan. Other agencies had their own specified technical functions. As a result, there was a de facto policy of catering to short-term objectives on an ad-hoc basis, rather than addressing overall goals (ref. 10).

25. A second conclusion was that the performance of the scheme could be significantly improved if certain physical and organizational changes were made with the active involvement of the system's managers and farmers. The key step was the establishment of an overall project management charged with achieving the long-term objective of making the best use of the limited water to maximize farmers' incomes, and with the authority to ensure that other departments contributed their efforts to achieving this objective.

26. The study team therefore made a series of specific recommendations aimed at restructuring the project management. A crucial recommendation was the appointment of a senior Resident Project Director to develop plans for achieving the long-term objectives of the project, oversee the establishment of decision rules for water allocation, set up mechanisms for making and implementing these decisions, and ensure effective cooperation among the supporting agencies. Other recommendations included the further reform and strengthening of the Irrigation Department's organization

for management of the system, the allocation of high priority to creating the conditions for the development of strong farmers' organizations in the area, and a number of specific measures to improve the performance of the irrigation delivery system.

27. Implementation of the study team's recommendations has occurred in several stages (ref. 11). During 1989, there were minor changes in the Kirindi Oya management structure in response to an earlier paper (ref. 12), in which an additional joint farmer-official committee was set up to bridge the gap between officials and farmers. After the first interim report of the study team, the Irrigation Department reorganized to put more emphasis on O & M as opposed to new construction. However, the most significant change occurred after the draft final report was published in early 1990, when Sri Lanka's State Secretary for Irrigation made a series of suggestions for improvements in the scheme's management. The recommendations, which are summarized in a report entitled "Kirindi Oya Project: Recommendations for Institutional Changes and Remedial Measures" (ref. 13), included several important proposals for changes in institutional arrangements, farmer organizations, and crop diversification practices. The report called for the appointment of a Project Manager responsible for management of the whole project with the help of a new Project Management Committee.

28. Although, in the Secretary's words, the proposals "are not intended to be the perfect solutions for the problems at Kirindi Oya", they "may serve at least as interim measures to put the project back on track and to ensure that the benefits intended at the project formulation stage are ultimately achieved". To assist in this process of implementation, a phase II of the project has been agreed to in principle by ADB, IIMI, and the Government of Sri Lanka. This proposed second phase would translate into operational terms the major recommendations of the study, help introduce irrigation management innovations in the procedures and practices of the various agencies concerned, and assist these agencies to bring about the procedural and organizational changes required to improve irrigation management.

LESSONS LEARNED
29. The two case studies and IIMI's experience with other research and development projects world-wide have taught the Institute staff at least three things about technology development and implementation in developing countries.

30. The first general lesson is that successful implementation of innovations requires a process of technology development, adoption and implementation that is both interactive and long-term. In particular, successful technology development and adoption requires partnerships

between researchers and practitioners. Such partnerships ensure the efficient use of financial and staff resources, facilitate researcher understanding of the constraints of implementors and implementing institutions (and vice-versa), generate opportunities for training and knowledge transfer in both directions, and above all provide a mechanism for jointly addressing implementation problems. The use of seconded agency staff as an integral part of the research team -- a technique employed to good effect in both the Sri Lanka and Indonesia case studies -- can be an important vehicle for forging strong research/practitioner partnerships.

31. Effective research/practitioner partnerships cannot simply consist of the preparation of reports by researchers and their acceptance (or otherwise) by practitioners. For partnerships to result in the emergence of ideas and attitudinal changes that are a pre-requisite to effective assimilation of innovations, partnerships must involve such interactive mechanisms as extensive day-to-day exchange of ideas, joint field visits, organization of brain-storming meetings, and preparation of working drafts for informal discussion. Trustful partnerships can be facilitated by longer-term consultative mechanisms that reach beyond any particular project or study team. For example, the effectiveness of the research/practitioner interaction in the Sri Lanka case study was in large part due to the fact that close relationships between the key parties had already been established through the "Sri Lanka-IIMI Consultative Committee", which has met regularly since 1985 to discuss research priorities and review the findings of a wide range of research and development projects in which IIMI has been involved in Sri Lanka.

32. Experience also suggests that to be effective partnerships must be long-term. The successful implementation of technological and managerial innovation in developing countries requires significant investment of time on the part of both researchers and practitioners to ensure that all steps - from development and evaluation to full acceptance and institutionalization - are carried out with ample opportunity for discussion and consultation. A key principle of IIMI's work, which undoubtedly has had a bearing on the results of its work to date, is an insistence on a long-term resident presence in selected countries which enables the Institute to participate in sustained action research on priority problems and develop familiarity with the environments and institutions that influence them (ref. 1). Both the case studies described in this paper were part of projects conceived for a duration of at least four years.

33. The second lesson is that technology cannot be effectively "transferred" without strong policy commitment at the highest government levels. Undoubtedly, the effective

implementation of innovations that shake the status quo requires policy intervention to provide both the context and the incentives for the acceptance of change. As was noted in the Indonesia case study, the team's recommendations at the provincial and national level have not yet been implemented since they require accompanying changes in operational objectives, procedures, policies and supporting incentive structures that can only be achieved by high level policy intervention. And in Sri Lanka, the implementation of changes in the management structure of the Kirindi Oya project required the intervention of very senior authorities of the Ministry of Lands and Irrigation and Mahaweli Development of the Government of Sri Lanka.

34. Policy commitment is also needed to ensure acceptance and budget allocations for the full array of ancillary investments that must accompany even the most simple innovations. Although the case studies demonstrate that significant improvements in the effective use of existing infrastructure can be accomplished by relatively low-cost measures -- be they the data-base improvement measures described in the Indonesia case study or the management structure changes described in the Sri Lanka case study -- they also demonstrate that the effective implementation of such measures requires substantial attention to institutional support activities that play a vital role in determining whether such measures will be accepted and institutionalized. For this reason, although low-cost measures do not require significant investment in physical hardware, they require investment in a number of institutional support activities (i.e. workshops, training programmes, and the like) that help facilitate institutional acceptance.

35. The third and perhaps most important lesson derived from IIMI's experience around the world is the need for strong and effective national systems of technology development and implementation. Although international organizations such as IIMI are playing a role in forging partnerships between researchers and practitioners in developing countries, there is an urgent need to develop national systems of innovation development and implementation that involve partnerships among the research and development community in developing countries (universities, research institutions, etc.), governmental and non-governmental agencies, and user groups. IIMI's work in Indonesia and Sri Lanka has only scratched the surface of the potential improvement of irrigation performance. National capacity must be strengthened if further improvements are to be developed and fully implemented.

36. Currently, the capacity of research systems in developing countries in many critical sectors (including but not limited to irrigation) is highly inadequate. Although in

some sectors there are well-established national research systems, in many others research is highly fragmented and/or under-funded. For this reason, national systems of research and development in developing countries with strong linkages to national implementing agencies need to be established, nurtured and generated. Development assistance directed at these goals would help ensure that support for other aspects of research and technology transfer in developing countries achieves the maximum possible returns.

ACKNOWLEDGEMENTS
37. The views and comments of Douglas Merrey, Hammond Murray-Rust and Douglas Vermillion of the IIMI staff are gratefully acknowledged. The results of their field research work, presentations at internal IIMI meetings, and general advice and counsel have contributed significantly to the ideas expressed in this paper. The editorial suggestions and comments of Marian Fuchs Carsch and Nanda Abeywickrema on an earlier draft are also acknowledged with thanks.

REFERENCES
1. WORLD BANK, "Irrigation and Drainage Research", Volume 1, The World Bank, April 1990.

2. INTERNATIONAL IRRIGATION MANAGEMENT INSTITUTE, The Strategy of IIMI, Colombo, Sri Lanka, 1989.

3. LENTON, ROBERTO L., " Linkages Between Irrigation Technology and Management", Presented at the Workshop on Irrigation and Drainage Technology Research, World Bank, Washington, DC, April 1990.

4. THE ECONOMIST, "The Slow March of Technology", January 13, 1990, pgs 99-101.

5. INTERNATIONAL IRRIGATION MANAGEMENT INSTITUTE, "Efficient Irrigation Management and System Turnover; TA 937-IND-Indonesia", Final Report, Volume 1: Summary and Recommendations, IIMI, Colombo, Sri Lanka, 1989.

6. MURRAY-RUST, HAMMOND AND DOUGLAS L. VERMILLION, "Operational Planning and Practices in Government Operated Irrigation Systems: IIMI's Results and Experiences from 1986-1989", Discussion Papers, Fifth IIMI Internal Program Review, Volume I, November 1989.

7. MURRAY-RUST, HAMMOND, and DOUGLAS L. VERMILLION, personal communication, May 11 and June 4, 1990.

8. MURRAY-RUST, HAMMOND, AND DOUGLAS L. VERMILLION, " Information Base for Irrigation System Management", forthcoming IIMI Research Paper, 1990.

9. INTERNATIONAL IRRIGATION MANAGEMENT INSTITUTE, "Irrigation Management and Crop Diversification (Sri Lanka)", Volume I: Synthesis of Findings and Recommendations - Kirindi Oya and Uda Walawe Projects, Draft Final Report on the Technical Assistance Study (TA 846 SRI), Colombo, Sri Lanka, January 1990.

10. SAKTHIVADIVEL, R., N. FERNANDO, AND D. MERREY, "Performance of New Irrigation Settlement Schemes: A Case Study of Kirindi Oya, Sri Lanka", Discussion Papers, Fifth IIMI Internal Program Review, Volume I, November 1989.

11. MERREY, DOUGLAS J., "Appropriate Management Practices", memorandum, 7 May 1990.

12. MERREY, DOUGLAS J., AND SOMARATNE, P.G., "Institutions under Stress and People in Distress: Institution Building and Drought in a New Settlement Scheme in Sri Lanka", International Irrigation Management Institute, Colombo, Sri Lanka, Country Paper - Sri Lanka No. 2, 1989.

13. DE SILVA, N.G.R., "Kirindi Oya Project: Recommendations for Institutional Changes and Remedial Measures", Draft Report, Colombo, 31 March 1990.

4. Practical implementation — value for money

A. C. REED, Engineer, Oxfam

SYNOPSIS. OXFAM's involvement in the developing world is primarily concerned with enabling people to help themselves. There has been a considerable requirement, over the years, to develop appropriate technical solutions to their problems. A Technical Unit has been established to meet these requirements as well as developing special equipment for emergencies. The emphasis is placed on community participation from the earliest stages of a project to ensure sustainability. The introduction of equipment that will be difficult to service in the long term is avoided as far as possible. Training of local staff is seen as an essential element of all programmes.

INTRODUCTION

1. During the period 1988-89 OXFAM allocated £36.3 million to 2,300 projects in 71 countries. Even though the amount given by OXFAM is often only a contribution to a larger fund it is clear from these figures that most of the projects are very small by civil engineering standards.

2. Out of this sum the larger amounts are spent on emergency/disaster type projects which would not fall into the category of development as defined by the conference title. The remaining funds are therefore spread even more thinly. We shall give some discussion to the disaster projects but will look more closely at the development side in pursuit of our present topic.

3. A closer look at the grants list for the past year will show that, with education, health and social organisation featuring very high on the list, the amount left for engineering, or even vaguely technical projects, is quite small. Of the actual technical input much goes on assistance to local organisations or other aid agencies who are working closely with local groups. The bottom line therefore shows a comparatively small sum spent on civil construction or plant

and much less on design and supervision fees. We shall therefore be concentrating on the low technology and the associated social factors rather than the high profile, possibly unsustainable projects.

PARTICIPATION

4. For OXFAM the emphasis is placed on local involvement, encouraging local communities and organisations to meet what they see as the real needs (a need perceived in Westminster may be less recognisable in the Sahel). This cannot be effectively achieved without a local presence to decide when and where the money should be spent. (We now have 54 field offices around the world). With the Armenian earthquake £315,000 was passed to the Red Cross for specific needs because we had no presence in the country. Despite considerable pressure to be directly involved, that was considered to be our best contribution. For the more recent Iran earthquake materials rather than personnel were the urgent need and the 2,000 shelters we had in stock were despatched within five days, via the Red Cross/Crescent. Where we have a presence and another organisation is looking for ways of disbursing funds, we may be asked to use or direct the funds to worthwhile projects.

5. A government to government donation for a rural water scheme may lack the community support or the health education back-up that is essential if the scheme is to have an effective future. If the funding for maintenance also dries up the hardware will soon be rusting into oblivion.

6. Village level operation and maintenance (VLOM) has been occupying pump specifiers and suppliers for many years. The developing world has more than sufficient boreholes fitted with pumps, hand or powered, which have ceased to function for want of a little maintenance or a minor spare. The same is also true of other items of equipment, from tractors to sewage works, trucks to power stations, and the resources are lacking to support the developed world's throw-away approach. The problems are not solely a matter of availability of spares and consumables. There is a much better chance of arriving at a sustainable solution when there is close association with the local community. Indeed, it is salutary to see how resourceful people can be in keeping vehicles on the road, against all odds, when they are personally motivated.

7. Although in some countries we still have expatriate country representatives, this is becoming more rare. Project staff are invariably local people in close touch with their compatriots. They will spend a great deal of time in consultation with local community groups, women's groups and committees of various types, to arrive at action plans which will have the full backing of the social grouping involved.

TECHNICAL INTEGRITY

8. Having arrived at a sensible community approach, our next concern is to ensure that any solutions are technically sound and appropriate. For this reason OXFAM maintains a Technical Unit in its Overseas Division headquarters, staffed by qualified engineers. Through liaison with other relief/development organisations, research and university departments and by working closely with manufacturers, a range of equipment particularly suited to relief/emergency problems, has been, and continues to be, developed. Alongside this is a steady programme of assessing and reviewing development projects, advising on techniques and equipment and recruiting engineering staff where the needs cannot be met locally. The Technical Unit, however, is part of a team and we often have to curb our technical enthusiasm in the light of broader issues, particularly the need to prioritise spending in favour of those most in need.

WATER SUPPLIES

9. Amongst the debris of inappropriate development lie many broken intakes, silted up dams, complex water treatment works and disastrous distribution systems. Apart from being drawn reluctantly into a major refurbishment programme for Phnom Penh water works by an unusually complex political situation, OXFAM has concentrated on much smaller water projects. Even at this level it is necessary to be cautious about introducing inappropriate solutions.

10. <u>Water sources</u>. We have tried to avoid drilling boreholes because of the inherent problems. These start with the high cost of the larger, more versatile machines and continue with the maintenance of the rig with its steady need of consumables and backup facilities, especially when the strata is variable or unfamiliar. The problems continue with the pump and the necessity for spare parts and mechanics previously discussed. Nevertheless there are situations where there is no alternative and an appropriate rig would be very useful. The simpler percussion rig finds a niche in some areas. A simple rotary rig, which meets some of the other criteria, has been developed in Cambodia and we are currently purchasing one of these for use in our rural programmes in that country.

11. We have put great emphasis on spring protection and well-digging techniques and have encouraged their use wherever possible. Where local methods of lining cannot be found precast ring moulds have been introduced (Fig. 1). Subsurface dams, which do not require extensive spillway works, avoid risks of flooding and increased risks from stagnant water, can be particularly useful for increasing water availability.

HOW APPROPRIATE IS DEVELOPMENT?

FIG.1 Well Construction - Ghana

12. Rainwater catchment, in all its simplicity, provides a great opportunity for improving supplies. Even in the poorest areas, steel or tiled roofs are replacing traditional materials providing good catchment areas at the point of demand. The additional cost and effort of adding gutters and storage often only needs a little impetus from outside agencies.

13. <u>Water lifting</u>. It has been necessary to install diesel driven pumps for refugee camps where comparatively large quantities of water are needed in a hurry. Even with the usually high degree of ingenuity that keeps the oldest of vehicles on the road in remote places, it would require a very special circumstance for a powered pump to be appropriate for a small community, remote from the usual channels of spares and consumables. A large project in west Africa with international government funding, has foundered as the resources for maintenance have been cut by IMF imposed controls. Five hundred tube wells rely on a fleet of twelve support vehicles and spares are difficult to procure.

14. Even hand pumps require spares and maintenance. There are areas where the establishment of the spare part route and the training and payment of pump mechanics is not sustainable and alternatives must be found.

15. Where aquifer levels permit dug wells allow the use of very simple water lifting devices which can be locally maintained. In Ethiopia one of our wells programmes, in a particularly remote area, moved to rubber buckets in preference to hand pumps which were proving too difficult to service. A current well programme in northern Ghana has only used ropes and buckets. The only concessions to more advanced technology have been the use of compressed air pumps for dewatering, rock drills and steel shutters for the well rings, none of which produce long term maintenance needs. Spring protection may obviate the need for lifting devices altogether where levels permit.

16. By contrast, a simple rope pump developed on Nicaragua, has provided a great improvement in well hygiene at minimal cost. The maintenance is very simple, mostly with local materials, and local industry has been encouraged (Fig. 2).

Fig. 2. "Rope" pump - Nicaragua

17. In parts of Angola, where there is ground water, there are many wind pumps out of action. In principle the wind pump can be very appropriate, provided wind conditions have been adequately researched, but when the maintenance routes

have been interrupted, there is little that can be done with the pump until local workshops can handle the necessary repairs. In the meantime the well is useless unless it is large enough to allow bucket entry.

18. <u>Water treatment</u>. The slow sand filter pack has grown out of our emergency programmes. Sudden movements of thousands, even hundreds of thousands, of refugees, call for hastily constructed water supplies. It is rarely possible to mobilise groundwater resources at short notice and river intakes are often the only solution. Where the quality requires more than straining, settlement (with or without flocculation) and chlorination, it has been useful to turn the rubber-lined steel tanks into slow sand filter units. This equipment was one of the products of a development project with a university post-graduate programme (Fig. 3).

Fig. 3. Water treatment - Sudan

19. Post colonial conditions in Angola have left a large number of treatment works inoperable or with serious defects. The present civil war means that parts of the country are difficult to access, especially for expatriates. A suggestion from a WHO engineer working with the ministry of health led on to an appraisal visit by the technical unit. The installation of a slow sand filter plant, constructed from OXFAM water packs, will provide training in the use of the Packs, which can then be transported to difficult parts of the country and installed by local technicians. The initial installation will also plug the gap caused by delays in civil work needed for the more complex plant - imported some years ago. The longer term benefits will be in the familiarisation with slow sand filter techniques to replace the many rapid filter plants which are out if action. There

are also many places using raw river water with little or no treatment, and waterborne diseases are at a serious level.

20. <u>Water quality monitoring</u>. Another useful piece of equipment, developed in a joint effort with the Robens Institute at Surrey University, is the OXFAM/DELAGUA Water Testing Kit. This very portable kit includes a controlled incubator for E.Coli determination and is supplied with conductivity, turbidity, pH and chlorine residual apparatus. It can be run from a car battery or will last a week in the field after charging. The kit was recently awarded the Appropriate Technology Award in the RSA's Better Environment Awards for Industry scheme. It is being used, by locally trained staff, in many parts of the world to monitor water quality, providing guidelines for selecting supplies which should be improved. It does have the disadvantage of requiring occasional servicing from U.K. but, for the present, is very good value for money (Fig. 4).

Fig. 4 OXFAM/DelAgua Water Test Kit

SANITATION

21. There are still many rural communities lacking sanitation facilities and there is a steady demand for assistance with pit latrines. These are usually for family or small groupings, with locally adapted designs. In urban areas larger communal facilities may be needed. In a crowded part of Addis Ababa, communal pits are squeezed in between the crowded houses and a suction truck has been added to the city fleet to ensure continued servicing of the facilities. For large numbers of refugees or displaced people, in very crowded camps, the OXFAM sanitation unit was designed. Many of these units were used in Bangladesh after independence.

HOW APPROPRIATE IS DEVELOPMENT?

AGRICULTURE

22. A rainwater harvesting programme in Kenya illustrates the need for community involvement. The technology could not be simpler - contour earthworks to make the most of the rainfall and to minimise erosion. Hundreds of kilometres of earthworks had been constructed under s "top down" project - few of the areas had been planted and fewer maintained. The farmers felt frustrated and alienated by the decision-making processes. Since the scheme has been resuscitated with full community involvement, two hundred improved plots have been completed (Fig. 5).

23. Another project in Kenya will benefit some 60,000 people with construction of simple water tanks (52 of 125 constructed to date), subsurface dams and training for the local farmers. The introduction of ox ploughing is appropriate in some areas, where tractors would not be.

24. In Cambodia, steps ahead of some parts of the developing world, workshops for the repair of irrigation pumps and training of the maintenance mechanics have provided a major step towards sustainability.

Fig. 5 Rainwater harvesting - Kenya

HOUSING

25. In the slums of Addis Ababa the housing is traditionally of 'chika' construction, eucalyptus poles woven and plastered with mud. This type of construction requires regular maintenance and will often be seen to be in a state of near collapse. Not surprisingly the City Council has recently imposed higher standards for new construction, insisting on concrete blocks to reduce maintenance, as well as larger minimum living areas. The increased cost for concrete is balanced somewhat by the reduction in timber. This is important in a country suffering from deforestation

on a large scale. Here a little technology could be said to be appropriate and value for money. The counter argument would need to take into account the parlous state of the country's cement industry and its power requirements. The introduction of fibre reinforced cement tiles to replace steel roofing is thwarted by the lack of sawn timber for the laths. The lack of space in the slum areas, coupled with increasing standards for floor areas, is resulting in the development of two storey dwellings. These require more timber or concrete but the trend will be inevitable, given the overcrowding.

26. However, in Tanzania as in other parts of East Africa, where timber is more available, cement roof tiles are halving roofing costs as well as improving heat and noise insulation and providing local employment.

27. In other parts of the world, and especially in emergency situations, the steel roof still has an important role to play. The material can be transported quickly, is easily installed, and can be as easily removed and stored if a hurricane is approaching. It also lends itself to additional insulation if other local materials are available.

28. In the post-hurricane areas of the Caribbean and Central America the first priority is to get a roof over your head as quickly as possible. The result is that the hurriedly erected houses are even more prone to damage from the next strong wind. The severity of the damage in these areas is a direct result of poverty and consequent low construction standards. The same effect was noticeable after the Armenian and Iranian earthquakes where the extent of the damage and injury was in stark contrast to that in California with much higher levels of affluence and building standards. It is too much to expect great leaps in levels of construction standards in these poorer areas so one is looking for some way to mitigate the damage from the next 'attack'. We had spent appreciable sums on an emergency water supply and the replacement of steel roofs. A very small amount was spent on the supply of 1000 copies of a simple, illustrated book on 'Hurricane Housing'. This shows how to minimise storm damage by a few simple and inexpensive construction techniques and has the potential for making the next storm much less traumatic.

29. One thousand houses were replaced in Bluefields, Nicaragua, by the Cubans using precast concrete and a high level of local labour. The houses are surprisingly in keeping architecturally and will most certainly withstand gale force winds. This type of solution could be criticised on the value for money scale, where timber is very available and cement has a long way to travel, but the maintenance problems should not surface for many years.

HOW APPROPRIATE IS DEVELOPMENT?

TRANSPORT

30. The question has been asked "is Africa in a state of development or decay?" (ref.1). The state of the roads in many parts of Africa is cited as one of the symptoms of reliance on unsustainable technologies. There is probably little scope for Non-Government Organisations' (NGO's) involvement in solving this massive problem except, perhaps, at a local level with short feeder roads to small communities. We do, however, have to use vehicles to maintain any semblance of progress and the least we can do is to make sure vehicles supplied by us are selected for the rough terrain and have adequate spares and servicing. Trucking operations for refugee/displaced food programmes require a substantial investment in vehicles and spares. Money spent on a vehicle consultant, recently seconded from Crown Agents, is considered as a good investment considering the large proportion of our budget spent on vehicles. .

31. Motorcycles or pedal cycles will often be provided. We have, in the past, provided assistance to the development of pedal-powered load carriers. One well-known British engineer could be seen pedalling around a Nicaraguan town during his three month stint as a REDR post hurricane volunteer, fuel being at a premium at the time. In Cambodia we have spent appreciable sums on the rehabilitation of vehicle ferries where these are a vital link in the transport system (Fig. 6).

Fig. 6. Ferry maintenance workshop Phnom Penh

SAFETY

32. There are clearly many risks to life and limb in all societies, at whatever stage of development. New techniques and materials, however appropriate, bring with them new dangers, even if only from unfamiliarity. A steel roofing sheet becomes a lethal weapon in a hurricane. A mechanical saw or grinding mill are no respecters of persons.

33. Well digging has its own particular dangers, as UK figures for below ground accidents illustrate. It is therefore particularly important that all the safety rules are publicised and implemented. Safety equipment should not be skimped on the grounds of inappropriate technology, and every effort should be made to maintain safety education. Dam construction may be a local traditional skill but may well need to be supplemented with safety guidelines. Saving lives with improved health facilities should not be at the cost of lost lives during construction. We have recently produced safety guidelines in several languages together with a safety kit for well digging programmes.

DEVELOPMENT AND EMERGENCY

34. Sadly a considerable part of our effort and funding is taken up with emergency/disaster responses. Inevitably in these situations the priority is to save lives and reduce suffering. Usually some elements of the "appropriate technology/value for money" ideal have to be laid aside. Trucking water 70 kilometres for 120,000 Somali refugees in Ethiopia, which we are currently doing, would hardly be described in those terms. As it continues nearly two years after the emergency it is clear that difficult political decisions have over-ridden the simpler engineering solutions. Why let a camp be established so far from a reliable water source? Why no pipeline? What of the master plan? Will the local authorities allow the use of 1,000,000 litres a day for an indefinite period? One has to be satisfied with details like road maintenance to reduce tanker breakdown, pumps to speed up loading/unloading and standby generators to cover power failures.

36. Emergency work often leads on to development projects once the urgent problems have been solved. The well digging programmes in Ethiopia grew directly from the drought emergency of 1984'5. Having reinforced our field teams to deal with emergencies there is a stronger base on which to build development programmes. There is also pressure for us to remain in the area, especially if our efforts have met with some success.

HOW APPROPRIATE IS DEVELOPMENT?

TRAINING

37. A large part of the cost of making anything anywhere is in the provision of labour if that labour has to be imported. Training of local people is therefore a major contribution to cost reduction provided the end product is of real value. "Give a man a fish and you feed him for a day. Teach him how to fish and you feed him for a week. Show him how to make his nets, repair his boat and market his produce and you help him to feed himself for life." The contribution of technology has, therefore, to include the training of local people to use the skills and develop the materials that are so expensive to import. There are very few of our programmes which do not contain this element of working our expatriates out of their jobs. The major water supply programme in Ethiopia described above, is presently staffed by refugees and supervised by an Ethiopian engineer. The village wells programme in Ghana will be handed over to local staff after the initial phase. The Ethiopian well programme has had to be abandoned during the present hostilities, but will hopefully be resuscitated by local staff when peace returns. The workshop for maintaining a large trucking operation, also in Ethiopia, is staffed by local mechanics.

38. A building programme for returnees in Namibia will only continue on a longer term basis if basic building skills can be left within each community. Higher level skills will have to be made available on a regional basis until the communities are sufficiently re-established to be able to afford contractors. The building brigade structure that worked in the refugee camps has not proved sustainable in the returnee situation.

39. The major contribution to keeping a project alive, maintained and productive is to train the community to value the elements of the project. They are unlikely to do this if the project has been, in any sense, imposed on them. The upheavals in the Eastern Bloc remind us forcefully of the weakness of government owned institutions which lack the staff motivation for efficient operations and maintenance. Our own nationalised industries provide the same illustration. It is not surprising to see the same principles at work in the developing world. Community participation must therefore be the first point in any scheme. If this is something they asked for in the first place and if they have been consulted at every stage in the development and if they have committed themselves with labour, money or materials, then there is a good chance they will be sufficiently interested to put effort, time and money into maintaining it. It is, of course, more difficult to follow this path with larger schemes such as a water supply in the control of the water authority, or a factory run by a department of industry. Even more difficult is when the

client government insists on an unsuitable technical solution. This need not be a problem for the NGO's as they can decline to give funding for such a project (although this approach might put at risk other parts of the programme!). It is much more difficult for the consultant to turn down a lucrative project which he knows will turn into a white elephant. Client training is therefore as important for the consultant as community training is for the NGO.

REFERENCES
1. Hansen and Twaddle. Uganda Now - Between Decay and Development. James Currey Ltd. 1988

ACKNOWLEDGEMENTS
The author would like to thank his colleagues in OXFAM for their contributions and comments. The views expressed are, however, the sole responsibility of the author.

Discussion

A. REED, Paper 4

In my Paper I stressed Oxfam's concentration on enabling people to help themselves. The actual investment in technical hardware is comparatively small. The figures for 1989-90 are shown in Fig. 1. Compared with 1988-89 there has been no significant change in the balance of spending and only a slight increase in the total figure from 36.3 million to 37 million.

The balance of staff in the field offices (81 expatriates to 632 national staff) underlines the emphasis placed on local participation and consultation. (A quarter of the representatives - country, regional or provincial - and a half of their deputies are nationals.)

The attempts to avoid unsustainable technology are not always successful. A recent survey of simple wells in Ethiopia showed that not all simple wells remain safely operable.

The Arid Lands Information Network has been set up to inform and promote appropriate solutions for the special needs of the more arid zones by means of a magazine called 'Baobab'.

Flood relief is another area of technology which is of major concern. The flood action plan for Bangladesh will

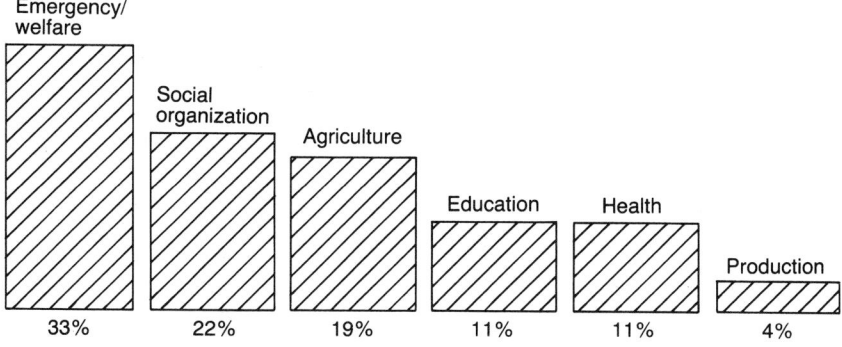

Fig. 1. Oxfam's allocation of grants overseas during 1989-90

eventually solve most of the problems but in the meantime practical and possible solutions (e.g. local bunding, floating hen coops and selective planting) could be started to assist those most at risk (ref.1).

I have endeavoured to stress the need for local consultation and participation to ensure the sustainability of technical inputs to development. The emphasis has been on small-scale projects but it should be noted that, even with the larger projects where sustainability is in the hands of a national or regional authority, there is always an interface with the local population where consultation and participation become crucial. Water wasted in distribution systems is one example, a significant proportion of the waste being at household/standpipe level. Likewise with large irrigation schemes supplying private/small-scale farms.

The UNDP workshop in Abidjan in May 1990 called for major changes in policy towards promoting and equipping local organizations, the formal and informal sectors, NGOs and communities.

'Safe water 2000' is placing emphasis on identifying and co-ordinating existing resources at country level. The manifesto of the External Support Agencies (Sophia Antipolis, 1989) laid the foundation for this emphasis. The Country External Support Information system data base has been set up to make this co-ordination possible. Research must continue in order to find even better solutions for financing and building new systems and keeping them in good repair (ref.2).

All these point towards a more sustainable future for technology but continued discipline and vigilance will be needed in order to get good value for money.

R. BELL, Consultant

A major problem with many irrigation projects is that there is no effective way of charging the farmer for the water used so that he values it. The farmer wants more water and may indeed (if he is at the top of a canal) get more by damaging the system. Certainly he has no interest in maintaining the infrastructure. A good citizen is one whose personal interest coincides with the communal good.

Typically, irrigation systems are designed technically before consideration is given to social factors and personal incentives. I suggest that consideration should be given to social factors first.

It is heresy to an engineer to suggest that water impounded above field level should not be fed by gravity to the field (at zero cost to the farmer) but should be led to level canals 1-2 m below field level and the farmer required to pump up what he needs. Farmers would then pump only what they need and indeed any excess would drain back to the canal.

A human-powered, or better, animal-powered pump could supply 1-2 ha at a rate of 1 m per 60 days (which should be adequate for rice production but which may not be enough to

DISCUSSION

control weeds by flooding). It would reduce consumption from the 3 m in 60 days used in some schemes.

This solution is not the most (mechanically) effective but it matches personal interest to communal interest and should reduce maintenance costs and lead to nearer optimum use of water.

SIR ALAN MUIR WOOD, Sir William Halcrow & Partners
In view of the strength of pressures by advertisement and marketing towards conspicuous consumption, is enough effort being applied to counter such pressures? The example from the USA is not encouraging; market forces have no respect for long-term considerations. Education must be the main weapon towards popular demand for sustainability.

I should like to enquire as to whether adequate monitoring is undertaken of successful and unsuccessful schemes, with the particular objective of defining specific criteria for success and, particularly, for failure.

Is enough effort applied to the setting up of appropriate management for projects? It is my observation that for well-established management with internal training to help sustainability, efficient operation can survive a high degree of collapse of a country's standards in other respects.

M. N. ISLAM, Department of the Environment, Bangladesh
Bangladesh is one of the victims of successive natural disasters in the form of floods within a few years (1987 and 1988). What do the Authors think are the major causes of such disasters and the possible consequences in the near future?

During the last devastating flood of Bangladesh in 1988, Oxfam played a vital role in emergency relief and rehabilitation programmes. Are there any further short-term or long-term programmes planned to overcome the disaster?

Do the Authors believe appropriate technology is no longer appropriate in terms of cost, lack of local expertise, maintenance difficulties and cost-economic and cultural points of view in developing countries? If so, how can this be overcome?

I should like to add the Farakka Barrage to the list of major causes of flooding in Bangladesh. Before the Farakka Barrage was opened (i.e. pre 1975), the Ganges carried 44 000 ft3/s of water; since then the Ganges (in Bangladesh's part it is called the Padma) has carried 34 000 ft3/s. During the devastating floods in 1988, the Padma carried 87 000 ft3/s of water. The Ganges originates in the Himalayas, then passes through Nepal, India and Bangladesh and into the Bay of Bengal. In the Himalayan region huge numbers of plants are disappearing every day; land is not managed properly and lacks grass cover. Soil types and other factors are also contributing to soil erosion and silted water. The river bed is silting up and broadening. The sudden rainfall and snow-melt and the consequent sudden opening of the Farakka

HOW APPROPRIATE IS DEVELOPMENT?

Barrage to relieve the tremendous pressure of build-up means at least three times the water flows through the river and make it impossible for the river to contain itself. The excess water overflows the bank and floods the low-lying plains. In the cause of development poorly planned soil roads are constructed without adequate culverts and bridges are built which disturb the waterways and worsen the flooding.

J. T. ARMSTRONG, Binnie & Partners
In the further development of hand-dug wells, there may be a danger of slipping from 'overgrown' engineering to 'primitive' engineering. I would suggest that work on hand-dug wells is restricted to rehabilitation as the yield is often sufficient for only a few families. In most developing countries the seasonal nature of rainfall results in rising and falling water tables and limited dry season yield. However, large drilling rigs for hand pumps are not appropriate and I commend Oxfam's development of an intermediate tool: the simplified rotary drilling rig in Cambodia.

DR I. A. SHIBLI, Third World Science and Technology Forum
From Papers 1 and 2 two development models appear to emerge

(a) the larger World Bank (and to a certain extent ODA) type projects - these are very costly, could bankrupt a developing country and could, and generally do, have political connotations
(b) smaller community-based projects advocated by well-intentioned people - these, however, do not have big money behind them and therefore cannot be replicated or made popular.

Both eventually fail.
I therefore suggest that engineers and professional institutions in the UK should help their counterparts in developing countries to build and strengthen their science and technology base and engineering institutions in those countries. The real development will be the one where engineers in those countries can come up with their own ideas of appropriate development and be strong enough to implement them. I believe that the Green Revolution in India succeeded because science and technology had a strong base there. However, in Africa it could not catch on because of the weak science and technology base.

DR G. K. BAMBRAH, Rofe, Kennard & Lapworth (East Africa)
It has been said a number of times that market forces are inadequate in themselves to get us out of the present state of affairs. I would suggest that recent trends in the world indicate that a move towards the free market is under way. Should we perhaps be addressing ourselves to the question of

DISCUSSION

appropriate modification of the decision-making tools such as CBA, EIA and other integrated approaches to this process?

PROFESSOR THRING, Paper 1

Sir Alan Muir Wood raises the key question: how can the developed and the developing countries jointly evolve the equilibrium engineering which is absolutely necessary if our descendants are to have a decent life in a stable world? It is certain that engineering has so shrunk the world that, in the long term all people will sink or swim together.

The essential components of equilibrium engineering are

(a) all humans living a good life in stable equilibrium with the ecosphere, i.e. no harmful pollution, stable forests and wildlife, and the reduction of deserts.
(b) permanently sustainable use of the world's limited resources, e.g. fuels, metals, limestone, clay, wood, fresh water and agricultural land.

In reply to Mr Islam's question about appropriate technology, I would say that I consider the concept of equilibrium engineering to have the advantages that it can be precisely defined and that it must be achieved, in both developed and developing countries, if humanity is to survive the next centuries. Equilibrium engineering is the old Greek principle of moderation in all things, which we have disastrously tried to replace with the impossible idea of perpetual growth.

The example of the USA is indeed not encouraging, nor is that of any country which has had the benefit of the Industrial Revolution, whether under market forces or any other system. Wherever the profit motive outweighs the human conscience, long-term interests are neglected.

I agree that the most important step to take is in education, both in developed and underdeveloped countries. In the former everyone needs to be taught about the long-term and worldwide consequences of their actions, about world limitations and the dangers of pollution of all kinds. Above all they need to be taught to think for themselves so that they do not accept uncritically the life-goal of a perpetually rising personal consumption.

In developing countries there is an equal need for this education but also for much more education in science and technology. However, it must be the technology of equilibrium engineering, otherwise there will be the same disastrous error made that has been made in developed countries.

The developed countries have sold their birthright (life of quality) for a mess of pottage (keeping up with the Jones). Many people listen enough to their conscience to worry about what we are doing to the Earth and its denizens, but this has almost no effect on policy decisions.

If the developing countries copy them by building huge

power stations, cities choked with commuters, mono-cropping and robot-operated factories they will destroy the traditional factors that have given them a life of quality, e.g. craftsmanship. If, however, they go straight to equilibrium engineering, they can earn a standard of living high enough to free them to enjoy this quality of life. They will be far ahead of the developed countries in the route which they will be forced painfully to follow, when disaster looms close.

Another practical step that needs to be taken is the establishment of the principles of equilibrium engineering and equilibrium economics in as much detail as has been done already for high technology and growth economics. Growth economics and high technology are failing to cope with unemployment, inflation, stress, fear, pollution, poverty, maintenance of drains, government indebtedness and so on, because they are based on an impossible concept. Every engineer knows that perpetual exponential growth is impossible, yet it is still regarded as the criterion of success by politicians and company chairmen.

In the hope of increasing the small number of examples of equilibrium engineering that already exist, a charity is being set up to do the work described in Appendix I of my Paper. This will aim to obtain funds from large sources and allocate them to established expert project groups. The project groups will be selected according to their experience in the use of equipment designed to provide power and other benefits to rural areas of the world. The aim is to use renewable energy, to avoid permanent damage to the environment and to make projects welcomed by their users, leading them to a situation where their standard of living can correspond to a permanent equilibrium with the world resources.

Each project will be based on a five-year pilot study set in a village. The project engineer and local engineers will co-operate with the villagers to develop the equipment to the point where it can fit their needs and be reliably maintained. The pilot plant, when established, will serve to demonstrate a viable solution to such problems.

J. B. WILMSHURST, Paper 2

In reply to Sir Alan Muir Wood, the ODA has a comprehensive monitoring and evaluation programme which is directed to modifying projects as necessary during implementation and learning the lessons thereafter. The evaluation studies are circulated widely outside the ODA and other donor agencies, governments of developing countries and interested members of the public.

I agree with Dr Shibli that official donors and non-governmental organizations in donor countries should assist developing countries with research into and the development of locally appropriate technologies. This has been happening for a number of years. Dr Shibli quotes the

DISCUSSION

excellent example of the Green Revolution in south Asia as the successful outcome of collaborative research and development along these lines - the product of both non-governmental and donor government financing and of diligent endeavours by agronomists in countries of the subcontinent. The Intermediate Technology Group is a non-governmental organization which benefits from official ODA support. Since the 1960s it has been developing and promoting a range of technologies in agriculture, manufacturing, mining, construction and energy use which are appropriate to the needs of low-income enterprises and households in developing countries.

Dr Bambrah is right to observe that current trends in thinking about the process of development favour a much greater reliance than was once fashionable on market forces and on the role of the private sector. There are, of course, limits to this such as those mentioned in my Paper in relation to the environment. If markets are to function efficiently many common price distortions also need to be rectified. There is no incompatibility between the use of cost-benefit analysis and environmental impact analysis and the free play (at least in most circumstances) of market forces. Cost-benefit analysis is an indispensable tool for governments in deciding which capital projects they should undertake and for private firms in compiling their capital spending programmes. To the extent possible, governments and firms should cost the environmental consequences of their projects into their cost-benefit assessments. Firms are increasingly aware of the adverse consequences to them of not taking into account fully the environmental damage which they may cause. Governments have a responsibility to the present generation and to future generations for the husbandry of the environment and so should also pay full attention in their project decisions to environmental considerations.

R. LENTON, Paper 3
In answer to Sir Alan Muir Wood about the monitoring of irrigation schemes, it is in fact far from adequate and in many developing countries there is virtually no reliable information on the extent to which irrigation systems are achieving their objectives. Since the availability of performance data is a prerequisite to effective management, this state of affairs is clearly a major constraint to the widespread adoption of appropriate practices in irrigation systems.

If adequate monitoring mechanisms for successful and unsuccessful schemes are to be introduced, indicators for assessing irrigation system performance will need to be generated. However, this in itself will not be enough. To ensure that such indicators are used in practice, methodologies to enable managers to obtain data on these indicators for irrigation systems in developing countries will need to be developed and field tested, and operating

A.REED, Paper 4
In reply to Mr Islam, the Bangladesh flood action plan holds promise of eventual improvement. In the meantime lower level technical solutions have been suggested (ref.1).

On the question of 'appropriate' technology, this can be made to work with strong community participation. Without this most solutions (technical or otherwise) will fail.

In reply to Mr Armstrong, there are still many areas where even basic well-digging techniques are not yet in use. Assistance is therefore still required where scattered populations can survive on the lower yields which hand-dug wells produce. An important element in the equipment is a dewatering facility which permits safe excavation to levels deep enough to maintain dry season yields.

Dr Shibli is over-pessimistic about smaller community-based projects. If carefully selected and implemented with full community participation they can be sustained and replicated without large financial inputs.

REFERENCES
1. BARRETT A. Floods in Bangladesh. Appropriate Technol., 1990, vol. 17, No. 1, June.
2. UNDP. Safe water 2000. 1990

5. Appropriate technological development for sustainable conservation and exploitation of natural resources in the SADCC region of Africa

M. L. KYOMO, Director, Southern African Centre of Co-operation in Agricultural Research, and C. L. KESWANI, Technical Adviser, Plant Protection Research Institute

SYNOPSIS. There is a wide diversity of ecosystems in the Southern African Development Coordination Conference (SADCC) comprising Angola, Botswana, Lesotho, Malawi, Mozambique, Namibia, Swaziland, Tanzania, Zambia and Zimbabwe. However, all these ecosystems can be very easily disturbed if heavy pressure is applied through human activities such as agriculture, mining, urbanisation, construction of roads, rail and ports, industrialisation and others. The fact that some soils in this region are easily eroded and the rainfall is erratic and often falls in form of thunderstorms which removed the top soil if there is little vegetation cover call for great care in the utilisation of these soils. Soil erosion, industrial effluents, too much reliance of artificial organic and inorganic fertilizers, herbicides and pesticides and others cause pollution and lead to health hazards. In this paper, the ecologies of SADCC have been described. The dangers caused by over exploitation of renewable natural resources without making allowances for their fast recuperation have been described. It is emphasized that the ecological diversity must be exploited judiciously for social economic development for the present generations and for posterity.

INTRODUCTION. The fragile environment in SADCC is being excessively exploited to satisfy human's social and economic needs. The ways to conserve the environmental elements such as soil, air, and water though known and appreciated in majority of cases are not being implemented judiciously for long term sustenance. In this paper, an attempt is being made first to describe the environment and the natural resources and to show the impact of various social and economic development endeavours on this environment. Before the first half of this century, the human populations in both rural and urban areas were such that there was a balance between the exploitation and regeneration of grasslands and forests. This meant that there was very little air and water pollution. This is not the case at present.

2. The SADCC region covers an area of 5.8 sq.km which is about 17 per cent of the African Continent. About 4.8 sq.km is land surface, while 0.9 million sq.km constitutes inland water systems. Table 1 shows that Angola has the largest area of 1.2 million sq.km followed by Tanzania (0.9 million sq.km) Namibia (0.82 million sq.km) and Mozambique (0.80 sq.km). Swaziland and Lesotho are the smallest countries in the region, with an area of 0.02 million sq.km and 0.03 million sq.km, respectively. Whereas, Lesotho, Malawi and Swaziland have the highest percentages of arable land 24.4 and 11.6 per cent, respectively), Angola, Botswana and Namibia have the least (about 2 per cent). Malawi, Tanzania, Zambia and Zimbabwe have the largest percentages of forest and woodland (47.5, 47.6, 27.6 and 61.5 per cent, respectively), while Botswana and

---
*SADCC is a political and economic grouping of ten countries in Southern Africa namely, Angola, Botswana, Lesotho, Malawi, Mozambique, Namibia, Swaziland, Tanzania, Zambia and Zimbabwe formed in 1980.

TABLE 1: Land Use in the SADCC Region (1980)

Country	Land Area Million sq km	Arable Land %	Perm. Crop %	Pasture %	Forest & Wood Land %	Other Land %
Angola	1.24	02.4	0.4	23.3	43.3	30.5
Botswana	0.60	02.3	-	75.2	1.6	20.9
Lesotho	0.03	09.6	-	65.9	-	24.5
Malawi	0.12	24.4	0.2	19.6	47.5	8.3
Mozambique	0.80	3.6	0.3	56.1	25.8	14.2
Namibia	0.82	*	*	*	*	*
Swaziland	0.17	11.6	0.2	72.7	5.8	9.7
Tanzania	0.95	4.6	1.2	39.5	47.6	7.1
Zambia	0.75	6.9	0.1	47.2	27.6	18.2
Zimbabwe	0.39	6.4	0.2	12.6	61.5	19.3
SADCC	477,122					
Africa	2,966,447	5.5	0.6	26.4	23.5	44.0

Source: SADCC Soil and Water Conservation and Land Utilisation Programme: Report No. 5, July 1986

Definitions: Arable Land is Land suitable for growing seasonal crops.
Other Land is land that does not fall into any of the four categories

* Not available at the time of the preparation of the paper.

CONSTRAINTS AND OPPORTUNITIES

Namibia are mainly deserts. The region is richly endowed with natural resources. Their distribution and abundance vary according to climatic, soil, altitude and latitude which in turn accounts for a diversity of bio-geographical zones. These range from moist forest to semi-arid savannah woodlands; grasslands, arid shrub thorn steppes, wetlands, and deserts. Due to this wide bio-graphical spectrum, the region encompasses a great diversity of ecosystems, many of which have yet to be fully studied, inventoried, evaluated and utilised. Some of the biomes and ecosystems are unique and are of great scientific and conservation importance.

3. The water resources of the region comprises eight major drainage systems (Figure 1) namely, the Ruvuma, Zambezi, Limpopo, Sabi, Komati, Orange (Sengu), Kunene and Okavango rivers; and some of the largest lakes on the African continent namely, Lake Malawi-Nyasa, Bangwelu, Tanganyika and Victoria. There are in addition, thousands of man-made reservoirs, amongst which the largest are lakes Kariba and Cabora Bassa, both of which are situated on the Zambezi River.

4. Wildlife in SADCC region, is of exceptional diversity. For example, out of the Africa's 84 species of larger herbivores, more than half are found in this region. Many of these species are economically important, while others have scientific medical or ritual significance. All wild animals are dependent on specific natural habitats. The wildlife resource, therefore, can best be seen in terms of the bio-geographical zones. Some wildlife and vegetation are able to survive in deserts of Kalahari and Namibia.

5. Economic development in general, and increased agricultural production in particular should aim at improving the living conditions of the population and at enhancing national and regional food security, and long-term conservation of the region's natural resource base.

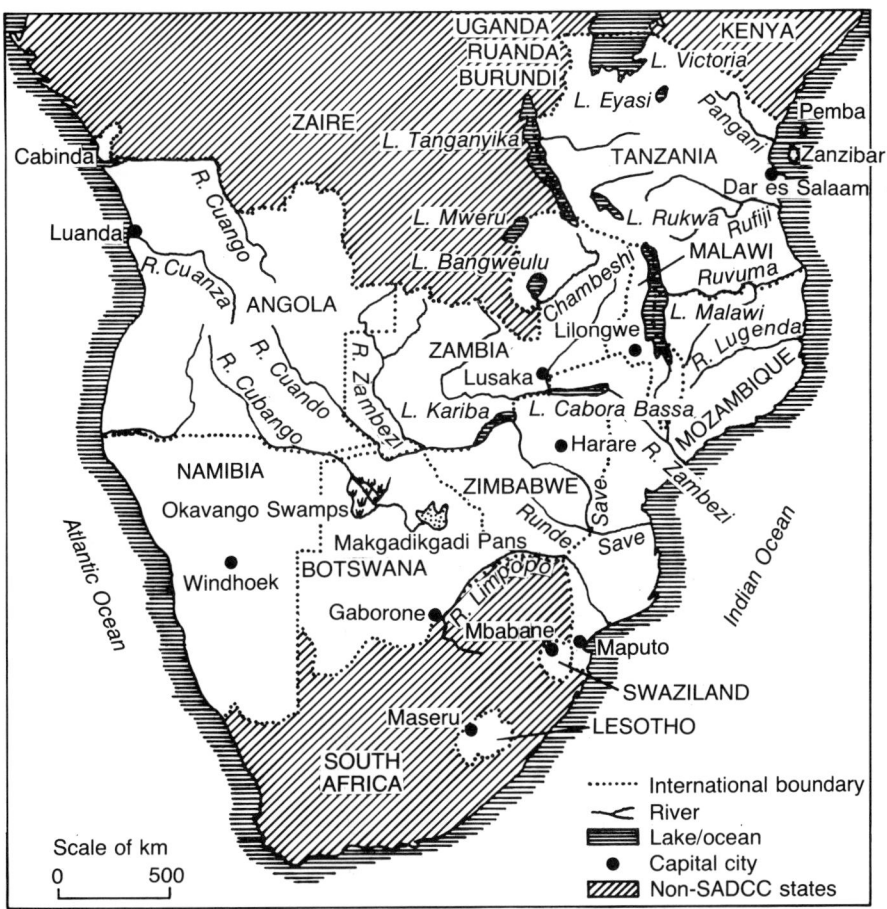

Fig. 1. SADCC natural resources - rivers, lakes and oceans

CONSTRAINTS AND OPPORTUNITIES

ACTIVITIES RELATED TO SOCIAL AND ECONOMIC
DEVELOPMENT THAT EXPLOIT OR HAVE IMPACT ON
NATURAL RESOURCES

Agriculture

Agriculture is a strategic sector in the economies of SADCC member states because a majority of the population lives and works in the rural areas. From 1980 to 1989, agriculture contributed 34 percent of the regions GNP, employed up to 80 percent of the total labour force and accounted for about 36 percent of the total exports. In the member states that are not dominated by mining, agriculture contributed about 60 percent of the total foreign exchange earnings (Table 2).

2. Before and during the early introductions of cash crops the human population pressure on the land was low. Communities used various methods of exploiting the land while leaving it to natural regeneration. There was, for example, the chitemene system in Zambia, parts of Malawi and Tanzania. It was a form of shifting cultivation for the production of finger millet. It involved the clearing of virgin forest. The cut trees and grass were burnt and the ashes were incorporated in the soil, which provided nutrients for two to three years of finger millet crop. When the fertility went down, cultivation was abandoned. This practice was repeated on new forest areas. In the meantime the old sites were given five or more years to regenerate naturally (fallow period). It was known that a shorter fallow period would not allow the soil to regain its fatility. In other parts of the region, various cultivation practices such as, the growing of crops on mounds, at the top or bottom of furrows, or in pits as a way of controlling soil erosion, and elimination of weeds was used. The latter practice allowed the decomposition of weeds with consequent built up of soil fertility. Yet, other communities evolved stall feeding as a way of controlling the collection and use of animal waste for fertilizing the soil. Residual moisture was effectively utilised in the cultivation of crops during the dry reason in valley bottoms and vleis which would normally be flooded during the rainy season in some countries of the region.

TABLE 2. Some Basic Indicators of SADCC Countries

Country	AREA ('000) Sq.km	POPU-LATION ('000000)	%POP DENSITY Sq.km	%POP IN AGRIC	AGRIC GDP	PER CAPITA GDP (US$)
ANGOLA	247	8.8	7.0	55	43	790
BOTSWANA	600	1.1	1.8	77	19	910
LESOTHO	30	1.5	50.0	77	34	530
MALAWI	118	7.0	59.3	81	45	210
MOZAMBIQUE	802	13.8	17.2	60	43	240
NAMIBIA	823	1.1	1.3	46	N/A	1470
SWAZILAND	172	0.7	4.0	69	33	800
TANZANIA	945	22.2	23.5	79	48	210
ZAMBIA	753	6.7	8.9	64	14	470
ZIMBABWE	391	9.0	23.0	56	16	740

CONSTRAINTS AND OPPORTUNITIES

3. In 1960's Sub-Saharan Africa, which includes SADCC region was a net exporter of agricultural produce. In 1970's the same countries became importers of food. This trend continued into 1980's and now Africa leads the world in reliance on food imports. According to Food and Agricultural Organisation (FAO) of the United Nations, this situation is likely to persist until some drastic measures are undertaken. It is aptly said that Africa as a continent, is losing its capacity to feed itself; using its little and scarce-hard currency in debt servicing of loans, import of food and fibre, consumer goods, machinery and equipment, technical knowhow and to a certain extent on manpower at the cost of basic national development including health, education, technology development, environmental conservation and infrastructure development. Consequently, the standard of living is either static or declining and in some countries of Africa it results in food shortages and malnutrion and in extreme cases starvation and even death.

4. The reasons for inadequate agricultural development could be traced in some of the following factors:

5. Rapid Population Growth: The population of SADCC region is increasing at an average rate of 3.5% per annum, whereas food production of food in the region is increasing at only 1.5% per year (SADCC, 1989). The FAO has projected that the region's food self sufficieny can be expected to decline from 95% in 1970-1987 to 64% by the year 2000. Therefore, in order to feed the increasing population of the region either the population growth rate should decline, or productivity must be more than doubled.

6. Land Pressure in small scale Farming Sector: Average land cultivated by a family in Sub-Sahara Africa ranges between 1.2 to 6.0 hectares (de Wilde et al, 1967, Upton, 1973, and Heyer and Waweru, 1976). But in Africa large families consisting of 7 to 15 members are not uncommon. This may be mainly due to polygamy and extended families in rural Africa. In addition to crop production, animals are an integral part of

farming system in subsistence farming. In the
communal areas of Zimbabwe the population
density is at an average of 25.2 person per sq.km
and goes up to 100 persons per sq.km in some
areas. In SADCC region about 70% of the population consists of subsistence farmers.

7. The consequence of increased pressure on the
land has resulted in deforestation, soil erosion,
water shortage, pollution and conflict in the use
of land (Kyomo and Keswani, 1987). Small land
holdings by subsistence farmers in SADCC region
precludes them from use of farm machinery for
ploughing, planting and harvesting due to
technical and economic reasons.

8. <u>Soil Erosion</u>: On World wide basis, soil
erosion is a serious constraint to agricultural
productivity, specially in the fragile tropical
soils. It is more serious in sub-Saharan Africa
in areas with slopes of more than 30%, in shallow
soils, in acid savannah soils as well as in sandy
soils. The situation is further aggravated by
over-grazing by animals (domestic and wild) as
well as deforestation caused by removal of wood
for fuel and commercial timber production. For
example, in Zimbabwe, excessive erosion especially
in communal areas is a common phenomenon. In
these lands, losses of fertile top soil at the
rate of 40 tonnes per hectare per annum are not
uncommon (Whitlow, 1980). Soil erosion is a
major contributing factor to silting of rivers and
water reservoirs.

8. <u>Low Soil Fertility</u>: Most of the subsistence
farmers in SADCC countries cultivate in marginal
lands with inherent low soil fertility. Perhaps,
this is because, during the colonial era, most of
the fertile soil was either appropriated to
settler farmers or was converted into estates by
multinational cooperations. Therefore, in order
to reap enough crop fodder from these marginal
lands, cultural practices such as green manuring
use of nitrogen fixing crops, crop rotations,
contouring, minimum tillage and others are the
alternatives to expensive and technology
dependent use of organic and inorganic fertilizers.

CONSTRAINTS AND OPPORTUNITIES

9. **Erratic Rainfall and need for Irrigation**: In Africa, 44% of the land area is desert, arid or semi-arid, 18% has low fertility and 18% has shallow depth and excessive water (Swaminathan, 1986). To successfully cultivate crops and pastures, it is necessary to have irrigation. The development of irrigation in SADCC region has lagged far behind the desired level. Table 3 shows the irrigated areas in relation to irrigation potential in some selected SADCC countries. Consequently, most of the farming in the SADCC region is rainfed. But, perhaps due to global environmental changes, the total rainfall distribution in recent years has been erratic. This rainfall sometimes comes in form of storms. This leads to fast sealing of soil pores and hence low water absorption and high water run-off and soil erosion. Therefore, soil erosion and rainfall are interlinked in one way or the other.

Table 3. Estimates of Irrigated Ares in 1982 in relation to Irrigation Potential (000'ha)

Country	Irrigation Potential	Commercial Farming	Small Scale or Traditional farming	Total	Irrigation Development % of potential
ANGOLA	6,700	0	10	10	<1
BOTSWANA	100	0	12	12	12
LESOTHO	8	0	1	1	13
MALAWI	290	19	2	21	7
MOZAMBIQUE	2,400	66	4	70	3
*NAMIBIA	*	*	*	*	*
TANZANIA	2,300	34	106	140	6
ZAMBIA	3,500	14	2	16	1
ZIMBABWE	280	140	6	146	52

* Statistics not available at the time of preparation of the paper.

Adapted from: Swaminathan (1986)

10. <u>Poor Infrastructure:</u> Agricultural areas in most of the SADCC region are characterized by poor rural infrastructure. These include lack of rail and road transport, dams and boreholes, lack of power supply and finally poor marketing systems. These deficiencies have generally resulted in low economic developments in respective countries.

11. Even, when farmers have managed to produce agricultural commodities, storage facilities have posed serious problems. The low farm productivity coupled with non-marketability of produce has continued or widened the gap between the rich and the poor. This situation has significant political implications resulting in unstability of political systems detrimental to the welfare of the nations.

12. To overcome some of the constraints and bottlenecks for improved agricultural production, technologically sound development strategies need to be formulated on short and long term basis. Basic aim is to develop sustainable agricultural base with the use of available technology and resources.

13. Some of the technological development required to improve the agricultural productivity of SADCC countries, to uplift the per capita income of their inhabitant could include:

14. <u>Irrigation:</u> The arid to semi-arid nature of arable land and unreliable rainfall in most of the SADCC countries, make the development of irrigation of paramount importance especially for the benefit of small holders or subsistence farmers. Irrigation development could take the form of canal construction to harvest perenial river water, drilling of boreholes and/or construction of small and large dams. In most of the countries of the region as indicated earlier, there are rivers with ample discharge for irrigation development.

CONSTRAINTS AND OPPORTUNITIES

15. However, there are several constraints in the development of irrigation system in SADCC region. Firstly, there is paucity of financial resources, secondly shortage of technology including technical manpower, and thirdly lack of equipment and machinery. Even if these resources were available, feasibility studies on water retention, properties of soils, underground water resources, effect of canal and dam construction on the environment including fauna and flora are lacking. In addition, the effect of irrigation and canal use and construction on water table are not known. Further, most of the countries lack water harvesting and storage techniques.

16. It should be noted that improper development of irrigation may create salinity problems similar to those that are being manifested in parts of India and Pakistan.

Production and use of Agro-chemicals:

17. In general the productivity of crops and animals in developing countries is low as compared to developed countries. For example, the average yield of rice in United States is between 8-10 tonnes per hectare (USDA, 1986) whereas, in most SADCC countries it averages between 2-3 tonnes per hectare. This is mainly due to low soil fertility, damage by pests, diseases and weeds as well as lack of moisture in the soil. In order to increase crop yields with the use of high yielding crop varieties, integrated pest management techniques are required.

Development of Transport Infrastructure:

18. Development of agriculturally based economy requires a satisfactory network of rail and road transport. Although most of major commercial centres in SADCC countries are interconnected with reasonably well maintained network of roads, there is acute shortage of roads and rail systems in rural areas where most of the agricultural production takes place. Again the development of these facilities require technology, equipment, materials as well as energy source, all of them scarce in this region.

19. The development of this infrastructure often leads to exposure of large tracts of land to wind and water erosion. This in many cases has been responsible for loss of valuable top soil as well as pollution and silting of rivers and dams. Unfortunately, in SADCC countries legislations to force road and rail construction companies to replant grass and trees on these exposed areas do not appear to be effective.

Expansion of Land for Cultivation:
20. Many countries around the world, including those in the SADCC region are expanding farming areas by indiscriminate clearing of trees from the land. This clearing makes the land prone to soil erosion, erratic rainfall, loss of catchment areas for rivers and lakes. The ultimate catastrophe is shortage of food and sometimes drought and famine. Although only 25 percent of potentially arable land in Africa is now under cultivation, it would be wrong to conclude that increase in food production can be achieved by bringing new lands under cultivation. In most cases the economic and/or ecological costs of doing so are very high and sometimes prohibitive (Strong, 1989). Therefore, there is a need for location specific cost-benefit assessment, before such and endeavour is undertaken.

Marketing and Storage Infrastructure:
21. The agricultural output specially for food and fibre produced by rural communities in SADCC region is often vulnerable to market forces due to lack of storage infrastructures. Consequently, there is wide seasonal fluctuation in prices, and in some cases produce is lost to spoilage by bacteria, fungi and insects. This results in unprofitable farming enterprise and in many cases, the farmers even give up the farming itself and look for stable source of income in urban centres. This migration from rural to urban areas is a serious threat to whole economic base of the countries.

22. But to develop rural marketing and storage infrastructures basic ingredients such as resources and techical know how is imperative.

CONSTRAINTS AND OPPORTUNITIES

Mining

23. The SADCC region in general is richly endowed with mineral resources. Table 4 shows the major minerals found in each member state of SADCC. In exploiting these mineral resources, various methods such as open cast or strip mining, deep shaft system are being used. In some cases the exhausted mines are left exposed to direct wind, rain and sun making them vulnerable to erosion and subsequently to air and water pollution. There is need for protection of natural resources from these activities by reinforcing legislation on the shaping of these areas as mining progresses and on containing the effluents from mineral processing plants.

Energy

24. Energy in one form of the other, is the basic requirement for every developmental aspect from cooking to driving the vehicles and trains, and to keeping the wheels of industry moving. Natural gas and oil, in most of the SADCC countries except Angola are non-existent, or where they have been discovered, their commercial exploitation has not been undertaken. In countries such as Botswana, Mozambique, Swaziland, Tanzania, Zambia and Zimbabwe there is significant presence of coal resources; but it is a non-renewable source of energy and cannot be relied upon on long term basis. At the same time 80% of the Africa's energy is derived from fuel wood, and the continent faces a severe energy crisis because harvesting already greatly exceeds planting. Twenty-nine trees are cut on the continent for every one that is planted. In 1980 about 146 million Africans did not have enough wood to heat their homes or cook their food.. Forecasts for the year 2000 put that figure at more than 500 million. This crisis is most urgent in rural areas, where 80 to 90 percent of those without sufficient wood supplies live. The bottom line of this issue is the development of alternatives such as nuclear, etc. Again most of these depend on availability of finance and technology and technical manpower

TABLE 4. MAJOR MINERALS FOUND IN THE SADCC REGION

COUNTRY	MINERALS
ANGOLA	Diamonds, Petroleum, Copper Gemstones, Iron-ore, Manganese, phosphates, Salt, Uranium. Natural gas.
BOTSWANA	Diamonds, Gold, Coal, Soda Ash, Copper-nickel, Iron-ore, Manganese, Chromite, Uranimum.
LESOTHO	Diamonds, Peat, Lead, Iron-ore, Uranium.
MALAWI	Coal, Bauxite, Lime, Asbestos, Graphite, Uranium, phosphates.
MOZAMBIQUE	Coal, Graphite, Elmenite, Bauxite, Coke, Iron, Mica, Tin, Gold, Nickel, Copper.
NAMIBIA	Uranium, Diamonds, Cadmium, Copper, Gas, Gold, Lithium, Pyrite, Silver, Zinc. Tin. Gemstones.
SWAZILAND	Diamonds, Asbestos, Coal.
TANZANIA	Coal, Diamonds, Gold, Kaolin, Gemstones, Gas. Phospates. Natural gas.
ZAMBIA	Copper, Cobalt, Lead, Zinc, Gemstones.
ZIMBABWE	Gold, Nickel, Coal, Asbestos, Copper Chromite, Iron-ore, Silver, Tin.

CONSTRAINTS AND OPPORTUNITIES

<u>Policies and Strategies on Natural Resources
Conservation, Management and Utilisation</u>

25. The SADCC organisation wishes to protect the environment for the present generations and for posterity. It has set up a Plant and Forest Seeds Gene Bank to preserve domesticated and wild plant species. It has policy and strategies for improving food security and for protecting the environment. The strategy for food and agriculture encourages small and large scale farmers to diversify their activities by engaging in both food and cash crops. This is expected to enable them to earn cash returns for the uplifting of their nutritional and living standards. The Natural Resources Policy and Strategy recognises three broad and inter-dependent classes of natural resources management, viz. conservation, utilisation and environmental monitoring:

- Conservation aims at ensuring long term availability of natural resources, for the benefit of present and future generations. Policies include the establishment of protected areas to preserve selected samples of region's flora and faunal communities or to protect areas of great beauty and species diversity.

- Utilisation is to derive benefits, on a sustainable basis, from natural resources, and

- Environmental monitoring involves assessment of the impact that development and other human activities have on the environment. Such assessments form the basis for appropriate measures to be taken to control and manage the environment.

26. This strategy argues that there must be a multidisciplinary approach to the conservation, utilisation and monitoring of natural resources and of the environment; aimed at achieving optimum sustainable benefits for all peoples, and in particular the rural communities. Natural resources conservation and management are viewed as distinct elements within the SADCC programmes dealing with conservation and land utilisation, forestry, fisheries and wildlife.

The multidisciplinary approach requires close collaboration among SADCC sectors especially, agricultural research and training, and development oriented sectors of; food security, livestock production and animal disease control, industry, energy, mining and tourism. SADCC also encourages initiatives in the formulation and implementation of similiar policies and strategies to take place at national level. SADCC was established in 1980 and although it has achieved a great deal in formulation of policies and strategies in various sectors the biggest challenge is the integration and harmonisation of the same for the benefit of the citizens and the future generations.

DISCUSSION

27. An overview of the past three decades of global economic development shows impressive gains in human welfare. People generally have more food to eat than they did in 1960's. The rate of population growth is either static, declining or in some countries like Singapore is negative. Similiar trends are visible in combating diseases and illiteracy and in creation of wider economic opportunity and posterity.

28. On the other hand, by almost any measure Africa is "odd man out". Africa has less today than it did 20-25 years ago, as population growth continues to overtake hard won advances in food production and economic growth. In this respect SADCC countries are still much better off than many other countries in the same continent such as Sahelian countries or Ethiopia and Sudan. There has been no famine in spite of occasional drought, locust invasion and unreliable rainfall.

29. In order to sustain and continue economic growth and social development in SADCC region, plans for restoration and improved management of natural resources, not only for the present generation and for posterity must be made.

30. Unlike, North America, Europe and some countries in South and East Asia, where the economic developments have been on the basis of industrialisation, in Africa it has to be based on

agriculture. In Africa nearly 40 cents out of each dollar earned comes from agriculture. Between 55-80% of the population in this continent is directly or indirectly dependent on agricultural activities. It is therefore, the biggest single employer of labour. All these attributes are equally applicable in SADCC countries. Past historical experience in Africa, shows that over emphasis on industrialisation at the neglect of agriculture can lead to low or negative social and economic development. For example the copper based economy of Zambia up until 1970's.

31. In some countries such as Zimbabwe agriculture has at all times received equal or better share of national resources in terms of research and development, training, infrastructures and marketing. In other words, a balance in investment between agriculture and industry is essential for social and economic development particularly in SADCC countries. In this respect, the region could learn from Japan, a small country with high population density and intensive agriculture which is now emerging as one of the leading economic powers in the world; second only to the United States. Japan can be proud of its record in reducing air and water pollution at home and its leadership in international environmental cooperation.

32. While, African countries are struggling on the drawing board with the concurrent agricultural and industrial development, there is a need to revisit the so called "Bio-intensive farming". In bio-intensive minifarming, crops are placed close together on comparatively small land areas. They use one-fourth the amount of water, one-one hundredth of the energy required for conventional farming and need little or none of the costly and potentially dangerous inputs of fertilizers and and pesticides. This saves the farmer money, while at the same time preserving soil quality and maintaining purity of ground water. The traditional African farming system of intercropping requires further assessment for the benefit of small farmer.

33. One of the major stumbling blocks in raising economies of SADCC countries is the scarcity of human capital. One should appreciate that when Africa started to undergo the process of independence in 1960's which continues till today, many of the trained and experienced professionals left the continent. The shortage of trained manpower which is still felt today has caused slow progress in the development of African nations. Education and training, therefore, should receive due emphasis.

34. Just 20 years ago, Asia was a continent of concern and Africa was not even a topic of discussion. Today, Africa is in the spotlight in man's struggle against economic under-development. Africa has many assets - land, mineral wealth, climate, water resources and above all hardworking and willing men and women. It is not too late to build an African version of green revolution based on twin foundations of ecological and economic sustainability, if policy makers and administers would use wisely the experience and knowledge gained in past 20 years from developed nations like Japan, India, South Korea, Singapore and others.

35. Swaminathan (1986) predicts that in the next 10 years, food problems of Asia will be a topic of discussion, rather than Africa; because Asia has more fundamental problems such as large population, growing unemployment, diminishing land resources and varying degrees of damage to lake and river ecosystems, in addition to change in environmental parameters. Hopefully, scientists, engineers, policy makers and administrators and the people of respective continents are able to prove Dr. Swaminathan wrong.

REFERENCES

de Wilde, J.C., P.F.M. McLoughlin, A. Guinard, T. Scudders and R. Mauboucha (1967). Experiences with agricultural development in tropica Africa. Vol. The Synthesis Vol. 2. The case studies. Jon. Hopkins Press, Baltimore.

Heyer, J and J.K. Waeru (1976). The development of the small farm areas. In Heyer, J. Matha J.K. and Senga W.M. (Eds). Agricultural Development in Kenya. Oxford University Press.

Kyomo, M.L. and C.L. Keswani (1987). Structure and distribution of land and corresponding yields of field crops in Eastern and Southern Africa. GCP/RAF/SWE. FAO, Rome. p.54-69.

Southern African Development Coordination Conference (SADCC) (1989). Food Agriculture and Natural Resources. Annual Report.

- SADCC Policies and Strategies on: Food, Agriculture and Natural Resources Annual Repots 1987 and 1988.

Strong, M.F. (1989). Ending hunger through sustainable development. Third Annual Arturo Tanco Memorial Lecture. The Hunger Project. Global Office, 1, Madison Ave. New York. NY10010 30pp.

Swaminathan, M.S. (1986). Sustainable nutrition security for Africa, Lessons from India. Hunger Project Paper No. 5. The Hunger Project. 1388 Sutter Street. San Francisco. CA 94109.

United States Department of Agriculture (USDA) (1986). Crop production 1985 summary. National Agricultural Statistics Service. Washington D.C. U.S. Government Printing Office February. 40pp.

Upton, M. (1973) Farm Management in Africa. The Principles of Production Planning. Oxford University Press. London.

Whitlow, J.R. (1980) Envionmental constraints and population pressures in the tribal areas of Zimbabwe. Zimbabwe Agricultural Journal 77:173-181.

World Bank (1987) World Development Report. International Bank for Reconstruction and Development/The World Bank. 1818 H. Street, N.W. Washington D.C. 20433 U.S.A.

World of Information: The Africa Review. The Economic and Business Report. 13th Edt. 256p. NTC Business Books - A Division of NTC Publish . Group. US Edt. Essex. U.K.

6. The social appropriation of technology

PROFESSOR A. REW, MA(Econ), PhD, Director, Centre for Development Studies, University of Wales

SYNOPSIS. 'Appropriate' means both suitability and taking possession. The focus of the paper is on how the world's poorer income groups can take possession of the benefits of technical change while avoiding the impact of its costs. Taking control of development requires participation in the design of projects and partnerships between technical and social science disciplines and between community groups and official sponsors. The likelihood of these requirements being met is examined in the specific case of resettlement projects and those for forestry conservation.

1. A SUITABLE DEVELOPMENT FOR THE WORLD'S POOR
The Standard of Survival

1. The idea of suitability or appropriateness necessitates the use of standards; in the case of the present conference the standard is survival. The starting point for this paper is that suitability and survival centre on the extent of world poverty. In this sense an appropriate development is a development suitable to at least the survival of the poor and, hopefully, to an improvement in their livelihoods and welfare.

The Magnitude of the Problem

2. Roughly one-third of people in the developing countries consume goods and services valued - at today's exchange rate - at approximately 50 pence or less per day. In absolute terms we can estimate that more than one thousand million people live at chronic poverty levels characterised by malnutrition, disease, short-life expectancy and high infant mortality rates. Of these people, in what I am terming chronic poverty, some 630 million people - or 18 per cent of the total population of the developing world - are **critically** poor with a total consumption level of less than 40 pence per day. In addition to the over one thousand million in critical and chronic poverty there is probably close to another one

thousand million living at a subsistence margin that, while not life-threatening, precludes attainment of much beyond the minimal necessities. Thus the lives of more than two thousand million of the world's five thousand million people are controlled by the conditions of bare (refs. 1-2) survival or its actual lack.

Southern, Rural and Poor
3.   The vast majority - over 85 per cent - of the world's critically and chronically poor people live in the developing countries of Africa, Asia and Latin America. At least 80 per cent of those living below or very near the level of chronic poverty in the developing world live in the rural areas. These people depend overwhelmingly on agricultural activities and the natural environment for (ref. 1) their daily subsistence.

Further Population Growth
4.   These magnitudes may already seem overwhelming. They give a picture of a major proportion of the world's human population as resident in the rural areas of the southern continents and suffering from the multiple deprivations of poverty. There has been some progress in tackling the causes and consequences of poverty in certain regions and sectors. Nonetheless, the level of poverty will grow in the next decade since the world's population is calculated to have increased by a further one thousand million by the year 2000. An estimated 90 per cent of that increase will occur in the developing countries. These magnitudes and rates provide an important context for any discussion of what is appropriate about forms of development and help (ref. 2) highlight the urgency of the development task.

2. THE POSSESSION OF TECHNOLOGY
5.   The term "Appropriate" also means taking possession and it is my contention that the key social issue in development is how the poor can take possession of the benefits of technical change while avoiding taking (ref. 3) possession of its costs. The critical issue is one of control - 'appropriate' can mean taking possession, taking control so that key decisions and arrangements for design and implementation are either in the hands of the most needy beneficiaries or can be substantially influenced by them. In other words, an appropriate technology and development requires public participation in setting the aims of projects and programmes and in the arrangements for determining the nature and flow of the benefits and costs arising from improved productivity and technical efficiency.

Criteria for Social Appropriation

6. Many of the detailed discussions needed to establish the scope for community participation and within which to address world poverty come later in the conference. There will be discussions of training, labour-based technology and of implementation in specific sectors of technology and development, for example, water and sanitation, energy and transportation. The tests of realism for poverty-focused planning and of community participation should be in specific areas of implementation. We know, for example, that it is generally easier to introduce community participation frameworks in water supply projects than in water harvesting and catchment planning. We also know that some social and cultural structures are more prone to factionalism and schism than others and that community participation will be harder to achieve in these cases. The purpose of this paper is not, however, to review the detailed prospects for poverty-focused planning and community participation strategies. It is, rather, to state three key principles or criteria for use in judging what is 'appropriate' in a given local context.

Development and Poverty Alleviation

7. The first of these three principles can be stated in a negative way – it is that people are neither constraints or opportunities to or for development, as the title to this session could imply. Put positively, people come (ref. 4) first and the aim of development policy analysis and development planning is the alleviation of poverty and the reform of the social and economic relationships which create it. Human welfare and poverty alleviation is the standard against which development outcomes should be judged. In other words, the minimum appropriate standard for development is the survival of the poor's livelihoods. Development cannot be thought appropriate if livelihoods are destroyed by insensitive development or by a development which places future uncertain gains accruing to unspecified groups and individuals above immediate needs.

Partnerships in Planning

8. The second and third criteria centre on partnerships in planning. One of these, the most important of the two, is the need to encourage a partnership between state agencies and community groups in the interests of implementation. The second of the two partnerships concerns the respective contributions of the technical specialist – the engineer and agricultural scientist for example – and the social analyst – usually a social anthropologist or sociologist.

9. Let me take this last partnership first and then with

this out of the way turn to the other two later in the paper as the main means and ends of the development process.

3. THE SOCIO-TECHNICAL MESH

10. There is much to suggest that the social analyst and the engineer have aims and activities in common. The sociologist in development work spends most of his or her time understanding how existing structures are held together by forces and dynamic pressures and how they are maintained or alternatively deteriorate and change over time. The output of this analysis is the design of new structures or recommendations for remedial action on existing ones. Both the engineer and the sociologist, that (ref. 4) is, deal in constructions and design. The sociologist is principally concerned, however, with social constructions, with the cultural and organisational templates that shape social behaviour and people's understanding of reality. There is a major difference, for example, between the way that most engineers on the Indian sub-continent in Egypt or Ethiopia understand project management and the way that British engineering institutions teach it. It is not at all clear that the differences can be dismissed as simply 'inefficiency'. There are social constructed realities in these management cultures which are not to be dismissed as simply 'poor national practice and sociologists will need special terms and concepts to analyse them.

11. Engineering education could contribute to the professional dialogue by assisting the production of guidelines on how to incorporate sociological inputs and sociological concepts into project planning. It is not so long ago that I was told by an engineering director wishing to save money and retain control of his team that a soil scientist might double up as rural sociologist. Apparently, the soil expert was a pleasant, sociable person and had previous experience of counting village huts on aerial photographs which the director thought ought to be relevant! Some engineers are also riotously unable to avoid playing to the gods about sociological language. They should pause at this point and ask themselves why the special terminologies of economics and engineering are OK as concepts and those of sociology are (always?) spurious.

12. There is a need for sociological and engineering partnership not denigration. Both disciplines need to demonstrate to sometimes sceptical publics that their professionalism is not, as Shaw might have it, a conspiracy against the layman but a commitment to the search for technologies capable of appropriation by the developing countries' chronically poor. The two disciplines need to demonstrate this in their choice of

research and development priorities and by critically challenging those projects and programmes which will jeopardise the poor's existing livelihoods.

4. POVERTY-FOCUSED TRANSPORT PLANNING
13. The need for these disciplines' partnership and a demonstration of the first criterion - the overriding aim of poverty alleviation - can be seen in the field of rural transport. Engineers have been particularly interested in the machines and structures which promote efficiency in transportation. Adam Smith gave great importance to transport, particularly transport by water for 'the extent of the market'. On some Pacific coasts and groups of islands the typical transport system for goods and passengers relies on initial footpower and headloading which then links to smallboat marine transport. Typically, however, the terms of reference and inputs for engineering consultancies stress assessment skills for roads and buildings. They show little interest in the techniques and organisational challenges needed to secure or improve footpaths and footbridges, to control the deep gullying of footpaths leading to jetties or in naval architecture. The stress on roadbuilding may appear correct from the perspective of the rural elite, offering them all-weather transportation of bulked cargoes. From the standpoint of the chronic poor new roads can be a threat; roads will not necessarily enhance their returns from trade and it will bring into the area those who can not only appropriate the technology but, most probably, the area's land as well. Transport design can contribute to appropriate development for survival by understanding the poverty context of rural transport activity.

5. A POVERTY-FOCUS TO MAJOR PROJECTS
14. This last observation should not be taken to mean that only small-scale engineering is beautiful. The magnitude of poverty, the rate of population growth, national aspirations and underutilised resources all lead to the search for larger solutions. Yet we are all familiar with the actual and perceived social and environmental deterioration with which large industrial and infrastructural projects are sometimes associated. The central social issue is not size but how the technology is appropriated and controlled.
15. In the case of mining and ore processing projects, for example, these are often located in more sparsely populated areas with marginal agriculture. It is precisely in these areas that great care should be taken to examine the actual and potential linkages of the new project with the non-project economy and society even though the gap may appear considerable and the prospects for integration seems unlikely at first glance. Often there is no

provision for training to prepare the local population for the range of jobs which the project will create. Even if there is a training programme there is only very infrequently the thorough-going regional investigations of linkage, vulnerability and capability which would alert related industries, departments and agencies to the opportunities to avoid polarisation in the local economy. Too often, major industrial and irrigation projects in marginal areas simply incorporate some of the able bodied locals as watchmen and labourers while the elderly infirm, many women and the extremely poor are further impoverished. It is usually possible, however, to mitigate the poverty creating outcomes provided there is monitoring of the detailed outcomes of project arrangements and the need to do so is accepted at policy levels.

Poverty and Resettlement Planning

16. The worst poverty impacts usually arise from non-existent or inadequate resettlement planning following land acquisition to develop the project. National departments and ministries eager to implement a major project are prone to state that they have land acquisition, compensation and the resettlement modalities (refs. 5-8) under control. The comparative evidence suggests most strongly that they do not and that donors and consultant engineers would be strongly advised not to take the usually bland assurances about land acquition and resettlement at face value. Frequently, the numbers of people who will be dispossessed through initial land acquisition and subsequent project development is understated often because of the failure to look closely at the details of the local economy and of land rights. The landless suffer disproportionately when compensation is offered in cash rather than in alternative accommodation and livelihood. Community organisation tends to unravel as resettlement proceeds even if there has been an attempt at the relocation of the community, or significant sections of it, in nearly locations. The executive agency often resists the preparation of a resettlement plan to give itself more flexibility only to find that the need to buy off discontent early in the project leaves it with insufficient funds to resettle people caught up in the development of ancillary infrastructure.

The Appropriation of Compensatory Development Potential

17. Engineers and planners may find themselves arguing that there are compensatory local benefits from the new development. Reservoir development, for example, may entail disruption and loss of land but it **may** also bring fishing and tourism potentials. Yet these theoretical

opportunities are not on open access; opportunities to take advantage of them are structured and biased according to the existing social structure and information channels and only a few who actually know about the possibilities will have the capital, social contacts and confidence to participate. It may take years to develop possible tourism opportunities and local operators will usually require urban contacts and substantial capital. Fisheries may be easier to enter but full-time fishery is frequently perceived as the occupational prerogative of special social groups, both in areas of south asia and also in Africa. In Rajasthan it is an occupation for tribals; in Sri Lanka for a specialised caste; in inland southern Tanzania for a tribe. There may be no-one from these groups in the dispossessed population. Moreover there may be resistance to outsiders from these or other groups coming to the reservoir area to available themselves of opportunities which have arisen from the local people's misfortune. The known costs of resettlement need to be balanced against the carefully judged likelihood of the realisation of potential benefits when social and microeconomic constraints are taken into account. If the full local costs of resettlement are taken into account the reservoir project with an apparently healthy rate of return on investment can suddenly become (ref. 9) more marginal. The World Bank has estimated the economic cost of resettlement per household in the Narmada Valley project at US$34,000.

6. INTERACTION NOT INTERVENTION

18. The style of development work that is increasingly needed is based on an interaction with local society and economy rather than an intervention from outside. Development specialists appear too often to think of development as a container they have brought in from outside and then opened up in a local community to demonstrate the technical wares and consumption goods on offer. An **appropriate** development needs – rather than this external packaging and containerisation – facilitators who can encourage interaction between the specialised scientific and planning knowledge brought in from outside and the indigenous technical knowledge and people's science on which local farmers and health practitioners have had to rely, usually successfully (ref. 10). The identification and implementation of solutions to poverty and survival require a partnership between these two forms of knowledge and also between the community, regional and governmental institutions which carry them within a given country. The partnership should then consist of both a sharing of knowledge and of arrangements to encourage joint governmental and community planning of key resources.

CONSTRAINTS AND OPPORTUNITIES

A Partnership with Indigenous Technical Knowledge

19. Partnership and community participation cannot work if the existing technical knowledge of rural communities is dismissed out of hand. Moreover, the less developed countries often face combinations of low export commodity prices, deteriorating terms of trade against essential imports and growing debt which encourage their national planners to support possible village-level solutions to social needs rather than solutions which depend upon additional public sector delivery systems and expanded recurrent budgets.

20. In the field of health, for example, the impact of external debt and the structural adjustment programmes required by donors have necessarily limited the ambition of LDC governments to expand both curative health and primary health care systems. Governments can no longer afford the health sector staff or the drugs. This creates the space within which to examine more closely the merits and disadvantages of indigenous health knowledge and the role played by other medical systems and traditional practitioners. Traditional medical systems in south India are already organised and often have written systems of knowledge. There is a need to record African traditional health practices and systems of knowledge. Certain membership organisations of traditional heath practitioners have already begun to do so.

21. Indigenous technical knowledge in agricultural production has been less well recorded, although social anthropologists have made a number of recent contributions in this field. The challenge in rainfed farming in arid and semi-arid zones, for example, is to integrate the design of participatory planning with farmers and their community institutions with plant breeding research and improved soil and water conservation. ODA is supporting participatory research and planning work in rainfed agricultural areas in both eastern and western India.

7. REGIONAL RESOURCES AND PUBLIC PARTICIPATION

22. These last illustrations of attempts to plan projects with a strong socio-technical mesh may appear small scale and they also involve interdisciplinary work with medical, plant science and agricultural engineering specialists rather than with engineers. But there is an increasing need to think about community participation on a much larger scale and to involve civil engineering in the range of professional partnerships. Many rural areas in the developing countries are so populous and fragmented in their landholding that solutions drawn from low-cost urban engineering may need to be examined. The pace and pressure of development also means that land use must be reconsidered in new, more imaginative ways.

23. Forestry conservation and development, for example, can involve very large land areas and major resource planning considerations. The recent announcement of a proposed new UK broadwood forest on the site of the old Needwood and Charnwood forests in the British Midlands envisages a forest of some 150 square miles with a population of five million within 30 miles of it and the planting up of major areas of low-grade farmland and derelict industrial sites and coal spoil heaps. There will need to be considerable public consultation and participation, finely-tuned incentive schemes and partnership between Government and private funding sources if the forest conversion is to succeed.

24. It is worth trying to view this proposed new forest development in reverse and in trying to imagine the progressive growth of the agricultural, human settlement and industrial activity which has reduced forest cover in many less developed countries which were previously rich in timber and non-wood forest products. If we can do so, we begin to see the scale of the problem that is faced by those charged with the conservation, rehabilitation and development of forest lands in Asia and Latin America. These forest lands still provide essential fuelwood and fodder for nearby and more distant agricultural and urban communities. They are also often rich in mining and hydro-electric potential and, because they are more sparsely populated, provide the sites for major projects such as power stations. These forest regions are relatively unknown both sociologically and environmentally. The exact status of rights concerning the collection of fuelwood and fodder are either sharply contested or are very grey and uncertain because the emphasis, hitherto, has been on the regulation of timber resources not other forest products. The balance of interests in forest use is usually not well known. There is potential for conflicts between forest users from adjacent and more distant communities and between officers of the forest service and local populations (ref. 11). The secondary towns within the forest region often provide some off-farm employment and service provision but also tend to have urban residents with very low incomes.

25. These more marginal lands are major challenges to poverty-focused planning partnerships and to the balance between development which is appropriated locally and development which is 'trucked in' by means of externally controlled infrastructural and industrial development. However well-meaning these last attempts at development they are - because of their scale and the perspectives of the political, economic and occupational elites - usually destructive of livelihoods. Many of the rights of land tenure and usage which underpin the livelihoods are

unwritten and are thus easily ignored. The challenge for 'appropriate development' is to field the multi-discipline teams and to encourage the partnership between external technical and local knowledge which will make it possible for the poor to appropriate their own futures.

REFERENCES
1. LEONARD H.J. Environment and the poor: development strategies for a common agenda, Transaction Books, New Brunswick and Oxford, 1989.
2. WORLD BANK World Development Report 1990: Poverty, Oxford University Press, 1990.
3. LAMB G. and SCHAFFER B.B. Can equity be organised? Gower, Aldershot, 1980.
4. CERNEA M. Putting people first: sociological variables in rural development, Oxford University Press, Oxford, 1985.
5. SCUDDER T. The development potential of new lands settlement in the tropics and sub-tropics: a global state-of-the-art evaluation with special emphasis on policy implications, AID Evaluation Discussion Paper 21: 1-46, USAID, Washington, DC, 1984.
6. REW A. and DRIVER P. Initial evaluation of the social and environmental impact of the Victoria Dam project, vol. III Overseas Development Administration, London, 1986, Evaluation Report EV 392.
7. CERNEA M.   Involuntary resettlement in World Bank projects: policy guidelines, World Bank Technical Paper, 22, 1988.
8. MOUGEOT Luc   Future hydroelectric development in Brazilian Amazonia: towards comprehensive population resettlement in GOODMAN D. and HALL A. (eds.) The future of Amazonia: destruction or sustainable development? Macmillan, London, 1990.
9. OWEN P.L., MUIR T.C., REW A.W. and DRIVER P.A. Evaluation of the Victoria project in Sri Lanka: 1975-1985 Evaluation Report, Overseas Development Administration, London EV 392 volume 1, 1986.
10. RICHARDS P. Community environmental knowledge in African rural development, IDS Bulletin 10, 2: 28-36, 1979.
11. NADKARNI M.V. et al. The political economy of forest use and management, Sage, Delhi, India. 1989.

7. The engineer's contribution

P. A. GREEN, ACGI, BSc, DIC, FGS, FICE, FIHT, MConsE, Partner, Scott Wilson Kirkpatrick & Partners

SYNOPSIS. The paper looks at the role of the civil engineer in development, with particular reference to his *
contribution in the LDC's. Appropriate Technology is examined with reference to employment generation, tools and materials, agriculture, energy and infrastructure. Examples are given of the successful application of this technology and the side benefits of its use. The pre-eminence of the agricultural sector in the LDCs is noted. Observations are made about the longer-term aspects of development with particular reference to the consequences of large-scale climatic change. The necessity of the Engineer working as a member of a team in order to produce develoment that is appropriate, affordable and sustainable is emphasised.

THE ENGINEER'S ROLE
  1. Historically, the engineer has played a paramount role in the development of society as we know it today. This role, both in terms of further development and in terms of alleviating environmental hazards, will continue to be a vital one for survival. He is the one person able to evaluate alternative technology strategies. Engineers cover many disciplines and each has his part to play; for example, the civil engineer for irrigation projects, the chemical engineer for water purification and treatment of power station gas emissions, and the mechanical engineer for the development of appropriate vehicles. This paper deals primarily with the role of the civil engineer.
  2. Whilst the engineer has the technical knowledge to propose new methods of solving problems, he must always be regarded as part of a team comprising, inter alia, economists, sociologists and environmental scientists. Sometimes he is an important member of the team and at other times he has only an advisory capacity. Although the engineer is the one person able to make technical valuations, the team, and society at large, must make the

---
* The use of the masculine gender in this paper is for brevity, female engineers are becoming increasingly important for survival.

Appropriate development for basic needs. Thomas Telford, London, 1990

CONSTRAINTS AND OPPORTUNITIES

economic, social and political decisions concerning how that technology is to be used. Clearly, the engineer's role is crucial on issues of affordability and only he can design projects in a way which makes them sustainable.

3. In looking at issues of survival, one may consider short-term issues (say 10 years) or longer-term issues (say 50 years) in which climatic changes start to become important. Most of this paper deals with the short-term. Also, it deals particularly with those countries where there are immediate problems of development and hunger associated with population explosion, the so-called lesser developed countries (LDCs). Almost all of the LDCs are in Africa, South Asia and South-east Asia. The economic environment for such countries is one of low GDP per capita (typically less than $400), a chronic shortage of foreign exchange and a rapidly expanding population. The situation in Africa has been graphically high-lighted in a recent World Bank study (ref. 1.)

4. Investment in infrastructure in the LDCs is almost exclusively public funded and typically absorbs less than 10% of the GDP. By way of example, Table 1 gives percentage breakdown of GDP by economic activity for Tanzania and Sri Lanka for 1986.

6. In the rest of the paper the engineer's contribution to development is examined in relation to general issues of employment generation, tools and materials, before looking at the more specific issues of appropriate development in agriculture, energy and infrastructure. The last part of the paper briefly high-lights the engineer's possible role concerning environmental issues and the part he could play in dealing with longer-term effects of climatic changes.

EMPLOYMENT GENERATION

7. Construction is often used by governments as an economic regulator insofar that public funding can be readily increased or decreased according to the economic situation. During the 1930s major infrastructure developments were used in the United States and in Europe for employment generation and this trend continues in the developing world today. It is often assumed that a major programme of construction will solve chronic unemployment problems. However, this is more a political view than a reality. In a typical developing country approximately 5% of the GDP will be used in construction and about the same percentage or less of the working population will be employed in construction. This should be compared with the typical figure of 50% employed in agriculture. Even if all construction work is carried out by labour-intensive methods, there is little that construction can do to solve large-scale chronic unemployment. In the longer-term, one of the most important roles of construction is to develop agricultural potential, thereby enabling the increase in population to undertake more geographically dispersed and/or more extensive farming activities.

Table 1. Percentage Breakdown of GDP by Economic Activity for 1986 (Based on data from the Europa Yearbook 1988/89 and the Europa Yearbook 1987 Africa South of the Sahara)

	Tanzania	Sri Lanka
Agriculture & other rural enterprises	38.26	22.92
Mining and quarrying	0.61	0.97
Manufacturing	7.37	15.61
Construction	2.18	7.65
Electricity, gas, water & sanitary services	1.99	1.78
Trade, restaurants & hotels	10.16	
Transport, storage & communications	7.19	11.40
Wholesale & retail trade		18.97
Banking, insurance & real estate		4.49
Finance, insurance, business services, etc	11.70	
Ownership of dwellings		1.50
Public Administration & defence		6.45
Community, social & personal services	20.54	
Other services		2.45
Import duties		5.8
	100.00	100.00
Total GDP (T.sh x 10^6)	26,258	
Total GDP (Rs x 10^6)		172,440
Est Population	22,462,000	16,177,000
Per capita GDP (T.sh)(Rs)	1,170	10,660
Av Exchange rate (T.sh/Rs per US$)	33	28
Per capita GDP ($)	35	380

8. Table 2 gives a breakdown of the total numbers and percentage employed in various sectors of the economy for our 'typical' countries of Tanzania and Sri Lanka. In Tanzania in 1981 the total number of people in <u>paid</u> employment was estimated to be 574,483, of whom 132,154 were employed in agriculture. This compares dramatically with the estimated number of economically active people (EAP) of 5,747,096 in 1967 and 7,845,000 in 1978. The corresponding total population for 1967 and 1978 was 12,313,469 and 17,512,611. It can be seen from Table 2 that in 1967 virtually all the EAP were in agriculture and other rural enterprises and only 0.6% of EAP were in construction. For Sri Lanka, based on the 1971 census, 3.8% of EAP were in construction.

9. In Sri Lanka, it has been estimated by Fields (ref. 2.) that in 1981 about 3% of the working population was employed in construction, ie 280,000 people. The current GDP is about US$6 billion and typically 8% of the GDP relates to the construction sector, suggesting that some 480,000 jobs are available if it is assumed that an average

CONSTRAINTS AND OPPORTUNITIES

construction worker's wage is US$400 and approximately 40% of construction costs relate to wages if all the work is carried out by labour-intensive methods. This indicates that, as is already known, the bulk of construction is already relatively labour-intensive but there is room for some further job creation; however, as indicated in Table 2, the potential for job creation is limited when compared with the EAP and the reported unemployment numbers.

Table 2 Economically Active Population (Based on data from the Europa Yearbook 1988/89 and Europa Yearbook 1876 Africa South of the Sahara)

	Tanzania (1967) Total No	%	Sri Lanka (1971) Total No	%
Agriculture & other rural enterprises	5,216,493	90.7	2,530,969	42.4
Mining and quarrying	5,017	0.1	66,727	1.1
Manufacturing	98,864	1.7	648,470	10.8
Construction	33,073	0.6	226,912	3.8
Electricity, gas, water & sanitary services	5,862	0.1	21,482	0.3
Commerce	78,804	1.4		
Trade, restaurants & hotels			513,871	8.6
Transport, storage & communications	46,832	0.8	220,025	3.7
Finance, insurance & business services			65,093	1.1
Community, social & personal services			631,410	10.6
Other activities & services	262,151	4.6	206,791	3.5
Unemployed			840,252	14.1
Total labour force	5,747,096	100	5,972,002	100
Total pop in 1967	12,313,469			
Total pop 1971 census			12,689,897	
Total pop 1981 census			14,846,750	

TOOLS AND MATERIALS

Tools

10. In construction, tools, equipment and material costs can represent anything from 40% to 95% of the total cost of the project, depending on the level of equipment intensity. At the labour-intensive end of the spectrum the wages typically account for 40% of the costs with the tools 1 - 2% of the cost and the remaining 58 - 60% being materials and equipment. In equipment-intensive operations, the costs associated with the purchase and running of the equipment can typically be as much as 90 - 95% of the total cost of the project. Therefore, if local tools and local materials

are used, as much as half of the construction costs will stay within the local economy.

11. The international market for equipment is very large and considerable sums of money are spent each year on the research and development of construction machinery. However, until recently little or no effort was made to improve the design and quality of tools for use on labour-based construction works. During the late 1970s the World Bank (ref. 3) and the ITDG (ref. 4) undertook studies of tool design and set out a series of specifications for different types of construction tools. Until that time, and even today, many of the tools used in construction are simply those found in local agriculture. The engineer's role in developing appropriate construction tools to high standards is one area where he has been able significantly to improve productivity and, at the same time, reduce costs because inferior tools have a considerably shorter useful life.

Materials

12. Equally important to minimising the use of imported equipment is the need to develop a local materials industry which is also likely to be environmentally beneficial. In the domestic sector, engineers have developed local materials for building purposes and have extended the use of masonry for structures associated with civil works. In the construction of roads, considerable work has been done on the use of low-cost, locally occurring gravels for servicing rural access roads where traffic densities are less than, say, 200 vehicles per day. This type of road is particularly important in agricultural development. Interesting research work undertaken by Henry Grace (ref. 5) and others has shown that considerable savings can be made if the engineer develops methods for using 'non-standard materials'. He quotes an example from Malawi where a saving of $30,000 per km (at 1982 prices) was achieved.

13. Another example of where the engineer has been able to exploit local materials is in the area of river crossings. For example, as illustrated in Figs 1 and 2, in Lesotho major projects have been undertaken by labour-based methods in which segmental Armco linings have been used as permanent shuttering for masonry arch construction. In this design the largest vehicle needed for reaching the site is a Land Rover (or equivalent) and the biggest piece of equipment needed is a small portable concrete mixer. Not only does such a design maximise the use of local materials, it also fits more aesthetically into the environment. In the development of a design such as this some basic engineering was undertaken at the site, but subsequently sophisticated computer analysis was used both to confirm the design principles and to refine the design using the latest analytical techniques.

14. These two examples illustrate specific cases where the engineer has been able to use modern and appropriate technology to solve specific problems.

CONSTRAINTS AND OPPORTUNITIES

Fig. 1. Masonry pipe/arch bridge in Lesotho

AGRICULTURE
15. Perhaps the most crucial sector of the economy in which the engineer's role is vital for survival is agriculture. With rapidly expanding populations, particularly in Africa, the need to sustain and increase agricultural production is paramount if under-nourishment and hunger are to be eliminated. The World Bank's recent report on Sub-Saharan Africa (ref. 1) states that any future strategy for development must include agriculture as the primary foundation for growth. In Africa, agriculture accounts for 33% of the GDP, employs two-thirds of the labour force and provides 40% of the export earnings. The engineer's direct contribution to agricultural development is mainly related to infrastructure which is dealt with in the next section of the paper.

16. Human power is likely to remain of prime importance in developing world agriculture for the foreseeable future; an FAO study in 1987 showed that in sub-Saharan Africa, 1% of farming was mechanised, less than 10% used animals, and the remaining 89% was undertaken by people. The best use of development effort must therefore be to improve the productivity and efficiency of the human being, often by simple mechanical engineering developments. That this could apply equally to civil engineering is often overlooked, and the greater use of labour for civil engineering works is discussed elsewhere in this paper. Again, the key is self-sustainability; the cost of purchasing and operating imported machinery is so far from being affordable by the average LDC as to seem a total irrelevance to the problems of the day. However, if tools and small machines can be

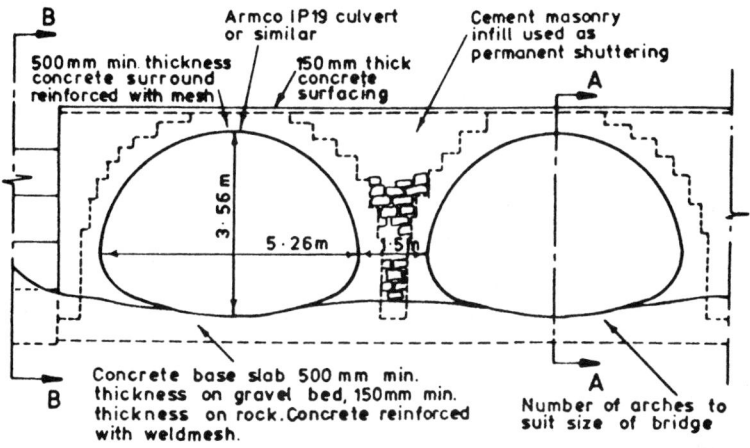
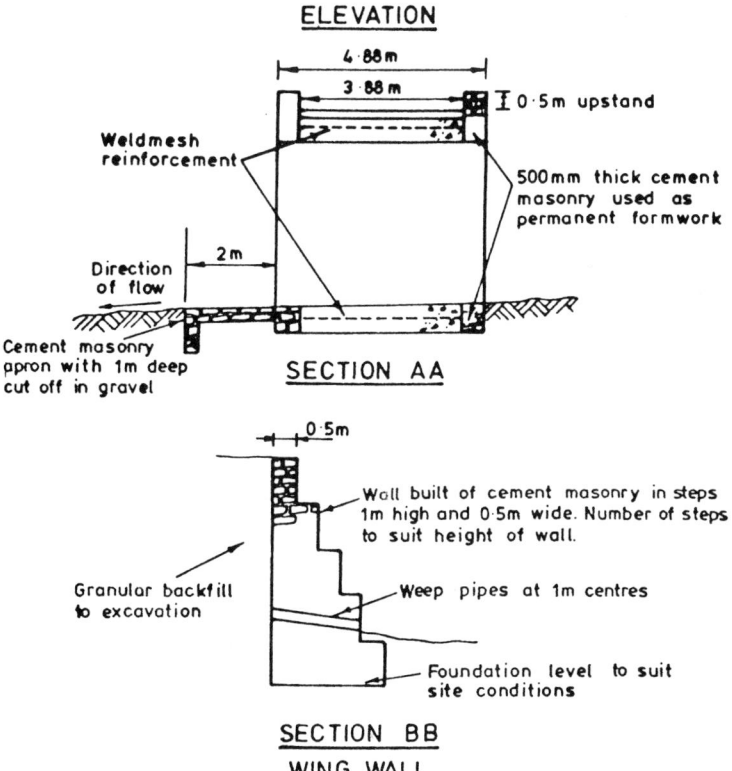

Fig. 2. Details of bridge shown in Fig. 1.

developed locally to ease the daily tasks of the farmer and so improve his or her ability to grow crops, or to build and maintain infrastructure, then wealth can be created in the community which can be used to good effect in a wide variety of ways.

17. Sometimes it may be possible to reduce the amount of effort needed to carry out a particular task by other than mechanical means; an example is the greater use of herbicides to reduce the need for weeding, although this must of course be treated with caution and with due respect for the environment. It is also essential to consider all aspects of the perceived need for cultivation such as the need for moisture retention and soil surface runoff, and the dangers of potential erosion if soils are denuded of surface cover and root growth.

18. The question of technical and engineering development touched on above, brings together a number of points which are relevant:
   (a) There is no mystique about the adoption of mechanical methods by farmers; simply, they will be adopted if, and only if, these methods can be proven to be profitable to do so, and persuasion will not lead to self-sustainable solutions.
   (b) The typical small farmer in a developing country is likely to be less well-nourished than his European counterpart, and the design of hand tools and implements should take this into account.
   (c) Mechanisation must be relevant to the conditions in which it will be used; design and testing should preferably be undertaken in the country concerned and take into account all the sociological, educational and environmental aspects of the situation.
   (d) In developing suitable tools and equipment for engineering or for agriculture it is just as important to learn from those who cannot cope with the new technology as from those to can; very often the former are more representative of the end-user of the equipment under development, and it is the fault of the equipment if it breaks down under usage.

19. Soil conservation is a critical area of concern for survival and the traditional approach, which has been practised and developed in Asia over thousands of years, requires extensive terracing of hill-sides. This approach is not the one normally adopted in most other parts of the world (particularly Africa) where the seasons are much more distinct, ie a very wet period followed by months of drought. The normal approach to conservation under these circumstances is to prepare graded bunds along contour lines to intercept rain water running down the hill-side; and to introduce small control ponds and dams as necessary to check the worst floods. Additionally, if erosion has taken place, gulley control structures can be built. As with irrigation projects generally, much work on soil conservation can be undertaken using labour-based methods and a paper by Subba

Rao and Dawson (ref. 6) describes some of the measures that have been taken by engineers working in Lesotho. In this work comparisons were made between undertaking soil conservation measures using both labour-intensive and equipment-intensive methods. The conclusions from this study were that it was both feasible and economical to undertake this type of work using the abundant supply of local labour.

20. In another example of land improvement in the northern Sudan several types of technology were used to improve production of fodder for cattle, sheep and camels for the lucrative export market. Early efforts to improve the farming conditions in this arid area centred on the construction of extensive earth bunds using heavy earth-moving machinery. This was an extremely expensive and impossibly unsustainable way of improving the land, and depended almost entirely on external donor funding. Over the last few years, however, with the assistance of British consultants, the emphasis changed from one which measured success by the extent of bunded area, to one which concentrated on the improvement of the water retention characteristics of the soil and the 'harvesting' of water by low bunds, directing water from sterile grassed collecting areas into areas where crops were planted into previously-tilled soils. The only real measure of success for such a project is the improved end product - in this case the quantity of animals produced for export.

ENERGY

20. The 1980 ICE conference on appropriate technology contained six papers dealing with issues of alternative energy and in the report of the working party it was concluded that perhaps the most important technology is that of motive power for agriculture; the use of liquid and solid fuels derived from biomass; the small-scale application of wind power; and small-scale pump hydro storage as an adjunct to energy sources such as solar and wind. The over-riding fact remains that energy usage is directly proportional to GDP and at a constant GDP per capita, energy use must increase in direct proportion to population. This means we are faced with at least a doubling of energy use over the next 20 years.

21. It has been estimated that firewood and biomass provide some 15% of the world's energy needs and in some countries more than 90%. Although with the diminishing supply of firewood, this source must eventually dry up. Additionally, animal power provides a very significant input to the energy supply; eg as recently as the 1960s the animals of India were estimated to provide 30,000 megawatts compared with an installed grid capacity of 26,000 megawatts. Additionally, human energy can be significant, both in agriculture and in construction and work has been done on the use of this source by Green (ref. 7).

CONSTRAINTS AND OPPORTUNITIES

22. The engineer's contribution to energy sources and the question of survival may be divided into two parts. Firstly, the engineer is the one person able to design efficient machines and systems which provide energy. Secondly, the engineer is a vital member of the team dealing with the undesirable by-products of energy generation, such as acid rain.

23. With increasing concern about the greenhouse effect in part caused by carbon-dioxide from the burning of fossil fuels, there will be a renewed interest in energy derived from the sun (solar power, wind and wave power); from hydro-electric schemes; and from atomic energy. Most of the engineering for these schemes is outside the role of the civil engineer and includes mechanical, electrical, atomic, and chemical engineers - to name but a few. The role of the civil engineer is most crucial in the design of structures for wind energy, barrages for wave and tidal energy and the design of dams and associated equipment for hydro-electrical schemes.

INFRASTRUCTURE

24. The engineer plays a crucial role in the develpment of the basic infrastructure. In most developing countries this consists of roads, (both the national network and for rural develoment), water supply, sanitation and irrigation.

Roads

25. It is a generally held view that roads are vital for proper development. Considerable effort was made in the 1960s and 1970s to build new national road networks, often at the expense of the less glamourous rural roads. Today many LDCs have a road network which is not sustainable and the emphasis has changed from new construction to rehabilitation and maintenance. For example in Sri Lanka there are some 83,000 km of road of which 25,000 km (the national network) are the responsibility of the central road authority. Of the 25,000 km, 21,000 km are paved - mostly with gravel. In the 1988 financial year approximately US $30 million were spend on the national road network which represented 2.6% of the government capital budget. In turn, the capital budget made up 36% of the GDP; therefore, the highway element of GDP was less than 1%. Studies of the national network have all indicated that the level of funding for roads is inadequate by a factor of 2 or 3.

26. The 1980 ICE conference on appropriate technology had four papers dealing with development of rural roads and other publications have dealt with specific rural roads development programmes, for example the Kenyan Rural Access Road Programme (ref. 8) and the Malawi District Road Improvement and Maintenance Programme (DRIMP). Sufficient knowledge now exists to enable the engineer to design and build relatively cheap low-cost roads linking villages and providing farmers with access to markets.

27. The first problem faced in planning rural roads relates to priority ratings and economic need. It is important that the road network is conceived to maximise agricultural development and increases in production, but all too often it becomes a major political issue and priorities do not always reflect the agricultural needs. Any method of priority ratings needs to be mechanical and objective to minimise political interference.

28. The construction of rural roads in labour-abundant economies lends itself to manual methods and the skills acquired in building the roads remain within the local community. However, there is always a (small) danger that road building will detract from agricultural development by taking away key labour. Additionally, if rural roads are built using local labour, there is a greater possibility that these roads will be maintained after the construction phase is finished.

29. Engineers have also carried out work on designing appropriate low-cost vehicles for the rural situation, eg see Barwell & Howe (ref. 9). Roads allow public transport systems, particularly buses, to develop and their impact on development must not be seen as purely a physical one. Greater mobility and exchange between villages and rural towns leads to the dissemination of ideas, better health care and a general up-grading of the development process.

Water and Sanitation

30. The LDCs are characterised by low investment in water supply and sanitation facilities. In the rural areas a long walk is often required to the nearest source of water, which may be contaminated, while sanitation is generally the responsibility of the individual. In the rapidly expanding urban areas facilities may exist, but they are frequently inadequate for the population they serve. A major effort is therefore required to provide potable water and sanitation facilities which are acceptable both economically and socially. Again, the engineer has an important role to play, once more as part of a team, as sanitation matters in particular have strong social overtones.

31. In providing facilities which are easily sustainable and require no foreign currency, slow sand filters are often the best answer for providing potable water. These filters are comparatively safe bacteriologically and there is little requirement for complex mechanical and electrical equipment, although they require more land than some other methods.

32. Pit latrines are often used for sanitation, particularly in rural areas. It is necessary, however, for them to be correctly designed in consultation with the users for them to be socially acceptable. In his design the engineer must ensure that their use is not ruled out by high ground water levels, or by potential pollution of local ground water. In some high density population areas such problems may make conventional sewerage the only feasible option.

33. In this latter case, sewage must be considered as a resource rather than a waste product. Waste stabilisation ponds can produce effluent of a high bacteriological quality which can be used in most irrigation applications. The sludge generated can be used as a fertiliser. The engineer will, however, need to prevent industrial wastes entering the system if there is a possibility of heavy metal contamination.

34. There is much published work on appropriate water and sanitation systems, for example books published by the Ross Institute (ref. 10)

Irrigation

35. The engineer's input to agriculture is most directly linked in work on irrigating crops. The 1980 conference had eight papers dealing specifically with this topic. The majority (80%) of irrigated land lies within the tropics and sub-tropics and therefore occurs in most of those countries where survival is critical. These same countries also have the 2,000,000,000 people who are reckoned to be under-nourished. Irrigation is the one area which can enhance the productivity of land quickly. The basic operation of irrigation usually requires straightforward simple engineering such as the excavation of canals, the construction of minor control structures and the building of small dams. The operation of irrigation schemes and their maintainence, however, are often less well-managed and to make irrigation projects successful, a number of support activities are needed.

36. The question of dam building raises serious environmental effects relating to siltation and increased health risks and detrimental effects to users down-stream of the dam. The engineer must take these environmental effects into account when planning his structure and considerable research (ref. 11) has already been undertaken in this field.

37. One interesting irrigation project is that of the Sategui - Deressia irrigation project which was carried out in the 1970s in Southern Chad. The project involved constructing unlined distribution canals, drainage networks and dykes and levelling land to irrigate 3,800 ha of rice. Initially the work was to have been done by a contractor using equipment-intensive methods, but the tender sums were considered too high and it was decided to execute the work by force account, again using equipment. Due to severe drought and chronic unemployment, it was subsequently necessary to investigate the possible use of labour in the work and two trial projects were undertaken to examine the economics and practicability of doing most of the work by labour. In general, it was concluded that labour-based technology was suitable for this type of work provided sufficient attention was given to training, administration procedures and the development of adequate logistic support. Using this technology benefitted the economy by savings in

foreign exchange, freeing the work from problems of fuel supply and creating employment in an area of chronic under-employment. Unfortunately, civil unrest has severely delayed the project.

38. The question of appropriateness and sustainability is of over-riding importance, as illustrated by a project in the Gambia, where equipment installed by Chinese experts some 15 years ago has been almost totally ignored by the farmers who were supposed to benefit from it. Large and inappropriate pumps were installed to pump river water into a number of individual perimeters. Whilst the idea behind over-sizing the equipment may have seemed attractive when viewed from the point of view of machine life, in practice it proved impossible to remove the pumps for routine maintenance without the large lifting equipment which had placed it during construction. Under the present rehabilitation project, with the assistance of British engineering and agricultural expertise, the perimeters are being consolidated so that several are served by a group of pumps, any one of which can be removed for maintenance.

ENVIRONMENT AND THE LONGER-TERM

39. Most of this paper is concentrated on the shorter-term needs of the LDCs. However the recently published report by the United Nations Intergovernmental Panel on Climatic Change (IPCC) (ref. 12) has indicated that there is a strong probability that climatic changes over the next 100 years will alter the environment of almost every part of the world, with Africa being worst affected. Some of the conclusions of the report point to the fact that wood supplies will be exhausted and there will be migration on an unprecedented scale as shore lines change and agricultural patterns are disrupted. The report states that "Many areas to which they (the refugees) flee are likely to have insufficient health and support services to accommodate the new arrivals." Additionally, drinking water supplies will be disrupted and changing weather patterns will accelerate soil erosion. The role of the engineer will be essential for such things as coastal protection works, new roads and bridges to meet changing patterns of habitation and to provide the basic infrastructure in the new conurbations of refugees.

CONCLUSIONS

40. The title of this conference is Appropriate Development for Survival. For the vast majority of people in the LDCs survival means an adequate supply of food which, in turn, depends on an efficiently functioning agricultural sector. Efforts to develop the agricultural sector in these countries have not been as successful as the promoters would have liked. Rapidly increasing populations therefore threaten to exhaust available resources and survival becomes an open question.

CONSTRAINTS AND OPPORTUNITIES

41. The reasons for failure are well-known. <u>Too often projects have been carried out at inappropriate levels</u> of <u>technology</u>, at costs that cannot be afforded and using resource levels that cannot be sustained. Often little has been done to blend political considerations and technical demands. Frequently little thought has been taken of the wider environmental and sociological consequences of what has been proposed.

42. To ensure that projects are appropriate, affordable and sustainable the Engineer must work as a member of a team. As part of the team he is uniquely qualified to examine the practicability of the technologies available to produce the low cost roads, the conservation measures, the irrigation works and the locally manufactured tools and equipment that are needed for the development of agriculture. With the sociologist and the economist in his team he can then look towards the wider political and social implications, with the environmental scientist he can examine the possible effects on the physical surroundings and so together they can produce schemes that will work, will increase the employment of local people, increase their skills and self-confidence and reduce dependence on foreign currency.

43. The nearly-new grader and the big pump may still rust in the plantyard, immobilised by lack of foreign currency to buy spares, but the sun will glint on locally made tools and equipment handled by local people who will be doing the job of the grader and the pump, and more.

44. While in the past decades survival has meant food to the people of the LDCs and protection from the bomb to the population of the developed world, now rapid environmental change is producing a threat which may soon be feared by all peoples.

45. The problems produced by global warming, with the vast changes of agricultural potential of some areas and coastlines of others, accompanied by attendant shifts in population will make the present problems of development in the LDCs seem small by comparison. Such changes will produce a great demand for new infrastructure; water supply and drainage, communications, housing and sources of energy. The engineer will play a paramount role in these developments, but here, as in the case of development in the LDCs, he must work with colleagues from other professions to ensure that what he builds is appropriate, affordable and sustainable.

REFERENCES
1. Sub-Saharan Africa: From Crisis to Sustainable Growth. A Long-Term Perspective Study. The World Bank 1989.
2. FIELDS GARY S. "Rural labor markets and the economic development of Sri Lanka". Unpublished World Employment Research Working Paper. ILO March 1988.

3. COUKIS B. & others. "Labor-based construction programs: A practical guide for planning and management". The world Bank, 1983.
4. ARMSTRONG W. "Better tools for the job". Intermediate Technology Publications Ltd 1980.
5. GRACE H. & ERRIDGE P.S. "The use of plastic lateritic materials as bases for bituminous surfaced low volume roads". IRF January 1980
6. SUBBA RAO G.V. and DAWSON J.R. "Appropriate technology for agricultural development in Lesotho". Proc. Conference on Appropriate Technology in Civil Engineering pp 196 - 199. ICE London 1981.
7. GREEN P.A. "The use of human energy in construction". Conference on Making Use of Renewable Energy. Solar Energy Society of Zimbabwe, March 1984.
8. DE VEEN JAN. "Rural Access Roads Programme: Appropriate Technology in Kenya". ILO Geneva 1980, 3rd impression with modifications 1984.
9. BARWELL I.J. and HOWE J.D.G.F. "Basic vehicles for rural transport". Proc. Conference on Appropriate Technology in Civil Engineering, pp 33 - 35, ICE London 1981.
10. FENCHEM R.G & CAIRNCROSS S. "Small excreta disposal systems". Bulletin No 8, Ross Institute of Tropical Hygiene, Information and Advisory service 1978. "Small water supplies". Bulletin No 10, Ross Institute of Tropical Hygiene, Information and Advisory service, 5th Edn. 1971.
11. INTERNATIONAL COMMISSION ON LARGE DAMS. "The consequences on the environment of building dams". Transactions Vol 1, Question No 40, Madrid 1973.
12. THE GUARDIAN "UN warns of global timebomb" 22nd May 1990.

8. Education and training - communication

J. C. BLACKWELL, MBE, BACertEd, MEd, Controller, Education and Science Division, The British Council

SYNOPSIS. Vocationalization in secondary schools, the introduction to multidisciplinary curricula in further and higher education and necessary changes in the attitudes to developmental research born of Western academicism all warrant more attention if technology is to contribute effectively to development. Continuing Professional Education (CPE) has a role to play but requires an institution infrastructure that does not exist in may developing countries. Several ways in which the professional institutions might stimulate change at home and overseas are suggested. The contribution of the British Council to education and training for appropriate development in more than forty developing countries is also described in outline.

EDUCATION AND TRAINING - COMMUNICATING
The British Council
 1. The British Council's Royal Charter dates back to 1940. As Britain's principle agency for the conduct of cultural relations overseas, the Council's aim is to promote an enduring understanding and appreciation of Britain in other countries. This we do by providing access to British thought, experience, achievement and expertise, notably in the areas of education and science - but also in the arts - and in fields important to technical co-operation with developing countries. The Council also has that ask of promoting the knowledge and use of the English language. As science, technology and engineering are integral parts of contemporary British culture, they are a crucial component of the Council's work in other countries, including the more than forty developing countries in which the Council operates.
 2. It is noteworthy that developing nations seek not only the transfer of technology, systems or ideas from industrialised countries such as Britain, but also wish to develop their own manpower and institutional resources. The Council's main role in this is in building bridges - aiding communication - between like-minded groups of people from Britain and overseas. On the one hand the Council's extensive network of overseas representations, staffed by British and local staff, have direct contact with both

Appropriate development for basic needs. Thomas Telford, London, 1991

CONSTRAINTS AND OPPORTUNITIES

high-level decision makers and development workers on the ground while, on the other hand, a team of specialist staff in Education and Science Division in Britain liaises closely with UK educationalists, scientists and engineers. So bridges can be build. In many countries, of course, the Council works in a close development partnership with the Overseas Development Administration (ODA) and Foreign and Commonwealth Office (FCO), who fund much of the Council's activity.

GENERAL EDUCATION
(In March 1989 the British Council was asked by the World Bank to undertake a study entitled "Educating for Capability: The Role of Science and Technology Education". The following section draws extensively on the report which emerged from that study.)

3. The rapid advancement of scientific knowledge, new social priorities, political imperatives and economic influences have all affected the contextual framework within which science education is delivered to schools. There remains, however, disenchantment worldwide amongst those who receive the products of secondary schools, although this manifests itself in different ways. In the less developed countries, where the need is to close the technological (and, by implication, economic) gap between themselves and others, to reduce dependence upon more industrialised countries and to enhance self- reliance, school science does not always lead to personal and collective empowerment in relation to urgent practical problems. Instead it frequently remains an arid and compartmentalized academic activity.

4. One possible alternative to the traditional academic curriculum has been adopted in some developing countries - diversification to include practical and occupationally-related subjects alongside academic ones at secondary school level. It has, however, yielded few, if any, of the advantages claimed for it, such as providing more equitable access to secondary education, or assisting school leavers to obtain jobs or become self-employed in conditions of widespread youth unemployment. Yet vocationalism continues to attract those who plan secondary education, despite discouraging evidence from such empirical evaluation studies as have been undertaken.

5. Vocationalization of secondary education today requires both academic and vocational subjects to change and converge on a new model. Academically, more regard for action and practical performance as an outcome of learning is necessary in whatever subject, be it mathematics, science or a language. Vocationally, the new technologies are reshaping the skill requirements of manufacturing industries and of commercial services. Secondary schools can provide only the basic elements. Insofar as there is a consensus on these, it seems to be centred on competencies such as communication skills, interpersonal skills, problem solving skills, and

personal qualities such as persistence and flexibility, and the ability to establish priorities, schedule tasks and complete them on time. Academic subjects can clearly contribute to the acquisition of these competencies as readily as putative vocational ones. The vocationalization of the curriculum of a secondary school is therefore achieved not by changing the combination of academic and vocational subjects, but by permeating all subjects with concern for practical capability. Knowledge is no longer king, if indeed it ever was.

6. Interest in and attention to technology in the industrialised countries is a comparatively recent phenomenon, arising from changing economic circumstances. Many developing nations now appear to be searching similarly for increased scientific, technological and practical capability. Inevitably, the paths of particular countries reflect their own traditions of schooling, the external infrastructure for science and technology, and the policies designed to privilege them. In other words, education for capability may not mean introducing a whole new subject but, rather, delivering some of the existing subjects in a new way. In many countries, therefore, the basic curriculum frame already exists on which initiatives for increasing the scientific and technological capacity can be based.

7. Educational initiatives in science, technology, craft and enterprise in recent years range from innovations in science education to a whole series of developments in craft and vocational education. Between these two points lie intermediate positions: the introduction of technological awareness and applications through reformed science; the identification of technology draws upon its triple roots of craft, art and design, and science. Whichever mode is pursued, emphasis should be placed on linking together action on curricula, staffing and institutional development, rather than treating them in isolation from each other.

THE FURTHER AND HIGHER EDUCATION SECTOR AND RESEARCH INSTITUTES

8. In the field of further and higher education, applied science all too often seems to address ever more esoteric problems - as perceived in the affluent Western institutions. There is, however, but little evidence of the application of science on a large scale in a manner appropriate to the alleviation of the problems of hunger, drought and disease that prevail in much of the so-called developing world. The Western tradition of academic isolationism has unfortunately led in some instances to vast international research institutes being set up in developing countries, in which the pursuit of scientific excellence takes precedence over the solving of such problems as these.

9. Because of the historical development of many scientific institutions there is still scant regard paid to the appropriateness of what is being taught, neither to

national development nor to the personal development of the students. Outdated, single subject curricula are still predominant and, even in the present age of environmental awareness, very little environmental work has found its way into curricula. It would appear that the major changes needed if we are to implement more multidisciplinary curricula is too difficult for entrenched, single subject specialist to embrace. It can fairly be said that, in that sense, most curricula in most institutions in the developing world remain inappropriate and would be unlikely, as they stand, to lead towards the survival of any species, let alone the hman species. The importance of encouraging the implementation of curricula more appropriate to the real needs of developing countries can therefore hardly be overstated. At their best, efforts by aid donors and lending agencies to relate further education and technician training to developmental needs have made a real local impact, but the sheer scale of the problem, the lack of resources and a pervasive unwillingness to abandon 'pure' academic values, thus favouring higher education at the expense of technical education, often make the task exceedingly difficult.

CONTINUING PROFESSIONAL EDUCATION (CPE) FOR UK SCIENTIST AND ENGINEERS

10. There is a plethora of areas in which continuing professional education (CPE) could help to meet the training needs of UK scientists, engineers and technicians interested in the contribution of technology to sustainable development overseas. Younger professionals need awareness programmes that point up the importance of ensuring that there is an adequate supply, from the most economical source, of raw materials, appropriate materials of construction, spare parts and servicing facilities. There is another, more general, need on the part of professionals at all levels of experience that CPE could meet: the need to understand how the economics of technology can be transformed in a developmental context by such factors as a lack of foreign exchange – or a strategic need to rely upon local resources that must themselves be developed. An appreciation of the implications of training or re-training of the local work force, the use of women workers, bureaucracy, and other culture-dependent considerations relevant to the socio-economic framework within which technology must function, is also amenable to the CPE approach. Nor should we neglect the opportunities for enhancing awareness of the value of re-cycling, the use of renewable resources and the costs of environmental damage in the developing world.

11. One way of utilising CPE in tackling these problem areas might be to establish a library of judiciously selected case studies with discussions, led by senior engineers with appropriate developing country experience and supported by commentary from experienced professionals from the developing world, to provide a user's insight and perspective. A group

of participants with varied backgrounds, though not
necessarily from different disciplines, would enable
particular aspects to be illuminated from several viewpoints.
Benefits would then accrue not only to the inexperienced but
also to the seasoned professional who could contribute as
well as receive.

FOR DEVELOPING COUNTRIES

12. The value of CPE for scientists, engineers and
technicians can only be fully realised, of course, in
situations where the necessary institutional infrastructure
has been established. Given that constraint, although a
collaborative regional approach to CPE might be feasible in,
say, East Africa, one requirement for the long term viability
of CPE in developing countries must surely be the existence
of soundly based national professional associations that work
in close liaison with local industry and the education and
training sector. The formation of strong partnership with UK
industry, and compatible organisations in developing
countries would provide one possible way of encouraging CPE
overseas. Training programmes in the UK and overseas for
local specialists in CPE could certainly help, too.

13. But what are the needs of developing countries when a
basic CPE system is in existence? Analysis of lifetime
career needs would probably demonstrate that in many
developing countries scientists, engineers and technicians
ought to be trained to recognise local needs and, through
CPE, to be kept aware of the full range of relevant
technological opportunities offered by the UK and other
industrialized countries - without overlooking local
constraints. With increasing age and experience, scientists
and engineers pass through the level of supervisor to that of
manager of technology. Such professionals need to be able
not only to identify and manage consultants effectively at
all stages including the drafting of terms of reference, the
interpretation of reports and the identification of sources
of funds, and to advise on staff development programmes. The
UK resource base could, in principle, assist with CPE at all
of these stages of the professional career, in many cases
usefully incorporating periods of academic or industrial
updating in the UK, subject to the availability of funds.
Also, local modular post experience training programmes at
engineer and technician levels could be set up with UK inputs
as necessary. The field is still wide open!

A ROLE FOR UK PROFESSIONAL INSTITUTIONS

14. Professional institutions in the United Kingdom, such
as the Institution of Civil Engineers which organised this
conference, are in a key position when it comes to promoting
the concepts of appropriate development. In particular,
professional institutions could encourage academic
institutions in the UK, and overseas (to a limited extent),
to incorporate relevant lecture topics, course options, and

laboratory and design projects into engineering curricula at undergraduate and postgraduate levels. Scholarships or prizes might be provided, too, at all levels and possibly in collaboration with industry, in order to promote through competition a knowledge of, and interest in, the appropriateness of technology for survival. The exchange of ideas and experiences between members and officers of professional institutions could be stimulated by exchanging publications and by encouraging visiting professionals to attend meetings of analogous bodies at home and abroad. Talks and discussions on appropriate topics could also be included in the programmes of UK centre meetings. In the UK, awareness-raising could be achieved by enabling practising engineers with overseas experience, and visiting engineers from overseas, to give lectures or seminars at secondary, further and higher educational institutions. Accredited workshops and short courses in the CPE domain could similarly include appropriate development topics.

15. Information is vitally important in education and training. If professional bodies were to collect and collate biodata on all members with expertise in appropriate development and then pool the information on a database for general access, I believe this would be a potentially useful exercise for those involved in education and training. I understand that the International Institute for Environment and Development (IIED) and the ODA have already established a database of appropriate developmental UK experts in natural resources. Assembling a complementary database in the broader field of engineering could also be invaluable.

THE BRITISH COUNCIL AND DEVELOPMENT

16. The British Council does not normally fund development projects in Science and Technology directly. However, the Council does manage a number of education and training programmes in science and technology that are intended to benefit the developing world. The majority of this management work is undertaken on behalf of the ODA. In 1988-89 the largest of the ODA programmes, the Technical Co-operation and Training Programme (TCTP), brought almost 12,500 trainees to the United Kingdom. This training, which can be academic, industrial or in combination as appropriate, is intended to alleviate manpower shortages in selected development related fields in aid-recipient countries. Training is increasingly provided as part of a large, carefully formulated project which includes aspects of training, consultancy and books and equipment provision as an integrated whole.

17. Another externally funded programme administered by the Council is the Foreign and Commonwealth Office Scholarships Award Scheme (FCOSAS). The FCOSAS targets the high fliers and future opinion leaders of a country and brings them to the UK to study.

18. There are also a number of smaller scale academic

links with developing countries which are managed by the British Council, advised by the Committee for International Cooperation in Higher Education (CICHE), on behalf of the ODA. These links facilitate exchanges and communications between departments and institutions in the developing world and related departments in institutions in the UK with the aim of encouraging sustainable institutional and academic development overseas. At the same time the links can often build long term relationships, of benefit to both partners, which remain in place whe the formal scheme has ended. Within a typical link in higher education, staff from the overseas institution are trained in the UK and joint research work is carried out. The training frequently ranges from training in specific, specialised research techniques to longer and more general training of technical staff to provide a support base for the overseas institution.

19. Such small scale academic links can sometimes act as the seeds for larger development projects funded by bodies such as the European Community (EC) and the World Bank. The British Council often undertakes the management of education and training components of projects funded by such agencies or by foreign governments. These components can include technical, secondary and higher education and draw on many parts of the UK educational resource to carry out the necessary work.

20. The origins of education and training projects and academic links vary widely. Many of them arise as the result of exchanges of ideas and experiences initiated by the British Council through its interchange of persons programme. This programme, which is funded from its own budget, enables overseas academics, government officers and educationalists, amongst others, to investigate the resources available in the UK and allows eminent UK specialists in development to travel overseas for seminars, lectures, advice and consultancy work.

CONCLUSION

21. In summary, it is almost a truism that the developing countries aspire to fostering and developing their own manpower and institutional resources. Education, training and research are therefore vital ingredients of development. Vocationalisation of secondary education curricula in the developing world has not yet yielded many of the hoped for benefits, owing to deep seated traditions of single-subject teaching. However, an integrated approach covering curriculum development, staff training and institutional development looks promising. There is also a need to introduce more relevant multidisciplinary curricula into further and higher education institutions overseas. This means avoiding inappropriate single subject specialisation and making research more relevant by breaking down entrenched attitudes reflecting the near obsessive Western pursuit of excellence for its own sake coupled with an academic isolationism that is anathema to development for survival.

CONSTRAINTS AND OPPORTUNITIES

The British Council endeavours to meet some of these needs by building cultural bridges. UK educational institutions in the further and higher education sectors and professional bodies, where possible in collaboration with industry, can also contribute. Particularly important areas are appropriate curriculum design, academic links with overseas institutions, CPE, and the collection, collation and dissemination of information. Collaboration with the British Council in much of this is already widespread.

Discussion

R. HOLLAND, <u>Intermediate Technology Development Group</u>
ITDG's Shelter programme has completed a study on building standards in Kenya. They are based on standards specified before independence and are not compatible with the need to develop low-cost urban housing. We are investigating, in co-operation with the Ministry of Housing and others, how those standards could be changed to be more appropriate for local conditions and locally perceived priorities. How should countries go about developing their own, locally appropriate, standards?

M. N. ISLAM, <u>Department of the Environment, Bangladesh</u>
In addition to the engineer's contribution as presented by Mr Green, engineers might think about fundamental needs such as food, shelter, birth control, health and education. To overcome the world's present crisis, the developing world has to spend more than 70% of its resources to meet basic needs. In developing countries, the population is growing fast and, if immediate measures are not taken, a major disaster is imminent. The population problem should be considered a priority, otherwise it will have far-reaching effects on ecology and economy as well as having social and cultural consequences and quickly outdating infrastructure development. Population growth is directly related to environmental degradation such as soil erosion and pollution with all its consequences. Engineers have been involved in development for two hundred years. Twenty years ago, engineers paid little attention to the environment. Now, environmental factors are among their top priorities. Therefore, we have to consider the global significance in the Third World.

DR P. G. L. WASS, <u>Intermediate Technology Development Group</u>
I should like to present a current example of constraints in appropriate building development: a UNDP project in a semi-arid zone of an African country, to put up appropriate project buildings (low-cost, improved local/traditional designs, minimum import component, sustainable energy use and so on). The concept is from the external agency; resistance

to such approaches often comes from national engineering decision-makers whose education, due to cultural lag, is often insensitive to appropriate technology, which they consider inferior or not up to standard. Could the Institution of Civil Engineers find ways of introducing more appropriate technology concepts into the engineering profession in one or more selected countries, for example, through a research and development project, an exchange of appropriate staff, or a panel of consultants who adopt such an approach?

A. STEYN, Development Bank of Southern Africa
Paper 5 highlighted the problems of Africa and mentioned the cost of settling one farmer (approximately US$200 000 per farmer). Some people are of the opinion that there does not seem to be any solution to Africa's problems. The DBSA has settled about 4000 farmers at a cost of approximately R200 000 (40 000) per farmer. Although development results were achieved, this typical settlement method proved to be very expensive and the bank realized that the world has not got enough funds to settle enough farmers in Africa at this cost.

The DBSA introduced a farmer support programme in 1987. Where, in the settlement approach, infrastructure was provided which enabled farmers to obtain maximum production, the emphasis was changed in the support programme to remove constraints which inhibit optimum production and therefore economic development. Furthermore, the support programme focused on the creation of and access to opportunities.

The results after three years showed that 25 000 farmers had been supported at an average cost of R5000 (1000) per irrigation farmer. It is estimated that 600 000 people are benefiting from this relatively small investment compared with the investment put into settlement projects. The constraints which were removed and the opportunities which were created allowed these small-scale farmers to contribute to the economic processes.

I want to link this to the question of appropriate standards. I believe that standards are variables which should be accessed and evaluated for each situation. They should be linked to criteria such as affordability and acceptability. Very often, one should forget about standards and just provide a basic service which will increase the living standards of people, or create new opportunities for the people involved.

E. MASANJA, Edinburgh University
Dr Kyomo's analysis on food security in the SADCC region distorts the true picture because of its lack of analysis on the effect of pressure on arable land due to emphasis on cash crop production. My experience is that the best land is always under cash crop farming and substandard land is used for food production.

DISCUSSION

DR J. M. JEWSBURY, <u>Liverpool Associates in Tropical Health</u>
I recently carried out an assessment of the training needs for graduate staff on behalf of the EC-funded regional tsetse and trypanosomiasis control programme in Central Africa. The programme is for the control of animal trypanosomiasis and is severely compromised by a shortage of professional (graduate) staff with appropriate training. This situation is deteriorating due to loss of senior staff with extensive experience (as a result of retirement, change of duty and so on) and shortage of national staff for training. The latter is the more serious for both the immediate and long term, and is substantially due to salary scales and conditions of service which are insufficient to attract and to retain the services of suitable staff. Until conditions of service are improved there is likely to continue to be a problem of staff shortage. It is unclear how this problem can be rectified as salary scales and conditions are fixed by governments.

Although applying specifically to this project, I suspect the same general issue applies to many other areas of professional expertise and staff shortage.

Education (including 'health' education) is frequently (and correctly) said to be the key to fundamental change, development and sustained independence. Education can be 'applied' at different periods, from primary to post-graduate. What does Dr Blackwell consider to be the period between the start of a change in education and the results/benefits becoming evident in the community?

R. D. BELL, <u>Consultant</u>
Commentators stress that western standards for works are often inappropriate and there is a need to develop local appropriate standards. It has been pointed out that resistance to lower - locally appropriate - standards comes from local decision-makers. None of the commentators considers the pressure on local executives to adopt accepted western standards. To advocate less than the best is for them to invite criticism that they are seeking to hold back their country or industry to a second-class status, and if the appropriate development should fail or need high maintenance the official risks his entire career. Nor does the Institution of Civil Engineers or any other major engineering institution do much to encourage the study of truly appropriate technology by positive statements that theses, research and study schemes with a strong content related to appropriate technology will be accepted - or even welcomed - by their qualifications boards. Academic boards are generally reluctant to recognize research in appropriate technology as of comparable standard with highly technical research programmes. To be appropriate for the developing countries technical research must encompass the human factor and western boards are not organized to do this.

Too many of the appropriate technology volunteers or technical staff from the West are young men who see the technical problems but do not understand the pressures on local staff. Mr Steyn refers to the remarkable success in development in his country by seeking out and relieving constraints to the efforts of the individual peasant. The institutions must seek out and relieve the constraints on the individual engineer, policy-maker and administrator.

DR J. BLACKWELL, Paper 8

Dr Jewsbury mentions one of the fundamental problems in harnessing education to developmental processes: that of the time span between the application of new approaches and the full evaluation of results in terms of benefits to the community. In this regard much will depend on the level and objectives of any innovation. If, for example, as has been claimed, improvements in primary education yield a higher rate of return in less developed countries than investment in other sectors of the education system, any evidence to this effect is likely to emerge from studies of primary school-leavers and their productivity only some years after the completion of their primary education - perhaps 7-10 years. At post-graduate level, again taking into account the period of study followed by a period of contributing to the community, a minimal period of three or, more likely, four years would be required. In general, the lower down the educational ladder, particularly if the objective is to improve performance at higher levels in the educational system with the overall aim of benefiting the community, the longer the evaluation span required. Many innovative projects in education now have built into them an evaluation cycle intended to yield early pointers as to likely effectiveness and it is often on the bases of these that decisions are taken as to future direction and scope.

9. Food: survival and appropriate development

S. MAXWELL, Institute of Development Studies, University of Sussex

The paper reviews data on the period since the last ICE Conference on Appropriate Development in 1980, to show that food insecurity persists despite aggregate increases in food production per capita. Five propositions are then put forward: (1) The priority is the food entitlement of poor people; (2) Increasing entitlement does not require food self-sufficiency; (3) Cereal market protection is largely counter-productive; (4) Trade is preferable to buffer stocks and government price stabilisation; and (5) Targeted interventions are required to reach the food insecure. Three implication of these propositions are: (a) the need for a new focus on sustainable livelihoods; (b) a new 'enabling' role for government; and (c) a new emphasis on urban and rural safety nets.

Introduction

The Institution of Civil Engineers last held a Conference on Appropriate Development in 1980. The subsequent decade has been described as the 'lost decade' in development. As far as the food sector is concerned, the agenda has been dominated by the African famine of 1984/85 and its aftermath. However, at first sight, the global picture may not be so gloomy. The evolution of the food situation in developing countries in the 1980's is summarised in table 1. In aggregate terms, this shows:

Table 1. Cereal production, imports, exports, total supplies per person and food aid in the 1980s (source: WFP 1990, Table 18)

	UNIT	1979/80	1980/81	1981/82	1982/83	1983/84	1984/85	1985/86	1986/87	1987/88	1988/89[1]	1989/90[2]
All developing countries												
Production[3]	mill.tons	630.7	644.7	682.8	699.3	750.2	775.0	778.3	794.1	784.7	826.0	827.9
Per-person production[3]	kg	194.1	194.3	201.5	202.0	212.3	214.8	211.3	211.2	204.4	210.7	206.8
Imports[4]	mill.tons	92.7	99.8	95.7	103.4	112.6	109.8	97.7	110.1	116.4	118.2	123.3
Exports[4]	mill.tons	27.1	21.3	32.2	36.4	34.9	36.9	38.0	34.0	27.3	33.7	26.9
Net imports[4]	mill.tons	65.6	78.4	63.5	67.0	77.6	72.9	59.7	76.1	89.1	84.5	96.4
Food aid[5]	mill.tons	8.5	8.7	8.7	9.2	9.8	12.4	10.9	12.6	13.5	10.0	9.8
Food aid as % of imports	percent	9.1	8.7	9.1	8.9	8.7	11.3	11.1	11.4	11.6	8.5	8.0
Total supplies per person[6]	kg	214.3	218.0	220.2	221.4	234.3	235.0	227.5	231.4	227.6	232.2	230.9
Low-income, food-deficit countries[7]												
Production[3]	mill.tons	477.1	483.5	500.0	518.0	573.6	589.2	578.9	600.1	587.5	625.0	641.7
Per-person production[3]	kg	183.3	182.1	184.4	187.2	203.2	204.7	197.1	200.2	192.1	200.2	201.3
Imports[4]	mill.tons	43.6	48.1	48.6	50.1	52.6	48.6	43.4	46.1	53.2	56.4	54.4
Exports[4]	mill.tons	4.3	3.7	2.9	3.4	3.9	7.3	11.4	9.0	7.2	8.9	8.2
Net imports[4]	mill.tons	39.3	44.4	45.7	46.7	48.8	41.3	32.0	37.1	45.9	47.5	46.2
Food aid	mill.tons	7.6	7.3	7.6	8.1	9.1	11.3	10.0	11.1	11.5	8.3	8.5
Food aid as % of imports	percent	17.4	15.3	15.7	16.1	17.3	23.2	23.1	24.2	21.7	14.7	15.6
Total supplies per person[6]	kg	198.4	198.8	201.3	204.0	220.5	219.0	208.0	212.6	207.1	215.4	215.8

Continued

PAPER 9: MAXWELL

	UNIT	1979/80	1980/81	1981/82	1982/83	1983/84	1984/85	1985/86	1986/87	1987/88	1988/89[1]	1989/90[2]
Least developed countries												
Production[3]	mill.tons	50.6	54.3	56.8	57.0	56.5	53.2	60.7	62.7	58.7	66.9	65.7
Per-person production[3]	kg	150.3	157.3	160.7	157.2	152.2	139.9	155.7	156.6	142.9	158.5	151.7
Imports[4]	mill.tons	6.4	5.8	6.3	6.1	8.5	10.9	8.1	8.3	9.2	8.3	8.6
Exports[4]	mill.tons	1.1	1.1	1.2	1.2	0.9	0.8	1.1	1.2	0.6	1.0	0.5
Net imports	mill.tons	5.3	4.7	5.0	4.9	7.5	10.1	6.9	7.1	8.7	7.4	8.1
Food aid	mill.tons	2.8	2.7	2.9	3.2	3.4	5.5	4.8	4.5	4.9	3.7	3.5
Food aid as % of imports	percent	44.2	45.8	46.9	53.0	40.0	51.0	59.8	54.8	52.5	43.9	40.7
Total supplies per person[6]	kg	166.1	171.0	174.9	170.7	172.4	166.4	173.5	174.4	164.0	176.0	170.4
Sub-Saharan Africa												
Production[3]	mill.tons	38.6	41.2	43.4	43.2	41.0	38.2	50.2	53.2	45.4	57.6	52.9
Per-person production[3]	kg	108.3	112.2	114.5	110.6	101.8	92.1	117.3	120.6	99.8	122.6	109.1
Imports[4]	mill.tons	7.5	9.2	9.4	9.0	10.3	13.7	9.7	9.2	9.1	7.7	8.5
Exports[4]	mill.tons	0.7	0.3	0.7	0.9	0.5	1.5	1.0	1.5	1.3	1.4	1.3
Net imports	mill.tons	6.8	8.9	8.7	8.1	9.8	13.5	8.7	7.7	7.7	6.3	7.2
Food aid	mill.tons	1.6	2.4	2.4	2.5	2.8	5.0	3.9	3.3	3.8	2.7	2.6
Food aid as % of imports	percent	21.3	25.9	25.5	28.2	26.7	36.4	39.8	36.2	41.6	35.0	30.6
Total supplies per person[6]	kg	127.4	136.5	137.5	131.3	126.0	124.6	137.7	137.9	116.8	136.0	123.8

1 Provisional figures.
2 Estimate.
3 Data refer to the calendar year of the first year shown. Rice is in terms of milled rice.
4 For total grain, season beginning 1 July of first year shown; for rice, calendar year of second year shown.
5 Excludes Israel, Malta, Poland and Portugal. Because of different sources, data differ slightly from Table 14.
6 All supplies per person are based on production and net imports, taking no account of stock changes.
7 As defined in Table 12, footnote 2. For country details, see Table 12.

IMPLEMENTATION

1. Cereal production in developing countries increased during the decade by nearly a third, or about 2.7% per annum;

2. Cereal production per capita increased very slightly;

3. Net imports rose by nearly 50%; and

4. Total cereal supplies per person rose by nearly 8%.

This global trend of increased food availability holds for all the main categories of countries: 'low income food deficit countries'; least developed countries; and even sub-Saharan Africa (though here the trends are more muted and per capita supply actually shows a small decrease, largely because of a shortfall in imports).

Of course, the aggregate data disguise differences between countries and the extent of malnutrition within countries. Tables 2 and 3 are taken from the new UNDP Human Development Report. The first shows variation between countries and groups of countries in the index of food production per capita, as well as the daily calorie supply and the food import dependency ratio. The second provides key data on child survival and development, including a point estimate of child malnutrition. The main conclusions of these tables are:

1. Food production per capita fell between 1979-81 and 1985-87 in no fewer than sixty nine countries, or more than half of those for which data is available*;

2. Aggregate daily calorie supply per capita is below 2200 calories per day in twenty five countries, or 20% of the total; and

3. More than a quarter of children under five are underweight in twenty seven countries, or 44% of countries for which data are available.

These new data suggest that hunger is still very much an issue and this is confirmed by the final set of data

---

* There are some inconsistencies with the previous table, caused by differences in reporting periods.

presented in tables 4 and 5. Table 4 is taken from the recently published World Bank World Development Report and shows the prevalence of poverty in developing countries by 1985. Table 5 is restricted to sub-Saharan Africa and gives estimates of 'food insecurity' in the region in 1988[*]. These tables show:

   1. Over one billion people in 1985 were 'poor' or 'extremely poor', with over half of these located in South Asia; and

   2. About a quarter of Africa's population does not consume enough food to allow an active working life.

Thus, first appearances are deceptive. Hunger and poverty remain at the heart of the development challenge in 1990, as they did in 1980. In considering approaches to hunger alleviation, the next section present five propositions. The implications of these are reviewed in the conclusion.

2. Five propositions on food security

1. The priority is the food 'entitlement' of poor people

At the time of the last ICE Conference in 1980, most of the attention in food policy analysis was focused on food production and national food supplies. In the 1980's attention shifted from the national level to the household level, with a new interest in 'food security' and in 'entitlement' to food.

The standard definition of food security is found in the World Bank (1986) policy study, 'Poverty and Hunger': 'access by all people at all time to enough food for an active, healthy life'. In this definition, food insecurity can be 'chronic' (all the time) or 'transitory' (only in certain seasons or certain years).

---

[*] 'Food security' is 'access to enough food for an active, healthy life'

IMPLEMENTATION

Table 2 (source: UNDP 1990: 150-151)

12 Food security

		Food production per capita index (1979-81=100) 1985-87	Daily calorie supply per capita 1986	Food import dependency ratio		Food aid in cereals (1,000 metric tons)	
				1979-81	1984-86	1981-82	1987-88
	Low human development	105	2,190	6.9	7.7	4,630 T	6,390 T
	Excluding India	97	2,130	12.2	12.9	..	..
1	Niger	98	2,430	7.3	12.6	71.4	18.9
2	Mali	108	2,070	7.1	16.2	66.4	25.9
3	Burkina Faso	121	2,140	6.6	9.7	80.9	38.2
4	Sierra Leone	89	1,860	18.6	15.3	28.9	57.9
5	Chad	105	1,720	2.3	7.5	28.6	14.5
6	Guinea	90	1,780	11.9	14.4	38.6	26.2
7	Somalia	98	2,140	33.6	26.4	185.9	152.4
8	Mauritania	91	2,320	53.0	63.3	86.4	51.4
9	Afghanistan	..	..	..	..	81.8	104.0
10	Benin	112	2,180	6.7	6.8	8.3	11.3
11	Burundi	102	2,340	2.1	2.4	9.0	4.3
12	Bhutan	118	..	..	..	1.1	2.1
13	Mozambique	84	1,600	..	..	148.5	339.6
14	Malawi	83	2,310	3.3	1.8	2.0	108.8
15	Sudan	100	2,210	9.6	12.1	194.1	604.2
16	Central African Rep.	83	1,950	2.8	4.9	2.0	6.4
17	Nepal	102	2,050	1.7	3.1	23.2	20.5
18	Senegal	103	2,350	34.8	31.8	82.7	109.0
19	Ethiopia	94	1,750	..	..	189.7	825.3
20	Zaire	94	2,160	5.6	4.5	97.5	176.5
21	Rwanda	75	1,830	1.6	4.0	12.6	7.8
22	Angola	85	..	..	..	74.5	102.9
23	Bangladesh	88	1,930	9.5	16.9	1,005.5	1,394.6
24	Nigeria	96	2,150	15.0	9.1	1.4	..
25	Yemen Arab Rep.	105	2,320	39.7	60.2	12.9	159.7
26	Liberia	93	2,380	25.2	23.4	42.4	55.7
27	Togo	87	2,210	10.9	14.5	4.6	16.3
28	Uganda	82	2,340	2.2	1.0	48.5	29.3
29	Haiti	89	1,900	19.7	20.9	89.9	153.5
30	Ghana	108	1,760	8.8	5.3	43.1	109.6
31	Yemen, PDR	86	2,300	62.4	71.4	25.3	31.2
32	Côte d'Ivoire	94	2,560	18.3	18.1	0.9	0.9
33	Congo	94	2,620	19.6	29.1	0.4	0.7
34	Namibia	..	..	..	..	..	..
35	Tanzania, United Rep.	86	2,190	4.7	4.9	307.5	71.5
36	Pakistan	104	2,320	10.2	11.9	347.4	657.4
37	India	112	2,240	2.7	3.4	337.6	223.0
38	Madagascar	91	2,440	8.6	7.0	87.1	75.8
39	Papua New Guinea	97	2,210	25.3	19.7	..	..
40	Kampuchea, Dem.	141	..	..	..	49.9	6.2
41	Cameroon	95	2,030	7.6	10.0	10.5	2.3
42	Kenya	90	2,060	10.2	12.8	127.2	118.8
43	Zambia	92	..	22.1	14.1	100.0	140.4
44	Morocco	122	2,920	38.2	30.8	477.5	339.6
	Medium human development	118	2,650	8.8	7.7	3,190 T	5,790 T
	Excluding China	108	2,680	15.0	14.4		
45	Egypt	120	3,340	40.6	46.9	1,956.6	1,737.8
46	Lao PDR	110	2,390	..	..	1.3	21.4
47	Gabon	82	2,520	21.9	31.9	..	..
48	Oman	..	..	..	..	..	..
49	Bolivia	95	2,140	20.9	14.9	44.2	290.4
50	Myanmar	124	2,610	0.9	0.6	5.0	..
51	Honduras	87	2,070	14.8	12.0	33.8	145.6
52	Zimbabwe	97	2,130	4.2	7.6	..	13.9
53	Lesotho	86	2,300	46.9	59.2	34.2	55.3
54	Indonesia	119	2,580	8.4	3.9	106.6	319.1
55	Guatemala	96	2,310	11.2	10.3	10.6	320.1
56	Viet Nam	114	2,300	9.6	3.6	43.8	65.0
57	Algeria	95	2,720	64.5	69.1	5.4	3.8
58	Botswana	75	2,200	65.8	79.5	6.5	52.8
59	El Salvador	88	2,160	..	..	129.1	177.3
60	Tunisia	90	2,990	42.8	41.6	96.0	393.1
61	Iran, Islamic Rep.	89	3,310	..	..	..	..
62	Syrian Arab Rep.	95	3,260	22.6	35.2	9.3	26.3
63	Dominican Rep.	91	2,480	31.2	30.0	57.1	278.1
64	Saudi Arabia	236	3,000	89.7	78.4	..	..
65	Philippines	88	2,370	7.6	8.5	54.5	470.9
66	China	127	2,630	4.0	2.4	78.4	347.1

128

		Food production per capita index (1979-81=100) 1985-87	Daily calorie supply per capita 1986	Food import dependency ratio		Food aid in cereals (1,000 metric tons)	
				1979-81	1984-86	1981-82	1987-88
67	Libyan Arab Jamahiriya	90	3,600	69.7	78.2		
68	South Africa	88	2,920	4.7	15.8		
69	Lebanon					9.0	58.3
70	Mongolia	95		27.4	2.6		
71	Nicaragua	65	2,500			103.6	86.6
72	Turkey	98	3,230	1.9	5.2	0.3	0.6
73	Jordan	117	2,990	91.0	97.3	72.5	28.8
74	Peru	103	2,250	30.1	27.6	76.2	355.4
75	Ecuador	92	2,060	15.1	16.1	8.3	32.6
76	Iraq	102	2,930				
77	United Arab Emirates		3,730	114.7	98.0		
78	Thailand	104	2,330	3.5	2.5	2.3	97.2
79	Paraguay	117	2,850	3.5	2.3	1.1	1.9
80	Brazil	111	2,660	9.5	8.2	3.0	20.7
81	Mauritius	99	2,750	76.0	63.6	42.5	31.5
82	Korea, Dem. Rep.	109		7.1	3.5		
83	Sri Lanka	88	2,400	26.3	27.5	202.5	360.5
84	Albania	95		4.5	4.4		
High human development		100	3,280	24.4	22.9		
85	Malaysia	138	2,730	42.0	48.5		
86	Colombia	101	2,540	12.2	14.0	2.6	89.9
87	Jamaica	98	2,590	57.3	63.5	82.8	208.2
88	Kuwait		3,020	110.9	103.9		
89	Venezuela	92	2,490	49.3	44.0		
90	Romania	110	3,370	10.6	4.3		
91	Mexico	93	3,130	18.0	14.8		32.1
92	Cuba	105		49.5	47.2		
93	Panama	93	2,450	25.6	25.7	3.1	0.1
94	Trinidad and Tobago	71	3,080	82.6	92.0		
95	Portugal	102	3,150	58.9	54.9		
96	Singapore	83	2,840	157.4	179.5		
97	Korea, Rep.	100	2,910	44.2	46.9	429.2	
98	Poland	102	3,340	14.7	6.4	417.4	0.7
99	Argentina	96	3,210	1.1	0.5		
100	Yugoslavia	98	3,560	8.5	4.9		
101	Hungary	106	3,570	6.5	2.2		
102	Uruguay	102	2,650	14.8	11.3		
103	Costa Rica	86	2,800	25.4	18.0	45.2	235.1
104	Bulgaria	102		11.9	15.4		
105	USSR	109		15.8	16.5		
106	Czechoslovakia	122		19.6	9.8		
107	Chile	108	2,580	35.2	18.0	18.3	13.9
108	Hong Kong	54	2,860	105.7	120.3		
109	Greece	100	3,690	17.4	15.9		
110	German Dem. Rep.	117		12.5	12.4		
111	Israel	100	3,060	71.1	71.9	0.2	2.1
112	USA	85	3,650	5.1	4.3		
113	Austria	104	3,430	12.9	12.1		
114	Ireland	98	3,630	21.8	21.1		
115	Spain	110	3,360	24.2	16.5		
116	Belgium	116		128.9	119.8		
117	Italy	98	3,520	29.5	27.8		
118	New Zealand	111	3,460	25.4	24.1		
119	Germany, Fed. Rep.	112	3,530	35.2	34.3		
120	Finland	99	3,120	21.9	13.5		
121	United Kingdom	105	3,260	37.3	31.7		
122	Denmark	119	3,630	15.7	15.3		
123	France	100	3,340	15.8	14.3		
124	Australia	97	3,330	4.0	5.5		
125	Norway	109	3,220	49.4	39.4		
126	Canada	93	3,460	15.5	12.6		
127	Netherlands	111	3,330	114.5	112.0		
128	Switzerland	108	3,440	50.1	47.1		
129	Sweden	92	3,060	19.4	19.8		
130	Japan	98	2,860	55.5	54.5		
All developing countries		111	2,480	9.6	9.2	8,410 T	12,770 T
Least developed countries		96	2,070	9.1	12.8	2,800 T	4,410 T
Sub-Saharan Africa		93	2,160	11.1	10.8	2,070 T	2,850 T
Industrial countries		101	3,390	23.1	21.4		
World		109	2,650	12.9	12.2		

Note: Summary data for regional and income groups are given in tables 23 and 24

IMPLEMENTATION

Table 3 (source: UNDP 1990: 146-7)

10 Child survival and development

	Births attended by health personnel (%) 1983-88	Low birth-weight babies (%) 1982-88	Infant mortality rate (per 1,000 live births) 1988	Mothers breast-feeding at one year (%) 1980-87	One-year olds immunised (%) 1987	Child malnutrition 1980-88 % of under-fives underweight	% of 12-23 months wasted	% of 24-59 months stunted	Under-five mortality rate (per 1,000 live births) 1988
Low human development	30	25	107	72	55	42	16	44	170
Excluding India	27	20	114	..	49	43	..	..	186
1 Niger	47	15	134	15	24	49	23	38	228
2 Mali	27	17	168	82	31	31	16	34	292
3 Burkina Faso	30	..	137	97	46	..	..	..	233
4 Sierra Leone	25	17	153	83	40	23	26	46	266
5 Chad	24	11	131	..	21	..	..	..	223
6 Guinea	25	..	146	40	23	..	..	..	248
7 Somalia	2	..	131	..	28	..	..	..	221
8 Mauritania	20	11	126	67	45	31	..	..	220
9 Afghanistan	8	20	171	..	27	..	..	..	300
10 Benin	45	8	109	76	35	..	14	..	185
11 Burundi	21	9	111	90	54	38	10	60	188
12 Bhutan	7	..	127	..	67	..	..	..	197
13 Mozambique	28	20	172	..	42	..	..	..	298
14 Malawi	45	20	149	96	83	24	8	61	262
15 Sudan	20	..	107	72	58	..	13	..	181
16 Central African Rep.	66	15	131	..	33	..	..	..	223
17 Nepal	6	..	127	82	71	70	..	..	197
18 Senegal	50	11	80	82	57	22	8	28	136
19 Ethiopia	14	..	153	95	18	38	19	43	259
20 Zaire	..	13	83	86	46	28	11	40	138
21 Rwanda	22	17	121	74	82	28	23	45	206
22 Angola	15	17	172	..	28	..	..	..	292
23 Bangladesh	5	28	118	82	18	60	17	59	188
24 Nigeria	40	20	104	60	62	..	21	..	174
25 Yemen Arab Rep.	12	..	115	29	32	61	17	69	190
26 Liberia	87	..	86	70	43	20	7	38	147
27 Togo	15	20	93	90	73	25	..	..	153
28 Uganda	45	..	102	20	52	7	3	32	169
29 Haiti	40	17	116	88	50	37	17	51	171
30 Ghana	40	17	89	72	42	27	28	31	146
31 Yemen, PDR	10	13	118	55	37	26	8	36	197
32 Côte d'Ivoire	20	14	95	78	37	12	4	10	142
33 Congo	..	12	72	95	76	24	13	33	114
34 Namibia	..	..	105	82	..	..	..	..	176
35 Tanzania, United Rep.	..	14	105	70	86	48	17	..	176
36 Pakistan	24	25	108	70	65	52	17	42	166
37 India	33	30	98	..	63	41	..	..	149
38 Madagascar	62	10	119	85	44	33	18	41	184
39 Papua New Guinea	34	25	57	..	55	35	..	58	81
40 Kampuchea, Dem.	47	..	127	..	47	..	..	..	199
41 Cameroon	..	13	93	77	52	17	2	43	153
42 Kenya	28	15	71	67	74	..	10	42	113
43 Zambia	..	14	79	93	84	..	12	41	127
44 Morocco	29	..	80	76	65	16	6	34	119
Medium human development	61	9	51	60	81	32	10	43	72
Excluding China	..	12	66	..	70	..	..	..	94
45 Egypt	47	5	83	81	85	17	3	34	125
46 Lao PDR	..	39	109	93	20	37	20	44	159
47 Gabon	92	..	102	..	76	..	..	..	169
48 Oman	60	6	40	20	90	..	..	..	64
49 Bolivia	36	2	109	..	38	15	1	46	172
50 Myanmar	57	6	69	..	24	38	17	75	95
51 Honduras	50	20	68	24	76	21	2	34	107
52 Zimbabwe	69	15	71	84	81	12	1	29	113
53 Lesotho	40	..	99	..	81	..	7	23	136
54 Indonesia	31	14	84	83	71	51	17	..	119
55 Guatemala	34	10	58	74	49	34	3	68	99
56 Viet Nam	99	8	63	..	58	52	12	60	88
57 Algeria	15	9	73	..	71	..	..	..	107
58 Botswana	77	8	66	73	90	15	9	51	92
59 El Salvador	35	15	58	55	63	..	..	54	84
60 Tunisia	68	7	58	71	88	21	3	45	83
61 Iran, Islamic Rep.	82	5	61	..	81	43	23	55	90
62 Syrian Arab Rep.	37	..	47	41	63	..	..	..	64
63 Dominican Rep.	57	16	64	..	70	13	3	26	81
64 Saudi Arabia	74	6	70	52	88	..	..	..	98
65 Philippines	57	18	44	53	82	33	7	42	73
66 China	..	5	31	..	96	..	..	..	43

		Births attended by health personnel (%) 1983-88	Low birth-weight babies (%) 1982-88	Infant mortality rate (per 1,000 live births) 1988	Mothers breast-feeding at one year (%) 1980-87	One-year olds immunised (%) 1987	Child malnutrition 1980-88			Under-five mortality rate (per 1,000 live births) 1988
							% of under-fives underweight	% of 12-23 months wasted	% of 24-59 months stunted	
67	Libyan Arab Jamahiriya	76		80	..	62	..	..	..	119
68	South Africa	..	12	71	..	..	..	..	..	95
69	Lebanon	..	..	39	15	88	16	..	..	51
70	Mongolia	99	10	44	..	67	..	..	..	59
71	Nicaragua	41	15	61	71	70	11	..	22	95
72	Turkey	78	8	74	51	71	..	..	..	93
73	Jordan	83	5	43	50	71	..	..	..	57
74	Peru	44	9	87	37	66	13	3	43	123
75	Ecuador	27	10	62	48	62	17	4	39	87
76	Iraq	56	9	68	..	84	..	..	..	94
77	United Arab Emirates	96	7	25	..	73	..	..	..	32
78	Thailand	40	12	38	68	79	26	10	28	49
79	Paraguay	22	7	42	49	65	..	..	..	62
80	Brazil	95	8	62	34	68	13	2	31	85
81	Mauritius	85	9	22	40	84	24	16	22	29
82	Korea, Dem. Rep.	65	..	24	..	59	..	..	..	33
83	Sri Lanka	87	28	32	81	79	38	19	34	43
84	Albania	..	7	28	..	95	..	..	..	34
High human development		94	8	20	..	76	..	..	..	27
85	Malaysia	82	10	24	..	74	..	12	33	32
86	Colombia	51	15	46	36	85	12	1	27	68
87	Jamaica	89	8	18	43	82	9	5	9	22
88	Kuwait	99	7	19	12	51	6	2	14	22
89	Venezuela	82	9	36	30	62	10	3	7	44
90	Romania	100	6	22	..	93	..	..	..	28
91	Mexico	94	15	46	36	74	..	..	..	68
92	Cuba	..	8	15	..	93	..	1	..	18
93	Panama	89	8	23	53	79	16	7	24	34
94	Trinidad and Tobago	98	..	20	14	78	7	5	4	23
95	Portugal	87	5	14	7	78	..	..	..	17
96	Singapore	100	6	9	..	95	14	..	..	12
97	Korea, Rep.	70	6	24	27	89	..	..	..	33
98	Poland	100	8	16	..	97	..	..	..	18
99	Argentina	..	..	32	14	68	..	..	..	37
100	Yugoslavia	86	7	25	..	90	..	..	..	28
101	Hungary	99	10	17	..	99	..	..	..	19
102	Uruguay	97	8	27	..	84	..	..	16	31
103	Costa Rica	93	10	18	22	89	6	3	8	22
104	Bulgaria	100	6	15	..	99	..	..	..	20
105	USSR	98	6	25	..	83	..	..	..	32
106	Czechoslovakia	100	6	12	..	99	..	..	..	15
107	Chile	98	7	19	17	96	3	1	10	26
108	Hong Kong	92	5	8	..	91	..	..	..	10
109	Greece	97	6	13	..	86	..	..	..	18
110	German Dem. Rep.	99	6	8	..	97	..	..	..	12
111	Israel	100	7	11	..	90	..	..	..	14
112	USA	99	7	10	..	48	..	..	..	13
113	Austria	..	6	8	..	83	..	..	..	10
114	Ireland	..	4	7	..	70	..	..	..	9
115	Spain	96	1	9	..	78	..	..	..	12
116	Belgium	100	5	10	..	83	..	..	..	13
117	Italy	100	7	10	..	59	..	..	..	11
118	New Zealand	99	5	10	..	59	..	..	..	12
119	Germany, Fed. Rep.	100	6	8	..	68	..	..	..	10
120	Finland	100	4	6	..	89	..	..	..	7
121	United Kingdom	100	7	9	..	82	..	..	..	11
122	Denmark	100	6	8	..	90	..	..	..	11
123	France	99	5	8	..	83	..	..	..	10
124	Australia	99	6	9	10	68	..	..	..	10
125	Norway	100	4	8	..	84	..	..	..	10
126	Canada	99	6	7	..	85	..	..	..	8
127	Netherlands	100	..	8	..	96	..	..	..	8
128	Switzerland	99	5	7	..	88	..	..	..	8
129	Sweden	100	4	6	..	76	..	..	..	7
130	Japan	100	5	5	..	84	..	..	..	8
All developing countries		42	17	79	64	68	38	13	42	121
Least developed countries		23	21	124	75	37	46	16	54	205
Sub-Saharan Africa		36	16	110	71	52	29	16	38	183
Industrial countries		99	6	15	..	75	..	..	..	18
World		51	15	71	..	69	..	..	..	108

Note: Summary data for regional and income groups are given in tables 23 and 24

IMPLEMENTATION

Table 4. How much poverty is there in the developing countries? The situation in 1985 (source: World Bank 1990: 29)

How much poverty is there in the developing countries? The situation in 1985

Region	Extremely poor			Poor (including extremely poor)			Social indicators		
	Number (millions)	Headcount index (percent)	Poverty gap	Number (millions)	Headcount index (percent)	Poverty gap	Under 5 mortality (per thousand)	Life expectancy (years)	Net primary enrollment rate (percent)
Sub-Saharan Africa	120	30	4	180	47	11	196	50	56
East Asia	120	9	0.4	280	20	1	96	67	96
China	80	8	1	210	20	3	58	69	93
South Asia	300	29	3	520	51	10	172	56	74
India	250	33	4	420	55	12	199	57	81
Eastern Europe	3	4	0.2	6	8	0.5	23	71	90
Middle East and North Africa	40	21	1	60	31	2	148	61	75
Latin America and the Caribbean	50	12	1	70	19	1	75	66	92
All developing countries	633	18	1	1,116	33	3	121	62	83

Note: The poverty line in 1985 PPP dollars is $275 per capita a year for the extremely poor and $370 per capita a year for the poor.
The headcount index is defined as the percentage of the population below the poverty line. The 95 percent confidence intervals around the point estimates for the headcount indices are Sub-Saharan Africa, 19, 76; East Asia, 21, 22; South Asia, 50, 53; Eastern Europe, 7, 10; Middle East and North Africa, 13, 51; Latin America and the Caribbean, 14, 30; and all developing countries, 28, 39.
The poverty gap is defined as the aggregate income shortfall of the poor as a percentage of aggregate consumption. Under 5 mortality rates are for 1980–85, except for China and South Asia, where the period is 1975–80.
Source: Hill and Pebley 1988, Ravallion and others (background paper), and United Nations and World Bank data 1989.

Table 5. Africa's food insecure (source: World Bank 1988: iv)

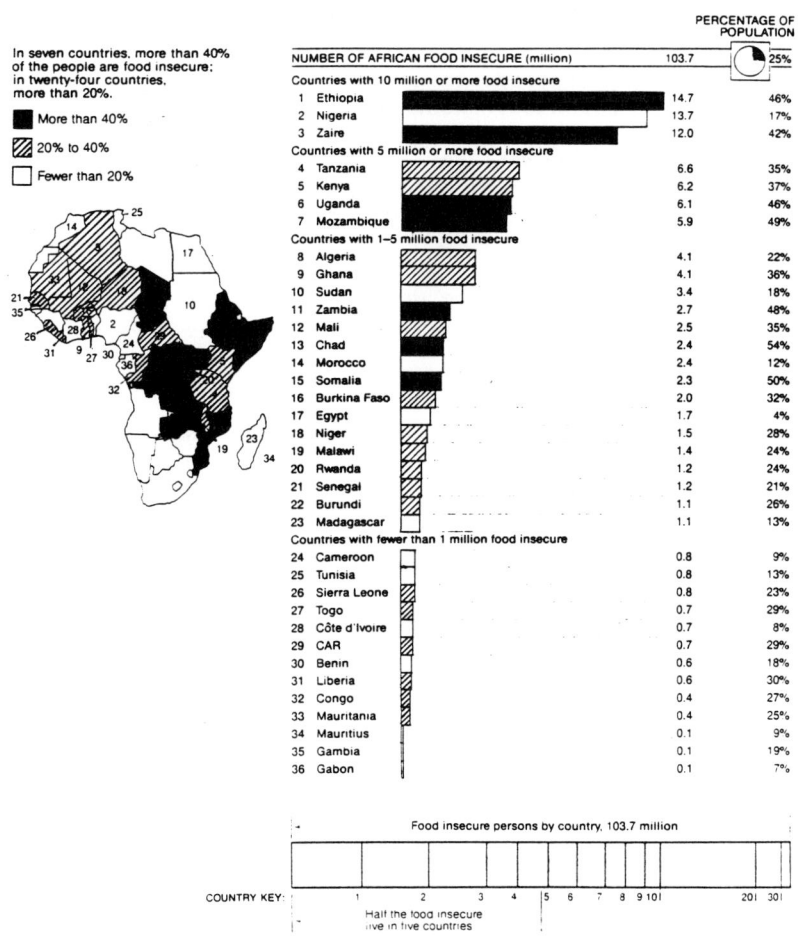

IMPLEMENTATION

The definition has many virtues: it stresses consumption over production, introduces the idea of temporal variation in access to food and requires not just a target number of calories but the number required by a functional diet for an active life (which will vary by location, climate and activity level).

The intellectual roots of the World Bank definition are to be found in the work of Sen (1981), who introduced the concept of 'entitlement' to food: command over food by production, purchase, exchange or gift. Food insecurity may arise if individuals or households fail to produce enough to eat; but also if they are unable to earn or sell enough to buy enough to eat; or if social welfare provided by the community or the state in some way fails.

Recent work has extended the definition of food insecurity to lay greater stress on the role of assets and on the perceptions of poor people themselves. A recent definition suggests that

> 'A country and people are food secure when their food system operates efficiently in such a way as to remove the fear that there will not be enough to eat. In particular, food security will be achieved when the poor and vulnerable, particularly women, children and those living in marginal areas, have secure access to the food they want. Food security will be achieved when equitable growth ensures that these groups have sustainable livelihoods; in the meantime and in addition, food security requires the efficient and equitable operation of the food system.' (Maxwell 1988).

The focus on sustainable livelihoods has led food security analysis to focus particularly on the food needs of four main groups: 'resource poor families' in rural areas; people living in marginal, mostly arid areas; small-scale nomads; and the urban poor. In each of these categories, a substantial proportion of the households will be female-headed.

2. Increasing entitlement does not require food self-sufficiency

The new focus on individual food entitlement rather than aggregate food production has led to a reappraisal of the importance of food production in general and food self-sufficiency in particular. There are cases where both may be desirable, but they are rare. The route to greater food entitlement for most poor people in most poor countries is most likely to lie through expanded cash cropping.

The reasons for this include the following (Maxwell and Fernando 1989):

1. Cash cropping results in faster growth, both because it exploits comparative advantage and because both upstream and downstream linkages to the rest of the economy are greater.

2. Cash cropping is generally more labour intensive than food cropping, with the consequence that the incomes of poor people and hence their command over food both rise.

3. Cash cropping at the farm level is often complementary rather than competitive with food cropping. This is because of technical and financial linkages within the farming system, associated with rotations, sharing of inputs or the greater availability of cash.

In general, this pro-cash crop conclusion applies both to households and to countries. There are, however, some qualifications: cash cropping may result in rapidly increasing social inequality; and it may, in certain circumstances, lead to an increase in food prices.

3. Cereal market protection is largely counter-productive

The implication of the previous paragraphs is that food production should be left to find its own level in a developing economy. This can be interpreted as meaning that protection of the food sector or special incentives to food production are unnecessary and can be counter-productive. Here again, the conventional wisdom differs markedly from that in 1980.

IMPLEMENTATION

If there is a case for protection, it lies in the protectionist policies of rich countries, which have artificially depressed world cereal prices; and in the need for a protective barrier behind which new technology can be introduced (the infant industry argument). However, there seems little reason to protect cereal production when other, more profitable avenues may be open to small farmers. Nor is there a strong, farm-level case for infant industry protection, though there may be one, especially in SSA on infrastructural or institutional grounds.

Where protection of food production has taken place in the developing world, it has largely been counter-productive, benefiting large farmers at the expense of small ones and producers over consumers, in both rural and urban areas.

4. Trade is preferable to buffer stocks and government price stabilisation

Another shift in conventional wisdom during the 1980's has been the gradual disenchantment with buffer stocks as the answer to national and regional production instability and price variability. These were found to be expensive, displacing of private trade and often inequitable. Cereal market intervention was justified on the grounds of market failure: barriers to entry to private trade; the development of monopoly situations; restrictions on international trade; or shortages of vehicles, spares or fuel in the private sector. However, there is now a more general recognition that private market agents are often efficient and that the emphasis should be on providing an enabling infrastructure.

As a result of this shift, the new conventional wisdom on grain market intervention can be summarised in three propositions: (a) public sector sales and purchases should be kept as low as possible, so as to provide incentives to traders; (b) stocks should be kept to the minimum required for emergency relief; and (c) inter-annual fluctuations should be handled largely by trade. The benefits of this model lie in reduced fiscal outlays, in a smaller burden on state administrative capacity and in an active private sector.

Nevertheless, there are also costs in the new approach: larger price fluctuations than would otherwise be the case, with a major impact on the real income of the poorest groups; and increased risk of food shortage in a bad year. These potential costs make the case for the last proposition, which is for strengthened social welfare safety nets in rural and urban areas.

5. Targeted interventions are required to reach the food insecure

Food security interventions by Third World Governments take many forms, from generalised food subsidies to highly targeted nutrition interventions aimed at vulnerable groups. The final shift in thinking in the 1980's has been the realisation that generalised food and nutrition subsidies - which command widespread political support and are relatively easy to administer - are unsustainably expensive. Generalised food subsidies have been a prime target of structural adjustment programmes.

The International Food Policy Research Institute have shown (Pinstrup-Andersen 1988) that the feasibility and desirability of targeting vary from case to case. The best case scenario is one in which the target group is small relative to the population; there is political support for redistribution; a targeted intervention can be implemented with little 'leakage'; the extra purchasing power delivered to households results in increased consumption by vulnerable groups; the cost is explicit rather than implicit; and the fiscal burden is offset by taxing the rich.

These conditions have proved very difficult to meet, especially in SSA. Nevertheless, the search for improved safety nets is underway, with particular interest in employment-based public works programmes, sometimes but not always supported by food aid.

Implications

Three important conclusions can be drawn from the above analysis:

1. The most successful solutions to hunger in the 1990's will be found in programmes which provide the poor with sustainable livelihoods, which is to say adequate current incomes and substantial buffers (in the form of disposable assets) against misfortune. Food production is not necessarily the first priority and even agriculture may take second place to non-farm rural enterprises. Increasing numbers of the target

IMPLEMENTATION

population will be functionally landless people in rural areas and the urban poor.

2. As far as the food system is concerned, the 1990's will be marked by a continuing retreat from intervention into an 'enabling' role for government: providing the infrastructure, setting the rules, regulating the market.

3. Nevertheless, food security interventions will still be required to provide a social welfare safety net, particularly through employment-based public works and targeted nutrition programmes for vulnerable groups. In Africa, especially, such programmes will require a large investment in target group identification and in programme design and management.

References:

Maxwell, S, 1989, 'Food insecurity in North Sudan', Discussion Paper No 262, Institute of Development Studies, University of Sussex

Maxwell, S and A. Fernando, 1989, 'Cash crops in developing countries: the issues, the facts, the policies' in World Development, Vol 17, No 11

Pinstrup-Andersen, P (ed), 1988, Food subsidies in developing countries: costs, benefits and policy options, Johns Hopkins for IFPRI

Sen, A, 1981, Poverty and Famine: an essay on entitlement and deprivation, Clarendon Press, Oxford

United Nations Development Programme, 1990, Human Development Report 1990, UNDP, New York

World Bank, 1986, Poverty and Hunger: issues and options for food security in developing countries, Washington

World Bank, 1988, The challenge of Hunger in Africa: A call to action, World Bank, Washington

World Bank, 1990, World Development Report, 1990, World Bank, Washington

World Food Programme, 1990, 1190 Food Aid Review, WFP, Rome

10. Energy consumption and generation

J. D. L. HARRISON, BA, Senior Renewable Energy and Engineering Research Adviser, Overseas Development Administration

SYNOPSIS. This paper will review the scale on which energy is used, what it is used for, some of the issues raised by the scale of use and the role that technology plays in contributing to an enriched and sustainable future for mankind.

ENERGY - CONSUMPTION AND GENERATION
INTRODUCTION
1. The development of human societies in all parts of the World has been intertwined with the development and application of means to harness a wide range of energy sources - from draught animals to uranium - for a range of uses - from cooking to computing. The availability of energy has become essential to the survival and continuing development of virtually all societies. The world has become dependant on the use of energy for the production and distribution of food; for water supplies; protection against extremes of cold or heat; for transport; the extraction and use of a host of materials and for communications - which have themselves become an essential part of the fabric of most societies.

USES OF ENERGY
2. Energy inputs enable us to carry out a whole range of tasks that, unaided, we could accomplish only with great difficulty, or not at all. It is an essential enabling factor which we employ in four separate guises at the final point of application. We use it as heat to provide warmth, to cook food and in a host of industrial processes such as metallurgical extraction and refining; distillation; manufacture of building materials and fertiliser manufacture.

Appropriate development for basic needs. Thomas Telford, London, 1990

IMPLEMENTATION

<u>Mechanical energy</u> is needed for agriculture, for transport, for industry and for domestic appliances from electric toothbrushes to vacuum cleaners. <u>Light</u> we need to extend the working and the convivial hours, to illuminate places where sunlight cannot ever reach, and, quite recently, for fibre-optic communications. <u>Electricity</u>, though widely and mainly used as a means to deliver heat or mechanical power and light is essential only for electrolysis, communications, and for computing.

3. Quite a large proportion of mankind's technical inventiveness over the last couple of thousand years has been concerned with finding effective ways to make these four useful forms of energy conveniently, safely and affordably available from a wide range of primary sources. These primary sources include draught animals; combustible fuels such as wood, coal, oil and gas; wind and flowing water; sunshine; nuclear fuels and geothermal heat.

4. The scale on which energy is used is now very large indeed, and likely to grow even further as the World population increases and as more people become able to afford the goods and services which, presently, are taken for granted only by the one third of people who live in industrialised countries. Last year's BP Statistical Review of World Energy estimates use of major sources as:

Source	1988 Consumption (MTOE)*
Oil	3038
Gas	1631
Coal	2428
Nuclear	438
Hydro	537

The total is 8073 MTOE. In 1978 it was 7000 and in 1968 4900 MTOE, a considerable rate of increase, averaging 2.7% over 20 years but currently 3.7%. In addition, woodfuels and other biomass fuels are used in substantial amounts - perhaps 10-15% of world primary energy use or 1100 MTOE annually. They are widely used in many countries for domestic needs and industries such as brickmaking, brewing and lime-burning. Geothermal sources contribute a small, growing, amount applied mainly for power generation.

* Million Tons Oil Equivalent

5. At present the industrialized countries, with a total population of roughly 1,200 million, are responsible for about 60% of the global primary energy use. This situation will change in the coming decades as the 3,800 million population of the rest of the world grows not only in numbers but in per capita primary energy demand. On present trends total world primary energy consumption will double, to about 15,000 MTOE, by 2020 as world population increases to about 7.5 billion. In practice this rate of consumption may not be reached since fuel price increases and concern for environmental effects seem likely to constrain energy use somewhat. Nevertheless, both the quantity and the proportion of energy used by the developing countries will increase considerably. Between 1971 and 1987 their primary energy consumption grew at an average annual rate of 6.2% compared to a rate of 1.3% within the OECD countries.

'SURVIVAL' ISSUES
6. In the context of the title of this meeting – 'Appropriate Development for Survival' – we can consider some of the important energy-related issues linked to the sustainable development of our societies and then go on to reflect on the roles which technology may play in enabling such development.

7. As I see it, there are two main topics that give rise to concern: resource depletion and environmental impact. At present we derive most of our energy from non-renewable fuels, oil, gas, coal and uranium. We shall undoubtedly discover further reserves of these and find means to extract and utilise these fuels more efficiently and cheaply. But, inevitably, a time will come when the remaining resources will be very difficult and expensive to access by current standards. The historic trend of ever-decreasing fuel prices in real terms will reverse – perhaps quite abruptly. This may not occur for many decades; but the issue cannot be ignored in view of the long lead times that are needed to develop, to introduce and to adjust to the widespread use of different energy sources; whatever those may turn out to be. In the shorter term there is international concern over the depletion of the forest resource. Although the majority of this depletion is caused by pressures which lead to forests being cleared either to make land available for agriculture or to obtain timber, the present demand for woodfuels in the urban areas of some developing countries does add to the other causes of depletion. The consequences of the reduction in forested land area include soil erosion and associated siltation problems; reduced availability of woodfuels; an increase in the output of carbon dioxide (CO_2) when forest is burned to clear land and a loss of

IMPLEMENTATION

habitat for those human beings, animals, and other living things that have become adapted to forest conditions. Of course, this is not a new circumstance. Mankind has been clearing forests for a very long time for much the same reasons albeit at a slower rate. Consider, for example what has happened in Europe during the last two thousand years and in North America during the last two hundred. The essential differences between present and past circumstances are that the rate of deforestation is much more rapid; the remaining resource is smaller than it has ever been in human history; and we perhaps understand better than in the past the likely consequences of what is occurring.

8. The second issue - the impact of energy use on the environment - has a high profile at present. We have become increasingly aware of several harmful environmental effects related to energy use including the release of carbon dioxide (CO_2); sulphur oxides (SO_x); nitrogen oxides (NO_x) as gaseous products arising from the combustion of fuels. CO_2 release is the major contributor to the global "greenhouse effect" on account of the huge amounts involved - about 18,000 million tons per year. SO_x and NO_x both contribute to "acid rain" and urban "smog" which are regional rather than global in their harmful effects. Methane (CH_4) is another important "greenhouse gas" and is released from leaking gas wells and pipelines, although releases from other sources, mainly agriculture and decomposition of natural and man-made wastes predominate. Domestic and urban atmospheric pollution, especially by smoke, arises due to the combustion of solid fuels for cooking and heating. In some cases, such as high sulphur coals; damp wood; animal dung; it is impracticable to burn such fuels cleanly on the domestic scale. Lung and eye diseases tend to afflict those compelled to live in such smoke-polluted air. Hydro-power schemes can lead to inundation of fertile or populated land by man-made lakes. The mining, processing and combustion of solid fuels can lead to the release of dust and ash and bad practice can lead to land and water courses being fouled by mine operation. As in the case of resource depletion, it is the present scale on which energy is used and the prospect of a substantial increase in that scale, that is the overarching cause of our difficulty. The larger the scale, the greater the rate of change imposed on the natural order - including human society.

CONTRIBUTIONS OF TECHNOLOGY

9. Let us now consider some of the contributions technology - and I include science in that term - can make to the satisfactory resolution of impending problems. Some of them are direct and some of them indirect. Technology

over the centuries - from the first harnessing of fire and the development of the stone axe - has played a vital role in freeing us from incessant toil and enabling us to diversify our lives, mental and physical, in ways which have been beneficial. It will continue to do so, provided that we develop it aright. Scientific research will lead to a better understanding of the nature and consequences of problems and so point the way for the development of measures to alleviate them.

10. Direct contributions will include more efficient ways to use energy; more effective ways to discover and develop energy resources, including the renewable ones; ways to avoid harmful pollution effects and to clean up some of the consequences of past mistakes that have damaged the environment. Indirect contributions, affecting especially the developing countries, will arise from the role that energy technologies play in increasing economic well-being.
People who at present live on the margins of survival have little freedom to change their lifestyles even though change may be needed to ensure long-term sustainability.

11. Technical advances have for a long time enabled us to use primary energy sources to greater and greater useful effect - with greater efficiency. The early, primitive, steam engine developed through the condensing engine and the triple expansion piston engine to the super-critical boiler and multi-stage turbine sets of modern power stations. They, in turn, are being displaced by combined-cycle gas turbine - steam units for power generation. The modern petrol or compression-ignition engine is both efficient and more reliable than the first commercially-successful versions used a hundred years ago. These great improvements in the efficiency of conversion of fuels into useful mechanical or electrical energy have been accompanied by great reductions in the emission, per unit useful output, of noxious substances. The provision of light from fuels has progressed from the open fire to the oil lamp, to the tungsten filament lamp and to the family of gas-discharge lamps, each stage being more energy-efficient than the earlier one. Cheap and effective insulating materials, allied to improved designs and construction techniques, have greatly reduced the energy-inputs needed to maintain comfortable living conditions in buildings. Much the same has hasppened to road transport vehicles which, for a given level of performance, are safer, more comfortable and more fuel-efficient than ever before. Many industrial processes now require much less energy input per unit of product than in the past - steel and fertiliser manufacture are good examples.

IMPLEMENTATION

12. Satellite remote-sensing techniques, improved data processing and display and mathematical modelling have improved the effectiveness of oil and gas exploration and, especially for offshore fields, new methods have reduced the costs of well completion. The price of photovoltaic modules, to convert sunlight to electricity, have fallen substantially in the last ten years and are likely to fall further over the next decade and the cost of power generation from the wind has also been reduced although not so dramatically.

13. In response to international understanding of, and concerns about, atmospheric pollution technologies have been developed to reduce the emission of sulphur and nitrogen oxides when fuels are burnt and to clean up fuels before they are burnt. However, we have as yet no practicable means to remove the CO_2 which is produced in huge amounts. This presents a major challenge for the future. It is unfortunate that of the known resources of fuels coal is much the most abundant since it is also the one that gives rise to the largest output of CO_2 per unit heat or power.

14. Thus, technologies have continually developed in response to our innate wish to do things that could not be done before, to do things better or more easily than they have been done before and to find solutions to those difficulties that arise in consequence. We shall surely continue this process in the future.

11. Water and sanitation

PROFESSOR J. PICKFORD, OBE, MSc(Eng), FICE, HonFIWEM, Leader, Water, Engineering and Development Centre, Loughborough University

SYNOPSIS. Floods and droughts make survival difficult or impossible, but clean accessible water and sanitation are keys to health, development and survival. Aspects of health, developing countries and limited resources are discussed. Technologies for water supply, drainage, excreta disposal and solid waste are outlined, with special attention to rural areas and low income urban communities. Software' is considered in relation to training, to management by communities, institutions and non-government organizations, and to maintenance. An adequate service for those who have greatest difficulty in surviving depends on a combination of technology and management that is appropriate for underprivileged poor people.

THE SIGNIFICANCE OF WATER AND SANITATION
1. Too much water and too little water cause some of the greatest disasters - by flood and drought. Floods cover much of Bangladesh every year so it is obvious that only a little extra water makes survival impossible and causes millions of people to become refugees. The 1988 floods in and around Khartoum were specially tragic because Sudan has been afflicted by the drought in the Sahel and the long civil war (ref. 1). About a third of the earth's surface is classified as arid or semi-arid and supports 600 million people and some of the fastest growing cities. The populations of Ouagadougou and Niamey on the edge of the Sahara had more than four-fold increase in the 1960s and 1970s (ref. 2).
2. In the right place and in the right quantity water of any quality can be used for hydropower and transport. As Robert Browning said beside the Grand Canal in Venice, 'water, as you see, for purposes of locomotion most convenient, for washing indispensable'. Water for washing has more relevance for good health than is often appreciated, although 'good drinking water' is the most felt need when water is difficult to come by. In terms of quantity, agriculture makes more demands than domestic use in rural areas, and industries' demands are high in urban areas. For example, water used in dairies is up to eight times the volume of the milk produced

IMPLEMENTATION

(ref. 3). In Saudi Arabia, hardly an agricultural country, irrigation is using 90% of the abstracted fossil water (ref. 4). Irrigation has a greedy demand for water, but without it there would have been no green revolution, which has enabled the growing population of India to survive without recurrent famine.

3. Getting rid of unwanted water by drainage is essential to prevent (or reduce) flooding and to allow irrigated land to survive - without proper drainage the soil is ruined by salt build-up.

4. Sanitation is defined as the 'use of means for protecting public health, especially by the removing and treatment of waste' (ref. 5). This waste is primarily human excreta (faeces and urine), sullage (wastewater not containing excreta) and domestic solid waste (refuse or garbage).

5. This paper focuses on water supply for personal and household needs and the treatment and/or disposal of excreta. These have been the concerns of the International Drinking Water Supply and Sanitation Decade - Water Decade for short. At the beginning of the Decade Peter Bourne said 'clean accessible drinking water and sanitation for all would have a dramatic impact on the economic status of the world's billion people who live in absolute poverty. Healthy people are productive people and productive people are the key to economic development' (ref. 6).

APPROPRIATE TECHNOLOGY FOR DEVELOPMENT AND SURVIVAL

6. All technology should be appropriate for its purpose, its location and the resources available (ref. 7). A major purpose of providing sustainable water and sanitation is the promotion of health and well-being. The focus is on developing countries in which resources are limited.

Health for survival

7. There is plenty of evidence of the increased chances of survival, or reduced mortality rates, when good water and sanitation is provided. For example, the death rate fell from 42 per thousand to 20 per thousand when a municipal water supply was installed in Burdwan, India, in 1890 (ref. 8). Well-designed projects with water supply, sanitation and health education have resulted in up to 50% reduction in mortality from diarrhoeas (ref. 9).

8. Francois Bernier in his travels in the Mogul Empire (1659-67) wrote about the water of Delhi 'the impurities of which exceed my powers of description' (ref. 10). His account of guinea worms and the care needed to extract them 'gently winding them round a small twig the size of a pin' exactly matches the situation in thousands of villages in the 1990s. This painful disease, which causes much loss of production (and so hinders development), can be eradicated simply by improving the quality of drinking water (ref. 11).

Appropriate for developing countries

9. At the meeting of bilateral donors held at Bonn in October 1984 one of the conclusions was that the approach of copying the norms and technologies of industrialised countries had not so far provided a solution to the problems of providing water and sanitation (ref. 12). Schulz and Okun (ref. 13) tell of a US consultant who boasted that everything in a new African water treatment plant (including inoperative instrumentation) was exactly as it would have been done in his own city.

10. Developing countries range from the very poor to those on the verge of being developed. Countries that were selected for 'primary focus' in the last years of the Decade were China, Ethiopia, Ghana, India, Indonesia, Nigeria, Pakistan and Zimbabwe (ref. 14).

11. Within countries too there is tremendous variation. In general, rural areas have less infrastructure, less provision for health and less chance of survival. But the needs of the urban poor are also now receiving more attention as the significance of worldwide urbanization is appreciated. Paul Harrison noted (ref. 15), that 'every Third World city is a dual city - an island of wealth surrounded by a black belt of misery.' Many of those in the black belts - the peri-urban or fringe areas - are squatters with totally inadequate water supplies and sanitation. Other recent squatters share urban slums in city centres with families who have never had another home.

12. Bulldozing slums has given way to slum upgrading, with provision of water supplies and sanitation. Some upgraded slums have become show-pieces, contrasting with the squalor of unimproved and unserviced areas.

Appropriate for limited resources

13. Technology that is appropriate for oil-producing developing countries may reflect their wealth. Water in Bahrain is twice as costly as petrol (ref. 16).

14. Lack of knowledge of lower-cost technologies and use of technologies inappropriate for developing countries was given in 1988 as one of the obstacles to Decade success (ref. 14).

15. The increasing availability of microcomputers in developing countries enables engineers to select resource-effective designs. However, there is a danger of unnecessary elaboration and accuracy. Simple rules of thumb may be more sensible. There is much to commend old methods like making culvert diameters in inches equal to the time in minutes it took for a horse-rider to go round the catchment.

16. A valid criticism of much aid is that too little is effective. Of the several hundreds of millions of dollars provided by bilateral and multilateral donor agencies for desertification control between 1978 and 1983 only 10 per cent went to operations in the field (ref. 17). In many countries confusion is caused by the multiplicity of donors. In the

IMPLEMENTATION

early 1980s in Zambia 69 donors were involved in 614 projects (ref. 18).

17. Underprivileged minorities are most at risk in the battle for survival. Least privileged in many communities are women-headed households. These are reckoned to be 30 per cent of all households worldwide with the proportion reaching more than 50 per cent in some Latin American countries (ref. 19).

WATER SUPPLY FOR SURVIVAL

18. Urban water supply is in many ways the same worldwide. As towns and cities expand the search for additional sources involves greater transmission distances and higher costs. Much effort is currently going into reduction of unaccounted water through leakage, waste at outlets and sometimes by illegal connections.

19. In developing countries public standposts (ref. 20) are widely used for low income urban communities and many people get their water from vendors. In Dar es Salaam protests from Moslem women caused the City Council to rescind a decision to move water vendors to rural areas (ref. 21).

20. Arlosoroff et al (ref. 22) suggest that 'the technology should give the community the highest service level that it is willing to pay for, will benefit from, and has the institutional capacity to sustain'.

Rural water supplies

21. Communities that have traditionally drawn their water from streams and other surface waters may be reluctant to abandon them. For example, a village in Sierra Leone used a highly polluted stream. 'There was a myth in the village that water from that stream was good for fertility, and it would be hard to disprove this myth as the water had been used for generations and people in fact had many children' (ref. 23).

22. Where the dry rainless season is short a roofwater collection system can provide good water which is under the control of individual householders. However, a storage tank may cost more than the roof (ref. 24).

23. Safe drinking water is most commonly obtained from groundwater. Considerable attention has therefore been given to hand-dug wells (ref. 25) and handpumps. ODA started and the World Bank continued a very comprehensive research programme during which commercial handpumps were tested in the laboratory and field (ref. 22) in relation to village level operation and maintenance (VLOM).

24. Survival primarily depends on availability of sufficient quality of water. Good quality is essential for good health. Accessibility can contribute to well-being and economic development by freeing people, especially women, from the time-taking burden of carrying water long distances.

25. Dr M G Candau, former Director-General of WHO, wrote that 'there is no more efficient means of transporting water than by a pipe. A small pipe, one inch in diameter, will

deliver in a day, without human effort, as much water as can be carried by 150 women working steadily for eight hours.' One of the most successful rural water supply schemes has been in Malawi, where hundreds of kilometres of pipes were laid by communal effort. The route was decided one year and no crops were planted along the line. Digging started in the next year after the rains had made the ground soft (ref. 26).

Water treatment
26. Storage is a simple method of water treatment that has been used for centuries. Samples of polluted dug-well water (with more than 2400 coliforms per 100 ml) had less than 20 coliforms per 100 ml after being kept in copper vessels (ref. 27). Slow sand filtration was popular in Europe before coagulation with chemicals and rapid filtration took over. It is particularly suitable for developing countries (refs. 28, 29). No chemicals or power is required; most of the labour needed can be semi-skilled; there is high removal of pathogens, resulting in water that is safe to drink without disinfection. However, a large area is required and pre-treatment is needed for turbid raw water (ref. 30).

DRAINAGE FOR SURVIVAL
27. In a survey in 1982 city councils in Mozambique almost unanimously gave rainwater drainage as the infrastructural problem for which they most needed help (ref. 31). The problems of drainage are aggravated in both rural and unsewered urban areas of developing countries by the common practice of discharging sullage into rainwater drains and inadequate solid waste collection. Poor removal of sullage may increase breeding of culex mosquitoes, leading to filariasis and sometimes to elephantitis. The extent of the problem is indicated by the record of over 700 mosquito bites per person per night in Calcutta (ref. 32).

EXCRETA DISPOSAL FOR SURVIVAL
28. Scattered rural communities may suffer little from defecating in the fields, especially if they follow the rules laid down in the Quran and Bible to cover up excreta. The spread of worm infection can be reduced by digging furrows for defecation and walking on the ridges. A point usually missed by the media in their diatribes against deforestation is that cutting down trees and bushes has resulted in women having nowhere to squat to defecate.
29. Open, indiscriminate or 'free-range' defecation within villages and in urban areas presents a very serious health risk. It is often difficult to find suitable out-of-the-way places, resulting in widespread nuisance on the sides of roads, railway lines, rivers and canals. Bucket latrines, and what is known in the Indian sub-continent as the dry latrine system, are now universally condemned because of fly nuisance, spillage of contents during cartage, the collectors' exposure

IMPLEMENTATION

to disease and the social unacceptability of the work.

Sewerage

30. Conventional sewerage can be entirely satisfactory in terms of convenience, health and the environment, providing the sewage is sufficiently treated to avoid harm to the water to which it is discharged. It deals with sullage as well as excreta, and can also cope with industrial wastewater. Both indigenous and international engineers are familiar with design and construction, so it would seem logical to continue a system which is proved beyond any doubt (ref. 33). Installing sewerage might initiate an upward spiral of improved health and development leading to increased productivity, higher standards of living and improved quality of life (ref. 34). Urban reuse of effluent could reduce the demands on limited water resources (ref. 35).

31. However, there are two major hindrances and several minor snags to the universal adoption of sewerage in developing countries. The first major obstacle is the very high cost. The second is the need for an ample reliable piped water supply right up to the WC. The two are linked, for when the cost of the necessary piped water is included, sewerage is shown to be up to ten times as expensive as some alternative methods of excreta disposal. Its cost exceeds that of the housing for low-income communities such as those living in slums and squatter settlements. Although small-bore and shallow sewers promise some cost reduction (refs. 36, 37), their effectiveness is only now being independently evaluated.

32. A common problem is poor connection rates, like the 29 km of sewers in Accra to which only 120 house connections had been made after three years (ref. 38). Sewers in developing countries often become blocked and most treatment plants for inland towns discharge effluents that are a serious health risk because receiving rivers have little natural flow in the dry season and whatever water reaches downstream areas is abstracted for people or crops.

Septic tanks

33. For low-density housing, like that commonly occupied by upper echelon civil servants, well designed septic tanks (ref. 39) provide a sanitation service little different from sewerage if the septic tank effluent passes to good soakpits or drain fields. However, effluents from tanks on small plots often discharge to open drains in spite of legislation like the Indian Code which strictly prohibits the practice (ref. 40). Drains receiving effluent present a serious health risk (ref. 41).

Rural sanitation

34. Rural sanitation often involves providing a service for people who are underprivileged in all respects. They have little cash. Their time is spent in the fields or in walking

long distances for water or fuelwood. Sanitation improvements in rural areas start from a low base. In many places there is virtually no existing sanitation foundation on which to build (ref. 42).

Pit latrines

35. In some areas with a record of poor construction, pit latrines are condemned because of smell, flies and danger of collapse (ref. 43). Nevertheless, for rural and peri-urban areas, and indeed for many unsewered urban centres, some form of pit latrine is the most satisfactory method of dealing with faeces.

36. A crucial factor in latrine selection is whether users clean their bottoms with water or solid material. Newspaper, corn cobs and stones are amongst the solids used (ref. 44). With these the pit is best located immediately below a "squat hole" in the latrine floor slab so that faeces and cleaning material fall directly into the pit.

37. A very low cost latrine can be made with a thin slightly arched concrete slab and a removable lid that fits tightly into the squat hole (ref. 45). The lid must be replaced whenever the latrine is not in use to prevent flies getting in and out of the pit. The ventilated improved pit (VIP) latrine (Fig. 1) deals with nuisance from flies and smell by a vent pipe or stack fitted with fly-proof netting at the top (ref. 46).

38. Where water is used for anal cleaning flies and smells can be prevented from escaping from the pit by a water seal in a trap. This may be cast under the floor slab with the pit beneath, but an offset pit connected to the trap by a short length of pipe or channel (Fig. 2) has advantages, including the possibility of locating the latrine inside a house (ref. 47).

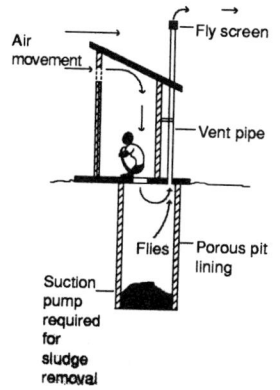

Fig. 1.
VIP latrine

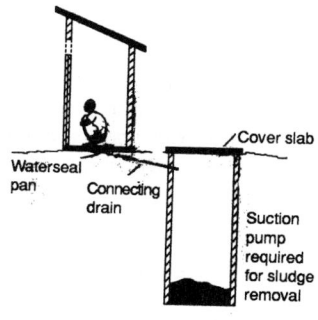

Fig. 2.
Pour-flush waterseal latrine

IMPLEMENTATION

39. Even the largest single pit eventually fills and it then becomes necessary to dig another pit. An attractive variation is to use two small pits (or two halves of a single pit) which are used alternately. Each has enough capacity to last two years. Retention of solids for at least a year ensures that viruses, bacteria and protozoa do not survive and doubling the capacity gives an ample factor of safety to allow for more people using the latrine than planned. Few roundworm eggs (the most persistent pathogen) remain after a year (ref. 48).

Bio-gas and compost latrines

40. As a method of dealing with human excreta bio-gas has not proved satisfactory. The cost makes plants out of reach of most people and operation is only successful where more animals than people contribute (ref. 49). Northern Vietnam has a long history of successful operation of batch type compost latrines where ash is used to cover faeces. Urine is collected separately to avoid high moisture content. Farmers in Guatamala preferred compost latrines to pit latrines (ref. 50). However, the use of compost appears to have an important role in the transmission of roundworm infection (ref. 51). In Africa compost latrines (ref. 52) have been far from satisfactory.

SOLID WASTE MANAGEMENT FOR SURVIVAL

41. It is often said that modern civilization is in danger of being buried in its own waste. In some low-income communities of developing countries little waste is left after animal and human scavengers have had their pickings. Elsewhere vast quantities of vegetable material cause nuisance by blocking open drains and providing a feast for flies. In the tropics high temperatures increase the rate at which organic waste becomes putrid, requiring frequent collection which municipal authorities are unable to effect. 'With few exceptions the systems and hardware developed and applied for treating, recovering and disposing of solid waste in developed countries are either unsuited or irrelevant to the conditions usually found in developing countries' (ref. 53).

42. Solving the problems of solid waste are largely a matter of management rather than technology, so it is now appropriate to consider 'software' in relation to water and sanitation.

SOFTWARE

43. The Princess Royal said in 1986 'irrespective of the size of a water and sanitation project . . . the importance of training, management and maintenance is paramount if all that money, effort and goodwill involved is not to be wasted' (ref. 54).

Training

44. The need for and value of appropriate training of professional and sub-professional staff has been a recurrent theme before and throughout the Decade (ref. 55). Having spent much time for many years providing training that is intended to be appropriate for people from developing countries I believe it has been a worth-while effort. However, training is only a part of proper human resources development (ref. 56). A major step in improving water supplies in Zaire came with a change of the promotion base from length of service and seniority to one of personal performance and response to training (ref. 57).

Management by communities

45. The Abidjan Statement affirmed that 'lasting health and economic benefits' [that is, development] 'for the rural and urban-fringe populations of Africa can be achieved through increased community management of water supply and sanitation systems based on proven low-cost techniques' (ref. 58).

46. More recently Wilson Ndolo Ayah, the Kenyan Minister of Water Development, said 'the time has come for us all to realise the role the rural population, particularly women, can play if they are trained in the operation, maintenance and repair of water supply systems' (ref. 59).

47. 'Community participation does not mean the participation of the community in a government project, but the participation of the government in a community project (ref. 60). Local people should understand the technology and also the reasons for the technology (ref. 61). Often there is too much government interference or too little state support (ref. 62). Useful participation may require little effort. In the Malawi piped water programme women have been encouraged to use pipeline routes as village paths and report leaks to water caretakers (ref. 63).

48. While the emphasis of community management is obviously the group, successful management by the community often depends on individual responsibility. In the Archeological Museum in Amman I noticed an inscription engraved about 830 BC 'there was no cistern inside the town at Qarhoh, so I said to all the people "let each of you make a cistern for himself in his house".' A disadvantage of some sanitation programmes is that people no longer have a choice of what sort of latrine to build or use (ref. 64).

49. A sociological input is essential for the technological success of water and sanitation programmes. However, just as some engineers delight in calculations to umpteen decimal places, some sociologists obscure their wisdom in claptrap. At a workshop on low cost sanitation last year a speaker used these gems: 'inventorizing the categories', 'dynamics of social interaction' and 'aggregation of social groups'.

IMPLEMENTATION

Management by institutions

50. Institution building has been a pet theme for international banks and bilateral donors. This is justified because of the limited capacity of many local bodies that are responsible in some way for implementing projects and programmes. Inadequate numbers of poor quality staff often result in failure to generate income or to use resources effectively. This in turn results in insufficient funds to pay for better staff.

51. Vast numbers of master plans have been produced by consultants. Their 'lack of realism is reflected in the period taken to prepare them. By the time of publication interim growth has rendered many of their recommendations impractical' (ref. 65). Development authorities 'frequently usurp all but low level functions and have been criticised for adopting an engineering approach and ignoring social and economic realities' (ref. 66).

52. Politics sometimes adversely affects the provision, operation and maintenance of schemes. Before they could remove a dead donkey from a water conduit in Karachi engineers were detained for three days because they had entered a curfew area without passes (ref. 67). Sometimes attempts to enlist support for communal efforts are ruined by pre-election promises of bounty by politicians. Inter-party rivalry can be a hindrance to efficiency.

Management by non-government organizations

53. Timberlake (ref. 68) quotes a UNEP report as stating that the high record of success of NGOs 'is related to the small-scale and local direction of their projects and the requirements for local community participation, as well as their flexibility in operation and their ability to learn from others' mistakes'. An 'Economist' leader suggested that 'dollar by dollar, the small bodies help more people than the big donors' (ref 69).

Management of expenditure

54. Expenditure on both water and sanitation has sometimes been limited arbitrarily to 5 per cent of income but in southern Tanzania most households are willing to pay 8 per cent of income for public taps in villages. Many are willing to pay more (ref. 70). The price paid to vendors is up to a hundred times that paid by those with piped water connections. In Burma the local government charged half the vendors' price for water and got enough revenue to repay capital costs and meet maintenance costs, with enough left over after a year to build a school (ref. 71). A balance has to be made between the service a community desires and what they can afford to pay (ref. 72).

Maintenance

55. An official of the Swedish Foreign Ministry said 'as a result of an inappropriate choice of technology, the Swedish rural water programmes in Tanzania and Kenya have reached what must be termed a dead end. After 15 years of quite considerable investment in piped water and mechanical pumping equipment, hardly more than 10% of our installations are still in use' (ref. 68). A national paper in Dar es Salaam reported that nearly 75% of all diesel or petrol driven pumps were out of action due to lack of maintenance or inavailability of fuel (ref. 73). In government funded schemes routine maintenance may get low priority because workers get paid overtime to repair broken-down equipment.

56. Local ability to cope with maintenance is proved by the ancient vehicles that are kept running in developing countries. Yet because this skill and ingenuity is not employed, maintenance of water and sanitation facilities is inadequate. Sometimes the fault lies with design, based on expatriate consultants' expectations that spare parts and manufacturers' service teams arrive soon after making a phone call. Where there are no spares, no manufacturers' agents and no phones, a different design may be required (ref. 74).

SUSTAINABILITY AND SURVIVAL

57. The large number of publications referred to in this paper reinforces the author's experience. Work concerned with low cost sanitation and water supplies in many developing countries of Africa and Asia during the past 36 years has given ample proof of the need for technology to be appropriate for the local people and that sociological and management factors are as important for successful implementation as technology. Provision of facilities is not enough. They must be sustainable so that those who are most at risk, the underprivileged poor people, are helped to survive.

REFERENCES

1. HANLEY Mary Lynn. Sudan: development vs war, drought and floods. World Development, 1989, vol. 2, 3 (May), 12-16.
2. GRAINGER Alan. Desertification: how people make deserts, how people can stop and why they dont. Earthscan, London, 1982.
3. CPHERI. Technical Digest 21. Central Public Health Engineering Research Institute, Nagpur, 1971.
4. VIDAL-HALL Judith. Wellsprings of conflict. South, 1989, May, 23-25.
5. LONGMAN. Dictionary of contemporary English: new edition. Longman, Harlow, 1987.
6. Thirsty Third World. Report of the Conference held in London 27 January 1981 to support the start of the Water Decade, p. 7.
7. PICKFORD John. Appropriate technology. World Water '83, p. 141-147. Thomas Telford, London, 1983.

IMPLEMENTATION

8. WALLACE John. Sanitary engineering in India, p. 36. Education Society's Steam Press, Bombay, 1893.
9. ESREY S.A., FEACHEM R.G. and HUGHES J.M. Interventions for the control of diarrhoeal diseases among young children: improving water supplies and excreta disposal facilities. Bulletin WHO, 1985, vol. 63, 757-772.
10. ALEXANDER Michael. Delhi and Agra: a travellers' companion, p. 243. Constable, London, 1987.
11. HOPKINS Donald R. Dracunculiasis: an eradicable scourge. Epidemiological Reviews, 1983, vol. 5, 208-219.
12. WORLD WATER, 1984, vol. 7, no. 12 (December), p. 9.
13. SCHULZ C.R. and OKUN Daniel A. Treating surface water for commuities in developing countries. J. American Water Works Association, 1983, vol. 75, 212.
14. UNDP/WORLD BANK. Water and sanitation: toward equitable and sustainable development: a strategy for the remainder of the Decade and beyond. UNDP, New York, 1988.
15. HARRISON Paul. The Third World tomorrow, p.109. Penguin Books, Harmondsworth, 1980.
16. WATER AND SEWAGE INTERNATIONAL, 1989, vol. 1, 1 (April), 8.
17. GROVE A.T. Some comments on the economics of dryland degradation and rehabilitation. In Environmental issues in African development planning (Ed J.A.Steeley and W.M.Adams), p. 71. Cambridge African Monographs 9. African Studies Centre, Cambridge, 1988.
18. HARRISON Paul. The greening of Africa: breaking through in the battle for land and food, p. 65. Earthscan - Grafton Books, London, 1987.
19. HARPHAM Trudy, LUSTY Tim and VAUGHAN Patrick (ed.). In the shadow of the city: community health and the urban poor, p. 12. Oxford University Press, Oxford, 1988.
20. WHO INTERNATIONAL REFERENCE CENTRE FOR COMMUNITY WATER SUPPLY. Public standpost water supplies. Technical paper no. 13. IRC, The Hague, 1979.
21. WHITE G.F., BRADLEY D.J. and WHITE A.V. Drawers of water: domestic water use in East Africa, p. 243. University of Chicago Press, Chicago, 1972.
22. ARLOSOROFF Saul et al. Community water supply: the handpump option. The World Bank, Washington DC, 1987.
23. BEAUJOT Roderic. Rural sanitation in Sierra Leone. In With our own hands: research for Third World development, p. 105. IDRC, Ottawa, 1986.
24. WIJK-SIJBESMA Christine van. Participation and education in community water supply and sanitation programmes. Technical paper No. 12. WHO International Reference Centre for Community Water Supply, The Hague, 1979.
25. WATT S. B. and WOOD W. E. Hand dug wells and their construction. Intermediate Technology Publications, London, 1977.
26. CHAUHAN Sumi Krishna et al. Who puts the water in the taps, p. 68. Earthscan, London, 1983.

27. DHABADGAONKAR S.M. Metallic copper for disinfection of water in rural areas. J. Indian Water Works Association, 1980, vol. 12, 43-48.
28. HUISMAN L. and WOOD W. E. Slow sand filtration. WHO, Geneva, 1974.
29. GRAHAM N. J. D. (ed). Slow sand filtration: recent developments in water treatment technology. Ellis Horwood, Chichester, 1988.
30. WEGELIN Martin. A pretreatment for slow sand filtration. In Developing world water (ed. John Pickford). Grosvenor Press International, London, 1987.
31. HARPHAM Trudy, LUSTY Tim and VAUGHAN Patrick (ed.). In the shadow of the city: community health and the urban poor, p.117. Oxford University Press, Oxford, 1988.
32. GUBLER D.J. and BHATTACHARYA N.C. A quantitative approach to the study of Bancroftian filariasis. American J. of Tropical Medicine and Hygiene, 1974, vol. 23, 1027-1036.
33. PICKFORD John. Conventional sewerage - the case for and against. In Sanitation in developing counties (ed. Arnold Pacey), p. 68-72. Wiley, Chichester, 1978.
34. OKUN D. A. and PONGHIS G. Community waste-water collection and disposal. WHO, Geneva, 1975.
35. OKUN Daniel A. Water reuse in developing countries. Water and Wastewater International, 1990, vol. 5, 1 (Feb), 13...21.
36. SINNATAMBY Gehan, MARA Duncan and McGARRY Michael. Shallow systems offer hope to slums. World Water, 1986, vol. 9, 1, 39-42
37. OTIS Richard J. and MARA D. Duncan. The design of small bore sewer systems. TAG Technical Note No. 14. World Bank, Washington DC, 1985.
38. ANNAN C.E. and WRIGHT A.M. Urban waste disposal in Ghana. Paper presented to Regional Expert Committee on Waste Disposal, Brazzaville, 25-29 October 1976.
39. PICKFORD John. The design of septic tanks and aqua-privies. Overseas building note no. 187. Building Research Establishment, Gartree, 1980.
40. INDIAN STANDARDS INSTITUTION. Code of practice for installation of septic tanks. Part 1: design criteria and construction. IS 2470. 2nd revision. ISI, New Delhi, 1986.
41. BRADLEY R.M. The choice between septic tanks and sewers in tropical developing countries. Public Health Engineer, 1983, vol. 11, 1, 20-28.
42. PICKFORD John. Rural sanitation and development. Waterlines, 1988, vol. 6, 3 (January), 2-4.
43. PICKFORD John. Slow sand filters and pit latrines. In Appropriate technology in civil engineering, p. 76-78. Thomas Telford, London, 1981.
44. WRIGHT A.M., OWUSU S.E. and HANDA V.K. Availability of latrines in a developing country. In Sanitation in developing counties (ed. Arnold Pacey). Wiley, Chichester, 1978.

IMPLEMENTATION

45. BRANDBERG Bjorn. Why should a latrine look like a house? Waterlines, 1985, vol. 3, 3, 24-26.
46. MORGAN Peter. Rural water supply and sanitation: Blair research bulletins. Macmillan, Basingstoke, 1990.
47. ROY A. K. et al. Manual on the design, construction and maintenance of low-cost pour-flush waterseal latrines in India. TAG technical note No. 10. World Bank, Washington DC, 1984.
48 STRAUSS Martin. Survival of excreted pathogens in excreta and faecal sludges. IRCWD News, 1985, No 23, 4-9.
49. VILLAGE ARTISANS AND SCIENCE. Proceedings of a Workshop, Sewagram (Wardha), 7-11 September 1978. Management Development Unit, Planning Division, CSIR, New Delhi.
50. HUNT Steven. Lucrative latrines. IDRC Reports, 1986, vol. 15, 4 (October) page 13.
51. CAIRNCROSS Sandy. Water supply and sanitation: an agenda for research. J. Tropical Medicine & Hygiene, 1989, vol. 92, 310-314.
52. WINBLAD Uno and KILAMA Wen. Sanitation without water. Macmillan, Basingstoke, 1985.
53. BETTS M.P. Trends in solid waste management in developing countries. Public Health Engineer, 1980, vol. 8, 78-81.
54. WORLD WATER '86: water technology for the developing world, p. 2. Thomas Telford, London, 1987.
55. PICKFORD John. Training people to meet the global need. In Water and sanitation: economic and sociological perspectives (ed. Peter G. Bourne), p. 199-219. Academic Press, Orlando, 1984.
56. CAREFOOT Neil F. Human resources development. In Developing world water (ed. John Pickford), p. 24-26. Grosvenor Press International, London, 1987.
57. WORLD WATER, 1984, vol. 7, no. 3 (March), p. 25.
58. WORLD WATER, Five-point plan for Africa agreed by 30 countries at Abidjan. World Water, 1986, vol. 9, no 10 (November), p. 6.
59. WORLD WATER, April 1990, p.24.
60. GUPTA Rajiv. Are community biogas plants a feasible proposition? World Health Forum, 1983, vol. 4, 358-361.
61. PICKFORD John. Water and people. In Developing world water, p. 23-24. Grosvenor Press International, London, 1986.
62. HUGHES Arnold. Alternative forms and levels of popular participation: a general survey. In Popular participation in planning for basic needs (ed. Franklyn Lisk), p. 63. Gower, Aldershot, 1985.
63. GLENNIE Colin. Village water supply in the Decade. Wiley, Chichester, 1983.
64. PARKER Ronald. Accounting for the individual. World Water, 1985, November, pages 22...27.
65. LOWDER Stella. Inside Third World cities, p 103. Croom Helm, London, 1986.
66. LOWDER Stella. Ibid, p 107.

67. WORLD WATER, 1986, vol. 9, no 5 (June), p. 14.
68. TIMBERLAKE Lloyd. Crisis in Africa: the causes, the cures of environmental bankruptcy. Earthscan, London, 1985.
69. ECONOMIST The. Leader. The Economist, 16 March 1985, vol. 294, no. 7385.
70. WORLD BANK. Sub-Saharan Africa: from crisis to sustainable growth, p. 68. World Bank, Washington DC, 1989.
71. UNITED NATIONS DEVELOPMENT PROGRAM. Internal financing of water supply and sanitation in developing countries. Decade case history No 5. UNDP, New York, 1981
72. FRANCEYS Richard and PICKFORD John. Beyond the Water and Sanitation Decade. Science, Technology and Development, 1989, vol. 7, 1 (April), 21-34.
73. SUNDAY NEWS, Dar es Salaam, 16 September 1979.
74. PICKFORD John. Water, maintenance and people. Water International, 1987, 12, 1.

12. Infrastructure

MARGARET J. HERATY, MSc, FCIT, FTS, MIHT, Independent Consultant in Transport and Tourism

SYNOPSIS. Infrastructure is generally regarded as the key to the long-term development of rural areas, cities and regions in all parts of the world. However, the imposition of inappropriate standards or the provision of infrastructure in an insensitive manner can lead to both a waste of resources and disbenefits to local society. The author points out some of the pitfalls and illustrates how infrastructure can be made more appropriate to local needs.

INTRODUCTION

1. The rôle of infrastructure in Survival during an emergency or disaster is to provide piping for water, roads for trucks and airstrips for airlifts: the emphasis of provision is on instant availability. This paper more concerns Appropriate Development in which infrastructure needs a long-term programme and when developmental benefits are its significant contribution to the long-term survival of the nation, region or town, and their population.

2. The main argument of the paper is that infrastructure, as being developed currently, often fails to meet the needs of the very people for whom it was hoped to provide benefits. The corollary is that the failure is often, if not usually, due to insufficient understanding of the social, cultural and micro-economic mores of the country or region concerned. This is not to say that infrastructure is a bad thing - obviously it is not. But the installation of it through the "development process" often leaves a lot to be desired.

3. The paper starts with some background observations before illustrating the argument with some cases drawn from experience.

THE INFLUENCE OF FUNDING ON INFRASTRUCTURE PROJECTS

4. Infrastructure is expensive. Few governments in developing countries can afford to pay for much of it from their current revenues and most turn to international funding sources, often international funding agencies and bilateral donors. In turn, these agencies have a great influence on the way in which infrastructure is provided and

IMPLEMENTATION

in the selection of projects for implementation. A brief discussion of this is important, therefore, to the broader considerations.

5. For example, in the transport sector alone, thousands of millions of dollars are loaned each year by international funding agencies for the construction of roads and ports, railways and airports, warehousing and other infrastructure. Millions more are given by bilateral donors, of which the largest is now Japan. Although there has been a recent trend towards more funding inputs to maintenance and training, infrastructure remains the largest sector for most agencies, not least because of the high capital costs involved.

6. It has already been pointed out in earlier papers that infrastructure is an attractive item for both the funder and the beneficiary country. It is usually straightforward to cost, the methods of establishing the benefits for use in feasibility studies are well developed. Implementation provides work for local people and sometimes hidden benefits to officials involved in the tendering process. And when implementation has been achieved, there is something tangible to look at and use - and to name after the leading politician of the day. However, it is also true to say that most of the "best" projects (in economic terms) have now been built; it is not surprising that the more obviously beneficial projects were the first to be carried out. These days, rates of return hover around the critical levels of 13 or 15 percent (depending on the funding agency) and the days of the 40 percent rate of return are generally long gone.

7. Funding agencies have also become more interested in the financial aspects of project repayment. Even a project with a high rate of return may be turned down if there is no obvious way of generating an income from it, to cover the debt charges. Some projects are more obviously amenable to user charges than others: ports and airports are (in principle) easy, rural roads much less so.

8. It is therefore becoming more difficult to find "bankable" projects in the infrastructure field, yet they remain the major indispensible items in the shopping lists of developing nations and the core of the agency lending programmes.

9. The nature of funding agency thinking leads to projects being assessed against sets of criteria which are necessarily established in isolation from the peculiarities of any local society. Savings in the costs of the operation of vehicles are crucial to highway appraisal, and shipping costs similarly form an important element of assessing port projects. These are readily identified, if less easily quantified. Softer elements, such as road accident costs, are more contentious, and all too often the developmental benefits are impossible to quantify and dismissed from consideration in a qualitative form. Socio-cultural disbenefits are often not even considered.

CASE STUDY 1: THE YAOUNDE-DOUALA ROAD

10. The capital of Cameroon, Yaounde, used to be only accessible from the country's main commercial centre, port and international airport at Douala by local airline or a tortuous drive on unmade roads, and that only when rivers were fordable, taking one or two days. Now a classy new blacktopped road joins the two and the journey can be made in three or four hours, depending on how intrepid the driver. The road was designed as a dual-two lane highway but in the interests of economy, and reflecting the extremely low levels of traffic flow, only one of the two carriageways has been built and it operates as a two-lane road.

11. Problem number one is that accident rates have exceeded all expectations; high speeds on a single-carriageway road which has sightlines and vertical curvatures at dual-carriageway standards often have fatal results.

12. More interestingly, from the social point of view, was the decision to build the road on a route running in between, rather than through, settlements. The rationale was that this was an inter-city road and not intended for local use; also that passing through settlements would present road safety problems due to the African habit of selling goods along the roadside, spilling on to the carriageway.

13. In practice, this meant that the road had no population to call on in the event of accident or emergency, nowhere to buy cold drinks or the other niceties of long distance travel. Then gradually a network of tracks developed from each settlement to the road, with unmarked "junctions" presenting extra safety hazards. Down the tracks came the local people, walking long distances each day through the forest to lay out their wares on the roadside; they are now beginning to consider undertaking the upheaval of moving home and settlements are developing away from traditional land and unplanned in relation to the road alignment itself.

14. Thus there is a new road which (while offering faster end-to-end journey times) is both more dangerous and more poorly served with the usual benefits of African travel than the old one, and which has led to disruption of the local communities. How much better it would have been all round had the planning taken account of these factors and run very near communities, with pull off points on short spurs or laybys for markets and the possibility of some form of public transport being provided to enable the villagers to take their produce into the cities.

15. I do not know why the decision was made but I can speculate that the characteristics (including the value of time) of the previous air travellers over the route (businessmen, politicians and international consultants) were used to define the "best" alignment using well-defined

IMPLEMENTATION

criteria developed on the basis of international experience. This is economics in the raw. Perhaps there was a well-meaning attempt to preserve the local culture and prevent environmental intrusion by avoiding impinging on settlements. Certainly the reasons for using the detailed alignment of a dual carriageway but only building one carriageway for the time being would be financial (lower construction costs from using tighter curves, etc., and 40 percent or so savings from only providing foundations and paving for half the width).

16. What is evident is that whoever designed the road and made the decisions at various stages knew little about the way that African society in the bush actually works and had little appreciation of the social dynamics of the situation.

TECHNOLOGY AS APPLIED TO INFRASTRUCTURE

17. The theme of this conference is the contribution of technology and we now have at our disposal the most formidable array of technology of all types. At the planning and design stages, for example, satellite imagery can map an area in a way that used to have to be done on foot: sites of aggregate deposits can be identified and old meanders traced. Computer Aided Design can minimise the amount of earth to be moved, and design a road within international standards, allowing options to be investigated in a matter of moments. Specialist programs allow costs to be calculated without the need for quantity surveyors to leave the comfort of their firesides. Economic models to relate costs and benefits which used to take days to work through can now produce rates of return in minutes.

18. One problem with using such sophistication is that it is easy to lose touch with the reality of the situation. The model or program is king and the thinking part may be omitted from the process - especially the choice of inputs and the interpretation of the output. What cannot be modelled falls out as an "unquantifiable" element and is often excluded from the final decision-making process. This is certainly true in my own field of transport economics: RTIM2 or HDM models for highway investment appraisal use certain parameters and these data are all that is collected. Anything outside this tends to be neglected or argued over fiercely as to its validity in the balance of feasibility.

19. In one such aplication of RTIM2 in the highlands of equatorial Africa, it was very apparent to me and my colleagues that up-grading the road under discussion would enable temperate and sub-tropical soft fruit to be trucked to the business and tourist hotels of the coast and capital without the damage to the fruit that was preventing this trade at the time. We could see that the local people were industrious agriculturalists, that strawberries would grow (and were grown on a small scale for local consumption) and that avocados were growing virtually wild and dropping off the trees for lack of demand; we also knew the prices

charged in the restaurants, hotels and luxury shops six hours' drive away for fruit air-freighted from Europe. The problem was that we had no way of forecasting the likely production and no way of calculating the benefits in a form that would allow easy input to the model, certainly not without large extra inputs of staff and time which were not available. The formal economic appraisal showed the road to be barely feasible and I tried to add the strawberries into the benefits pan of the balance as an unquantifiable extra. Our client laughed us to scorn. The good news is that the road was, in the event, up-graded but for reasons other than the study, following a major natural disaster which demonstrated all too graphically to the world aid community the poor highway links to the region. And I understand that highland strawberries and other soft fruits are indeed now on sale in the cities, with cash benefits to the poor highland growers (and no doubt many middlemen).

20. And that is all before the building starts. In the main, major infrastructure (and a lot of minor infrastructure) no longer uses the old fashioned methods: one really has to go out of the way to find people hand chipping aggregate and sieving it for size. There are those who think this "development" is perhaps not such a good thing and their arguments are well rehearsed. Even at the simplest level of technology, the tendancy is to use the easy way out without thinking through the basic needs and problems.

CASE STUDY 2: ROAD MAINTENANCE IN PAPUA NEW GUINEA

21. In the Highlands of PNG, anyone over the age of 50 saw their first wheel underneath an aircraft. This primitive tribal society had no fire and no wheels, and contained people who painted their faces with mud, put feathers in their hair and tusks through their noses, and wore little in the way of clothes. That isolation was all changed with the building of the Highlands Highway. Now they even have satellite television from both Australia and the USA. Striking juxtapositions of old and new are evident everywhere. The electrical fitters still sometimes wear mud and feathers and tusks under their hard hats as they wire up the new national grid along the road; villagers hire pick-up trucks to carry them to tribal fights - packed like sardines standing up in the back, with their spears and full war regalia - or aircraft to take them and their pigs and cassowaries to neighbouring feasts and celebrations.

22. This is all due to a length of graded (in places gravelled) road, perhaps 300 miles long and 15 feet wide. But how is this Highlands Highway maintained? By the Australian Army, using plant that would not disgrace the M1 on a good day and would be terrific on a bad one: cynics might say that the road needs more maintenance to support the maintenance plant and associated traffic that passes over it. The argument for using this approach runs as

follows: each village will not allow anyone from any other village to maintain "their" piece of road. Each village wants to negotiate the price for the maintenance of their piece of road from a standing start. Thus to obtain maintenance agreements for the whole length of the road requires individual negotiation with perhaps 100 villages and sets of village elders - and that in one of the more than 600 languages of PNG. Once the price has been fixed (and New Guineans are hard bargainers) there has to be inspection and quality control, and some form of penalty clause. It is all too difficult and the road is regarded by both the Government and the international "development set" as too important to be left to such ad hoc methods.

23. So in comes the Australian Army with its massive bulldozers, rollers, trucks and other equipment, its operatives and mechanics and support staff and housing and overseas allowances, and maintains the road. The plant is imported as are the spares. The local people are deprived of one possible source of cash income and exposed to an alien culture at first hand. It cannot be cheaper. It is certainly not better in social terms. But it is easier.

24. To be fair it may also be maintained to better standard and thus there must be some transport and development benefits (although the population of Lae, the town at the bottom of the road who have experienced the increased crime and other problems of rural in-migration and uncontrolled urban accretion may not agree). But it does also strike one as a decision made by someone who could not cope with the original problem and went for technology as a solution.

WHO IS TO BLAME?
AT FAULT: THE FUNDING AGENCIES

25. It is one view that decisions on funding are made by people who live in air-conditioned or centrally-heated offices in major capital cities, with large tax-free salaries. Of course it is not a simple as that. But it is true that the guidelines and strategies on lending and donating are determined by people who, even if they came originally from the developing world, are its elite.

26. Funding agency staff are not immune to the seduction of infrastructure: it is a glamorous and high-cost item, it looks good in the lending programme and is easily appraised using standard formulae. But this can lead to a blinkered approach.

CASE STUDY 3: URBAN MOTORWAYS

27. There is one capital city in Africa where an international funding agency had become convinced of the need for a type of Boulevard Péripherique, along a waterfront of about 10 miles either side of a peninsular. At the southern end two inadequate bridges led across the mouth of the bay to the major industrial employment area.

At the northern end of the peninsular, and wrapping round on the the main coastline to a point facing the industrial area across a mile or so of sea, lay the new (agency-funded) low-cost housing areas and shanty town. In between was a five-mile long smart residential and commercial area, to be bypassed by the new road but also provided with much easier access by cars using the road and taking turnings off it with the new traffic lights (with, therefore, possibly greater benefits accrueing to the rich). Consultants were appointed who spent two years designing the road and traffic signals to match, with - to be fair - some bus lanes for the workers' buses to use, and produced a nine-volume report.

28. On the Mission going in to appraise the project, two previously unreported elements were discovered: an old and underused freight railway line down through the peninsular and over its own bridge from the shanties of the north to the industry of the south, with its own right of way and old passenger stations still in place; and some decrepid and legendarily unsafe privately-owned ferry boats running across the bay directly from the new housing areas to the industrial area. Why not, I asked, upgrade the railway to take passenger trains? And why not make available loans to local people to improve the quality and capacity of their boats?

29. The answer was that the agency's department concerned with the project does not have a remit to look at mainline railways, and the mechanics of lending to small local businessmen is very complex. Happily, after protracted discussion and rethinking the railway was upgraded (with secondhand European stock rebogied to suit) and now carries massive loads, the ferries are now the African equivalent of the Star Ferries of Hong Kong, and the poor can get to work more quickly than they would have done by a tortuous bus journey. The country has not incurred massive debt. The roads have been improved but not by cutting off the seaside promenades from pedestrians with a new dual-three highway carrying fast-moving traffic. It may look less glamorous but the result is more satisfactory, more cost-effective and efficient, safer and better environmentally and in terms of energy use.

AT FAULT: THE GOVERNMENTS

30. Governments cannot be blamed for wanting what they perceive as the best. But even they are not immune from thinking that infrastructure is the best solution and to some extent they are coloured in their thinking by aid agency philosophies and protocols, and by the demonstration effect of western values. The undoubted attraction to some officials of the benefits of having a major construction project for letting to companies owned by friends or relatives has already been mentioned.

IMPLEMENTATION

CASE STUDY 4: JETTIES IN VANUATU

31. Vanuatu (formerly the New Hebrides) is a country of 200 islands (50 or so inhabited) between New Caledonia and Fiji in the Pacific. Its staple export is copra (dried and processed coconut, used for oils and soaps and animal feedstuffs) which is shipped to factories (mainly in Germany) for processing, in large ships which call irregularly at the two main ports.

32. The small island growers dry their copra and send it by small ship ("copra boat") to one of the two central collection points for storage until the large ocean-going ships call. Under a national marketing scheme, the producer can sell his copra for cash at a fixed "beach" price to the inter-island copra boats. These arrive at intervals of once a week to once in six months, have on-board stores where the money obtained from the sale of copra can be use to buy items such as matches, stick tobacco, fish hooks, canned fish, rice, salt and sugar, tea, kerosene for hurricane lamps, batteries, soap and lengths of cloth. The boats also carry wholesale goods (rice, flour, tinned foods and drinks, washing powder, anything and everything) for the local stores in more important settlements and significant quantities of government supplies (building materials, medical and school supplies).

33. At present there are few jetties or quays and few safe anchorages: Vanuatu is rugged, lies in both cyclone and earthquake zones and has three active volcanoes. The copra boats anchor off shore outside the reef or, more commonly, (because of the depth of water) stop with engines running and await arriving sacks of copra - copra arriving in outboard motor boats, dug out canoes or even on the heads of swimming producers. The boats may stop every mile along a coastline as there are few links (tracks or roads) between the settlements.

34. It was felt by the Government, encouraged by a well-meaning international agency, that it would be A Good Idea to consolidate the collection of copra at major settlements, most of which have been built at traditional safe anchorage points. A jetty or quay could be provided for the boats to load and unload over the side, the shipping costs would be reduced, the site would become a bigger focus of local activity with a store, clinic and primary school provided if not already in place. Of course a road would be needed to link the coastal strip with the jetty site but this could be of simple construction and would provide motorable links for journeys which at present have to be made, if made at all, on foot through the jungle.

35. In practice, who wins and who loses? The biggest winner is the local rich man with a pick-up truck who can use the government road (free of charge) and charge the copra producer a lot of money to carry him and his sack of copra to the jetty, or will buy the copra at a knockdown "farmgate" rate below the official beach price and then sell

it on at the quayside at a profit. The shipowner gains on the operating costs but loses on the sales from his onboard stores. And if the wind gets up his boat can be smashed against the jetty where it would not have been damaged riding out at sea.

36. The store keeper should win as he has more activity in his settlement and possibly more regular supply lines. The producer loses except insofar as he has the opportunity to reach the local settlement more easily but at a cost in ready money and in spending time taking his copra to the jetty or making more copra to raise the same amount of money from the pick-up owner who collects it. The very person who was supposed to be helped comes off worst.

37. And what of the Government: the jetty has to built, as has the road, and both have to be maintained through cyclones and the rainy season. There is no agregate. Plant is stationed on only three of the 200 islands and has to be brought by the one Government-owned barge (landing craft) or by chartering in an expensive barge from elsewhere. The "imported" work force has to be housed and fed. The cost is high and resulting international debts have to be serviced. The road maintenance budget is already only 10 percent of what is needed for essential routine maintenance. So why not introduce user charges for the copra boats to use the jetty - a docking fee to be collected by the local headman?

38. What happens? The owners will not pay and the boats cease to tie up at the jetties. The blasting of the reefs to provide channels and other works associated with the building of the jetties have destroyed the safe anchorages. The local stores lose their supply lines. Boats go elsewhere and whole coastlines or islands lose their only link to the outside world. The copra producers lose their only source of income and have to withdraw their children from school (the major cash expenditure), can no longer buy radio batteries and listen to cyclone warnings and educational broadcasting; they no longer have access to anything other than the most basic essentials of life. The road decays, the jetty or quay is destroyed by natural forces, and still the debt has to be serviced.

AT FAULT: THE CONSULTANTS

39. I must conclude by pointing the finger at some of my fellow colleagues. We all make mistakes: we would not be human if we did not. But the process of international competitive bidding (ICB) leads to large international firms with impressive track records winning contracts and then applying totally inappropriate staff. Some of the team members are often independent consultants with no previous experience with the firm: they are chosen for their relevant experience in the pertinent geographical area or type of project. Other are the firm's staff (often more junior) who may have little such experience but who are used for obvious commercial reasons. The proposal is won or lost on the

IMPLEMENTATION

strength of the experienced outside personnel and the profits are then made by using cheaper members of staff.

40. These commercial factors which are led by the ICB process can cause hideous results. I can cite one recent experience (and I could have picked a dozen others). Again an equatorial archipelago, with a couple of dozen grass airstrips in amazing terrain and two paved airports, where an aviation specialist was to be provided from the parent firm. His remit was to identify and cost the priorities for extra navigational aids (typically non-directional beacons or VOR/DME), for forced drainage of grass strips, for installing something slightly better than a roof on stilts as a terminal building at the busiest strips. The institutional aspects included the process of contracting a local man to cut the grass each week and provide him with a mower and a means to service it.

41. The expert supplied had never worked outside his (developed) home country. He had never been on a propellor driven aircraft. His first "recce", in an eight-seat Islander flown by an ageing Australian bush pilot and with crabs and pigs in the luggage, flying through mountains in cloud on visual flight rules, was a revelation. His previous job had been an extension to Dallas-Fort Worth and his next was to be the third international airport at Chicago. Small wonder that he failed totally to come to grips with the simplest of concepts and wrote a report which confused pounds with kilos and baggage with air freight.

CONCLUSION

42. This all sounds very negative but I hope that by highlighting some examples, and I think not extreme ones, I have raised a few points of conjecture:

(a) Don't be hidebound by procedures and the rule book. Think them through and be prepared to adapt them: the putative funders of the African Boulevard Péripherique had to be prepared to hand the project over to another department of the same agency.

(b) Specifically, if an important parameter does not fit the model, change the model. Values of time are a crucial issue here in transport planning and provide scope for another three day conference: suffice it to say that again one risks benefiting the rich.

(c) If the appropriate technology does not exist, adapt it or invent it: provide wheelbarrows as a mid-point between headloading and the JCB.

(d) Don't stay in the air-conditioned hotel and only talk to high ranking officials. Get out and meet the people who live and work in the communities and see what makes them tick and how they can become involved (not just in planning or building but also in simple care and maintenance). Talk to people who know about the local religion, social customs and culture and don't try to change them: another complication of the Vanuatu copra boats was the division of the fleet into those owned by the Chinese, the Vietnamese and the Seventh Day Adventists. No shipping policy based on allocating one ship per island could ever work, because of divided loyalties, and the debt base and "truck shop" nature of small island communities.

43. Technology offers everyone a means of providing appropriate development in a more rational and cost-effective way. But it should be our slave not our master.

13. Management and planning

J. HENNESSY, President, International Commission on Irrigation and Drainage, and Director, Sir Alexander Gibb & Partners Ltd

SYNOPSIS. Sustainability and enhanced performance from infrastructural developments represent prime objectives for the decade. Management and planning have crucial implications on the success or failure of such systems. Management is a pragmatic matter, depending entirely on people and how they react and the holistic approach deserves greater attention from both developing and industrial countries alike.

INTRODUCTION
1. Appropriate technology may be defined as a method or technique that provides a socially and environmentally acceptable level of service or quality of product at the least economic cost (Ref. 1). Accordingly, appropriate technology - or development - is not necessarily "low technology" or "labour intensive methods" for example but rather is the selection and adoption of the right solutions to meet the developmental needs in the particular environment.

MANAGEMENT
2. In many cases project failures in the Third World are ascribed to technological faults; either the facility does not function or if it does, the operation and maintenance requirements are beyond the local capability for sustained performance. However, such cases are really management failures because with good management practices and control systems the choice of, for example, inappropriate technologies would simply not arise.
3. A further factor with particular relevance to survival or subsistence economies is that the development returns - either economic or financial - are generally so marginal that the risk of failure is much greater than like situations in industrial countries. This strongly suggests that management skills and practices of the highest order are essential pre-requisites for sustainable project success in the development economies.

IMPLEMENTATION

4. It also follows that of the many definitions of "management" in current usage (Ref. 3) it is important to explicitly emphasise the social factor when dealing with Third World economies. Thus, an appropriate definition to adopt would be:

> Management is a pragmatic matter depending entirely on people and how they react ...... and in particular, management is not about the preservation of the status quo, but is about maintaining the highest rate of change that the organisation and the people within it can stand (Ref. 2).

5. To meet such a yardstick, it is clearly necessary for the typical project development team to possess management science knowledge and skills as well as the other professional disciplines - sociology, agronomy, economics, environmental sciences, engineering - pertinent to the task. This can be achieved either by the recruitment of management specialists or by the enlightenment and development of the natural scientists and engineers through management training and support programmes. Wherever possible the latter course of action will provide for increased chances of success.

MANAGEMENT OF OPERATION AND MAINTENANCE

6. In the particular case of irrigated agriculture, the performance of Third World irrigation systems is generally described as being below expectation and in many cases poor. To reverse the decline a number of actions are in hand which may be of interest and applicable to other sectors.

7. Firstly, the International Irrigation Management Institute (IIMI) was established (headquarters in Sri Lanka) to develop innovative management techniques for enhanced system performance. Good progress has been made in the few years since commencement and Paper No. 3 of this Conference by the IIMI Director General, Dr. Lenton, is commended for widespread attention.

8. Secondly, the structure of the International Commission on Irrigation and Drainage (ICID) was modified in the mid-1980's by the creation of new working groups to give proper emphasis to the importance of sound management in successful crop production. Inter alia management topics have been introduced and debated more frequently at both national and international meetings of ICID.

9. Thirdly, the ICID raised these issues with the World Bank on behalf of the member national committees. Through joint ICID/World Bank efforts and much hard work, the following documents are now available for all to use:-

> World Bank Technical Paper No. 99
> Planning the Management, Operation and Maintenance of Irrigation and Drainage Systems (Ref. 5)

> EDI Technical Materials (World Bank)
> Irrigation Training in the Public Sector (Ref. 6)

10. Fourthly, the International Programme for Technology Research in Irrigation and Drainage (IPTRID) has been launched in response to the need to improve the performance of irrigation schemes.

Planning the Management, Operation and Maintenance of Irrigation and Drainage Systems (Ref. 5)

11. This joint ICID/World Bank publication (1989) was prepared with significant inputs from actual practitioners in developing and developed countries alike. It is constructively pragmatic in approach and is widely applicable to organisations and project authorities concerned with infrastructural development and operation. Rather than being rigidly prescriptive it is written as "A Guide for the Preparation of Strategies and Manuals" with the aim of assisting the responsible authority to develop strategies and prepare plans for effective operation and maintenance (O&M).

12. The Guide also discusses the formulation of the corporate plan (including essential references to the organisations's Mission statement and level of customer service objectives for example) and describes how to integrate the O&M plan therewith.

Irrigation Training in the Public Sector (Ref. 6)

13. This World Bank/USAID/ICID publication (1989) is prepared as "Guidelines for Preparing Strategies and Programmes" and is the companion to Ref. 5. Here again strong inputs have been made by key organisations from a number of developing countries. Fundamental to the adoption of the Guidelines are two premises:-

> A continuous system of training for all levels of management and staff is an essential component and cost in any successful business.

and; A sound training strategy cannot be proposed until all those involved clearly understand and agree on the context in which it is to function and the scope of training required for Managers and Staff.

14. As with Ref. 5, the Training Guidelines is widely applicable to other sectors as well as irrigation and drainage organisations.

MANAGEMENT OF PROJECTS

15. Whilst ICID (for the irrigation sector) has given particular emphasis to the management of O&M, it is also important to best ensure that the project delivery process is properly effected. In practice the creative and systematic application of management controls will permit the key elements - quality, cost and time - to be quantified and predicted.

IMPLEMENTATION

16. Throughout the project delivery cycle of pre-design, design, procurement, construction and commissioning the principal project management functions are:-

    Contract and Information Management
    Quality Control
    Cost Control
    Programme Control

However, it is particularly important (especially for developing countries) to plan and design the operation and maintenance programme during the design phase. Such action will best ensure that appropriate and therefore sustainable technologies are selected (Ref. 7).

17. Project management is necessarily a lengthy and involved task and the following check list of activities is offered as a guideline for success. Whilst it is appreciated that some projects may not require such comprehensive attention, it is nevertheless recommended that elements should only be omitted following explicit decisions to that effect by senior management responsible for the project.

Pre-design Phase

18. <u>Develop Project Delivery Strategy</u>. Analyse project requirements for function, quality, cost and time. Evaluate environmental, socio-economic, operational and legal constraints. Recommend a design and construction strategy that best addresses all of these issues all in accordance with the owner's requirements.

19. <u>Manage Programme Development</u>. Work with the owner, financing agencies and the various user groups to develop functional programmes for the project.

20. <u>Develop a Project Budget</u>. Prepare a detailed project budget. Clearly identify all categories of cost. Include construction cost, land cost, legal fees, consultant fees, building permits, testing laboratories, furnishings, fixtures equipment, landscaping and project management fees.

21. <u>Manage Selection of Consultants</u>. Develop selection criteria and procedures. Receive and evaluate written proposals and conduct interviews to assist the owner in selecting architects, engineers and other consultants. Assist in the negotiation of these contracts.

22. <u>Identify Applicable Construction Methods</u>. Select alternate construction systems appropriate for the project. Review function, price and local construction practices to determine compatibility with the facility programme.

23. <u>Prepare a Preliminary Cost Estimate Based on Historical Models</u>. Establish a preliminary budget for the project, based on a statistical analysis of similar completed projects adjusted for current conditions.

24. Develop Cost Models. Develop budgets for each major element of construction and/or manufacture. Compare these cost models with design estimates as the project progresses.

25. Document Project Organisation and Procedures. Develop organisation charts for owner and consultants and contractors. Prepare a project directory with names, addresses and responsibilities of all individuals and organisations associated with the project. Document procedures for decisions, communications, distribution of reports, billings, etc. Prepare a quality assurance plan.

26. Develop a Master Programme. Prepare a master programme showing duration, responsibility and precedence for major activities. Establish the duration of the project and identify the most critical activities. Update and magnify/ expand the level of detail as the project progresses.

27. Develop and Decision Tracking System. Identify, monitor and report on the status of key decisions and issues which influence the progress of the project, especially during the various design phases.

Conceptual Design Phase

28. Advise on Phased Construction Techniques. Decide the division of work into separate contractors to permit phasing. Consider such factors as construction durations, construction document preparation, long-lead-time materials and equipment, labour availability, trade jurisdictions and interface problems between contractors.

29. Establish and Monitor Detailed Design Programme. Expand the design schedule indicating milestones for each phase. Monitor and report on progess and problems.

30. Develop Preliminary Procurement Programmes. Prepare a programme for the tending or negotiation of construction contracts. Develop programmes for the bidding, shop drawings fabrication and delivery of direct-purchased equipment.

31. Develop Design Phase Programme. Produce a detailed programme of activities for each of the design phases. Include both graphic and numeric reports.

32. Prepare Final Budget. Establish a final budget for all categories of work. This will become the basis for all financial reporting as the project progresses.

33. Initiate Project Accounting Reports. Based on the final budget, initiate a reporting system which includes detailed budget categories for consultant fees, construction costs, owner costs, contingencies and reserves. Produce monthly project accounting reports to compare the budget to current estimates, contractual obligations, changes and anticipated changes.

IMPLEMENTATION

34. Estimate Alternative Construction Methods. Estimate the cost of alternate construction systems and methods in order to finalise selections prior to design development.

35. Estimate Design Concepts and Compare to Cost Models. Estimate conceptual design in progress and compare to preliminary cost models.

36. Identity Value Engineering and Life-Cycle Cost Savings Areas. Identify areas for value engineering study as the design progresses. Where energy, maintenance and operational considerations dictate, perform life-cycle costing studies to evaluate the most cost effective systems.

37. Report on Escalation Changes. Monitor the rate of inflation for labour, materials and equipment. Update unit costs accordingly.

38. Identify Interested Contractors and Suppliers. Investigate and prequalify contractors and manufacturers interested in tendering for the work. Review plans with them and promote their interest in the project.

Design Development Phase

39. Monitoring the Design Development Programme. Review the preparation of tender documents and compare to programmes developed during the conceptual design phase. Report on activities which are on or behind programme. Recommend corrective action as required.

40. Review Drawings and Specifications for Technical Accuracy and Co-ordination. Review drawings and specifications as they are being developed. Check construction feasibility and co-ordination of all design disciplines. Advise on contract provisions for controlling construction programmes. Advise on special and general conditions sections of the specifications.

41. Conduct Value Engineering Review of Design Development. Conduct a multi-disciplinary value engineering review to evaluate alternatives for construction systems and methods that are not within budget.

42. Operations and Maintenance (O&M) Requirement Planning. Analyse long term O&M requirements and ensure designs are implemented in following phases.

43. Report on Escalation Changes. Monitor relevant rates of inflation in the construction industry and update cost projections accordingly.

44. Estimate Final Design Development Costs. Prepare a cost estimate for all construction and site development in categories comparable to previously developed cost models and budgets.

45. Compare Design Development Estimate to Cost Models. As drawings progress, compare estimates to cost models and budget by category.

46. Update Project Accounting Reports. Prepare current project accounting reports, including project cost summaries and detailed cost status reports.

47. Identify Long-Lead Delivery Items for Early Purchasing. Identify materials and equipment which require long delivery times and are critical to the progress of the work. Develop a strategy for purchasing these items directly and later assigning them to a contractor.

48. Identify International Contractors and Suppliers. Maintain contacts developed during conceptual design phase. Continue to promote interest in the project.

Construction Documents Phase.

49. Establish Final Procurement Strategies. Finalise project strategies considered during the conceptual design stage. Finalise all bid packages and phasing techniques.

50. Review Drawings and Specifications for Technical Accuracy and Co-ordination. Review drawings and specifications as they are being developed. Check construction feasibility and co-ordination of all design disciplines. Advise on contract provisions for controlling construction schedules. Advise on special and general conditions clauses of the specifications.

51. Recommend Contract Provisions. Prepare contract provisions for inclusion in the construction specifications. Require performance by the contractors to support quality, cost and programme objectives.

52. Prepare Tender Documents. Advise on general and particular conditions and develop bid forms for all packages.

53. Bid Long-Lead-Time Materials and Equipment. Organise and manage the bidding of long-lead-time materials and equipment. Prepare bid forms and distribute bidding packages. Review and analyse bids.

53. Update Master Programme. Update the master programme to reflect the current project plan. Prepare both graphic and numeric reports. Distribute to all members of the project team.

54. Establish and Monitor Detailed Construction Document Programmes. Update, expand and review programmes which identify individual areas of responsibility for the preparation of construction documents. Monitor and report on progress.

IMPLEMENTATION

55. <u>Establish Submittal Procedures</u>. Document all procedures required for the submittal of materials, samples and shop drawings. Develop and maintain programmes and logs.

56. <u>Report on Escalation Changes</u>. Monitor the relevant rates of inflation in the construction industry. Update cost projections accordingly.

57. <u>Compare Current Design to Cost Models</u>. As working drawings proceed, compare current estimates to cost models. Recommend modifications as required.

58. <u>Estimate Final Construction Documents</u>. Prepare detailed cost estimates of final construction documents. Display cost information in categories that can be compared to budgets, cost models and tender results.

59. <u>Update Project Accounting Reports</u>. Prepare current project accounting reports. Include project cost summaries and detailed cost status reports.

60. <u>Develop Operation and Maintenance Plan</u>. Prepare a detailed computer driven operation and maintenance plan for all aspects of the facility.

61. <u>Identify Interested Contractors and Suppliers</u>. Maintain contacts development during the development phase. Continue to promote interest in the project.

Procurement Phase

62. <u>Conduct Pre-Bid Conferences</u>. Organise and direct conferences and site visits prior to the receipt of tenders. Include all tenderers, the consultants and the client.

63. <u>Manage Issuance of Addenda</u>. Work with the consultants in the preparation of any addenda to the construction tender documents. Handle the issuance of addenda to the tenderers.

64. <u>Receive Tenders</u>. Assist the owner in receipt and evaluation of tenders. Make recommendations on award of contracts.

65. <u>Negotiate Contracts on Behalf of the Owner</u>. Where elements of work are not competitively bid, negotiate on behalf of the owner to establish a fair and equitable price for the work to be accomplished.

Construction Phase

66. <u>Conduct Pre-construction Conference</u>. Organise and direct a pre-construction meeting with the contractors, consultants and owner. Review project organisation, lines of authority and project procedures.

67. <u>Maintain On-Site Staff</u>. Maintain a field staff to administer the work of the construction contractors. Inspect the work for conformance with plans and specifications.

68. **Manage Testing Agencies**. Assist in the selection of independent testing agencies. Co-ordinate their work, review their reports and make recommendations regarding their findings.

69. **Prepare Detailed Construction Programme**. Develop a construction programme outlining start and finish dates for procurement and construction activities. Establish major milestones for each segment of the work.

70. **Monitor Progress of the Work**. Review contractor's construction programme. Observe construction progress and report deviations from the programme which will jeopardise job progress. Work with contractors to develop recovery plans.

71. **Control Construction Quality**. Review capabilities of proposed subcontractors and evaluate proposed procedures and equipment prior to use. Observe work in progress and report defects and deficiencies.

72. **Maintain Site Records**. Maintain a current record of contracts, drawings and specifications. Inventory handbooks, technical standards and operating manuals. Log shop drawings and samples. File correspondence directives and minutes of meetings, etc.

73. **Certify Payment Requests**. Develop and implement a procedure for the review and processing of contractor applications for payment. Require a contractor's schedule of values for use in processing payments, prior to commencement of the works.

74. **Recommend Variations in the Work**. Make recommendations for variations in the work which are dictated by field conditions or will save time or money or improve quality.

75. **Maintain Project Accounting System**. Maintain an accurate, up-to-date construction cost accounting system. Include costs of contracts, direct purchased materials and other appropriate items. Make revisions to incorporate approved variations as they occur.

76. **Process Variation Orders**. Develop and implement a system for the preparation, review and processing of variation orders. Estimate the cost of all variation orders and negotiate them with the contractors on behalf of the client.

77. **Co-ordinate Processing of Shop Drawings**. Monitor submittals and expedite approvals of shop drawings. Maintain logs and sets of documents.

78. **Conduct Regular Job Meetings**. Arrange and conduct regular meetings at the construction site. Include all owner and contractor representatives and appropriate consultants. Discuss job progress. Track and record decisions.

IMPLEMENTATION

79. <u>Assist in Claims Defence</u>. Support the owner in the defence and resolution of claims related to the project. Assemble and analyse data.

80. <u>Prepare Field Reports</u>. Maintain daily job site reports. Record weather, numbers of workmen, equipment in use, general activities and special occurrences. Prepare monthly status reports which record the progress of the work and comment on quality, cost and time issues.

81. <u>Monitor Safety Programme</u>. Review the safety programmes developed by each of the contractors. Make recommendations and monitor the adherence to such programmes.

82. <u>Manage Insurance Programme</u>. Manage the processing of claims, payments and rebates for client sponsored project insurances.

83. <u>Arrange for Photographic Record of the Project</u>. If required, arrange for sequenced video coverage or monthly photographs of the work in progress.

84. <u>Complete Final Operations and Maintenance Plan</u>. Update previously developed computerised O&M plan, listing all installed equipment with such requirements and set requirements for preventive maintenance and work order processing.

Commissioning Phase

85. <u>Develop Commissioning Programme</u>. Produce a detailed programme of commissioning activities. Include key activities lists, equipment testing, start-up procedures and occupancy.

86. <u>Assemble Operating Manuals and Warranties</u>. Collect and catalogue all procedures manuals and instructions for the operation of mechanical, plumbing, electrical and special equipment. Collect all warranties.

87. <u>Co-ordinate Acceptance Inspections</u>. Work with each contractor to monitor the completion of defects list items to finalise all outstanding changes in their scope of work. Ensure "As Built" documents are completed by each contractor. Verify the payment of retention monies.

88. <u>Co-ordinate Systems Testing Programmes</u>. Organise and manage the testing of mechanical, plumbing, electrical and special building systems.

89. <u>Implement Start-up Procedures</u>. Plan and monitor the start-up and adjustment of all plant and building systems.

90. <u>Initiate Operations and Maintenance Plan</u>. Instruct and train O&M staff to utilise the computerised O&M system. Install furniture fixture and equipment inventory lists and drawings, through Computer Aided Drafting and Design (CADD) data links when available.

91. <u>Co-ordinate Occupancy</u>. Schedule the installation of furnishings, fixtures and equipment as well as phasing the relocation of personnel.

92. <u>Participate in Management of Warranty Work</u>. Work with the owner and the designers to ensure that the contractors honour their warranty responsibilities in a timely manner.

CONCLUSION

93. In this paper it has not been possible to review institutional factors in as much as they affect the management and output of the development activity. However, an irrigated agricultural development typically involves ministries of planning, agriculture, irrigation, commerce or industry and finance, together with research establishments and regional/rural development agencies etc.

94. Other infrastructural sectors will have similarly complicated inter-government and parastatal relationships and it is easy to understand how a secular approach to project implementation can fail. For holism - the whole being greater than the sum of the parts - it is therefore vital that the management team for each component activity be kept comprehensively aware of its place in the development chain together with the full knowledge of the project objectives and benefits. By the same token, a holistic attitude to the leadership of multi-disciplinary teams is the recipe for universal success.

ACKNOWLEDGEMENTS

95. I gladly acknowledge the contributions of my ICID colleagues, Professor David Constable and Jerry Schaack to this paper. I am likewise indebted to my fellow Director, Joseph Horn, for his many views on the management of projects. Finally, the editorial suggestions of Zena Haines have been gratefully accepted.

REFERENCES

1. Appropriate Technology for Water Supply and Sanitation: A Summary of Technical and Economic Options: World Bank December 1980.

2. Making it Happen: Sir John Harvey-Jones
                        William Collins 1988

3. IIMI Review Vol. 2 Nos. 2 August 1988;
   The Changing Concept of Management in Irrigation; Mark Svendsen.

4. ODI - IIMI Management Network Paper 90/1f April 1990

IMPLEMENTATION

5. Planning the Management, Operation and Maintenance of Irrigation and Drainage Systems - A Guide for the Preparation of Strategies and Manuals.
World Bank Technical Paper No. 90 (1989)

6. Irrigation Training in the Public Sector - Guidelines for Preparing Strategies and Programmes
The Work Bank/USAID; EDI Technical Materials (1989)

7. Water and Sanitation for Health; Progress Report No.13 March 1990 USAID.

8. Selection of Appropriate Technology in Irrigation Canal Systems; Herve L. Plusquelec - World Bank 1987.

14. Technology choice

Dr G. A. EDMONDS, Head, Infrastructure Programme and Engineering, Infrastructure and Rural Works, International Labour Office

Introduction

A few years ago, driving into Dar es Salaam from the airport it was possible to observe a very modern grass-cutting machine efficiently dealing with the tufts of grass that managed to grow at the side of the road. In its progress the machine passed the hundreds of Tanzanians who were walking into Dar in the vain hope of being able to obtain a job.

It would be nice to think that the choice of technology was made in an objective and neutral manner and that the final choice was dependent only on being able to use the available resources in the most effective manner to achieve the required result. Unfortunately this often does not happen due to a variety of political and other factors. If a donor as part of a large aid package offers some modern grasscutting machinery it may seem churlish to refuse it, however inappropriate it may be.

There are a variety of reasons why the choice of technology is not necessarily made in a totally unbiased environment. These can be grouped under a variety of headings:

1. Political - the choice of technology may be restricted by a strict adherence to a certain ideology. Such an ideology may classify local resource-based technologies as backward or even neo-colonialist.

2. Economic - often the price tags placed on foreign imported goods bear no relationship to their actual value to the economy. Equally overvalued exchange rates, and wage rates which do not reflect the actual cost of labour all result in an economic framework which favours the choice of imported goods against the use of local resources.

3. Institutional - the systems and procedures related to the administration and organisation of infrastructure projects are generally modelled on

IMPLEMENTATION

those used in the developing countries. Consequently, they are not designed to fit the environment in which they operate. The payment, for example, of large groups of unskilled labour is something which most public works departments have difficulty coping with.

4. Attitudinal - whilst this factor has no basis in either fact or reason it is often the most important element in the effective application of a new technology. If the technology has not been part of either the education or experience of those who are asked to apply it then there is no real motivation to give it a reasonable trial.

In the following pages, two specific examples of the attempt to introduce a new technology are described. One has already been relatively successful, the introduction of the other is relatively recent and therefore it is too soon to say whether it will be successful or not.

Labour-based methods of roads construction and maintenance

Labour-based methods of road construction and maintenance are now appreciated as being viable alternatives to the use of equipment. We have come a long way since the initial studies by the ILO and the World Bank attempted to assess the technical and economic feasibility of labour-based methods in the early 1970's. The conclusion of that work was that in those countries where the agricultural wage rate was less than US$4 a day labour-based methods should be seriously considered. This of course covered a very large number of countries. Since that time this more general conclusion has been refined in relation to the supply of labour, the population density and constraints relating to administrative procedures.

Nevertheless one can now count some 20-25 developing countries which have initiated major labour-based programmes. Perhaps more significantly labour-based methods are no longer considered as second rate alternatives useful only to create employment. They now figure naturally in the range of techniques available to the road engineer. This is reflected in a variety of ways viz:

(a) Specific references in national development plans.

(b) Their inclusion in the project documents of financing agencies.

(c) The setting up of training courses on labour-based methods for road engineers.

Perhaps the most obvious area for the use of labour-based methods is road maintenance. This has become a major issue over the last 5-6 years. As governments have built up their road networks the previous lack of attention to maintenance has become apparent in the declining state of the existing network. In many cases investments are having to be made into rehabilitating the existing system which had so painstakingly been developed. In parts of Africa, the road network seems to be deteriorating at a faster rate than it is being constructed. Funds for maintenance are generally spent on improvement and emergency works rather than on routine maintenance. Public works departments are caught in a vicious circle. Budgets for road maintenance are insufficient and are spent on putting the network into a maintainable condition, there remains no funds however for routine or periodic maintenance thus the network continues to deteriorate. Because of inflation the maintenance budget covers less and less and more and more of it has to be spent on emergency repairs.

Certain major international donors, the World Bank being one, consider that the situation is critical. In particular they believe that:

(a) Any new construction should be paralleled by a major effort to improve the road maintenance system.

(b) Construction programmes should be limited to relate to the size of a maintainable network.

This situation seems chronic and it is worth trying to understand the underlying causes of such a situation.

During the 1960's and 1970's it was logical for those countries trying to develop their economies to place a major emphasis on building up a viable road network. Indeed this fitted neatly into the then current development theories which, inter alia, related transport improvement to development. Moreover there was no doubt that the road networks of many countries were inadequate. Both financial agencies and donors supported the policy and consequently foreign exchange funds were readily available for road construction projects. To illustrate the point, World Bank lending to the roads sector in 1965 amounted to $283 million, by 1977 it had risen to $636 million. This major investment in roads over a considerable period of time was not constant in its focus. With the completion of the primary network and the emphasis on rural development in the 1970's the emphasis shifted dramatically to rural roads. Thus in 1965 the World Bank's road lending included only 3,500 km of feeder road. By 1977 this had risen to 37,000 km.

In terms of maintenance, this major investment and its focus had several important consequences:

(a) The burden of road maintenance was dramatically increased.

IMPLEMENTATION

(b) It was increased in a sector (rural roads) for which no effective administration existed.

(c) Unlike construction costs, maintenance costs had to be borne by the Government.

It is fair to say that little thought was given to future maintenance. It was considered to be a minor cost element (which is true) and thus would provide no difficulty (which is untrue). For a whole variety of reasons discussed below, road maintenance is rarely effectively carried out. Thus, whilst the cost may be low, typically 1-3 per cent of the construction cost per annum, if it is not done the results are disastrous.

In most countries rural roads were either the responsibility of local councils or were maintained by community self-help. Rarely did there exist an organisation for maintaining rural roads. Thus the greatest investment was made in roads for which there was no maintenance organisation nor technical guidance. In many countries, previously governed by colonial powers, the idea of a lengthman or community maintenance had existed, but this was often swept away as it seemed to represent a symbol of forced labour.

Maintenance costs were accepted to be wholly borne by the governments, most donors until recently feeling that this was a responsibility they could not shoulder. Thus whilst maintenance costs are relatively small, any increase in their attribution has to be obtained from a treasury which is attempting to meet demands from all other sectors of the economy. In the case of construction, the funds came from abroad and therefore was not in competition with other funds.

The first reaction to the evident lack of maintenance in many countries was a call for increased spending. However this can be taken so far. Road maintenance is important, but in the national context how important is it in relation to health services, schools, maintenance of buildings or even defence? Most developing countries spend up to 0.33 per cent of their GNP on road maintenance. Industrialised countries, whose networks are generally well established spend more, up to 0.5 or 0.6 per cent. It would be unrealistic to expect developing countries to spend more than say 0.35 per cent. If we assume a reasonable average figure for routine and periodic maintenance of about $750 km for the whole network the results are interesting. For middle income countries like Thailand, the Philippines and Indonesia it would in theory be possible to maintain their networks if they increased maintenance expenditure to this level (i.e. 0.35 per cent of GNP). However for lower income countries like India, Bangladesh and Sri Lanka even if they increased their expenditure to this level they would only be able to maintain between 30 and 60 per cent of their networks. At the present level of expenditure there is no possibility of maintaining the whole network.

Clearly therefore money is not the only solution and in the case of the low income countries it may be necessary to make harsh decisions about what size of network it will be possible to maintain.

The next reaction was to look at what funds are spent on. This has certainly achieved results and is well documented elsewhere. Suffice it to say here that the major problem has been to try and reduce the amount of maintenance funds tied up in permanently employed labour forces.

A further refinement has been to attempt to redistribute the activities upon which funds are spent. Presently little or no money is spent on routine maintenance. Programmes therefore have concentrated investment funds on rehabilitating roads so as to put them in a maintainable state and then install a regular routine maintenance system.

	Actual size	Size of network at expenditure of 0.35 GNP and $750/km	Size of network at present expenditure and $750/km
	km/1000 pop.	km/1000 pop.	km/1000 pop.
Philippines	2.9 3.0	3.54	2.1
Thailand	3.3 3.0	3.8	1.7
Indonesia	1.3 1.0	2.6	0.37
India	2.0 2.0	1.2	-
Bangladesh	0.2 1.5	0.6	0.2
Sri Lanka	1.6 4.5	1.5	1.0

It is clear that governments are having to look more and more at their own resources and to encourage methods which minimise the use of foreign exchange. Equally governments are having to make hard choices about the level and scope of maintenance that the country can afford.

Given therefore a commitment by governments to a rational maintenance strategy which relates levels of maintenance funds available to a defined maintainable network a variety of opportunities present themselves for the use of labour-based techniques in order that funds will stretch to the maximum.

* Road Deterioration in Developing Countries
  Table A-2 (World Bank 1984)

IMPLEMENTATION

All these are concerned with developing cheaper, more effective approaches to road maintenance. They can be categorised as follows:

1. The classical approach of employing direct labour supported by equipment.
2. Individual or collective responsibility for the maintenance of a road section.
3. Agreements between the Government and communities.
4. Petty contracts for selected activities.
5. Use of private contractors.

The classical approach is of course not new. What has been attempted recently here is to (a) improve the manner in which equipment is costed in order that managers are aware of the cost of a machine standing idle and (b) reorganise and motivate the, often permanent, direct labour staff. Both have proved extremely difficult. The idea of accountability and profitability is a difficult concept for PWD engineers to assimilate. Some progress has been made by operating separate plant pools which "hire" their equipment to the PWD. Equally repairs and maintenance of equipment should be carried out on a cost recovery basis. This is a step forward. However as long as the financial transfers are merely on paper within government it is difficult to see how full accountability can be installed.

The reduction, or improvement of the productivity, of the permanently employed direct labour force has proved similarly intractable. Certain countries have attempted to decentralise the labour to their district or location of origin. Others have tackled the problem head on by reducing the staff with all the attendant costs, personnel battles and legal complications. It is clear however that PWDs should aim to reduce their permanent labour force to an absolute minimum.

The use of individual or collective agreements has been successful in many countries. The concept of a "lengthmnan" is not new of course. However it is only in recent years that it has been seen as a major element in a routine maintenance strategy. In general the system is effective, it reduces costs and ensures a continuous attention to the road. The problems relate to the need for supervision, the natural tendency of lengthmen to tackle only the easier tasks such as grass cutting and the logistics of payment. Nevertheless roads that previously had no maintenance whatsoever are now receiving attention through this system.

The question of agreements between communities and governments for road maintenance could be the subject of a separate paper. Suffice it to say here that possibilities do exist, however some form of motivation for the communities, be it financial or other, is necessary. The idea that villagers will maintain extensive lengths of road on a self-help basis is difficult to sustain in practice. As with any self-help projects questions of who benefits and what exactly constitutes self-help are critical.

In various projects with which the ILO is involved small or petty contractors are being used for defining routine maintenance tasks. The advantages of using the private sector are clear in terms of reduced administrative and bureaucratic procedures and improved efficiency. Various problems however present themselves. In the first place, small contractors in many countries are inexperienced, have poor financial control and limited technical knowledge. Routine maintenance is more difficult to adapt to the standard "measured work" contract system. Thus special effort has to be put into adapting the working environment so that contractors can work effectively. This means modifying the contractual arrangements, having solid data on maintenance activity productivities and effective supervision.

The use of labour-based methods in road construction has of course now been introduced in a large number of countries.

As long ago as 1979 the World Bank was arguing that in countries where the wage rate is less than $4 per day, then L.B. techniques should be seriously considered. Clearly with the increase in the price of machines and spare parts and the general inflation this figure is now considerably higher. Certainly the more stringent economic situation that prevails nowadays has pushed countries to look more closely at the resources available to them.

The ILO alone is implementing labour-based projects in more than 15 countries. The economic case has for some time been proven. The ongoing projects are making the parallel case for their technical viability.

At this stage therefore it is no longer necessary to make a case for labour-based methods. What is of interest is to look at the innovations that are being made in the introduction of the technology in various situations and disperse geographical locations.

The two major innovations that have occurred in the last 5 years have been:

(a) the involvement of the private sector;
(b) the development of simple equipment.

As regards the private sector, it has often been suggested that one way of promoting the local contracting industry was to have small contractors involved in the use of labour-based methods. This was based on the idea that small contractors had limited amount of plant and could adapt easily to the use of the techniques. It tended to ignore the fact that small contractors

IMPLEMENTATION

are generally in need of proper financial management. One thing however is certain; there is no real future for the use of L.B. techniques if they are are not taken over by the private sector. Work carried out by the ILO over the past few years in Ghana, the Philippines and Madagascar has shown that the constraints to the use of LB techniques by the private sector have more to do with the problems of small contractors in general than with any basic difficulty with the methods themselves. Small contractors face a variety of constraints in their activities. These relate to problems of obtaining credit, of keeping an effective cash flow, of being paid on time. These problems remain the same whatever the technology. The real problem posed by the use of LB methods is whether the contractor can still make a profit. Our experience shows that it is insufficient to merely tell contractors that the techniques are profitable, it is necessary to actually take them through the construction process to let them experience the methods.

In Ghana, a number of contractors were initially selected for training. They were informed that at the successful completion of the training they would be able to bid for labour-based projects. It was also made clear to them that there would be a flow of such projects, thus a supply of contracts was assured. During the training process the contractors were closely supervised not only from the technical point of view but also in relation to the contractual aspects of the work. At the same time the basic tender documents were modified to make them appropriate to the new techniques. Thus the usual insistence on a certain minimum plant holding was waived, specific points were inserted in relation to labour rates etc. In addition a special category of labour-based contracts was identified for which contractors who had passed the training programme could apply even if they were not on the list of recognised contractors.

The number of LB contracts is now growing and whereas before we were having to search for potential contractors they are now queueing to be trained.

When a contractor is presented with the possibility of using L.B. methods, he automatically has in mind a number of possible problems:

(a) can he still make a profit?
(b) labour is more difficult to handle than machines;
(c) labour implies concern with labour laws, unions etc.

In his mind (a) and (b) are linked. Machines don't answer back and their productivity does not vary (as long as the machine is working!) It is therefore incumbent upon us to show the private sector that with proper incentives and with effective organisation labour productivity can be competitive. This can therefore ensure that the methods are profitable. In addition, LB methods do imply a greater level of supervision. This will not solve all personnel problems but it certainly helps. As far as (c) is concerned, it is true the labour laws have to be respected but this is true in any case. There is a certain measure of the fear of the unknown involved here. Certainly the problems of the lack of spare parts, the cost of transport to remote sites, the inflexibility of machines compared with labour are no less onerous problems to a contractor - they are just problems that he already understands.

We certainly see a major area of development for LB in the private sector. In general what is required is that government makes it clear that there will be a supply of such projects thus making it worthwhile for contractors to invest time in learning the new techniques.

The development of simple equipment - one of the major misconceptions about labour-based methods is that no equipment is used. In fact one of the basic principles surrounding LB is that one should use the technology that is appropriate to the economic environment. Thus the technology appropriate in Thailand is unlikely to be the one that is equally suited to Tanzania. As the economy develops the wage rates increase and the LB methods become less appropriate for a range of activities. In those countries with more advanced economies therefore one would expect to see a range of equipment being developed to replace at least some of the labour. As we shall see below this is exactly what has been happening.

One reason for the use of simple equipment is then purely economic. The second reason is technical. In the early years of the use of the techniques emphasis was placed on equalising the excavation across the cross section of the road. This was to eliminate the need for hauling equipment. Equally compaction was avoided if possible, again to reduce the need for machines. The success of LB methods has also resulted in their use on roads carrying larger amounts of traffic. These roads have larger cross sections and require compaction. Another point here is that where roads have to be constructed in deep cut there is need to evacuate the soil. This is not very efficient without machines. Consequently, it has been necessary to look for both hauling and compaction equipment which harmonise with the use of LB methods.

Paradoxically this has been easier in the more economically advanced countries, principally because they have the potential to manufacture intermediate forms of equipment which the poorer countries do not have. In the poorer countries it has been necessary to look again at the possibility of using animal traction and improving the designs of wheelbarrows and carts. The ILO has recently produced a technical memorandum on the design and manufacture of animal-drawn carts which is one step in addressing the problem.

IMPLEMENTATION

There has also been a series of major developments in the use of simple equipment related to the use of tractors and power tillers.

In the case of tractors, the tendency has been to use them principally for hauling. More recently towed graders have been used. These simple yet often neglected machines can be extremely effective both for providing the final shape to the road and in its subsequent maintenance.

The power tiller is a new machine which has enormous potential for LB methods. It is simple. It can be produced locally if there is a basic manufacturing capacity. It works at the same rhythm as LB. So far it has been used in the following applications:

(a) with bowsers
(b) with rollers
(c) with scraper blades

Thus for a relatively small increase in cost the technical scope of LB methods is increased.

In more general terms, the more widespread use of labour-based methods has allowed a comparison of costs between countries. Whilst comparisons between LB and equipment is very difficult it is useful to have an indication of the overall profitability of LB methods. Equally a global comparison of the cost of building roads by LB is necessary to convince planners of their viability. A basic monitoring and reporting system has been produced which provides a project manager with a simple way of:

(a) keeping a control of his resource inputs;
(b) giving an overall indication of costs per kilometre.

Table 1 gives the results of some of the projects with which the ILO has been associated.

One has, of course, to take into consideration the different design standards, the type of terrain and the levels of supervision when comparing the figures. Nevertheless two points are significant:

(a) The consistently low cost as compared with equipment.
(b) The direct correlation between wage rates and total cost.

As far as comparisons with equipment are concerned, one has to be cautious. Nevertheless in all cases quoted in Table 1 the costs of labour-based was less, and in many cases considerably less, than for machines.

TABLE 1: Labour-based road construction - Cost comparison

Country	Cost	Type of road	Wage Rate
Ethiopia	$10,000	5 m gravel	$1.0
Ghana	$11,600	4.5 m gravel	$1.2
Tanzania	$ 3,500	4 m gravel	$0.4
Lesotho	$18,500	4.5 m gravel	$3.5
Philippines	$18,000	4 m gravel	$3.0
Thailand	$12,000	6 m gravel	$2.5
Kenya	$ 7,000	4.5 gravel	$1.0
Botswana	$ 9,250	4 m gravel	$2.6
Malawi	$ 5,000	5.5 m engineered earth	$0.9

It is perhaps not surprising that there is a straight correlation between wages and cost given that wages represent 30-40 per cent of the total cost. Nevertheless the equipment cost is not normally so constant a percentage in machine-based projects.

Labour-based technology is now an accepted fact of life. It has a proven track record in a variety of environments. It is supported by a mass of documentation dealing with every facet of its planning, design, implementation and evaluation. The one major element that is still missing is its introduction into the curriculae of faculties of engineering and technical colleges. Only when engineers are taught the use of these methods will they accept it naturally rather than it being forced upon them or treating it as something second rate to be endured rather than effectively utilised. Given its potential it is important that the technology finds it place in our institutions of learning so that engineers can give us the full benefits of its use.

Rural transportation

It is becoming increasingly apparent that the conventional approach to rural transport planning cannot respond to the actual transport needs of the

IMPLEMENTATION

mass of the rural population. This is because the traditional approach concentrates on the <u>national</u> transportation system which stops at the end of the last, well-maintained feeder road. It totally ignores what can be termed the <u>local</u> transport system. The latter is the means whereby the mass of the rural population transport their goods to market, their children to school and themselves to health clinics and government offices. The local system consists of a track and a vehicle, the latter ranging (depending on users and condition of the track) from head loading through human and animal-powered vehicles to simple mechanised means of transport. The tracks range from narrow footpaths to roads of a reasonable width, although usually not constructed to defined design standards.

The fact that these local transport systems abound throughout the developing world in all their diversity demonstrates two realities: (i) they are the rural people's answer to their transport problems and satisfy their most essential transport requirements, and (ii) they are sufficiently flexible to respond to transport demand of a very varied nature both for social and economic purposes. This being said, it is necessary to look much more closely at the forms of off-road transport that are used and, in particular, the types of vehicle.

Very little attention has so far been paid to the vehicle, basically because it has been assumed that there is no alternative to European-style motor vehicles. However, by any standards, these are totally inappropriate to the needs of the rural population. They are extremely costly; they are not available to the rural population; they require a particuar type of track which is expensive to build and maintain; their technology is far removed from that used in the rural areas; they must be either imported or manufactured in mass-production factories; and they need to transport large loads to jutify investment in them. If no alternative existed to vehicles of this type one would, sadly, have to accept their inappropriateness. However, as the World Bank and UNIDO have recently pointed out, there is a large range of vehicles presently in use, which could be made more effective if serious attention were paid to improving them. Animal-drawn carts, the bicycle and its numerous derivatives and simple motorised transport are prevalent in most developing countries. However, they are seen as quaint, second-rate substitutes for the car or pick-up. They should, however, be regarded as a real solution to the lack of mobility of rural people. They meet the criteria of affordability, availability, utility and compatibility with local conditions which the European motor vehicle does not. Moreover, they could be manufactured locally.

For those who find it difficult to believe that any form of transport is a luxury to the majority of people, the following figures from a study made in the northern region of India provide food for thought: during the reference period (July 1977-June 1978) 73 per cent of rural households did not own any type of vehicle, nor did 89 per cent of households having holdings of less than 5 hectares. Of the total quantity of goods transported from the village to a recognised road, 92 per cent were taken by head load or animal cart. Even on farm-to-market access roads as much as 63 per cent of goods were transported by cart.

On-farm transport

Very few studies have actually addressed themselves to the real transport demand in the rural areas. What we do know is that the bulk of such transport actually takes place on farm and is far removed from any road. Again, the India study shows that 80 per cent of all goods were transported within the confines of village lands. The need is thus for vehicles capable of transporting relatively small loads (less than 150 kg) over relatively short distances (up to a maximum of 15 km). In many countries the bulk of on-farm transport is done by women and children, typically for the collection of wood and water. Interestingly enough most of the developments in on-farm transport have related to easing the burden of men in their agricultural activities; thus simple machines do exist for crop spraying, land clearance and seeding. In addition, a great deal of work has been done on reducing the strain on bullocks pulling carts. Little or nothing, however, has been done to reduce the burden of head or back loading -

IMPLEMENTATION

traditionally women's work - which accounts for the majority of on-farm transport, and which can seriously impair health from the severe strain that is put on the spinal column. An example of what can be done, conspicuous by its uniqueness, is the <u>chekee</u>, an improved back-loading device, developed in the Republic of Korea. It is thus not beyond the wit of man to reduce the strain of this type of transport, provided that a concerted research effort is made.

Off-farm transport

"Off-farm transport" is usually defined as the movement of goods along a road from the farm to the market. However, this is merely the second stage, the first being the movement of goods from the farm to a recognisable road. As mentioned before, many - if not most - of the rural population of developing countries live at a considerable distance from roads. A study in India noted that where goods had to be transported further than 1 1/2 km (the effective limit of head or back loading) the majority had to hire a bullock cart for transportation. In spite of the obvious limitations of head loading, some 20 per cent of off-farm transport is executed in this way. These findings only confirm the need to improve the techniques of "human transport".

When the load actually reaches a recognisable road, there are, of course a wide variety of transport modes, from small human-powered vehicles to large trucks. It is unfortunate, however, that the emphasis on road planning and design has generally obscured the existence of anything save motorised transport. The Indian study mentioned above, however, concluded that only 0.5 per cent of all rural transport was carried out by motorised trucks. If on-road transport was separated out, trucks still accounted for only 6 per cent of the total tonne-kilometrage. It seems, therefore, that the gulf between what transport "experts" are planning for and what people really need is fairly wide. The figures suggest that it is far more important to improve the efficiency of animal carts, bicycle derivatives and very simple mechanised transport than to worry about the effects of poorly maintained rural roads on "conventional" mechanised transport. Even so, the development of these simpler forms of transport will not necessarily bring them within the financial means of the majority of the rural population. What it may do, however, is to bring transport down to their scale and more nearly within their control. For example, although the work on improving the bullock cart in India has shown that it is certainly possible to improve its efficiency dramatically, the cost of improved carts is almost double that of the traditional ones. As the majority of rural households cannot even afford the latter, it is clear tht the improved carts can be justified only in terms of increased efficiency and lower hire charges on the road. Nevertheless, they do provide an alternative to truck transportation, which is generally in the hands of middlemen and not the farmers themselves. This is important when it is remembered that the cost of transporting crops is substantial, averaging around 20 per cent of the retail price in the case of truck transport.

Location of essential services

It has been generally assumed that essential services such as schools, health clinics, administrative offices and market centres should be concentrated in one place serving a particular area. It has also been assumed that these services must be on a road network. This assumption needs questioning. Certainly some basic services such as education have a high degree of immobility and therefore the idea that a school should be centrally placed appears valid. However, as far as health facilities are concerned, it would appear that certain types of simple vehicles, such as modifications of motorised three-wheelers, which do not require conventional roads, could be used as mobile clinics.

I have drawn attention to the fact that the mass of rural transportation does not take place on a road system in the generally accepted sense. However, rural transport is planned as if the end of a road into a rural area were the starting point for the transportation of goods, services and people. In fact, it is already a long way down the chain which starts in the small farmer's field. We have concluded that it seems impracticable and financially impossible to provide road access to the mass of the rural population. If it is assumed that this is our objective, then, of course,

IMPLEMENTATION

the conclusion is a depressing one. If, on the other hand, it is recognised that conventional road transport is just a small - and generally the final - link in the whole rural transport system, there is less reason for discouragement, although we must radically reappraise existing top-down strategies and work from the bottom. This implies decentralisation of transport planning and a move towards greater emphasis on socio-economic factors in transport appraisal. More precisely, we must make genuine efforts to assess the actual transport demand; identify various ways of improving human, animal and simple mechanised transport and put them into practice; and evaluate the suitability of certain simple vehicles for use in both on-farm and off-farm transport.

There is no doubt however that a great deal needs to be, and can be done, to improve local transport systems. If the greater part of the rural populations in developing countries is to have access to low-cost forms of transportation, supportive measures to develop and improve the local systems will be indispensable. Examples of such measures are (i) the wide-scale promotion and dissemination of information on (successfully improved) forms of rural transportation, (ii) the development of a local capability to manufacture and maintain such forms of transport, (iii) the provision of credit facilities to develop and maintain local transport systems, (iv) the development of self-sustained community organisations responsible for local track networks and communal use of vehicle fleets.

Obviously, the resources required to realise these activities would be considerable, both in terms of finance and manpower. This the more so as no standard solutions exist and each area would require its own, specific approach. It is also evident that a shift of attention and resources from the conventional transport systems to the local systems implies major policy changes in most developing countries. It appears, however, that this approach may be the only alternative available if long-term solutions to the transport needs of rural areas are to be found.

In practical terms, this could mean that one would have to think in terms of a choice between spending money on road (re-)construction and maintenance or on the local transport system or (most likely) on a mixture of the two.

Before this phase is reached however considerable experimentation work will be required. Policy changes are only likely to be made once innovative appoaches have proven to be successful in an economic sense and to be socially acceptable. The great virtue of well-developed local transport systems is of course that, after (considerable) initial investments, they would be self-sustaining with minimal or no recurrent government inputs. The economic and social justification for the initial investments would be an improved personal mobility of rural poeple with all the social benefits that this entails - and increased opportunities to develop the agricultural potential in the rural areas concerned.

15. Maintenance

R. ROBINSON, Assistant Director, Rendel Palmer & Tritton Ltd

SYNOPSIS. In many developing countries, infrastructure is decaying and disintegrating, and expensively constructed facilities are not working. Much of this infrastructure has reached an age where major refurbishment and rehabilitation is needed, the situation having been exacerbated by a lack of attention to maintenance in the past. Poor maintenance can be attributed to several factors including: the attitudes of politicians and engineers, an economic recession that has destroyed the fragile economies of many developing countries, a lack of finance, poor management, a lack of attention to human resources, and an over-emphasis on technological issues without recognition of the underlying institutional constraints. Fundamental institutional changes are necessary if improvements to maintenance are to be made. Three steps are needed to address the situation: obtaining commitment for change, isolating and understanding the problem, and developing and implementing action plans. It must be recognised that, although there are technical issues to be tackled in the area of maintenance, the vast majority of problems are of an institutional or human resource nature. Failure to appreciate this will result in the continuation of the decline in the serviceability of existing facilities and of the further massive economic losses that are now being witnessed.

INTRODUCTION

The current maintenance situation

1. The provision of energy, transport, water supply and other forms of infrastructure in developing countries has provided the engineering industry with a massive global workload over the last 30 years. Since the end of the colonial period, governments have expanded and improved their countries' infrastructure in order to provide a platform for national economic development. These activities have also provided engineers from industrialised countries with opportunities, challenges and

Appropriate development for basic needs. Thomas Telford, London, 1990

responsibilities in an environment for personal development which they would have been unlikely to find at home.

2. Despite the huge investments that have been made over this period, many developing countries now find themselves with infrastructure that is decaying and disintegrating, and with expensively constructed facilities that are simply not working. In the road subsector alone, the World Bank have identified current expenditure need of $40 billion for rehabilitation, with further similar sum needed over the next ten years to prevent roads currently in good condition from falling into disrepair. What is even more alarming is that the rate of deterioration of much infrastructure is accelerating.

3. What has caused this poor state of affairs? There is no doubt that several factors have come together at the same time to cause the situation that is now being witnessed. Much infrastructure is now 20 to 30 years old and has reached the point where major refurbishment or rehabilitation is needed. This has been coupled with economic recession and a downturn in terms of trade that have destroyed the fragile economies of many developing countries, resulting in shortages of available funds and a virtual absence of foreign exchange. The situation has been exacerbated by a lack of attention to maintenance in the past which has led to the current condition of infrastructure being worse than it might otherwise have been.

Scope of maintenance
4. The objectives of maintenance are to ensure that a facility is kept in serviceable condition for users and to protect investments that have been made in the past. Maintenance is sometimes classified in terms of the frequency of its application such as 'routine' or 'periodic', or in terms of whether it is 'planned' of 'responsive'. There is some dispute as to whether refurbishment and rehabilitation should be classed as 'maintenance', since they are often funded from capital rather than recurrent budgets. Similarly, there is doubt as to whether the upgrading of facilities should be included as a maintenance activity.

5. The key issue is that, once a facility has been provided, there will be a need to keep it operating at a satisfactory level of service for as long a period as it is cost-effective so to do. Failure to maintain in a timely manner can result in a loss of original investment with unnecessarily high repair costs. For certain types of facilities, lack of serviceability can also result in greatly increased costs to users which can far exceed the loss in capital investment.

Development of the present situation

6. The background to the present situation with regard to maintenance of most kinds of infrastructure has followed a similar pattern in many developing countries. At the time of independence, the facility was operating reasonably efficiently with management carried out by a mixture of expatriate and local staff. Following independence, many expatriates left and others left slowly throughout the post-colonial period. Operations were handed over to local staff, many of whom had inadequate training, and most had insufficient experience to manage effectively or to control the tasks for which they were responsible.

7. As demand for the expansion of facilities arose, multilateral and bilateral aid donors were often keen to support capital works on either a loan or a grant basis. Emphasis was placed on the new investment programme with little attention being paid to keeping the existing facilities serviceable or operational. After a time, the available funding from aid sources tended to be reduced following the world recession and this coincided with many facilities ageing and becoming needful of extensive rehabilitation.

8. As the extent of infrastructure increased, there was typically no commensurate increase in maintenance funds and, in many countries, funding levels in real terms have actually declined over the years.

DIMENSION OF THE MAINTENANCE PROBLEM

The attitudinal dimension

9. Maintenance has traditionally been considered to be an unglamorous activity. In many organisations, it has become the preserve of the incompetent and those who lack motivation. It has been seen as a dead-end job, often based in the poorest available office accommodation and with allocations of budget that are too low and are arbitrary. There has been little political commitment to the subject, since maintenance provides few opportunities for 'cutting tapes' and gaining kudos. There is no prestige or grand opening ceremony associated with obtaining 85 per cent availability of mechanical equipment over a 12 month period, even though this may represent a major engineering achievement which could have a dramatic effect on the performance of the operating organisation as a whole. Similarly, donors in the past have often preferred to be associated with grandiose, prestige projects involving new investment rather than with the routine and apparently humdrum works of maintenance.

IMPLEMENTATION

10. The same attitude has also been seen among Engineers. Many people in the profession see their job purely as one of designing and building. Maintenance, all too frequently, is not given consideration when these activities are taking place. This often results in facilities being both difficult and expensive to maintain because of a lack of foresight during the engineering design process. This problem is not helped by an educational and training system for engineers that concentrates almost wholly on analysis and design, and where the concepts of management and maintenance receive scant attention, even if they are acknowledged to exist at all.

11. These background issues come together to result in the situation that now exists, with crumbling infrastructure and many engineers with the responsibility for repairs having neither the resources, the skills, nor the interest in tackling the problems that exist.

The economic dimension

12. Compared with the cost of new investment, maintenance is relatively cheap for most types of infrastructure. The cheapness of cost, coupled with the consequences of lack of maintenance in terms of reduced level of service, or complete breakdown, usually result in the economic return from investment in maintenance being very high - and nearly always higher than those for new investment.

13. Again, the road subsector provides quantification of this. Improvements in road maintenance normally lead to reductions in vehicle operating costs of between 15 and 50 per cent, and have led to internal rates of return on donor-financed maintenance projects which are generally above 100 per cent. Few maintenance projects have had rates of return as low as 50 per cent, whilst the return on new construction projects rarely exceeds this figure.

14. Existing facilities will normally be more important economically than new ones otherwise they would not have been built first. Thus, maintenance of existing facilities should normally have the first call on resources before the building of new ones. Additionally, once construction costs have been sunk in an existing facility, the economic return from carrying out maintenance will be very large, if this prevents the benefits associated with the facility being lost.

The financial dimension

15. Maintenance does require an ongoing commitment of funds which are available on a regular and reliable basis. However, the actual size of these funds is relatively small when compared with the cost of the initial investment. Although the cost will vary for different types of infrastructure, figures of less than ten per cent of the initial investment cost are normal.

16. For example, Lethbridge from the World Bank, in a paper to the 1986 Institution of Civil Engineers <u>Conference on Maritime and Offshore Structures Maintenance</u>, quoted annual costs for an African port with six general cargo berths, one coastal berth and typical back-up facilities. Maintenance costs for mechanical equipment were roughly $2.50 million compared with a value of the equipment of about $25 million at today's prices. For the port infrastructure, the replacement cost was estimated at $150 million with annual maintenance costs estimated to be $1.50 million, or one per cent. When the maintenance cost of the port's floating craft is added to this, annual costs for maintenance are likely to be of the order of $4-5 million.

17. Thus, although annual maintenance costs are only a few per cent of the value of the facility, the sums of money required by an organisation can still be considerable. For private organisations, it is normally possible for adequate provision for such sums to be planned for and put aside out of revenue. However, most infrastructure in developing countries is controlled by government or parastatal organisations. These tend to operate with budgets that are controlled externally to the organisation and, even those organisations that generate their own revenue, such as railways, are often forced to work within a government-imposed tariff structure that is unrealistic in terms of recovering operating and maintenance costs.

18. As a result, many organisations responsible for infrastructure are unable to fund basic levels of maintenance. The situation is exacerbated because of the demands for foreign exchange. Although much maintenance can be funded in local currency, items such as spare parts for equipment and certain building materials must be purchased with foreign currency. Even where cement is manufactured locally, its production usually depends heavily on the need for imported heating fuels. There are many examples of developing country maintenance organisations who, even though they can generate sufficient local revenue to cover maintenance costs, are unable to obtain foreign exchange allocations from the National Bank in order to purchase imported items.

IMPLEMENTATION

The managerial dimension

19. Availability of finance, both local and foreign, is a major constraint to carrying out maintenance of facilities. However, there is evidence to suggest that, even if more funds were available for maintenance, many organisations would still have difficulty in using these effectively. This is because maintenance is essentially a management problem of getting the right people, materials and equipment, to the right place, to carry out the right remedial or preventive work, at the right time.

20. Management is concerned with:

o   Defining activities
o   Planning
o   Allocating resources
o   Organising and motivating personnel
o   Controlling work
o   Evaluating performance
o   Feeding back results.

Included within these general management processes are the essential tasks for managing maintenance operations which are normally carried out as a sequence of steps:

o   Establish policies
o   Define standards
o   Assess needs
o   Assess options
o   Determine priorities
o   Allocate resources
o   Implement works
o   Monitor and review performance.

The process is essentially cyclic, with lessons learned from one annual cycle feeding back into the next year's planning process.

21. Unfortunately, experience has found that it is much easier to build new facilities in developing countries than to manage existing ones; similarly, procurement of maintenance equipment has usually proved to be simpler and quicker than its management and its operation. In general, planning and co-ordination have been among the most difficult areas in which to achieve an acceptable level of performance. Part of the reason for this may be that maintenance is usually the responsibility of Engineers who have rarely had any formal training in management and whose approach is dominated by a technical outlook. Few Engineers have had the opportunity for their careers to develop in an environment where a strong management culture dominates.

22. It is difficult to manage effectively without data and this has led to various attempts to introduce management information systems into developing countries. The success of this can best be summarised by a quotation from a 1981 World Bank publication.

" A great deal of emphasis has been placed in many Bank-assisted projects on the application of modern management systems for planning, programming, budgeting, scheduling, control and data collection, and it is difficult to avoid the conclusion that it has often been overdone. In some instances, the management information systems introduced by consultants have simply proved too complex to function or to be used beyond headquarters. In others, they were excessively dependent on computers that were unavailable of functioned poorly. More often, elaborate reports have continued to be produced at lower levels of the hierarchy, but there has been no effective system for checking them, and they have been little used, for lack of qualified headquarters personnel to handle them or for lack of interest. The effort seems to have been spread over too many systems, with too much detail, and with insufficient attention to the structural constraints on the ability of management to act. "

The human resource dimension

23. As has already been noted, the lack of personnel who have adequate skills and motivation is a major constraint to carrying out maintenance in an effective and timely manner.

24. Training has often been seen as a panacea for solving problems in this area, but the record of training in developing countries has been disappointing. One reason for this is that, too often, training has been seen in isolation from the broader subject of human resource development. Usually, too little attention has been paid to manpower analysis before training is planned, or to manpower management after training has been completed. Insufficient analysis of manpower resources and needs carries the risk that the wrong type of training may be given, or that people are trained for jobs that are of low priority or do not exist. Poor manpower management means that trained staff are unable to apply effectively what they have learned, and their training is wasted.

25. The availability of trained engineers, technicians and managers varies from country to country. But even where well-trained staff exist, institutional performance has tended not to improve significantly because these personnel have not been effectively utilised, developed and retained.

Where the earlier focus was on training, it is now becoming apparent that the human resource problem is more a problem of utilisation, motivation, development and retention.

26. There are a variety of factors which may cause ineffective use of manpower including personnel policies resulting from the application of Civil Service rules, conditions of employment and pay within public sector agencies, the lack of accountability and incentives, the level of the organisation's efficiency and structural complexity. Such factors can affect the general ability to attract, retain, train and motivate technical and managerial staff. These human resource problems seem to be exacerbated when considering maintenance, because of other institutional constraints inherent in the maintenance process, as discussed earlier.

27. This state of affairs contrasts to some extent to the situation within the construction industry in developing countries, where considerable attention has been paid in the past to questions of motivation and incentives. Site allowances, overtime and productivity bonuses have all been used as tools to motivate the engineering staff to perform. It is hard to find examples of similar schemes being adopted within organisations in developing countries concerned with maintenance. The result is often a demoralised work force, with apathy pervading everyone from senior management through to equipment operators and labourers. Against such a background, human resource performance, and indeed training, is always likely to be ineffective.

The technological dimension

28. There is undoubtedly a dimension to the infrastructure maintenance problem that is concerned with technology and it is this dimension that has very often been seen by Engineers as the key issue. This has resulted in the definition and preparation of projects in the past aimed at tackling these technological issues.

29. Engineers approach to technological solutions in connection with infrastructure has, as noted earlier, usually concentrated on the areas of conception, design and construction. The approach in these areas has most often been concerned with achieving a timely and low cost product, rather than with consideration of the difficulties and costs that would be associated with the resulting necessary operation and maintenance. The introduction of sophisticated high-tech designs may possibly be appropriate in the well-developed industrialised environment of the designer's own country, where labour may be expensive and technology relatively cheap. However, in many developing

countries, with a humid, tropical and dusty environment, such technology is often unmaintainable and unsustainable with the human and financial resources that are actually available.

30. The provision of equipment for maintenance purposes has often resulted in short term increases in productivity, only to be followed by longer term disrepair and the familiar equipment graveyards that are so common in developing countries. This would seem to apply whether the equipment is for carrying out the work itself, for inspection and assessment, or for laboratory testing. The maintenance of mechanical equipment in most developing countries is made much more difficult as a consequence of the multilateral and bilateral aid that has been received over the years. In the railway subsector, for example, this may result in perhaps six or more different makes of locomotive. This presents a maintenance nightmare that would probably not occur in an industrialised country where procurement would concentrate on the output of many fewer manufacturers. Similarly, in the field of water supply, the provision of pumps and distribution systems from many different countries can result in basic incompatibilities that make maintenance a much more complex operation than should be necessary.

31. The results of attempts to introduce computerised management systems have already been discussed. Unfortunately, attempts at addressing other technological issues have often met with a similar lack of success. It is difficult to avoid the conclusion that, although technological solutions are attractive to Engineers, their implementation seems invariably to founder because of underlying institutional constraints that are all pervasive.

THE WAY AHEAD

Steps to making change
32. Recognising that there is an infrastructure maintenance problem in developing countries is the first step to making progress in finding a solution. Three further steps are then needed in order to make the fundamental institutional changes necessary to increase the accountability and motivation that are necessary. These fall into the following categories:

o Obtaining commitment for change
o Isolating and understanding the problems
o Developing and implementing action plans.

IMPLEMENTATION

Approaches to carrying out these steps and considerations that should be taken into account are discussed in the following sections.

Changing attitudes
33. No improvements in maintenance performance are likely to take place unless those responsible for organisations grasp both the importance of maintenance and the necessity for the efficient use of resources. Steps are needed to make the institutional changes that are required to increase accountability and to improve maintenance organisations, by firstly obtaining commitment at the highest level. Without such commitment, it is entirely unrealistic to expect any improvements in performance to be obtained.

34. For organisations within the public sector, commitment needs to be obtained from politicians. This can be particularly challenging because maintenance timeframes are long, whereas those for politicians tend to be short. However, there are examples in developing countries where interest groups of users of facilities have come together and placed pressures on politicians for changes in policies and funding, with the result that the priority of maintenance has been increased, and improvements in performance and levels of service have been obtained. There is no reason why Engineers should not be involved in such pressure groups with a view to facilitating the development of a constituency interest in the subject.

35. In industrialised countries, attitudes to maintenance are changing as the activity is tending to move 'up-market'. The recognition that business management skills are needed for the job, plus the introduction of sometimes sophisticated computerised management information systems and high technology methods of assessment in many areas, is now often attracting the brightest and most committed of Engineers into a field that is offering a whole range of new challenges. There is hope that a similar change in attitudes may be seen in developing countries over the years to come.

Construction and maintenance
36. It is important to recognise is that there are fundamental differences between construction and maintenance as engineering activities, and this is emphasised when donor-assisted projects are undertaken for these activities. This has been discussed by Brooks et al in their paper to the Institution of Civil Engineers Proceeding, Part 1, in December 1989, and is illustrated in Table 1.

Table 1. Essential differences between aid projects for construction and maintenance

	New construction	Routine maintenance
Duration	Tend to be short term	Long term
Technology transfer	Incidental	Crucial
Local capability	Relatively independent	Very dependent
Contractor's organisation	Designed for rapid completion: independent of local organisation	Integrated with and dependent on local organisations
Donor administration	Straightforward	Complex

The consequence of these differences is that a fundamentally different approach is necessary for tackling maintenance than is required for new construction.

Developing human resources

37. Human resource development within a maintenance organisation is needed to increase staff accountability, motivation and competence, to strengthen overall manpower performance and to build a core staff of competent professionals. Changes in each of these areas will affect the other, as the performance of organisations cannot be divorced from the performance of the manpower within them. There are two main approaches to building up a competent core of managerial and technical manpower that can perform effectively:

o   Create a Personnel Unit within the maintenance organisation to strengthen its capability for manpower planning, recruitment, training needs analysis, organisation of training, management of promotion and career development schemes and administration of compensation and benefits

o   Strengthen the ability of line managers to utilise, supervise, motivate and develop their staff effectively.

IMPLEMENTATION

38. In order to follow these approaches, the Personnel Unit and line managers will need to adopt special skills and to install supporting administrative systems. In particular, management skills will need to be acquired, including those for setting objectives, allocating work, delegation and follow-up, standard setting, establishing accountability and the provision of on-the-job training, recognition and feedback to meet subordinates' needs. The personnel and line management responsibilities should be integrated into a single long-term manpower development programme. In order to implement this, maintenance organisations may need to introduce changes in hiring, promotion and termination practices to strengthen motivation, retention of talent, accountability and performance.

39. The development of human resources can take place much more effectively when the maintenance organisation can operate in an autonomous or semi-autonomous manner, and where it can hire only those people that it actually requires to do its job. It will not become overburdened financially with staff on the payroll that it does not really need. Cuts of unnecessary staff can free money for operation, supplies and equipment, and can improve the effectiveness and efficiency of the remaining staff. As funds become available to secure the equipment and supplies necessary for them to do their job, the management, motivation and retention of competent people are enhanced.

40. A semi-autonomous agency also has more flexibility to pay people at the level required to retain the talent it needs, in competition with the private sector. Even without autonomy, a maintenance organisation can still institute innovative compensation schemes, such as remuneration that is linked directly to quantities and qualities of outputs and results produced. Such a compensation system is an important tool for strengthening manpower management. Effective manpower utilisation also requires a good system of job descriptions, management by objectives, appropriate workload allocations and effective staff supervision. These are basic personnel and work management tools.

41. When strong manpower management and utilisation are in place, in-service training schemes make an indispensable contribution to staff development. In addition to qualifications and experience that staff bring to the job, they need to develop additional job-related skills and specialisations. Careful training needs analyses should be conducted to determine precisely what knowledge and skills are needed by each category of staff. Arrangements should be made for the development and delivery of suitable, applied, in-service courses targeted on the most essential

technical, professional and managerial topics. Training that is planned within the wider context of human resource development should be designed to meet clear objectives with achievement that is measurable and, wherever possible, training choices should be made on the basis of cost-benefit analyses. Training needs of organisations are frequently underestimated by a considerable amount.

Organisational change
42. Steps can sometimes be taken to increase the accountability and motivation of individuals by changing the nature of the organisation. Particularly with government-controlled maintenance organisations, this can be achieved by focusing on the factors of 'specificity' and 'competition' as they affect the organisation. Specificity is defined as the extent to which it is possible to specify for an activity the objectives to be obtained and their time frame, the methods of achieving those objectives, and the ways of controlling and rewarding achievement. Competition is defined more broadly than in traditional economics: in addition to external competition from others, competitive pressures can be exerted on an organisation by the political establishment, regulatory agencies and users of the facility, and by managerial measures that create a competitive atmosphere within the organisation.

43. In order to instigate organisational change, there needs to be a commitment to this from those responsible for the organisation at top management level, and within controlling or regulatory bodies, where these have influence. Without this commitment, no changes are likely to take place, and no improvements in maintenance are likely to happen.

44. Organisational change should not be attempted without a detailed appraisal of the maintenance organisation in order to obtain a thorough understanding of its strengths, weaknesses, efficiencies and bottlenecks. Although institutional appraisals can be carried out by the organisation's own staff, experience suggests that it is usually more effective if management reviews are carried out by external consultants who are freer to recommend the more difficult changes that would be a problem for insiders. Such appraisals can be difficult to undertake since the way an institution works may not be what is said formally, and is often obscure to the outsider. Political and cultural issues will often assume a much greater importance than in more developed countries.

IMPLEMENTATION

45. An approach to the appraisal of roads organisations has been proposed by Brooks et al, ibid and the fundamentals of this could also be applied to organisations in other sectors. Assessments need to be made of capability in the following areas.

46. Institutional capability:
o Legal powers to undertake maintenance
o A rational and functional administrative structure
o The employment and training of staff of a sufficient calibre
o Funds to undertake maintenance and for administration, salaries and expenses
o Financial control.

47. Managerial capability:
o Existence of an up-to-date inventory
o Works effectively planned, programmed and monitored
o Budget related to actual costs and ability to disburse
o Effective cost control
o Adequate plant and equipment available and effectively utilised
o Availability of materials as required.

48. Technical capability:
o Appropriate criteria for planning
o Materials test facilities
o Effective quality control of all operations
o Implemented pavement inspection and monitoring systems
o Access to research and information.

49. Results of assessments carried out by Brooks et al suggest that there is an inter-relationship between the institutional, managerial and technical capability of a maintenance organisation: sufficient capability must exist in each of the three areas before an organisation can become effective. Further investigation, however, leads to the perception that improvements at the institutional level are prerequisites to improvements in managerial and technical capability, as shown in the conceptual pyramid in Fig 1.

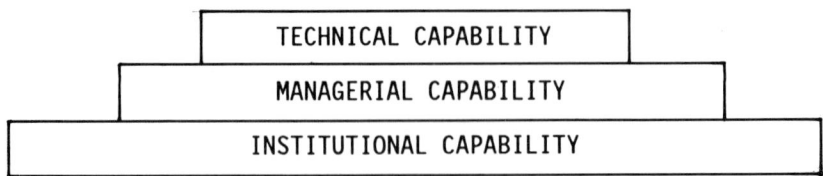

Fig. 1 Interdependence and Hierarchy of Institutional, Managerial and Technical Capabilities

50. It is notoriously more difficult to effect institutional improvements than to introduce specific managerial or technological advances. Nevertheless, unless a sufficient level of institutional capability exists, projects aimed at managerial or technological improvements are unlikely to be successful. Engineers designing maintenance projects should, therefore, recognise this hierarchy and carry out institutional appraisals to assist in targeting key areas of need. In the longer term, this will help to lay a better foundation on which to build a management culture and maintenance capability and, unless this is recognised, permanent improvements in performance are unlikely to be successful.

51. The levels of specificity and competition can be increased for many organisations by separating their planning and control functions from those for maintenance execution. The separation of these functions can be achieved in three areas:

o   Equipment management
o   Maintenance execution
o   Maintenance management.

52. Equipment can be managed through a separate Departmental plant hire scheme or can be privatised. Such an approach encourages specific accounting of costs, thus encouraging greater cost-consciousness and generating pressures for more efficient utilisation. By making financing dependent on revenues produced from hirings, strong incentives can be generated to keep plant in operation, since broken down plant provides no revenue for equipment replacement and spare parts purchase.

53. The effectiveness of maintenance can also often be enhanced by letting maintenance works on contract to public, private or parastatal organisations. Creating a separate maintenance enterprise that still enjoys a monopoly position is unlikely to provide the full advantages since, although the specificity is increased, the key issue is whether the organisation operates under a competitive or monopolistic situation, rather than whether it is publicly or privately owned.

54. Some success has also been achieved by inviting tenders for the management of maintenance in certain sectors, thus again increasing both the specificity and competition of the maintenance operation.

CONCLUSION

55. There is an increasing awareness of the problem of maintaining infrastructure in developing countries. What is needed now is a concerted effort by the countries themselves, supported by co-ordinated and appropriate actions by bilateral and multilateral donors, to build up institutions and to develop maintenance capability.

56. Engineers must recognise that, although there are technical issues to be tackled with the maintenance of infrastructure and facilities, the vast majority of problems are of an institutional or human resource nature. Failure to appreciate this will result in the continuation of the decline in the serviceability of existing facilities and of the massive economic losses that are now being witnessed.

57. It may well be that, as time goes on, the role of Engineers will increasingly become one of managing and of maintaining existing infrastructure, rather than one of designing and of building new facilities, as has been the case in the past. Engineering skills are no less relevant in this area, but it will be necessary to build on these and to add to them new skills in the case of management, human resources and institutional development. Armed with such an array of talents, perhaps Engineers will be able to occupy a place in society that has been eluding them in recent years.

16. Education and training — issues and roles

J. E. THEAKER, Director, Manpower Development Services

SYNOPSIS. Training is but one component of manpower based solutions to corporate and developmental issues. To understand how and when training can be effective is a skill which requires cognizance of cultural, environmental, economic, trading patterns, and demographic issues. How these factors relate in development terms and how best to encourage local institutional developments are the issues to address.

1. The role of training and education in developing situations is often confused or treated as a simplistic solution based formula which will solve a multitude of manpower and organisational problems. There is an every growing trend to treat training in an isolated fashion without fully realising the interrelated components which make the complete picture.

2. Ever increasing technological development, market place demands and economic factors necessitate continual assessment and readjustment of corporate strategies and business planning. The role of training in such dynamic situations is now widely recognised as an essential factor in ensuring that the work force is able to identify with the organisation during change, can understand their role within the organisation and readily adapt to learning and the practising of new skills by recurrent methods of training.

3. There are further issues to address within organisations facing development phases. These issues are concerned with economic, labour market, and demographic considerations which can effect the level of corporate or regional development possible.

4. In many development situations the prospect of individuals being exposed to too much irrelevant training is very real. The present wave of commercial training programmes, computer-aided learning and

distance learning packages often demonstrate curriculum with little adaption to cultural requirements or job related needs of individuals and organisations. It is often unfortunate to witness that 'training experts' often turn our to be 'retired' managers of industry. The pedagogical skills and understanding of training issues of such individuals are too often minimal. The "undertstanding" of relating learning back to people, labour markets, job performance, and individual requirements is often an unpractised and foreign skill.

5. To play a meaningful role within organisations it is important for managers of the training function to be aware of more than the psychology of learning, presenting sessions and using audio-visual aids. The following key attributes are essential for a training manager:

Understanding that line management often sees training as a solution to corporate or individual problems when reality demonstrates that systems, procuedures or other management issues are the real problem. So, beware of individuals who perceive training as a solution to ill-defined situations. It should be the training manager's role to help analyse corporate issues and give advice on the suitability of training.

Understanding corporate aims and aspirations and how training can best be used to achieve corporate goals. This is the true performance indicator of organisations and training should be evaluated in a symbiotic manner. It is important to recognise that individuals should aspire to achieve self-development in the broadest sense. However, this valuable and wider role of education should not be confused with the more mercenary necessity to ensure individuals are able to behave in a corporate manner and recognise their role within an organisation so that they can perform with the maximum of skill and reliability.

Understanding parallel issues of the manpower function and how this can affect training design and wider manpower issues - for example, detailed job specifications, selection procedures, performance monitoring, ensuring correct people are in the correct jobs, wage structures, career progression, succession planning, labour market trends and the role of external educational and training institutes.

5. The development of imaginative and flexible plans utilising the best training resources and methods to achieve agreed targets of performance is also essential. Experience has shown that a careful assessment of:

- corporate aspiration
- organisational and individual training needs
- related manpower issues

is necessary before training can be offered as a solution to organisational problems or specific skills development.

6. In many development situations training issues are often centred on changing of attitudes to accommodate new trends in work or economics - these attitudinal changes require a more sophisticated and longer term solution than pure skills based training. The risks associated with training being effective are also greater when dealing with attitudinal problems.

7. In financial and development terms, training managers have to accept that their role is central to management. Top management also have to recognise the valuable role training managers can provide in helping achieve corporate targets.

8. With specific reference to the theme of the conference I would advocate training in developing countries is best inspired by local and regional needs, and as such the initial demands and design should come from a local focus. This is especially so in many African States where real difficulties have been faced in sustaining often ambitious projects.

9. One way forward is to help strategic thinking nationals to be involved in bringing forward ideas and suggestions which encompass issues and needs as they perceive them. This could then present a focus for local institutional development where, in conjunction with partners from other nations (both developing and developed), training programmes can be developed around the needs and considerations of the local labour markets, industry and community needs and considerations.

10. The recently announced African Capacity Building Initiative which aims to improve policy analysis and management of development projects by having its own professional policy analysts, managers and institutions for training and advice is one crucial move to help in this process.

Discussion

PROFESSOR M. W. THRING, Fellowship of Engineering
There are two ways of looking to the future: one can extrapolate present trends or look at the conditions for a stable world where everyone has a good quality of life. The Industrial Revolution was based largely on cheap fuel and the exploitation of colonies as sources of raw materials. I query the belief of the Author of Paper 9 in export crops. I believe that as fuels get more expensive villages will export the necessary food to the local town and grow their own. I believe that in equilibrium engineering there will be no private cars in towns and probably no cars at all. I would like to ask the Author of Paper 12 about the problem of people migrating into slums. Would electric light, television and jobs in the village reduce this?

P. C. BARLOW, Binnie & Partners
I welcome the change in ODA policy to support long-term sustainable development projects. I assume that this policy must include the funding of maintenance programmes as part of the main project, which has not been so in the past.
Paper 11 refers to a Swedish programme in Tanzania and Kenya which failed drastically due to poor maintenance. Was this a result of lack of commitment by the donor for the training of local staff and maintenance? Can this problem be the root cause of the failure of other schemes?
How can engineers strive to change the present policies of donor agencies and convince them that training and maintenance are a necessity if a project has any chance of succeeding, so that recipient countries are not burdened with further expenditure?

A. L. L. REDA, Imperial College of Science, Technology and Medicine
I should like to suggest having a conference on appropriate survival methods for development: development in a broader view (i.e. beyond just survival), so that the First World is not only keeping markets 'just surviving' as a means of keeping markets for their manufactured goods, but also helping them to become self-supporting.

IMPLEMENTATION

DR G. K. BAMBRAH, Rofe, Kennard & Lapworth (East Africa)
On the question of aid agencies becoming increasingly interested in financial aspects as opposed to economic considerations in project appraisal, it would appear that this is not in keeping with the general trends in the history of the appraisal process. These trends show that this process has evolved from no formal accounting at all to cost-benefit analyses, environmental impact assessment and other integrated multi-disciplinary methods. Would the Author of Paper 12 comment on why the opposite trends are being adopted by the aid agencies?

J. E. GOULD, International Rainwater Catchment Systems Association
The emphasis of Paper 10 on energy efficiency is praiseworthy, but should not the potential importance of reusing and recycling materials and green economics, including the introduction of a carbon tax (e.g. a 1-2% per annum tax on all fossil fuels increasing steadily on a rising scale), have also been given specific consideration?

DR R. E. SOWDEN, The British Council
It has been said that a holistic approach to appropriate development is necessary. What forms of training, in the view of the Authors, are most appropriate for those staff in developing countries whose task it is to appraise critically the project proposals of consultants from the more developed countries?

A. STEYN, Development Bank of Southern Africa
Every aspect in a development proposal should be evaluated in terms of the development objective of the project, which is hopefully based on the needs of the area concerned. For example, 99% of the time the development need is not a road as such, but an asset or opportunity which will stimulate economic activities or provide access to activities. Therefore, the proposal should not be evaluated in terms of the technical aspects of the road, but in terms of the real development needs.

It can be concluded that overseas staff's training should be based on the problems of developing countries, how to identify the needs of developing areas, the identification of constraints which inhibit economic development, and solutions which will stimulate economic development.

A. J. COLEMAN, Consultant
It is important that the political dimension should not be underestimated, particularly with regard to the maintenance of infrastructure.

Good maintenance (i.e. the preservation of an asset in its original state) does not win votes, and rarely does it bring much kudos to the maintenance organization. Bad maintenance, however, loses votes. Further, raising the standard of maintenance also raises public expectations. As a result of maintenance managers and their staff can expect constant criticism from both politicians and the public, however satisfactory their performance. Such criticism should be regarded as an occupational hazard, which may be offset by personal satisfaction if improved standards of maintenance can be achieved.

However, there are limits. Since local government reorganization in the UK in 1974, and earlier in Greater London, the provision of day to day services has been subject to increasing political interference. Many staff responsible for those services have experienced public criticism, ridicule and vilification. It is little wonder that as opportunity has arisen, appreciable numbers have chosen to leave the public service.

For equivalent staff in developing countries the situation is usually far worse. The constraints under which they operate are well documented in the Papers. In addition many are subjected to threats of violence against themselves and their families if they fail to divert resources as requested. Sadly it is often their political masters who exert the most pressure in this respect. Maintenance organizations with at least some operational capability may be rendered virtually ineffective as a result of this outside interference.

What can be done to alleviate this situation? First, all management staff must go into the field regularly to familiarize themselves with the assets they maintain and to monitor on-going field operations. These may be different from what has been programmed or what they are told by others. Second, the management process must allow for regular and formal discussion of operational and policy issues by management and supervising staff at all levels. Staff who are left to operate in a vacuum are those most prone to yield to outside influences. Managers must also build up working relationships with politicians to promote a greater awareness of management and operational issues in the political mind.

H. GUNSTON, Institute of Hydrology
In the context of rural transport what part do the Authors feel that rail systems should be playing in national transport programmes?

A. T. LEHOBO, Ministry of Works, Lesotho
It is a fact that at this stage it is no longer necessary to make a case for labour-based methods. In Lesotho, the technology has been applied satisfactorily since 1977. Initially there were many constraints which included institutionalization of these methods and their limited support on the part of the government of Lesotho and the donor community.

Today the government is fully committed to support labour-based technology. The Labour Construction Unit - a

IMPLEMENTATION

branch of the Ministry of Works - has the full status of a government department and is charged with upgrading and maintaining a rural road network of approximately 2500 km using labour-based construction methods. A 20 year development programme has been devised; it started with a three-year consolidation period from January 1990.

The most important experiences of Lesotho in the construction of rural roads using these methods are as follows.

(a) One must achieve the right mix of labour and equipment for economic reasons, e.g. for haulage of materials over a distance of 200 m, tipper trucks are used instead of wheelbarrows, and to achieve satisfactory compaction, vibrating pedestrian rollers are used instead of handrammers.

(b) One must make optimum use of locally available construction materials such as stones and river sand for the construction of cross-drainage structures.

(c) One must appreciate the need to involve private contractors in the implementation of a rural road programme. Unless the private sector gets involved the technology will be applied only on a limited scale. Already with its present capability of handling 3000 labourers on the current maintainable road network of 500 out of 2500 km, the Labour Construction Unit is experiencing serious administrative problems in the handling of huge sums of cash for pay-rolls and the efficient control of its pool of plant and vehicles. For the individual contractor these problems should be small. The government should invest in manpower supervisory capacity for contractors. It is therefore important and urgent to introduce labour-based techniques into the curriculae of faculties of engineering and technical schools to enable engineers and technicians to appreciate and use the technology fully.

MS M. HERATY, Paper 12

In reply to Dr Bambrah, I am not sure that the aid agencies are adopted opposite trends so much as imposing an additional necessary condition: that of financial viability, which often means affordability. Projects still need to have an appropriate rate of return and satisfy the other criteria implicit in the question. However, the aid agencies are trying to get away from the situation of a decade or longer ago when almost any economically feasible project was likely to be granted a loan, and yet many Third World governments and parastatals could not service their debts. Many projects are now expected to raise revenue internally to cover the costs of the loans. In effect, the aid agencies are becoming just like any other commercial bank, although often with lower interest rates.

On Dr Sowden's point, there is a great need for training;

DISCUSSION

certainly, in transport there is remarkably little formal training available in all areas of project preparation and appraisal, as well as in the tasks of drawing up terms of reference and assessing proposals. This is very evident to those working as consultants. Training needs to be based on relevant real-life case studies and practical experience will also be desirable, if not essential. Courses in any field of development would have a common basis of theory but would be more comprehensible if they were based on broad disciplines (e.g. highways or water supply) or, at least, type of project (e.g. infrastructure or planning). They would probably best be organized on a regional basis (e.g. one every year or six months per discipline for East Africa) and run in a centre in the region.

Mr Gunston asked about rail systems. They are expensive to build but if they are already in place they may be maintained fairly economically. The biggest cost can be the replacement of the traction units and stock. Some remarkable work has been done in Africa on refurbishing old steam locomotives. New lines have to follow corridors of heavy demand, either from growing urban populations or from new industrial or port developments. For rural transport the demand on any corridor is unlikely to justify the building of new lines, and thus one is left with making the best use of whatever railways are already in place; these were often built some time ago by colonizing powers and may serve corridors or areas which are no longer active. The answer therefore hinges critically on how the present-day patterns of demand are served by existing track. In countries with cheap hydro power, the balance of the equation may be different, and this will certainly vary with the fluctuating price of oil.

R. ROBINSON, Paper 15
In reply to Mr Barlow, many donors, including the ODA, already fund maintenance programmes. However, maintenance projects are fundamentally different from those for new construction, as indicated in Table 1 of my Paper. The Paper also notes that these differences mean that the formulation of maintenance projects needs to recognize that the lack of maintenance capability in an organization should be tackled in a hierarchical manner: unless the institutional setting is appropriate, there is little point in mounting projects to address managerial weaknesses; unless there is sufficient managerial capability, projects addressing technical issues stand little chance of success. Unfortunately, most maintenance projects in the past have addressed technical problems, and apparently recognized the lack of institutional or managerial capability necessary to provide the foundation for technical success. Until those formulating projects recognize the existence of this hierarchy and address fundamental issues first, I believe that maintenance projects will continue to founder. The Paper also discusses my belief

IMPLEMENTATION

that training is often seen as a panacea for improving performance but, unless it is considered within the wider context of human resource development, and unless this is considered within the hierarchical approach discussed, training will have little impact on the overall performance and success of projects in developing countries.

In response to Dr Sowden, project proposals can only reflect the quality of the terms of reference to which they are responding. Many terms of reference appear to be badly conceived, poorly structured and unrealistic in their requirements. Training in writing terms of reference would help to ensure that project requirements in terms of outputs and deliverables were much more clearly defined, and that project activities needed to produce these outputs were understood more fully. Such an approach would lead more directly to the formulation of evaluation criteria against which project proposals could be assessed in a quantitative manner. I therefore believe that much greater benefit would result from training in the preparation of terms of reference than from training in appraisal methods for project proposals.

I agree with all the points made by Mr Coleman, which I believe complement and reinforce the issues discussed in my Paper.

J. E. THEAKER, Paper 16

Individuals from developing countries require the technical skills and experience which match the project proposal under consideration. They also need to appreciate the role of consultants and mechanisms of project work.

It is feasible to assume that some projects will fit into this category, and in such cases a participative workshop style of course for 10-15 individuals, held preferably in the country or inter-regional, would be a suitable option.

However, there are cases where for technological reasons external assistance in evaluation would be desirable, e.g. a proposal involving complex design considerations for a plant or services unfamiliar in the country concerned. In such events training local staff to make value judgements would not be an effective solution; training can rarely be used to supplement understanding built up from a base of research, design and past experience. It should fall on the executing funding agency to recommend in the pre-project feasibility study when specialist expertise is needed to work with local evaluation teams. The executive authority of the external inputs should depend on the strategic or critical nature of the issue concerned.

Fossil fuel energy and the survival of mankind

P. GARRATT, Knight Piesold and Partners

SYNOPSIS: The adverse environmental effects of fossil fuel combustion products have been widely publicised. The paper makes broad comparisons between industrialised nations and industrialising nations (for example, as between the U.K. and China) to illustrate the potential threat to the global environment posed by fossil fuel energy generation in developing countries. Anticipation of the problems and a bold approach to their amelioration are advocated. In conclusion the role of the engineer is highlighted in alerting politicians to the benefits of renewable energy and the long term hazards associated with reliance on fossil fuels.

INTRODUCTION:
1.   The recent dramatic upsurge of interest in the earth's atmosphere, sparked by the discovery of "holes" in the ozone layer, has spawned a new vocabulary. The popular press dwells on acid rain, the greenhouse effect and global warming, with the interest and concern of the UK public in these latter issues heightened substantially by the recent sequence of mild winters and hot summers. In the technical press the terminology is no less colourful, SOX gases (oxides of sulphur) abound but no one seems over-impressed with FGD (flue gas desulphurisation) as a means of removing them. NOX gases (oxides of nitrogen) are also a problem and now a solution to our environmental problems is sought through BATNEEC (Best Available Technology Not Entailing Excessive Cost).
2.   The fashionable preoccupation with European issues tends to obscure the broader picture, the greater global factors which will predominate in determining whether or not we will succeed in preserving the essential wrapping to the planet upon which our environment, climate, health and very existence ultimately depend.
3.   This paper focusses on one of these major issues, namely the burning of fossil fuels to generate electricity in the Third World.
4..   The related problems require for their solution a radical approach to energy policy in developing countries, an approach which embodies the key themes of this conference: Appropriate Development and the Contribution of Technology.

THE ATMOSPHERE AND MAN'S INTERVENTION
5.   Firstly it is important to view the problem in context: our concern is for a rather fragile mantle of gases only 50 km thick and comprising the troposphere and stratosphere. Relative to a typical table globe about 400mm in diameter the atmosphere, to scale, would be only 1.6mm thick. Almost all of this layer, some 99.95%, is made up of nitrogen and oxygen. The impact of man's activities is principally on the remaining 0.05% of which about half is carbon dioxide, the dominant greenhouse gas.
6.   As further brushstrokes in painting the background we should note that long before man appeared on earth carbon dioxide concentrations were similar to those of today and that natural phenomena, in particular volcanic eruptions, can significantly affect man's environment regardless of his own intervention.

7. The emissions from Krakatoa are considered to have decreased solar radiation arriving at the earth's surface by some 10 to 20% causing cold and wet conditions for several years. Furthermore the chlorine compounds emitted by the Krakatoa eruption may have caused a depletion of up to 30% in the ozone layer. This represents twice the depletion which would be expected to occur by the year 2010 if the release of chlorofluorocarbons (CFCs) continued at the present level.

8. Our attention is attracted to the more dramatic manifestations of the forces of nature. Longer term but more significant natural climatic changes are brought about by the earth's orbital eccentricity and it's axial tilt. Ice ages and warm periods clearly identified over geological time are attributed to such influences and sunspot and solar magnetic cycles are also cited as causes of substantial climatic effects, albeit less well defined.

9. Against this backdrop of awesome natural forces and the climatic changes to which they give rise, why should we be concerned about the relatively small changes in atmospheric composition wrought by man over the time period, insignificant in geological terms, since the industrial revolution?

10. The reasons are as follows:

i) The relatively short term atmospheric changes being measured today are almost entirely caused by man's activities.

ii) The measured changes are not cyclical or temporary, as in the case of the predominant natural influences, but represent the beginning of an insidious and accelerating process of deterioration unless there is a dramatic change in these activities.

11. Geographers and climatologists are divided as to the changes which man's intervention will cause and the timescale over which they will manifest themselves. In our preoccupation with these divisions of opinion we tend to overlook the remarkable consensus that global warming is definitely with us. It is also beyond doubt that other deleterious effects to health and the environment caused by man's activities, such as acid rain and photo-chemical smog, are already serious problems in many parts of the world.

ENERGY IN THE THIRD WORLD:

12. Man has extraordinary endurance to live in all climates, everywhere consuming carbonaceous resources for cooking, heating, lighting and transport. These resources are drawn mainly from timber in the less developed parts of the world and increasingly from fossil fuels, coal and oil, as the process of development advances. The former source can be regarded as renewable if properly managed, but the latter two cannot.

13. The ingenuity of man is such that he has in general found sufficient food and fuel not only to survive, but over the centuries, and particularly in the past few decades, to substantially extend his life span and reduce infant mortality. The resulting population growth in developing countries is coupled with ever more rapid growth in the demand for electrical energy as their citizens strive for a "quality of life" comparable with that already achieved in Europe and elsewhere in the developed world.

14. The simplest and cheapest means of meeting this demand growth is invariably through the burning of fossil fuels, even where, as in many developing countries, there is substantial hydro-electric potential. The current trend for smaller communities is to use diesel driven plant which in relatively small unit sizes can be installed for $600 to $800 per kw with the powerhouse located conveniently close to the load centre. The capital cost of hydro development typically would be at least four times higher, often with substantial transmission line costs to be added. Similar considerations apply to coal and oil fired power stations to serve larger communities and heavy industry.

15. Third World politicians are obliged to meet the aspirations of rapidly growing populations, usually with severely limited financial resources and often against a background of crippling debt. It is hardly surprising under these circumstances that fossil fuels will be the favoured energy source, with global environmental considerations overwhelmed by the national or local political issues of the day.

THE POTENTIAL THREAT

16. The implications of Third World energy policies driven by short term political considerations may be examined by comparing the potential generating capacity of rapidly developing regions with that of developed and fully industrialised parts of the world.

17. China has been selected for such a comparison for two reasons. Firstly, the size and population of this country are such that her own contributions to global fossil fuel emissions is potentially very large and secondly, her energy resources are well documented.

18. Even before the large scale combustion of fossil fuels for the generation of electricity, coal was long established as a fuel for domestic heating and cooking and by the mid-1980's air pollution in and around Beijing (measured as suspended particulate solids) had already reached more than four times the UN recommended limit.

19. The energy resources available within China are enormous. Theoretical hydro-power potential is estimated at 680,000 MW of which some 55% or 370,000 MW is considered to be exploitable (as against a total thermal, nuclear and hydro generating capacity in the UK of some 70,000 MW in 1987).

20. Fossil fuel reserves are plentiful and planning by the Chinese energy authorities for the period 1980 to 2000 has been based on an increase of 60,000 MW in hydro capacity and 120,000 MW in thermal capacity.

21. Since the pollution problems arising from the UK power industry are well reported, it is useful to compare the predicted position in China at the turn of the century with the current position for the UK:

	Year	Installed Capacity (GW)	Population (Million)
U.K.	1987	70	51
China	2000	240	1200

22. It will be seen that China, already apparently set upon a course of modernisation and industrialisation, has a great deal of leeway to make up if the past in Europe can be taken as any kind of yardstick as to the ultimate position in terms of energy consumption per head of population.

23. It is acknowledged that the quest for improved energy efficiency, cultural differences, the changing pattern of industrial development and other factors call into question the validity of this yardstick but we are seeking no more than a broad indicator as to the scale of the problem which has to be faced.

24. If China achieves a level of development which turns out to be as demanding as our own in terms of energy consumption, we could be confronted in the 21st Century by a scenario under which installed capacity will be at least 1600 GW with perhaps 1200 GW derived from fossil fuels.

25. According to UN estimates, some 4,000 million people currently live in the "Third World". The increasing energy demands of an industrialised society are dramatically illustrated by the growth in per capita energy consumption in the UK over the past 70 years:

Year	Energy per Capita (kwh)
1920	90
1940	520
1950	980
1960	2100
1970	3560
1980	3990
1988/89	4603

26. Even without allowance for the rapid population growth predicted in developing countries, a crude extrapolation from the UK figures suggests that the total generating capacity of countries currently at an early stage of industrialisation could substantially exceed 5000 GW by the time this process is complete (assuming adequate available fuel reserves).

27. This amounts to more than ten times the current total generating capacity of the European Community.
28. Given the concern voiced by environmentalists today about the level of harmful emissions from European fossil fuel combustion, it is clear that if the developing countries rely substantially on fossil fuels to meet their future energy needs we will face global environmental damage on a massive scale.

CONCLUSIONS:
29. The simplistic approach adopted above to illustrate the potential scale of the problem overlooks many complex political, socio-economic and demographic effects which will no doubt influence actual future trends in Third World energy production. However, it is clear that a radical approach is required, involving the cooperation of politicians, engineers, economists and environmental scientists in a determined international initiative.
30. It is concluded that this initiative should be taken up as a matter of urgency by the international engineering community through the following key actions:
1. Using the lessons learned from past experience, encourage international cooperation at the political and technical levels to face the global environmental challenge.
2. Encourage energy conservation and the use of environmentally acceptable sources with particular emphasis on the large untapped resources of hydro and tidal power.
3. Urge the international community to take a long term view of energy economics, recognising the future costs associated with environmental damage caused by fossil fuel combustion.
4. Press forward with the development of cost-effective technology for the treatment of flue gases.
5. Keep the nuclear option under review.
6. Continue and intensify research into new energy sources.
31. The greatest benefits in the short term probably can be achieved through providing financial and technical assistance to developing countries for the exploitation of hydro-electric resources in preference to fossil fuels.
32. The development of large hydro power projects has been heavily constrained in recent years by local environmental issues. Whilst these are important in themselves they must be weighed against the contribution to global environmental damage which will occur if the fossil fuel option is pursued.
33. Close cooperation is necessary between neighbouring states at the political level if the potential benefits of large hydro projects as regional energy resources are to be fully realised.
34. Engineers must assume the responsibility for ensuring that the politicians fully recognise these benefits and that they are made aware of the grave long term consequences of excessive reliance on fossil fuel energy.

ACKNOWLEDGEMENTS:
35. The provision of source material for this paper by Dr R.J. Laburn, Dr G.F.K.Herrmann and Mr D.D.A. Piesold, CBE is gratefully acknowledged.
U.K. energy consumption data are based on the Handbook of Electricity Supply Statistics (Electricity Council, 1990).

Low-wattage electric cookers - making the most of micro-hydro power

L. J. MacKAY, United Mission to Nepal

SYNOPSIS A low-wattage electric cooker has been designed by the United Mission to Nepal, with assistance from the Intermediate Technology Development Group, in order that electricity can be used economically for cooking in rural areas of Nepal. The cooker is being manufactured in Nepal, and may be operated continuously at a low power to store heat in water, which is later used for cooking food. Technical tests of the cooker show that it is energy efficient. Trials have demonstrated that villagers can adapt their cooking practices, and there is a high level of satisfaction among users.

ENERGY IN NEPAL

1. Nepal is among the 10 poorest countries in the world. The majority of the population are subsistence farmers, and besides increasing problems of food supply, there is also an energy crisis. This is because the forests are being felled at an increasing rate, largely to provide cooking fuel.

2. The largest natural resource of Nepal is hydro-power: the potential is some 83,000 MW, out of which less than 300 MW is currently tapped. The last ten years has seen a marked growth in the supply of electric power to the rural areas of Nepal. Much of this development has been through extensions to the national grid; however there are also a growing number of isolated micro-hydro plants. The United Mission to Nepal (UMN), an international Christian Mission, has played a leading role in both spheres. Up to the end of 1989 31 micro-hydro electricity generation plants, in the size range 1.5 to 50 kW, have been installed. The UMN is also involved in grid-connected rural electrification; the Andhikhola project involves the construction of a 5 MW hydro-electric plant, and rural electrification in the area round it. A key feature of both types of installation is the use of low-wattage cookers, in order to reduce the demand for firewood.

NORMAL ELECTRIC COOKERS

3. Electric cooking is widely used throughout the world. However, normal electric cookers are unsuitable for domestic use in Nepal, particularly with isolated micro-hydro plants. This is because of their pattern of energy use: during the time when a meal is being cooked, a high power is used (typically

1 - 2 kW); for the rest of the time (18 hours per day), no power is consumed.

4. In a typical Nepali village, with say 50 houses, this electric cooking would require a power installation with a capacity of 50 kW if every household were to cook with a single 1 kW electric ring. The greater the installed capacity, the higher will be the capital costs of the generation equipment and distribution system. The interest on this capital expenditure is the major cost of running a hydro-electric plant. If the amount of energy sold is low compared to the maximum possible output (i.e. the load factor is low), then unit energy costs will be high. Conversely, with a high load factor the unit costs will be reduced. With normal electric cookers the load factor will be poor (of the order of 25%): thus the cost of electric energy will be so high as to make electric cooking uneconomic.

THE NORWEGIAN EXPERIENCE

5. Norway is a country which faced the same problem in the early years of this century. In order to encourage the efficient use of electric energy from isolated hydro-electric schemes, a maximum demand tariff was introduced: the charges to consumers were based on a subscribed level of power; thermal cut-outs were installed in consumers' houses, in place of a kWh meter: these were adjusted to the consumer's subscribed power, and disconnected the supply if this subscribed power was exceeded. This meant that the unit cost of energy was not fixed, but depended on each consumer's load factor. They were thus encouraged to use their subscribed power for as long as possible, as it made no difference to their charges whether they used it for 1 hour or 24 hours per day.

6. This tariff structure prompted the development of electric cookers which would minimise the cost of electric cooking, by operating at a low power. These were cast iron storage cookers: a relatively low-wattage element was used to heat a cast iron block. This was insulated to reduce heat loss. The cooker was permanently connected to the electric supply to heat the block, except in the evenings when lights were used. For cooking, pans were placed on the cast iron block, and could then draw heat at a fast rate, reducing the temperature of the block. Many of these cookers were used in the early years of this century.

A NEPALI SOLUTION

7. This example prompted the search for a similar solution to the cooking needs of Nepal. It was soon realised that the Norwegian cookers would be too expensive for Nepal because of the amount of cast iron needed: also the weight would make transport to remote villages difficult. However, since most cooking involves boiling (of rice or lentils) the same principle could be used with water as the storage medium: water could be preheated, and used for cooking.

8. The maximum power of the cooker was set at 250 W; this figure was chosen on the understanding that wealthier households could be expected to subscribe to that level of power for lighting. In order for this power level to be practicable, it was important that the cooker should be energy-efficient.

9. The solution which has been adopted takes the form of a double walled aluminium container, with a 200 W element attached to the inner wall. This has a much higher heat transfer efficiency than radiant cookers. Loss of heat is reduced by the air between the walls. The design is thus very energy-efficient. The container is made out of 2 different sized locally available cooking pans which are crimped together. They are sold in sets of three, with capacities of 2, 4 and 8 litres respectively. Between meal times energy is stored by heating water in the largest pan: this preheated water is then used for cooking the main staples of rice and lentils. At any time only one of the pans is connected to the supply, while a thermostat prevents it overheating. This is set at 120°C, except for the 8 litre pan: this pan is used for heating water overnight, so the thermostat is set at 80°C, to prevent water boiling away. The construction of the cookers is illustrated in Fig. 1. This cooker is now being manufactured by a Nepali entrepreneur.

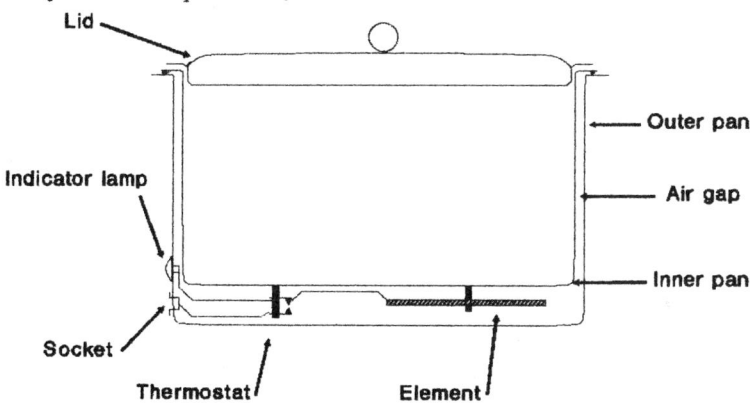

Fig. 1. Construction of low-wattage cookers

USE OF THE COOKERS

10. With the use of these cookers, electric energy may be used effectively throughout the day; they are being introduced in conjunction with maximum demand tariffs, similar to those used earlier in Norway. These ensure that there will be no extra running costs for consumers who require at least 250 W for lighting.

11. A number of tests have been carried out on the performance of the cookers. In these tests they have been compared with locally available 1 kW radiant cooking rings, which are widely available and very inexpensive. Although they use a much lower power than radiant cookers, the times taken to cook

rice with the low-wattage cookers are comparable with those of the radiant cookers. One of the reasons is because the largest energy input, heating the water, is spread over a longer time.

12. If higher power elements are used (300 W, 450 W and 600 W for the 2, 4 and 8 litre pans respectively), the cooking times starting with cold water are similar to or better than those of the radiant cookers; however the energy consumption is only 30%. This is because of the much more efficient thermal transfer. Such cookers are therefore suitable for urban use.

13. Tests have also been made of their insulation efficiency: it has been found that rice may be kept warm for 2 hours, which is an advantage when cooking is often done several hours before the meal time.

14. As well as technical performance, the social acceptability of the cookers is a key factor. Because of their design a number of changes to traditional cooking methodologies are needed if they are to be successfully introduced into rural Nepali communities. These are:
- the cookers must be closed during cooking, otherwise too much heat will be lost: this is in contrast with traditional practices in which food is cooked uncovered.
- rice and lentils must be cooked in a measured amount of preheated water, rather than cold.
- different foods must be cooked sequentially, rather than at the same time, since only one pan can be connected to the supply (with a maximum demand tariff).

15. Training villagers in the proper use of the cookers is being done by motivators, who are able to demonstrate how to adapt traditional cooking practices. Also, when a cooker has been broken, one of the motivators returns it to the consumer after repair, and explains again how to use it properly. There is little doubt that the motivators are essential to the successful introduction of these cookers.

FUTURE POTENTIAL

16. Up to the present time these cookers have been introduced on a trial basis in one rural electrification project area. About 50 families have used them, and this experience has indicated that they will find wide acceptance with those villagers for whom obtaining cooking fuel is a problem. Indeed there is a strong demand from many villagers who have not yet had the cookers. They are also being used in a number of isolated micro-hydro installations. When the manufacturing and marketing is well established, there is wide potential for their use in other areas of Nepal.

17. Cookers with higher power elements are expected to find a market in urban situations, and in lodges on tourist trekking routes. This is because of their lower running costs than other means of electric cooking.

Fossil fuels, air pollution and sustainable development issues and priorities

P. J. G. PEARSON, University of Surrey

SYNOPSIS. The paper discusses Third World energy-environment issues and priorities in relation to fossil fuels, electricity and air pollution, and examines them in the context of nationally and internationally sustainable development.

1. Air pollution and its consequences have the potential significantly to damage the capacity of people in Third World countries (TWCs) to maintain and improve the quality of their lives. If TWCs are to develop, their energy use and pollutant emissions will increase - particularly the use of fossil fuels and pollutants such as CO, CO_2, N_{ox}, SO_2 and hydrocarbons. Moreover, apart from their domestic problems, TWCs will also play an increasing part in contributing to, and perhaps cooperating in the resolution of, international environmental issues - global problems like the enhanced greenhouse effect and damage to the ozone layer, and transnational problems like acid rain.

2. The scale of fossil-fuel related air pollution emissions is expected to grow substantially in TWCs. Although it is as yet a relatively small proportion of global consumption, TWC commercial energy (CE) consumption has been growing much more rapidly than in industrialised countries and this trend is expected to continue.[1] For example, the Inter-Governmental Panel on Climate Change (IPCC) 'business-as-usual' scenario is said to envisage the following increases in CE consumption over the next 35 years: Africa, 124%; Latin America, 145%; India, 273%; China 158%; with OECD and Central Europe at between 45% and 90%, and with carbon emissions more than doubling (although it must be said that these figures have been questioned because of the enormous capital funding requirements implied).[2]

3. The explanation for rapid increases in energy consumption lies in the fact that TWCs tend to have relatively high rates of growth of both population and domestic product, and many are experiencing processes of urbanisation and industrialisation. Furthermore, while existing consumers of CE wish to use more as output and incomes rise, this demand is augmented by potential users who will make the transition away from dependence on traditional energy (TE) sources - e.g. biomass fuels like woodfuel, charcoal and agricultural residues - when they have the opportunity and resources to do so. In Asia, for example, the relations between GDP and CE, on the one hand, and the size of the biomass fuel share on the other suggest that CE demand will go on growing very quickly [3]. Newly industrialising countries (NICs) like Taiwan and South Korea offer striking illustrations of past growth: e.g., in less than 20 years (1961-80) Korea transited from nearly 60% dependence on woodfuel (and serious deforestation problems) to 90% dependence on CE, mostly oil and coal; and in the same period total energy supplies grew at an average rate of more than 8% per year. Moreover, growth will not be confined to the NICs. If structural change associated with development means that 'energy intensities' (CE/real GDP ratios) continue to

increase in many TWCs, CE consumption will be dragged up even faster as output grows. This contrasts with the experience of industrialised countries after the first two oil shocks, when energy intensities fell.

4.   There is considerable switching between TE and CE both in the short and long term. For example, households substitute from TE towards CE where the fuels/appliances meet their requirements and where they can afford both capital and running costs - and they switch back if relative prices change, their incomes fall, or if CE supplies become seriously unreliable. There are also longer-term transitions to CE in agriculture, manufacturing, services and transport. In many countries the transport sector is growing particularly quickly and is responsible, directly or indirectly for a large proportion of fossil fuel consumption.

5.   Electricity demand in particular is expected to continue to rise very rapidly in many parts of the Third World.[4] Moreover, air pollution is not only associated directly with electricity generation but also indirectly with electricity-consuming appliances like refrigerators and air conditioners, which use CFCs, and for which demand rises rapidly with income. The average annual rate of growth of electricity generation for 1971-86 has been estimated to be 8.7% for TWCs but only 3.5% for OECD countries, while the share of TWCs in world electricity generation rose from 9.9% to 18% over the same period. Moreover, the share of TWCs in incremental generation is nearly 45% and increasing - in the near future the international power plant market may be mainly a Third World market.[5]

6.   When environmental issues originally attracted attention in the 1970s, it was in particular Third World representatives who argued that they embraced much more than problems of wildlife conservation and loss of green-and-pleasantness: poverty and its attributes - bad health and housing conditions, defective water supply and sanitation, damaged soils, polluted air, etc. - are crucial aspects of the quality of a person's environment. The poor, with their limited stocks of human and physical capital, are especially vulnerable to environmental degradation. Concern with the impacts of environmental degradation has focused attention on how economic development paths can be made compatible with the pursuit of environmental quality and hence with 'sustainable development'. Recent work in this area has emphasised how present choices about pollution can have major impacts on the stock of wealth, including environmental assets, that will be available to future generations to help them meet their needs.

7.   When we analyse the issues of energy and environment in the context of TWCs, a number of specific questions arise. A first question is:

   (1)   How are the energy-environment problems of TWCs different from those of the developed countries?

Any attempt to answer this would, of course, need to consider the economic, demographic and social differences between TWCs and developed countries, including: the dualistic nature of TWC economies; their rapidly-growing, increasingly urbanising populations; their low incomes, levels of industrialisation and mechanisation; their ageing stocks of often poorly-maintained, energy inefficient equipment; their limited ability to afford imported energy and energy-producing and consuming technology; and in particular the significant role played in TWCs by TE. Furthermore, to assess actual and potential air pollution problems and the benefits and costs of controlling them requires a demanding range of sound scientific and economic data, much of which is not available in TWCs.

8.   The next two questions are interrelated:

   (2)   Should we expect the environmental policy targets of TWCs be the same as those of developed countries?

   (3)   Should we expect the same mix of policy instruments to achieve environmental policy targets?

Firstly, given the striking heterogeneity of TWCs, we should not expect either the targets or the mix of policy instruments to be the same between different TWCs, let alone between TWCs and developed countries. Secondly, the differences between both the socio-economic and energy situations of the TWCs and the developed countries would lead us to expect some differences in environmental quality targets. The question has long been posed as to whether environmental quality should be the aim only of richer countries. Put another way, if environmental quality is a luxury commodity then poorer countries should postpone their 'consumption' of it. However, this argument not only assumes that all consumption of environmental services is dispensable, it also ignores the impact of environmental degradation on productive capacities. Environmental quality matters to people in TWCs not only in their roles as consumers (e.g. through the experience of bad health or amenity losses) but also in their roles as producers (e.g. through inability to work because of impaired health, or reduced farm or fishery output). If people have few assets, their ability to use and have continued access to well-maintained natural resources (land, water, air, forests, and so on) may be necessary for their survival. Thus whether particular environmental quality targets should have high priority is partly an empirical question, depending both on the nature of the problems experienced and on which sections of the population are experiencing them - both now and in the future. Consequently, in the interests of sustainable development some types of environmental control are likely to be postponable luxuries for TWCs, while others will be necessities.

9. On the mix of policy instruments, even if the quality targets were the same, we would not expect different countries necessarily to use the same mix of instruments to achieve them. For example there are differences in political and legal systems and in the available or adoptable methods of implementing environmental controls. These differences are particularly significant between TWCs and developed countries. In many TWCs effective institutional arrangements for pollution control are not in place - weaknesses of institutions, laws and administration restrict the possibilities for the effective implementation of environmental policy.

10. The options available to a country that wants to reduce pollutant emissions below what they would otherwise be include: switching from the existing, and in some sense preferred, mix of fuels to a less-polluting mix (e.g. leaded to unleaded petrol, high to low-sulphur coal to reduce SO_2, coal to oil, gas or renewables to reduce CO_2); for any given fuel, to use less of it (e.g. burn fuel more efficiently in electricity generation, use fuels more efficiently in each end-use); reduce the emissions per unit of fuel used (e.g. flue-gas desulphurisation to clean stack gases, or catalytic converters in cars).

11. An important feature of all these options is that insofar as they involve doing what would not otherwise be done in the existing policy environment, they are less-preferred choices for energy users. Often the less-polluting choice is more expensive to the fuel user, at least in the short term, although it may be less expensive to the pollutees. The 'polluter pays principle' (PPP) is, of course, the rationale for policy intervention. Using policy instruments to implement the PPP (such as regulations or charges) may, however, involve difficult tradeoffs between the pursuit of efficiency and equity, depending on the ways in which particular groups and interests are affected.

12. Most of the options listed concern technology choices and involve, for example, investments in more energy-efficient (and often less-polluting) technology. It can be argued that there will be cases where, rather than increase (fossil fuel) energy supply and pollution, it might be better to reduce pollution by reducing the demand for energy through investments in energy efficiency. It is clear that TWCs (and indeed industrialised countries also) have not always chosen energy policies (e.g. pricing policies and investment incentives) that have encouraged a sensible choice between expanding the supply of energy and reducing demand through efficiency.

13. It has to be acknowledged, however, that the pursuit of energy (and pollution) efficient technology requires substantial funding. There have been suggestions that by taking advantage of the latest technologies of energy production and consumption, TWCs might be able to avoid following the energy-

intensive histories of the industrialised countries and move rapidly to much more energy-efficient strategies. However, it is unlikely that TWCs could afford to finance such a strategy themselves; nor until recently has there been much motivation for the industrialised countries to help them to do so.

14. The transnational nature of a number of fossil fuel related air pollution problems means that international cooperation is necessary if they are to be controlled. The greenhouse effect illustrates the extreme difficulties that can arise: there is much scientific uncertainty; the impacts of climatic change are complex, hard to predict and likely to be uneven in their spatial distribution; and the economic valuation of the likely societal costs and benefits of control will be particularly problematic and speculative. As TWC delegates to conferences on global warming and the ozone layer have not been slow to point out, because of their low levels of per capita income and energy consumption, the participation of TWCs in global limitations of emissions cannot be assumed. And when measures like carbon taxes or tradable permits to limit fossil fuel use are discussed, the TWCs understandably question why in equity they should pay high prices now for their use of the atmosphere (or accept equivalent physical limits on fossil fuel use) because the industrialised countries in the past added so rapidly (and without charge) to the stock of carbon dioxide while their economies were maturing. Thus the TWCs are likely to cooperate with the industrialised world only at a price - if they are, in various ways, subsidised or otherwise compensated, whether financially or through the transfer of technology. As Anderson has pointed out, the fact that subsidies to agriculture in Europe, Japan and the US cost these countries $75 billion per year, more than twice the level of official development assistance, has not been lost in the discussions.

15. Help here might come in two ways - one is simply funding to enable the TWC to buy or forgo what it could not otherwise afford, including imported technology. The other is making it possible for technology transfer and local production of the latest technology. A problem here for the development of international agreements can be the understandable but unhelpful reluctance of companies in the industrialised world to transfer their most up-to-date technology to TWCs. These issues have been well illustrated by the recent agreement on limiting CFCs - and they have been only partly resolved by the setting up of a global aid fund. Everything we know about the nature and scale of global warming suggests that it will be much more difficult to establish a global warming fund and to ensure successful technology transfer. What will be needed is a system of international public finance to implement and monitor all these arrangements for regulating the global commons. The suitability for this task of the existing institutions for international financial cooperation has been widely queried.

References

1. PEARSON, PJG (1987) 'Energy Demand in the Third World', Ch. 2 in Stevens, P (ed) **Energy Demand: Prospects and Trends**, Macmillan, London.
2. Boyle, S. (1990) 'Energy and Development', **Oxford Energy Forum**, 1(2), 3-5.
3. MADHAB, J (1987) 'Energy and Economic Development: Experience and Issues in Developing Asia', **Asian Development Review**, 5(1), 60-82.
4. PACHAURI, RK (1989) 'Energy Efficiency in Developing Countries: Policy Options and the Poverty Dilemma', paper presented to RIIA/BIEE/IAEE Conference on 'Environmental Challenges: the Energy Response', London.
5. DE OLIVEIRA, A & MACKERRON, G (1990) 'British Privatisation of the Energy Industries, the World Bank and Implications for Third World Countries', in Pearson, PJG (ed) **The Future Conduct of Energy Policy in the Third World**, Surrey Energy Economics Discussion Paper SEEDS 50, University of Surrey, Guildford.

Energy in the developing world

D. D. A. PIESOLD, WLPU Consultants (International) Ltd

SYNOPSIS: The paper focusses attention upon the benefits which can result from a modest supply of energy to remote parts of the developing world by way of higher living standards, water supply and treatment, better use of human resources, improved working environment, creation of a longer and less tiring working day, food production through irrigated agriculture and animal husbandry, fertilizer manufacture, population growth control, cold storage and refrigeration, beneficiation of raw materials thereby adding value and export of energy. Methods of achieving a supply of energy are proposed, following a review of some of the successes and failures of energy producing installations of bygone years, including case histories where appropriate. Both large and small electricity supply installations are considered not only for local use but also for the export of energy surplus to requirements.

1. Survival in many parts of the developing world is seemingly a matter of chance and the international community has nobly risen to the challenge once the crisis point has been reached, whether it be famine in Ethiopia, flooding in Bangladesh or earthquake in a remote part of Asia.
2. Can these tragedies be avoided or mitigated by a supply of energy? The answer must be yes. This topic is very wide ranging and will be considered in general terms in the first instance and then illustrated by case histories, suitably abbreviated.
3. Each community has different needs for survival in the face of adversity and a source of energy would supply many of these needs which collectively may be referred to as the "standard of living".
4. First and foremost, to sustain life a potable water supply is necessary and whether this be achieved by extraction of groundwater or from surface water, the availability of energy for pumping would normally transform the way of life in rural areas.
5. Normally groundwaters need little or no treatment and when surface waters are used for drinking purposes energy provides a facility for boiling until such time as forms of treatment involving filtration and chemical dosing can be introduced. The latter would require further supplies of energy for back washing and water transfers.
6. To be able to pump water makes it possible for the community to divert its human resources into other forms of activity including the production of food and clothing, house building, community projects, and redistribution and the handling of surpluses in good times. It is not uncommon in many parts of the developing world to see the women with urns of water balanced on their heads and the men and women with poles across their shoulders to balance several water containers, walking long distances each day to provide water needs for their families. The transformation of their lives by the introduction of even one single standpipe in a village is immeasurable.

7. A pumped water supply and some illumination by electricity provides a longer and less tiring working day, thereby creating new avenues for innovation and activity to safeguard the future.

8. The increased production of food through irrigated agriculture using sprayer systems is well-known and this can only be achieved with a reliable and inexpensive source of energy. Flood irrigation is more difficult to control and restrict losses of water.

9. Critical to survival is the ability to store food. For centuries this has been achieved by processes involving drying, the use of various salts or preservation with sugar and spices. The first method requires a suitable climate, the other methods require appropriate ingredients which are not available to many countries of the developing world. The most satisfactory method of storage is based upon cooling systems requiring insulation and energy. It is significant that in the early half of this century the colonial administrators introduced ice plants in countries with fishing traditions in the oceans or inland lakes; in land-locked countries without expanses of water, cold storage commissions were established to preserve food.

10. Despite the first successful development, almost simultaneously, of electric lamps by Joseph Swan in England and Thomas Edison in America in 1879, there remain many locations around the world where the working day is restricted to the hours between sunrise and sunset. Illumination beyond these times inevitably raises the standard of living by providing a more flexible and improved working environment as well as a time for leisure. It has also been suggested from studies carried out in India as far back as the 1960's that a modicum of illumination has the effect of depressing the birthrate thereby reducing population growth. This no doubt is a subject upon which comments should be invited from a sociologist.

11. Where large quantities of environmentally friendly energy can be generated from water power, the contribution of technology towards development for survival is inestimable and may include:

- The manufacture of nitrogeneous fertilizer from the atmosphere by filling the depressions in the load curve, thereby increasing the ability to produce food. This has already been achieved in Iceland by harnessing the water from glaciers.
- The beneficiation of important raw materials near their source without pollution thereby creating added value for the developing country and protecting mankind from the products of combustion. Also by having energy available during the primary and secondary crushing processes it is possible by means of pumping, cyclonic separation and/or sub-aerial deposition to dispose of particulate wastes in a manner which is not damaging to the countryside in any way. In some instances such materials can be used for landfilling or reclamation. All these processes require energy.
- The export of energy from such sources to neighbouring countries can contribute not only to the survival of the supply country but also to that of the recipient. Recent political changes between East and West and in several European countries with emphasis upon the freedom of the press and media generally and the introduction of democracy, have created an atmosphere of cooperation against the common enemy: environmental damage. Inter-change of energy between developed countries is already a reality. Is there any reason why the developing world should not do likewise?

12. The foregoing provides in outline some of the benefits achievable by a source or sources of energy. It now remains for us to consider appropriate development in terms of energy for survival of communities in countries with modest financial resources and an infrastructure partly developed and maintained with difficulty. Two cases will be reviewed, one relating to small rural development the other to larger scale development in the context of the preceding paragraphs. To avoid too many permutations and combinations the examination will be limited to electrical energy generated in an environmentally acceptable way. The two cases having been reviewed, an attempt will be made to summarise the lessons learned following by some thoughts as to how implementation of appropriate projects can take place.

Case 1:
13. The Bemba plateau in the north-east of the Republic of Zambia (formerly Northern Rhodesia) some 4,000 ft above sea level measures about 38,000 square miles. In 1950 the Bemba people numbered some 150,000 giving a density of 3.95 per square mile.
14. The plateau land is of poor agricultural soil derived mainly from the breakdown of feldspathic sandstones with little or no vegetable content from decomposition of leaves of trees. The leaves tend to be destroyed annually by bush fires while the trees survive. Rainfall is ample and the country is open and well watered.
15. The Bemba are not a pastoral people. The country is infested with tsetse fly and cattle are not often seen. Wildlife and particularly game have been decimated by hunting, the muzzle loader having taken its toll in the early part of the century. The Bemba follow a system of shifting cultivation known as "chitimeni". They make circular gardens by lopping off the tops of trees piling them to a height of about two metres and then setting them on fire. Seeds are planted in the ashbeds. Weeds are thus burned and no further hoeing is needed during the year. Gardens once made are planted for four or five years and a system of crop rotation is followed.
16. Characteristic of the men is their lack of interest in agriculture. They were warriors by nature and in days gone by they lived largely from tribute brought by other peoples. To live by chopping off branches of trees was considered belittling to a hunter and it was said that when he wished to opt out he would sit on the branch which he was chopping. When both had crashed to the ground the branch would end up in the garden and the man would become an outpatient in the local clinic. Reference was often made to the Season of Broken Limbs.
17. With the development of the copper mines of Northern Rhodesia (now the Republic of Zambia) during and after World War II the Copperbelt towns of Nkana (now Kitwe), Nchanga (now Chingola), Luanshya, Mufulira and the commercial centre of Ndola became very attractive to the rural people. The move southwards by young men was of such proportions as to cause concern to the Government of Northern Rhodesia. The difficulties were exacerbated by the worthy tradition that hospitality is rarely refused to blood relations. Those that worked and earned well were joined by others who did neither.
18. Sir Arthur Benson, very soon after his arrival as Governor in the mid-1950's, sought to change the centre of gravity of development in favour of the rural areas. Benson wanted more immediate and widespread availability of electricity and was prepared to spend some of the limited funds set aside for the Kafue Hydro-Electric Project now abandoned in favour of development of the Kariba Project on the Zambezi River as promoted by the bordering country of Southern Rhodesia.
19. Enquiry revealed that some years before District Commissioners had been instructed to report on any rivers with substantial waterfalls. The Boma records were duly searched. Although the officials were neither hydrologists nor civil engineers they were dedicated and duty-bound people who provided valuable references in their notebooks as well as maintaining rainfall records at many district centres. Consultation of these records provided a starting point which in turn was followed by a reconnaissance extending over the Luapula and Northern Provinces.
20. In the absence of hydrological and topographical data other than those at District centres reliance had to be placed upon records of rainfall, correlations with other rivers and recollections of aged inhabitants at mission stations followed by the extensive use of reconnaissance instruments including Abney levels, prismatic compasses, aneroid barometers and pedometers.
21. More than fifty potential project sites were visited and within an overall financial constraint of £1M, three schemes able to provide in the order of 6,000kW were constructed and commissioned by the early 1960's. There have been many visible benefits to the Bemba resulting from these schemes over the past thirty years. Further schemes have been built and electrification of the region has continued.
Case 2:
22. In the rural areas of Zambia south of the Copperbelt small scale urbanisation followed the development of the railways. Electricity supply to rural populations grew as an adjunct to the needs of commerce, industry and mining activity.

23. Starting in the south, Livingstone derived its electricity supply from a small hydro-electric power station, initiated in 1935, at the Victoria Falls. Some 8 MW served the town, the hotel and railway workshops on the south bank of the Zambezi River.

24. Between Livingstone and Lusaka at roughly equal intervals along the line of rail, there came into being some six very small townships each, like Lusaka, equipped with an electrical system which depended upon diesel electric generating plant dependent upon the importation of relatively expensive diesel fuel. These townships included Kalomo, Choma, Monze and Mazabuka agricultural centres, Kafue and Chilanga. The latter served the new cement factory and the Mount Makulu agricultural research station.

25. North of Lusaka were the mine and associated townships of the Broken Hill lead and zinc mine and a very small township known as Kapiri Mposhi. The supply of electricity came from the Mulungushi and Lunsemfwa hydro-electric schemes established in 1924 and 1943 respectively.

26. Further north on the Copperbelt the four main copper mines each had a 60 MW coal fired thermal power station interconnected into a 66 kV network. Later this network was first to draw some additional supply from water power sources from Shaba Province in Zaire and later from the south bank power station at Kariba on the Zambezi River.

27. In the above scene an electricity supply was necessary to support enterprises funded from overseas. The benefits were observed by the people in the rural areas but not enjoyed by them except as itinerant workers. However, the seed was sown and rural electrification followed and living standards improved. The concepts and benefits of international transfers of power and energy were also displayed in these remote areas.

28. There are several lessons to be learned from these case histories:
a) Political and engineering initiatives are needed to encourage the development of energy systems to raise living standards and increase expectation of life or survival.
b) Appropriate technology is necessary to obtain the best value for money. If concessional funds are provided then particularly careful management is required. There is no future for example in developing a scheme where the site investigations and feasibility studies exceed in cost terms the capital value of the schemes! For small hydropower schemes this can be a serious problem. The ideal solution is to use experience and judgement at the outset, with the sponsors prepared to recognise risks associated with modifications during construction. For small scale work this should not be too serious a challenge.
c) Experience has shown that the use of water power in remote areas has special merit with regard to serviceability and long life. The Mulungushi scheme mentioned earlier has been operating for nearly 70 years, with small maintenance requirements.
d) For the larger scheme on international waterways the engineer needs political support to ensure that the energy benefits are appropriately distributed.
e) The use of local labour and materials greatly enhances any initiative to provide energy.

29. Most important of all is the need for the more developed world to consider providing concessional finance or soft loans to assist in the implementation of energy systems and particularly those which are environmentally friendly.

30. The author would like to acknowledge assistance received from Mr W. Le Page who was Chief Electrical Adviser in Zambia over some of the period of the above case histories.

Small hydro systems using pump impellers as turbines and local materials for casings and bearings

T. SANCHEZ, Intermediate Technology Development Group, Lima

SYNOPSIS. This paper intends to show the posibility of using very small pumps as turbines for battery charging, using non conventional materials such as wood for casings and bearings in order to lower the price and make it available to poor rural inhabitants. A very brief look at some principles and experimental figures extracted from reference 1 are included; in addition, some economic social remarks as refers to energy for rural poor in Peru are included too.

PERFORMANCE OF PUMPS AND TURBINES
1. One of the most common expressions of performance for pumps and turbines is the following:

$$\frac{gH}{N^2 D^2} = f(Q/ND)$$

Where:
g, acceleration of gravity (m/s)
H, head (m)
N, rotational speed (rps)
Q, flow (m /s)
D, impeller diameter (m)

2. The previous relation is very much used for pumps where the known parameter is the source of energy (the motor) with known velocities. For turbines the known parameter is head H. Therefore, it is more convenient to use the following non dimensionless relations.
Q/ H, unit flow
N/H, unit speed
W/H , unit power

SELECTION OF A PUMP TO RUN IN REVERSE
3. Manufacturers supply H-Q performance curves for each pump and turbine, for a number of fixed rotation speeds which are useful to users when selecting the appropiate machine. Note: maximum efficiency point varies according to use, as pump or as a turbine.

Appropriate development for basic needs. Thomas Telford, London, 1991

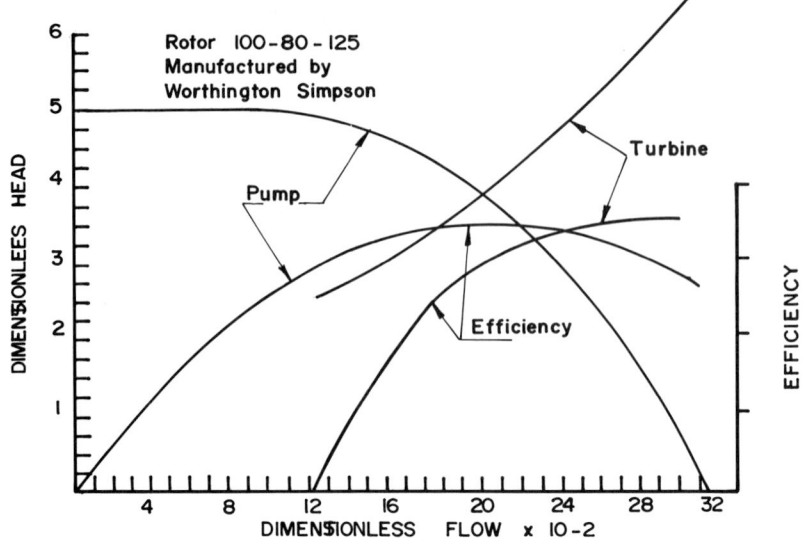

Figure 1. Performance curves of the pump impeller used as pump and as turbine

4. According to the previous figure Ht > Hp and Qt > Qp. Recomended values are the following:

Ht ≈ 1.3 Hp,   Qt ≈ 1.35 Qp

Where: Ht, head when the machine works as a turbine
        Hp, head when the machine works as a pump
        Qt, flow when the machine works as a turbine
        Qp, flow when the machine works as a pump.

Wooden case for small pump impellers and bearings

5. The proposal for the casing is the same used in reference 1 (see figure 2) in addition - wood bearings are cheap in rural areas and peasants are more familiar with wood than with metallic materials.

6. The idea is to buy a commercial impeller and make the case using two round discs of wood (could be marine ply wood as in reference 1), which are separated by a piece of aluminium sheet to form the shape of the outer wall of the volute.

7. The design of the volute must take into consideration logarithmic shape, wood is grooved in order to hold the aluminium sheet. The assembly is done using long bolts and plastic/rubber for sealing.

8. The inlet of the volute consists of a hole made in the top piece of wood. Figure 3 shows the assembly of the unit.

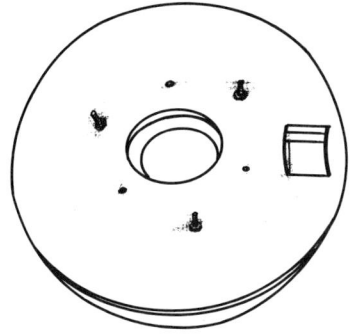

Figure 2. Wooden case used at the experiments

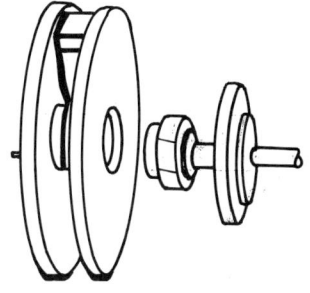

Figure 3. Assemble of the unit

Performance of the unit

9. The following figures show the performance of the 139 mm diameter impeller tested in the laboratory of Fluid Mechanics at Reading University (see ref. 1).

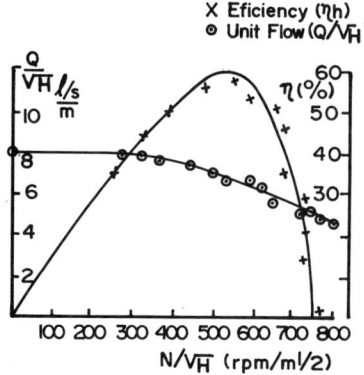 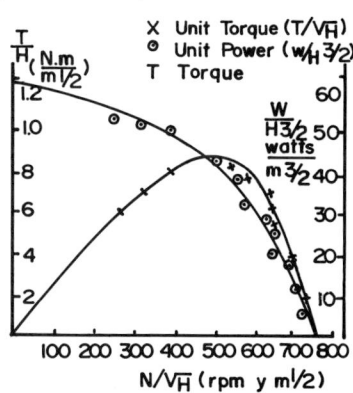

Figure 4. Performance curves of 100-80-125 pump impeller used as turbine (Laboratory tests)

Costs

10. The costs of a small complete unit of 300 w (electrical) will be divided as follows (in Peru):

Impeller	80 US$
Volute	40
Bearings	10
Axis	30
Labor	20
Alternator	80
Other materials	60
	----
	300 US$

11. Similar units (in power) are being offered in the peruvian market at prices over 900 US$ which is expensive for rural peasants.

Table 1. Cost of energy in Peru for rural inhabitants

System	Costo (US$/kwh)
Battery charging carried out in the urban areas for rural inhabitants	0.4 - 0.8
Small Diesel unit 8 hours/day (fc=60) oil (0.2 US/l)	0.30
Small petrol unit 8 hours/day (fc=60%) petrol (0.2 US$/l)	0.19
Wind generators (200w - 2000w) homemade	0.09 - 0.19
Microhydro (more than 2 kw (fc=30%)	0.08 - 0.15
Battery charging using pumps running in reverse **	0.08

** cost is calculated assuming 300 electrical watts, to charge 5 batteries a day, with the unit having a 10 years life span 10% interest rate.

REFERENCES

1. Sánchez T., Performance of Centrifugal Pumps Running as Turbines. MSc. degree thesis, University of Reading, Reading - England, June 1988.

2. Kittredge C.P., Centrifugal Pumps used as Hydraulic Turbines. Journal of Engineering for Power, Princeton, N.J. January 1961.

3. Wong W., Aplication of Centrifugal Pumps for Power Generation, World Pumps, London 1987.

Rehabilitation of estate hydro schemes in Sri Lanka

R. M. YOUNG, Binnie and Partners

SYNOPSIS. Over the last 20 years a large number of small hydro schemes in Sri Lanka have fallen into disuse. A project for their rehabilitation was started in 1986 and this paper reports some of the findings of the first phase, which included the detailed design and preparation of contract documents for 8 "advance schemes". The project did not proceed further but was re-appraised in 1988 by which time both the price of oil and the exchange rate of the Sri Lankan rupee had altered significantly, affecting the project economics.

BACKGROUND
1. The central region of Sri Lanka is steep and hilly with a high annual rainfall, conditions well-suited to the cultivation of tea and rubber. The conditions are also suitable for the generation of water power and in the 1920's and 30's a number of estates installed small hydro-electric schemes to provide a proportion of the power needed by their processing factories. This continued until the 1960's, by which time an estimated 500 schemes had been installed. Towards the end of the decade the Ceylon Electricity Board (CEB) began expanding its network to the tea and rubber estates. Power from the CEB was convenient, maintenance-free and, at the time, relatively cheap. As a result many estates discontinued independent power production and allowed their existing equipment to fall into disrepair.

2. In the late 1970's and early 80's the cost of power from the CEB rose considerably while at the same time the security of the supply dropped. As a result the Sri Lankan Government decided to rehabilitate as many of the estate hydro-electric schemes as was economically viable. Salford Civil Engineering Ltd (SCEL) in association with Binnie & Partners (B&P) were appointed to engineer the project in 1986 under an agreement with the British Government's Overseas Development Administration (ODA) which funded the foreign element of the costs.

3. The project has to have been carried out in two phases. Technical and economic guidelines were to be drawn up in Phase 1 together with detailed designs and contract documents for a small group of "advance schemes". Full implementation of the project, expected to cover about 120 schemes, was to be carried out in Phase 2 which was to start in early 1987. Phase 1 was completed on time but the start of Phase 2 was delayed and in the interim there was a substantial fall in the international price of oil. Consequently in 1988 the project was re-appraised with the result that the estimated number of economically viable schemes (defined as schemes having an economic internal rate of return (EIRR) greater than 10%) dropped to between 20 and 50. No further work has been carried out and therefore this paper reports only the results of the studies, not the problems of implementation.

CONDITION OF "ADVANCE SCHEMES"
5. About 30 schemes were inspected while collecting the data needed to draw up the technical and economic guidelines for the project. Detailed designs and tender documents were prepared for 8 of these during Phase 1. These "advance schemes" cover the full range of capacities (40 to 300kW) and overall head (45 to 172m) likely to be encountered during Phase 2. They are all run-of-river schemes, normally comprising a small weir diverting the flow to a leat or low-pressure pipeline leading to a header tank and high-pressure pipeline. In general the concrete and masonry works were well-built and in reasonable repair. The pressure pipelines were either of cast iron spigot and socket pipes with run lead joints or of steel pipes. The former were generally in adequate condition but all the steel pipelines had corrosion problems.

6. The condition of the mechanical and electrical equipment was not as good as that of the civil works. All the generators needed complete replacement as did 5 of the turbines; the other 3 were capable of being rehabilitated. The switchboards in the factories gave serious cause for concern due partly to inadequate construction and partly to ad hoc modifications. Many were considered to be in a dangerous condition and all needed replacement.

MODE OF OPERATION
7. Two possible modes of operating the hydro-power plant were considered. They were:

- as isolated generator units feeding sections of the factory via manual change-over switches used to select the source of power, either CEB or hydro,
- in parallel with the CEB system, requiring synchronisation with the CEB supply but eliminating the need for change-over switches.

Parallel operation enables surplus power to be sold to the CEB and therefore offers potential financial advantage. However at the time of the Phase 1 studies the CEB were not prepared to accept this because of perceived technical difficulties and therefore only isolated operation was considered. When the project was re-appraised some 2 years later these objections were not pressed as strongly so both modes of operation were examined.

SOURCES OF EQUIPMENT
8. A major design decision concerned the sources of materials and equipment needed for the work, particularly the high-pressure pipes, turbines, generators and electrical equipment as these were the major cost items. Two options were considered:

- the use of locally manufactured items and
- the use of items imported from the UK.

In all cases the imported items were preferred on grounds of quality. The only pressure pipes produced locally were of welded steel which could not be continuously protected internally. As these would suffer from corrosion problems imported ductile iron pipes were specified. Turbines could be manufactured in Colombo but the materials used were poor and the design and quality control inadequate so that there were serious doubts about their efficiency and reliability. The same comments applied to locally manufactured switchboards with the added fear that they would not pass basic IEE standards and would therefore be unsafe, perpetuating the risks associated with the existing boards.

COSTS AND ECONOMICS
9. The average scheme costs (taking the 8 schemes together) determined during the Phase 1 studies are given in 1986 prices in Table 1. This shows that the two major elements are the overseas M&E costs, essentially the costs of importing the turbines, generators and switchboards, and the design and supervision. Since the Phase 2 implementation programme was planned to be very rapid it was assumed that a considerable expatriate input would be required, with the result that about two-thirds of the design and supervision costs would be in sterling and the total overseas costs would amount to about 70% of the total scheme costs. Nevertheless the economics appeared promising, with only one scheme having an EIRR less than the target of 10% and the average being just above 15%.

10. When the project was re-appraised in 1988 a number of changes had taken place. The most important of these were:

- the international price of crude oil had fallen, causing the cost of energy from CEB to drop from Rs 1.55/kWh to Rs 1.23/kWh,
- the exchange rate had changed from Rs40 = £1 to Rs57 = £1,
- there had been a substantial increase in the sterling prices quoted by manufacturers for turbines and generators (but not for other imported items). The increases were more than 100% in some instances and were not due to any change in specification,
- parallel operation with the CEB was considered as well as isolated operation, giving the opportunity of increasing revenue by selling surplus power.

These changes affected both the scheme costs and the scheme economics, as shown in Table 1. The overseas M&E costs increased dramatically, as did the engineering and contingencies (although this was partly due to the latter being based on a percentage of the other costs and therefore influenced by the M&E cost increase). The total cost went up by more than 60% and the overseas element increased to nearly 74% of the total. Only 3 of the schemes had EIRR's greater than 10% using the same mode of operation as in the 1986 study, the average being 9%. If parallel operation was introduced the number of viable schemes rose to 6 and the average EIRR to about 13%, still less than estimated in 1986.

CONCLUSIONS

11. Three points come out of the study. The first is the perhaps obvious conclusion that on such rehabilitation schemes the most costly items are the M&E plant, particularly turbines and generators, and the design and supervision. The second is that as envisaged the foreign element of the project cost is very high. This is largely due to the decision to import equipment from UK rather than using local items. The decision was taken on grounds of reliability, durability and efficiency but prompts the question of whether for countries with limited overseas currency it would be worth sacrificing some performance for a reduction in overseas costs. The difficulty is knowing how much of a sacrifice is being made - reliable indications of performance can only come from experience and this is not normally available for locally manufactured items in a form that can be quantified.

12. The final point is how vulnerable the economic assessment of such schemes is to changing world conditions and particularly to the price of oil, a parameter which seems unlikely to be particularly stable in the future. In such circumstances there is reassurance in the development of indigenous renewable resources - they look expensive at the time but seem cheap a decade later.

Summary of discussion

R. E. HOLLAND, Director of Operations, Intermediate Technology Development Group

SYNOPSIS. The Energy Workshop tried to concentrate on appropriate development for <u>survival</u> but considered all aspects of energy for all uses. This was rather a wide brief and tended to focus on problems of the poor, but most forms and scales of generation of energy were considered. The recent oil price rises and future price uncertainty are causing extra problems for poor people in the use of energy for agriculture, transport, industry and domestic use.

SUMMARY OF ENERGY WORKSHOP DISCUSSION

1. The household use of energy is affected by the increasing scarcity of fuelwood caused by pressure on land use. The importance of planning for combined agriculture and forestry (wood-lots, intercropping etc) to make biomass a truly renewable resource was mentioned - not strictly an engineering problem but it highlights the social and management dimensions and emphasises the need for community participation.

2. The inevitability of greater use of fossil fuels by developing countries was emphasised (an expected doubling over the next 10 years just to keep pace with population). This would give rise to greater pollution - CO_2, NO_x and SO_x and there would thus be even more pressure for industrialised countries to bring their excessive consumption of fossil fuels under control, perhaps through carbon taxes if oil price do not continue to rise.

3. Because of this inevitable increase in demand in developing countries it was suggested that the most significant and well established renewable energy technology - large hydro - should have a major part to play. The adverse environmental effects of large dams should be evaluated in the light of the harmful effects produced by alternative sources such as coal and oil power stations.

It was suggest that perhaps more effort should be put into reducing the harmful effects of large hydro instead of dismissing it as being environmentally damaging. Large hydro currently provides 70% of electricity for Sub Saharan Africa and 30% of all developing countries' electricity. The workshop was reminded of the great contribution to development by large dams in that country and of the benefits of rural electrification for development (irrigation pumping in particular). Thus is was suggested that large scale plants can have an important part to play in some circumstances - particularly for providing power to urban centres and areas of dense population. Smaller scale, decentralised plants are particularly suitable for areas of low population density. Nevertheless we should take account of the tendency in industrialised countries towards smaller distributed power stations.

4. On the subject of other renewables the impact over the last 10 years has been small but a lot of progress has been made and there is a lot of very valuable experience, particularly with wind and solar. Costs are still falling, though solar is still only economic in small units, but is playing a vital role in communications and vaccine refridgerators for remote areas for example. Wind generation is now a well established energy resource in the USA (4,500 wind turbines at the Altamont Pass) Some very valuable experiences have been gained with wind diesel sets and wind stand-alone systems on islands off Britain. Wind power it has been estimated could generate up to 30% of the current UK power needs.

5. There is great potential for joint research and development in partnership with developing country institutions in the area of renewable energy sources, for application and eventual manufacture in developing countries. It was recommended that greater resources could be put into this joint work.

6. Potential for biomass powered systems needs to be taken into account (eg producer gas, Stirling engines). These are yet to go into commercial production but potential is there. Their development will depend on the establishment of a market in biomass fuel and some lessons could be learnt in certain Far East countries (eg Philippines). Ownership can cause several problems if controlled by an elite but that depends on how freely available the technology is.

7. As an example of fuel efficient energy use and the useful applications of renewables the experience of using low wattage heat storage cookers was noted - possible use with hydro (large and small) and wind power. ODA is continuing to fund R and D in this area. Another area is low wattage lighting.

8. Re-iterating the points about maintenance made in Dr Robinson's paper we had a paper on the maintainability of energy systems concentrating on the need for taking a long term view of maintenance needs - choosing equipment that can be maintained at an acceptable cost over the life of the plant and taking account of local maintenance facilities and capabilities. Institutional development action is needed in some cases to develop a commitment to maintenance at an organisational level and achieving good levels of reliability. This approach to maintenance is necessary for all energy systems. It requires committment from funders and project holders/ participants to ensure sustainability and not just the initial construction of a plant (Recommendation for Appropriate Development Panel to take up with funders etc).

9. On the subject of local manufacture versus imported equipment it was recommended that the most suitable equipment for the job be chosen but projects should consider at the outset whether local manufacture is a possibility and if so take steps (mid-term) to ensure that local production can take place. Often short term project time horizons are not compatible with the timescale for technology transfer.

10. It was recommended that a long term view be taken in project design so that while short term action may be needed for survival reasons, the social and development goals of local manufacture can be taken into account and if necessary built into the project design. This is a process approach to project design. Clearly there are constraints from funders but they should consider this approach.

11. There were examples of where short term considerations or unrealistic project design had resulted in inappropriate choice of technology and the elimination of the possibility of local manufacture or the local project cancelled because it was too expensive as a result. (eg, mini hydro in Sri Lanka - Paper by Binnie and Partners).

12. A matrix approach to project design was recommended that included consideration of local needs/goals on one axis and the local human/natural and social resources (such as local artisans) and the other. The starting point should be available technology. We were reminded that choice of energy technology (fossil/renewable, large/small scale) should start with demand. There is a suspicion that there are still energy technologies looking for applications. It was suggested the institution could have a role in helping to present technology choice and to assess demand.

RECOMMENDATIONS

13. Opportunities for more joint research and development - new energy technologies should be promoted through the institution eg Rutherford Appleton Laboratory keen on partnership with developing country researchers in wind power.

(Would need cooperation of ODA/British Council) and funding research in developing countries. (Note ODA and British Council reps while supportive pointed out that they do already promote such cooperative research).

14. Life cycle costing and maintenance. Funders and project holders should have a commitment to the whole life of a plant being planned and commit resources to ensure sustainability - maintenance, training, institution building. This also has implications for choice of technology (Appropriate Development panel to take up with funders - a guide book on appropriate development was proposed).

15. Local manufacture. If the choice of technology is considered at the outset of a project then the potential for local manufacture should be considered at that time. It requires planning and resources to ensure local capacity is established or strengthened, and requires a sufficiently long time horizon.

16. Longer term view of project design implies greater emphasis on local resources and local social considerations (eg involvement of local artisans) at the project design stage. (Appropriate Development panel to provide guidance in this, drawing on specialists).

17. Review of the Appropriate Development Panel experience and production of publications on technology choice was suggested.

18. An appropriate approach to technology - could involve the other engineering institutions - through the Appropriate Development Panel.

Observations on the plight of urban water supply in Nigeria

J. T. ARMSTRONG, Binnie and Partners

Preface
1. This paper is derived and developed from the concluding report made by a team of consulting engineers from Binnie and Partners of a pre-engineering study for the National Water Rehabilitation Fund (NWRF) of Nigeria. This study was undertaken for the Federal Government of Nigeria and the World Bank (International Bank for Reconstruction and Development) and was funded by the British Government's Overseas Development Administration. The study of urban water schemes was made over 6 months in 1989-1990 and complimented an earlier study 2 years before. The author was a member of the study team but views expressed here are the sole responsibility of the author.

2. Nigeria is a federal country comprising 21 states and the Federal Capital Territory For brevity this paper refers to them collectively as "states".

Summary:
3. Over recent decades Nigeria has made appreciable and commendable investment in urban water supplies. Hovever these schemes are now in variable states of repair with significant operation and maintenance problems such that few schemes are providing design flows. As a result of this and coupled with rapid population growth, urban areas are inadequately supplied with potable water leading to an increased risk to public health. The paper identifies and examines reasons for the shortcomings. Institutional and human resource limitations are discussed. The importance of correct selection of raw water source and treatment process is emphasised. The relative merits of slow sand filtration are reassessed. The paper concludes that the choice of the technology which is employed to supply potable water, and to sustain it's supply, in the context of a developing country such as Nigeria, is of overriding importance, to which all engineers must be sensitive.

Introduction

4. The technology for the provision of potable water supply to urban areas in Nigeria and indeed throughout the developing world has frequently been imported piecemeal from the developed western nations which are characterised by high technology. Pickford(1) identified that the technology of advanced industrial countries is capital intensive, labour saving, complex and highly productive. The technology prevalent in the less developed countries is conversely generally labour intensive and simple with relatively low productivity. Technology employed for development should be appropriate for its location and suit domestic resources using local knowledge and skills. This has not always been the case with the imported technology for urban water supplies.

5. Engineers who have been involved in the selection and specification of treatment processes and plant have often been trained in the more developed countries. People have often equated "development" with emulation of the so-called developed countries and thus acceptance of high technology processes and equipment is encouraged. In developing countries with limited resources, training and access to spares, operational problems are soon encountered and water supply is impaired.

Urban Water Supply in Nigeria

6. Nigeria with a population of approx. 120 millions has some 20% of the population of Africa. It's population is particularly burgeoning in the urban areas. Nigeria is a developing country which has benefitted from being an oil exporter. Availabilty of foreign exchange has enabled considerable development of infrastructure and public services including improved water and sanitation facilities. However although public funds have been deployed for the construction of new works, less attention has been paid to securing recurrent costs for the efficient running of the schemes once built.

Nationwide Study

7. Following recognition of a need to appraise the state of the Nigeria's urban water supplies and sanitation, in late 1987 consulting engineers Binnie and Partners were appointed to make a nationwide study. A detailed study was made of 4 states of Nigeria and information was collected from the remaining states in order to assess the condition of the country's urban water supply and sanitation, including the state water agencies (SWA) responsible for them.

8. It was established that there are approximately 1000 urban schemes which serve populations greater than 5000, 40% of which serve populations greater than 20,000. About 80% of the water supply systems use groundwater and 20% surface

water. However 80% of the surface water schemes serve populations greater than 20,000 and few of the major urban centres are served by groundwater sources; Port Harcourt and Calabar being notable exceptions. Nearly half of the surface water schemes have full "conventional" treatment processes (including chemical coagulation and pH correction, clarification, filtration and disinfection); the remainder being package type units or units which provide only partial treatment.

9. This nationwide study estimated that physical rehabilitation would require almost US$800M and an overriding conclusion was that the human resources and institutions required significant support. A World Bank loan of US$220 M was agreed with the Federal Government of Nigeria for the rehabilitation of urban water supplies; US$10 M being allocated to each state.

Pre-engineering Study
10. Between October 1989 and April 1990, Binnie and Partners undertook the Pre-engineering Study, for the NWRF. The field team of 4 engineers visited all the 22 states of Nigeria inspecting treatment works and schemes, and meeting with the state water agencies (SWA) to agree the priorities and budget costings for the rehabilitation works to be undertaken.

11. This Pre-engineering study tour provided the team with a unique overview of the present condition of Nigeria's urban treatment works and related operational difficulties. Although the study was specific to Nigeria, it is considered that such problems are common to many developing countries.

12. The data on levels of service is unreliable but it is clear that population growth has kept ahead of the installation of new water supply schemes. In response to such growth, reticulation systems have often been expanded beyond the maximum design capacity of the treatment works. To illustrate this with albeit an extreme case, Saki a town in Oyo State in southeast Nigeria, had a modest (approx 1Mld) but robust conventional treatment works built in the mid to late 1960s for a population of 20,000. This works is now impossibly trying to supply a reported population 10 times the original number.

13. Although there are significant regional differences the conclusion of the study found in general that all SWAs are strained to capacity to meet their obligations. Of all state organisations SWAs have perhaps the most technically demanding function, yet they have little control over policy to set staffing levels, renumeration and tariffs. Limited funds has affected staff development and morale. It was notable that staff responsible for the operation of the

treatment plants were poorly motivated and lacked training. This has resulted in poor operational practices and inadequate maintenance which has contributed to insecurity of water supply.

14. The poor financial status of the SWAs is due to a combination of factors such as:

- reduced levels of income, including state subventions, concurrent with rapid devaluation of the national currency:
- much increased costs of power, chemicals and imported equipment;
- State Governments reluctance to approve tariff increases on the basis that water supply should be a social service;
- inadequate records and people not being billed coupled with a reluctance of consumers to pay for poor service and a common public attitude that as water is a naturally occurring element it should be free.

Institutional improvements to alleviate the above will take substantial time and the politcal will to implement.

15. Securing adequate power to run treatment works is often problematic. In comparison to many African countries, the electricty supply from the Nigerian national grid is relatively developed. However it does not reach all treatment works and is not yet able to provide a reliable and stable supply. The price of ectricity has also increased 8 fold over the last two years. A significant number of works are dependant upon their standby generators which age rapidly and do not receive adequate preventative maintenance.

16. There is a complete range of treatment processes engaged in Nigeria to treat surface water which include hopper and flat bottomed clarifiers, horizontal flow sedimentation, pulsating clarifiers, accentrifloc clarifiers. Both gravity and pressure filtration is utilised. Some works commissioned in the last decade were found already in disrepair however some relatively old works were still giving good service.

17. Most treatment plants inspected demonstrated operational problems and most were running below capacity. The majority of works are not likely to be producing water of such quality that would meet WHO standards. Indeed water at a several of the works inspected merely passed through the works en route to the high lift pumps with little or no treatment at all. This was due to one or more reasons for example: lack of chemical stock, failure of chemical mixing/dosing equipment, failure of the desludging arrangements, failure of automated control mechanisms and instrumentation, defective filters

and/or unserviceable backwashing plant.

18. At Birnin Kebbi, a relatvely remote rural town in Sokoto State in the north-east of the country, a centrifloc clarifier had a defective desludging system. At the time of the first visit in 1987, a group of local convicts were engaged to manually desludge the clarifier. On the second visit in 1989 the situation had not improved and a sort of youth employment project had been devised for similar manual cleaning. Complete with a band and "disco" on the clarifier bridge, young people were dancing in the mud to put it into suspension so it could be pumped out!

19. Of particular note in Nigeria is the not uncommon permanent installation of package treatment plants. Over 20% of surface water treatment works are of this category. Most of these package plants, if functioning, were invariably not being operated correctly. Such units are complex and often utilise plant which operate at high rotational speed thus prone to short service life.

20. One of the foremost conclusion of the study was that the greatest care should be given to secure the best possible raw water which requires the least treatment. It was identified that the preferred selection order of raw water sources should be :

        First Preference   Groundwater from deep boreholes

        Second Preference   Shallow tubewells in reiver sands or adjacent river sands

        Third Preference   Surface water from reservoirs lakes rivers and streams.

21. Many of the water supply projects in Nigeria heve been caried out as turnkey projects. For turnkey contract to be successful the SWA must:

- ensure sufficient control over the contractor
- have adequate impartial advice and review of the design
- effect uncompromised supervision of construction and commissioning.
- maintain regular payments to contractors

The study concluded that whilst many turnkey schemes are satisfactory others are not owing to a deficiency in one or more of the above areas.

22. Many schemes have been built with obvious regard for speed of construction and least cost. It must be recognised that higher capital cost and time for construction may have

to be borne as both long life and simplicity of operation are far more important than possible initial savings.

23. The study surmised that for Nigeria the most appropriate design of treatment works for long life with the minimum requirement for spares and complicated maintenance would incorporate whereever possible:

- gravity dosing of chemicals;
- hydraulic mixing of chemicals into the main water flow and hydraulic flocculation;
- conservatively rated clarifiers and filters in concrete structures;
- rapid gravity filters (or slow sand filters where appropriate) in preference to pressure filters, in which the media condition and effectiveness of wash cannot readily be inspected;
- manually operated valves
- mains/grid electricity supplies with dedicated sub-station and transformer and uncomplicated safe electrical instalations

Slow Sand Filtration

24. In Nigeria only one state was seen to be utilising slow sand filtration (SSF) as a water treatment process. In Cross River State are three small SSF works, constructed in the 1960's, which serve Obubra (0.4 Mld), Obudu and Ogoja (both 1 Mld). At the time of inspection, all three were operational and appeared to produce good quality water. The plants were treating river water and for periods of high turbidity there are pre-treatment arrangements for dosing with aluminium sulphate followed by horizontal settlement. The operating staff demonstrated an understanding of the process and expressed their appreciation of the quality of the water produced and of the simple operation of the works.

25. In view of the relative success of these treatment works it is worth reviewing in detatil the application of SSF in developing countries.

26. Since the 1930's construction of slow sand filters has been less common and other treatment processes have been generally preferred by decision makers. This may be due to the large land area required for SSF, high labour input required for cleaning, high building costs and inability of SSF's to cope with appreciable incidence of algae, colour and turbidity in the raw water.

27. SSF has not been widely applied in developing countries despite their simplicity and the relatively inexpensive land and labour therein. The dominant trend has been to specify a modern "state of the art" process for prestige reasons or

following external advice.

28. The advantages of SSF have been reassessed in recent years, particularly in the context of developing countries:

- The operation of SSF is not complicated and does not require complex mechanical and electrical equipment and instrumentation.
- Algal problems may be less critical in developing countries where artificial fertiliser use is not widespread thus there is less ingress into the source water of the nutrients which promote algal growth. Furthermore the intensity of ultra violet light in the tropics may deter algal growth. Schellart(2) states that Algal reproduction may be controlled by shading or covering the beds.
- Many developing countries have seasonal rainfall and the turbidity of the source water may vary considerably between the dry and wet season. Pre-treatment may be employed for periods of high turbidity. Pre-treatment processes have become more developed in recent years and include storage, sedimentation, microstraining, rapid roughing filters or pebble matrix filtration. Rajapakse(3) notes that this last method can reduce suspended solids from 5000 to 25 mg/l
- The cost of imported chemicals for water treatment is a significant burden for a developing country. There is no chemical requirement for SSF and thus there are no operating problems for mixing/dosing equipment, which is prone to breakdown.
- A conventional treatment works has a significant power demand whereas a slow sand filter may rely on gravity if there is a fall across the site. SSF requires minimal mechanical and electrical equipment.
- In developing countries, land and labour remains relatively cheap and SSF construction costs should not be a limiting factor. Visscher(4) notes that experience in India showed that construction cost of SSF is less expensive than a rapid sand filtration up to 3 Mld and when recurrent operational costs are considered SSF is cheaper up to 8 Mld.

29. In Nigeria, a water utility under pressure from insufficient resources, will strive to maintain a minimal service to provide a certain quantity of water even if good quality is not attainable. A slow sand filter under such same pressure will tend to produce better quality water than a conventional works as SSF is not dependant on chemicals and can cope with variable flow through the works. Many source waters are from impounded reservoirs which are particularly suited to SSF. As compared to other conventional processes, SSF has less potential problems and thus the production of potable water is more sustainable. Decision makers in

Nigeria should therefore reconsider to further utilise SSF.

Conclusion

30. I have intended in this paper by observing the status of urban water supply in one developing country and by reviewing the relative merits of SSF, to urge engineers to carefully consider the choice of technology for water treatment in the context of a developing country. Although engineers have the engineering ability at their finger tips to design and construct water supply schemes, they may not be able to establish locally the ability to efficiently manage them, within in the same timescale. The different operational conditions, between a developed country which may have had urban water supplies installed for centuries in contrast to a developng country which may only have had such for decades, must be carefully analised. The technologies chosen must suit the particular site, in both the physical and socio-economic context.

31. The extended application of appropriate treatment processes in Nigeria, or any developing country, is not a panacea. There remain institutional and human resource constraints common to all treatment processes which must be overcome. Operating staff must be sufficiently trained and receive satisfactory incentive and supervision to be able to run potable water schemes effectively. An adequate institutional framework of the water utility is a critical prerequisite for successful operation and maintenance of water supply installations. Revenue collection must be efficient and based on realistic economic tarriffs in order to generate suffient funds to cover recurrent costs.

References:

1. Pickford, J. "People and the Decade - Technology and Community", Waterlines 1982 Vol 1.2.

2 Schellart J A. 1988, "Benefits of Covered Slow Sand Filtration" in Slow Sand Filtration edited by N J D Graham.

3. J P Rajapakse, K J Ives, 1990, "Prefiltration of very highly turbid waters using pebble matrix filtration" in J.IWEM 4 April 1990.

4. Visscher J T. 1988, "Water treatment by Slow Sand Filtration - considerations for design operation and maintenance" in Slow Sand Filtration edited by N J D Graham.

Environmental monitoring and institutional roles in post-disaster development

J. BARTRAM, BSc, AIMLS, University of Surrey, M. SUAREZ, Edificio de Gobernacion, Ibague, Tolima, Colombia, and E. QUIROGA, BEng, and G. GALVIS, BEng, MSc, Universidad del Valle, Colombia

---

SYNOPSIS An environmental surveillance programme was developed in Colombia following a major disaster. The programme provided support to the local Health Service and enabled identification of problems and shortfalls in the water supply and sanitation sector. These were used to develop a strategy for prioritising remedial actions according to public health criteria. The programme is now an ongoing activity of the local Health Service. Disaster relief may weaken local institutions and it is therefore crucial that these fulfil their roles in post-disaster development aid. Non-involvement of such agencies may affect the viability of investment in infrastructure. Similarly, individual and community attitudes may be created which influence the success of post-disaster development initiatives.

BACKGROUND

1. On the 13th of November, 1985, the glacier-covered volcano 'Nevado Del Ruiz' in central Colombia erupted. Part of the avalanche produced by the melting of the glacier cover flowed down the valley of the river Lagunilla and swept away the city of Armero. In total about 22,000 died and more than 5,000 were made homeless.

2. Following the disaster, national and international agencies involved in disaster relief provided substantial support for resettlement and improvement of living conditions, including improvement of basic services.

3. Investment in sanitary infrastructure included the construction of two wastewater treatment lagoons for the towns of Lerida and Guayabal and improvement of water treatment and distribution.

4. Following immediate disaster relief and expansion of basic sanitary infrastructure, the British Red Cross identified the need to consolidate the investments made and ensure their long-term contribution to public health (ref 1).

METHODS

5. A team of Health Promoters was trained in basic aspects of public health, water supply and sanitation and water supply surveillance. Teams were based in the four Regional capitals and provided with basic equipment including portable water testing kits.

6. Basic information regarding the state of sanitary infrastructure was not available. Further, the Promoters had little experience of sanitary inspection or systematic data collection. A preliminary study of a sample of urban and rural communities was therefore undertaken.

7. The local Health Service was supported to undertake inspection and sampling of water supplies and investigate excreta and waste disposal facilities. Preliminary contacts were made with local institutions involved in

water supply and sanitation. Furthermore, a survey of public attitudes to water supply and sanitation following the disaster was undertaken. The approach to systematic data collection has been described previously (ref 2).

RESULTS

8. A number of important findings were derived from the preliminary study (ref 3):

8a. No water treatment plant was in operation. This included those constructed in the wake of the disaster. Furthermore, most systems supplied grossly contaminated water and water supply services were gener deficient as shown in Table 1.

Table 1: Quality of Water Supply Services in a Sample of Communities, Tolima, Colombia, 1989

Population Type	System Type	Number visited	Coverage	Quality (faecal coliforms/100ml)	Continuity of service hours/day
Urban	surface water source with treatment	4	83-96%	3 with >50 1 with 11-50	1 with 1-10 2 with 11-23 1 with 24
Rural	surface water source with treatment	1	96%	>50	24
	surface water source, no treatment	7	65-96%	3 with >50 3 with 11-50 1 with 1-10	1 with 1-10 6 with 11-24

8b. Although water quality was generally very poor, considerable infrastructure existed for water treatment and little additional investment would be required to enable operation of existing water treatment plants, see Table 2.

8c. Public perception of the importance of water quality was high and many households claimed to regularly treat drinking water at home, buy bottled water or collect treated water from nearby industrial premises.

8d. Considerable investment had been made in wastewater treatment by lagooning, a technology which is generally considered low-cost and requires little operation and maintenance, but the Municipalities who 'inherited' this infrastructure showed little interest in it.

8e. Despite tariff levels below the minimum necessary for operation and maintenance, public attitudes to tariffs varied widely. In one district, users refused to pay any tariff because the water supply system had been given to them as disaster survivors by an international aid agency.

9. In light of these findings, a series of activities were initiated to promote the undertaking of remedial actions. These included training in urban water supply administration, organisation and tariff structuring; fostering of a link between the local University and the Municipalities for monitoring and optimisation of the wastewater treatment lagoons; rehabilitation of a pilot rural water treatment plant; and promotion of information dissemination to promote awareness both amongst the general public and local authorities.

10. These were undertaken not by direct intervention by outside agencies,

but by promoting remedial actions to be taken by the appropriate local agency. These activities were largely targeted through the local Health Service at the Service itself and the Municipalities.

Table 2: Actions Needed to Enable Functioning of Water Treatment Infrastructure

Town	Actual Status	Actions needed
Armero-Guayabal	Construction started 1987, still non-operational	* eliminate toilet sited on clear water tank; * repair coagulant mixing and dosing equipment; * finish construction of second storage tank and filter-storage tank inter-connection; * purchase chlorine cylinders; * operator training; * complete lab equipment and train user.
Lerida	Construction started 1987, commissioned but now non-operational	* repair pumping equipment and prevent repeat of flooding; * operator training; * complete lab equipment and train users; * purchase chlorine dosing equipment.
Mariquita	Functioning since 1986, coagulant and chlorine dosing practised irregularly; rehabilitation begun in 1988 now paralysed.	* repair coagulant mixing and dosing equipment; * initiate lime dosing to counter acidity of source water; * complete rehabilitation works (expansion of sedimentation and filtration capacity); * initiate chlorine dosing; * operator training.

Footnote: All plants comprised coagulant dosing, flocculation, sedimentation and rapid sand filtration. Most also had chlorine dosing equipment.

DISCUSSION

11. The exercise outlined above can be analysed as a success. Problems were identified and solutions applied. These included aspects of institutional development of local institutions and the perspectives for long-term benefit are good. Furthermore, the project attracted national attention and the National Director of Environmental Sanitation is now seeking means to replicate the experience nationally.

12. It is important to distinguish between disaster relief and post-disaster development. During disaster relief the need for action, for instance to save lives, is immediate and urgent. However, once immediate relief has been successful, actions should be governed by developmental criteria. There are a number of aspects of this project which merit analysis in this context.

13. Aid itself may influence local institutions which may be by-passed, especially during disaster relief and short-term aid, although it is these agencies which will be expected to operate and maintain any infrastructure developed.

13a. The funding received in an area following a disaster may be much greater than the budgets of the local agencies. Furthermore, much disaster relief is administered by external agencies with considerable independence, often without reference to local agencies or procedures and with specially contracted staff. In these conditions, local agencies may appear impotent when external support is withdrawn, along with budget and 'experts'. Positive action should be taken to mitigate this. In this project local staff were supported to manage the project themselves; workgroups included appropriate local institutions and established procedures (for example for water quality monitoring) were respected (ref 4).

13b. The failure to involve local institutions in the initial phases of projects may also lead towards problems. In this case, the initial disinterest of the Municipalities in the wastewater treatment lagoons and the non-functioning of much water treatment plant appear to be related to some extent to the non-involvement of these agencies.

14. Disaster relief may also affect community and individual attitudes.

14a. Cases of 'divided' communities where the new residents attained a higher standard of living (thanks to aid) than the original residents occurred. Contrasting attitudes were seen in some such communities. In the settlement of Lerida, the population refused to pay even the low local tariff for water; during interviews, inhabitants commented that they should not pay at all as the system had been donated to them and rather, the other users of the system should be grateful to be able to use the system. Also here, the original residents were resistant to the idea that the water sources (which their families had used for generations) were contaminated; while new residents were far more ready to accept and act on this idea.

15b. Attitudes created in response to the disaster relief and subsequent development aid also affected the project which was managed by the local Health Service itself. Health Promoters were initially reluctant to become involved because they were to receive only Ministry of Health travelling allowances, rather than the enhanced rates known to be paid by most international agencies active in the area.

16. Perhaps the best example of the success of the strategy of involving local staff and agencies in order to ensure project acceptance and transfer of ideas is that the Departmental Governor and the local Health Service decided during the final phase of external support to fund the rehabilitation of a demonstration rural water treatment plant, incorporating technologies new to the area, from their own resources.

REFERENCES
1. Lloyd, B.J. The Development and Control of Hygiene, Health and Sanitation Services in the Municipalities of Lerida, Guayabal and Mariquita. Consultancy Report to the British Red Cross Society, September 1987.
2. Lloyd, B.J. and Bartram, J.B. Surveillance Solutions to Microbiological Problems in Water Quality Control in Developing Countries (in press) in: Proceedings of Symposium on Health-Related Water Microbiology, IAWPRC, Tubingen, April 1990.
3. Anon. Proyecto Sobre Vigilancia y Mejoramiento de Sistemas de Abastecimiento y Remoción de Agua en la Regional de Armero del Servicio Seccional de Salud del Tolima, CINARA-SSS-Tol-Robens Institute, December, 1989.
4. Anon. Disposiciones Sanitarias Sobre Aguas, Decreto 2105, Ministerio de

Appropriate vehicles for municipal services in developing countries

M. COFFEY, Manus Coffey Associates Ltd

Low cost vehicles for hygienically emptying pit latrines have been developed in association with the World Bank/UNDP Tag leading in turn to lower cost latrine designs with dramatic cost savings for urban and peri-urban sanitation. Refuse collection vehicles and container systems used in industrialised countries are unsuited to the wastes in developing countries. Studies carried out for UNCHS/Habitat identified the cost and social factors relating to refuse collection and computer software has been developed for the selection of cost effective systems. This has led to the development of appropriate refuse collection vehicles.

1. INTRODUCTION.

There is perhaps no field of overseas consultancy where more costly mistakes have been made by well intentioned but poorly informed consultants from the industrialised countries than in the area of municipal services and in particular sanitation and refuse collection. My work in this field evolved out of the recognition by the World Bank that existing sanitation technology based on waterborne sewerage was inappropriate and totally inadequate for the problems emerging in a world where the combination of population growth and urban migration is creating problems on a scale never before encountered. Mexico City, for example, is increasing by more than 100,000 people per month, all of whom have to housed and provided with the services essential for their very survival.

Sanitation and refuse collection go hand in hand and our work with Dr. Gehan Sinnatamby of UNCHS/Habitat, resulted in their report "Refuse Collection Vehicles for Developing Countries" identifying the cost factors relating to solid waste collection and showing why refuse vehicles with a life of 10 years or more in industrialised countries often last only two or three years in developing countries. The Habitat report led to the development of computer software to provide cost comparisons for all the options available for any particular refuse situation.

2. SANITATION.

Only 17% of the worlds population have the piped water without which any form of waterborne sanitation is not possible and there is simply not enough money or water in many countries to make any form of waterborne sanitation feasible for more than a small elite group of people. The UN has a target of providing water and sanitation for 2.0 billion people by the end of this century and if these people are to have any sanitation at all it will consist of some form of pit latrine. In urban areas these latrines must be emptied when they are full.

Conventional vacuum tankers designed for the liquid wastes from septic tanks are incapable of sucking the dense wastes in dry pit latrines and early attempts at making vehicles to suck these wastes used massive vacuum pumps requiring up to 40 kw to give an "air drag" or hoovering effect. These larger trucks could only reach the periferal areas of the poor parts of the cities at costs far beyond the means of the countries concerned. Our work started with a study of the problems of pumping dense wastes showing the fundamental requirements to keep the suction hose pipes as short and straight as possible to reduce the pipe friction and for low tank heights to reduce suction heads. All good vacuum tankers achieve much the same vacuum with nominal suction heads of about 8.0 metres of water. However with wastes densities as high as 1.6 the nominal suction is down to 5.0 metres. A conventional truck with a tank height of 3 metres will have a theoretical below ground suction of only 2 metres but in practice about half this due to pipe friction and the thixotrophy of the wastes.

What was required was a vacuum tanker vehicle with a narrow width and tight turning circle to reach right up to the pits, a low tank height, powerful vacuum pump, easy servicing and capital and operating costs within the means of the poorer countries. We searched the world for a suitable truck chassis and ended up designing our own. We were able to almost double the theoretical below ground head by reducing the tank height to 1.5 metres and the shorter hoses possible with the smaller truck & greater manoeuvrability gave a dramatic increase in performance enabling dense wastes to be sucked from deep pits. Speed was not important for short-haul urban traffic and by reducing the top speed we were able to reduce the power/weight ratio and dispense with any suspension.

60% of engine problems in developing countries relate to the cooling system and the low revving air cooled diesel engine without radiator, hose, thermostat, or water pump, and the dumper transmission and rigid chassis give a life expectancy about four times that of a conventional truck.

In Kenya a latrine emptying service is now being operated
by the Kenya Water and Health Organisation in a squatter area
near Nairobi at a cost, including full depreciation on the
vehicles, of less than 0.08/capita/annum. We are now looking
at the design of the latrines to improve hygiene, reduce
construction cost and speed up the emptying process, reducing
sanitation costs for urban and peri-urban areas dramatically.

3. REFUSE

Domestic refuse in industrialised countries is light, inert
and non-abrasive so compactor trucks are used to compact it to
perhaps 1/4 of its original volume so that an economic load
can be carried on a truck. In most developing countries the
wastes are dense, abrasive and acid and compactor trucks with
a life of 8 to 10 years in the United States or Europe last
less than 4 years in Mexico and only 2 years in Haiti. There
is no logic whatever in trying to compact wastes which are
already so dense that an economic load can be achieved without
compaction but even so consultants and high pressure salesmen
from the industrialised countries have been recommending
compactor vehicles for developing countries with disastrous
results.

In the past there has been a choice of either using the
latest technology or improvising with open trucks, tractors
and trailers or other agricultural or construction vehicles
none of which are designed for the purpose. This inevitably
results in costly and short lived vehicles or inefficient
systems with slow loading speeds and high costs.

The lowest cost refuse system will almost always use communal
containers to which people bring their wastes. However
existing systems using large containers, although effective
for market & industrial wastes, do not work for household
wastes in developing countries. Studies in Brazil showed that
people will not carry their wastes more than 160 metres but
in a typical situation with a waste generation of 0.3 kg/
capita/day and a waste density of 450 kg/m3, a 10 m3 container
will hold the daily wastes from 15,000 people and only high
rise developments have this population density.

Our studies for Habitat showed the need for a low cost refuse
container vehicle to collect small containers, (1 m3 to 2 m3),
from areas with difficult access. Where the haul distances
are long this vehicle can bring the containers to a main road
and a separate vehicle can transport a number of containers
at a time for disposal. As the chassis requirements for the
container vehicle are the same as those we had identified for
the latrine emptying vehicle, (low chassis height,
manoeuvrability and simple long life construction), we
developed a container handling system for the same chassis
and a special hoist for fitting to a standard flat bed truck

enabling eight of these containers to be transported at a time for discharge at the disposal site.

Studies in Karachi showed that wastes in communal containers reduce in volume by as much as 50% over the original household volume but if these containers are then emptied into a larger container or open truck the wastes expand back almost to their original volume. Thus the volume is lowest in the communal containers and it is not cost effective to transfer these wastes into larger containers or open trucks with all the inherent hygiene and management problems of transfer stations.

4. COMPUTER SOFTWARE

We have now developed for Habitat dedicated computer software to enable consultants or local authority officials to assess all the factors effecting the life expectancy of different vehicles for any particular situations and provide cost comparisons for any number of alternative systems (from a wheel barrow to the most sophisticated compactor truck) for that particular situation. This programme is at present under test before being released by Habitat.

References.

1. UNCHS/Habitat. Refuse Collection Vehicles for Developing Countries. 1989

2. COFFEY M. Cost Effective Refuse Handling Vehicles. Proceedings of 15th WEDC Conference. Kano, Nigeria 1989.

3. COFFEY M. Low Cost Latrine Emptying Vehicle. Proceedings of 14th WEDC Conference. Kuala Lumpur, 1988.

4. IRCWD. Emptying On-site Excreta Disposal Systems. 1985.

5. COFFEY.M. Low Cost Systems for Refuse and Faecal Waste Collection. Proceedings of 2nd World Congress on Engineering and Environment. Delhi. India 1985.

6. COINTREAU S. Environmental Management of Urban Solid Wastes in Developing Countries. World Bank. 1982.

Appropriate development: the contribution of rainwater catchment systems technology

J. E. GOULD, MSc, Consultant, and Honorary Secretary, International Rainwater Systems Association

SYNOPSIS. This paper examines the current state of rainwater catchment systems, recent developments and the potential contribution of this technology in appropriate development. Using examples from projects in East Africa and S. E. Asia the "software" aspects (community organization/ participation, financing and management) of project implementation and the "hardware" aspects (construction and design) are considered.

INTRODUCTION.
1. Rainwater catchment systems (RWCS) have been used for millenia to provide water for both domestic and agricultural purposes (ref. 1-2). Despite its long history of scattered use around the world, the widespread adoption of RWCS as a serious water supply alternative in regions suffering water shortages is a recent phenomenon. Two trends, the transition from thatch to corrugated iron or tiled roofing in the rural parts of many developing countries and the development of cheap, simple, effective ferrocement tank designs are in part reponsible for the recent success of this technology for domestic water supplies from roof catchments.
2. Although RWCS may often provide the most appropriate domestic water supply option on technical, social, economic, health and environmental grounds the technology is still all too often overlooked. Meanwhile huge quantities of clean rainwater pour unused off millions of roofs thoughout the developing world while women continue to walk long distances to collect water.

THE STATE OF THE ART OF RWCS
3. A renaissance of RWCS technology is currently occurring throughout the developing world where it can now be found somewhere in almost every country. Two countries, however, Kenya and Thailand have lead the way on their respective continents. In Thailand around 10 million 1-2m^3 roof catchment tanks were constructed between 1985-1990 resulting in it being one of the few nations to even approach the IDWSS Decade targets for the provision of rural water supply. Apart from quantity, the quality of both the design and construction techniques and the effectiveness of

implementation strategies is also improving. The successes in Thailand and Kenya, where scores of community projects are in operation (ref.3), provide a useful demonstration of the potential of roof catchment technology for domestic water supplies in areas lacking clean, cheap, reliable alternative sources. The main advantages and disadvantages of roof catchment systems are summarized in table 1.

Table 1. Advantages + Disadvantages of Roof Catchment Systems

ADVANTAGES	DISADVANTAGES
Convenience	High Initial Cost
Simple Maintenance	Water Supply Limited
Neglible Running Costs	Relatively Expensive
Relatively Good Water Quality	Complex Administration
Low Environmental Impact	Risk of Contamination
Ubiquitous Supply	
Simple Construction	
Flexible Technology	

4. The potential of RWCS technology to provide water for crops and livestock in semi-arid areas through the construction of large sub-surface tanks and bunds for runoff farming has been demonstrated by several successful projects Eg. Yatenga in Burkina Faso and Turkana in Kenya where it is also helping to reduce soil erosion (ref.2, 4).

THE IMPORTANCE OF BOTH SOUND HARDWARE AND SOFTWARE.
5. In the 1970's and early 1980's a great deal of research and applied experimentation was directed towards the development of cheap, robust and easy to build rainwater tank designs. Unfortunately, this pre-occupation with the hardware side (design and construction) of RWCS projects lead to insufficient attention being paid to the software side of project implementation. These software aspects involve the promotion of individual and community awareness, motivation, organization, skills and resource generation (ref.5). Although a sound, affordable and easy to construct tank design is essential to the success of any project, good hardware alone, is not sufficient to insure a clean, reliable, well maintained, longterm water supply.

LESSONS LEARNT REGARDING RWCS HARDWARE
6. In efforts to minimize costs and maximize the use of local materials, tens of thousands of bamboo reinforced tanks were built in Thailand and Indonesia in the mid-1980's (ref.2). Within a few years a series of failures were reported. The cause for these was fungal, bacterial and termite attack of the bamboo. Similar problems were associated with the Ghala basketwork reinforced rainwater tank design developed in Kenya (ref.3). Unfortunately, a

great deal of literature promoting these designs is still in circulation which could potentially result in new projects springing up using these now obselete and discredited designs, Eg.(ref.2). Another design still under-going field tests is the interlocking brick tank which showed initial promise but is now clouded in doubt following leakage problems. Although these examples illustrate well the dangers of 'under-design', many examples of 'over-design' resulting in the lack of replication of RWCS technologies on cost grounds also exist (ref.2).

7. Most ferrocement tank designs appear to have survived the scrutiny of widespread field testing in the 1980's very well, and where levels of workmanship have been high and proper curing procedures followed problems have been few. The general lesson learnt in relation to promising new RWCS hardware in the 1980's has been that new designs need very thorough field testing over a long period of time, before wider scale replication should be encouraged.

LESSONS LEARNT REGARDING RWCS PROJECT SOFTWARE

8. Most successful projects have:
- started small and grown slowly, developing and modifying both designs and implementation strategies all the time.
- been predominantly run by local people.
- involved the local community from the outset in planning, implemention and maintenance of systems.
- generally been associated with communities where a real 'felt need' for water has been expressed and where the local community has contributed funds, labour and ideas.
- been subjected to constant apprasial, evaluation and modification to overcome problems as they arise.

Numerous case studies supporting these points have been documented (ref. 2,3 and 5).

LESSONS LEARNT REGARDING RWCS WATER QUALITY

9. Rainwater is susceptible to contamination by heavy metals such as lead used in some paints, roofing material and pipes and these should be avoided at all cost. Contamination of stored rainwater from bird and animal droppings and other organic material is a potential health hazard (ref.6) and should be avoided by removing overhanging trees above roof catchments and employing foul flush and coarse filter systems when possible. Water collected from ground catchment systems and stored in sub-surface tanks is not generally potable and is unsuitable for human consumption unless boiled.

GUIDELINES

10. The following questions may help to establish whether or not RWCS warrants further investigation in any community.
a. Is there a real need for an improved water supply?
b. Are present water supplies distant or contaminated.
c. Do suitable roof or other catchment surfaces exist.
d. Does rainfall exceed 400mm per annum?

WATER, SANITATION AND FOOD WORKSHOP

e. Does an improved water supply figure prominently in the communities list of development priorities?

If the answer to these five questions is YES, rainwater collection may be a feasible water supply option and further questions to be considered include:-

f. What other water sources are available in the community?

g. What are the economic, social and environmental implications of introducing RWCS?

h. What experience has the community had with water supply projests in the past?

The minimum technical requirements for low-cost rainwater tank designs are well documented (ref.2).

CONCLUSION

11. During the last decade great improvements have been achieved both in refining the design of RWCS 'hardware' and with innovative new 'software' for project implementation strategies (ref.5). The success of RWCS technology in Thailand leaves no doubt about the potential it offers elsewhere. Water Engineers and Planners need to consider RWCS on equal terms with other small scale water supply alternatives and not as a technology of last resort. The development of affordable, durable ferrocement tanks by a few progressive engineers willing to challenge conventional wisdom and standards has already made a substantial contribution to the success of RWCS to date. Despite the simplicity of the technology further efforts are still required in the refinement and application of computer models to optimize the volume of tanks for given rainfall regimes in order to maximize their economic appropriateness. The continued development of methods for improving water quality standards is also needed. As RWCS technology matures and continues to spread during the 1990's it is essential that the lessons learnt so far are both disseminated and applied. Provided they are RWCS techology is likely to play an important part in supplying clean drinking water to the 1 billion people still lacking it.

REFERENCES

1. ENENARI, M. et al. Ancient Agriculture in the Negev. Science. 1961, Vol.133, pp976-966.
2. PACEY A. and CULLIS A. Rainwater Harvesting, p.216. I.T.Publications 1986.
3. McPHERSON, H. et al. Low Cost Appropriate Water and Sanitation Technologies for Kenya., G.T.Z. report to the Min. of Water Development, Maji House, Nairobi. p.257. 1984.
4. HARRISON, P. The Greening of Africa. p380. Paladin 1987.
5. GOULD, J.E. Strategies for Overcoming the Obstacles Associated with 'Software' Aspects of Rain Water Catchment Systems Implementation. Proc. 4th Int. Conf. on Rainwater Cistern Systems, Manila. 1989, B3 1-16.
6. WIROJANAGUD, W. et al. Evaluation of Rainwater Quality: Heavy Metals and Pathogens. Faculty of Engineering, Khon Kaen University, Thailand. p114. 1989.

Participation in health for survival

D. M. B. JAGNE, MSc, Gambia College

SYNOPSIS.   The Village of Kerr Seringe lacked clean water supply and basic facilities to keep their environment clean. A tripartite project was launched to introduce simple technology to the village through the efforts and participation of the villagers and disseminate the ideas and findings to other villages. Concrete lined wells were dug to provide ample and safe water and fly proof VIP latrines built utilised and efficiently maintained.

Some few years ago the World Health Organisation publish figures which illustrated the community water supply situation in most of the developing countries. The rural population of the countries that were surveyed amounted to 72% of the total population of those countries. Among this rural population 1.11 thousand million people or 86% were without reasonable accsess to safe water.

The obvious need to look into ways of reducing the high incidence of water borne diseases due to inadequate protection of sources, methods of collection and storage, lack of proper, adequate and accessible sanitary structures used for the disposal of human wastes were the main factors that brought together the International Development Research Centre of Canada, the School of Public Health and the little village of Kerr Seringe, which is 20 Kms from Banjul the capital of The Gambia.

1. It is a well established fact that in any Health Education Programme in which a change in behaviour is required, the predisposing factors should be initially identified closely followed by provision of the enabling, motivating and reinforcing factors to give a meaningful and effective change in behaviour. The Kerr Seringe Project was therefore well equipped to provide all those requirements. The project erected seven ventilated improved pit latrines and seven protected sanitary concrete lined wells. It also

WATER, SANITATION AND FOOD WORKSHOP

provided the resource personnel for the Health Education Programmes. The village community were charged with the resplonsibility of providing unskilled labour and local materials.

2. MAIN OBJECTIVES

1. To introduce simple sanitary structures in the rural community of Kerr Seringe which the inhavitants and other rural dwellers can afford to build, use and maintain.

2. To ultimately improve the sanitary environment of the community through the provision and utilisation of such structures.

3. To provide training opportunities for students who would use the area as a model ground for demonstration purposes.

4. To make any findings achieved from the project available to National and International agencies, and also facilitate the extension of the models to other villages in the country.

CONDITIONS BEFORE THE PROJECT

3. The ethnic composition of Kerr Seringe is mixed and virtually all large ethnic groups in the country are well represented. Pre-project survey showed that there were 247 inhabitants in the village while post-project data revealed that the number increased to 800 people.

The village lacked adequate water supply to meet the general needs of the inhabitants. The few wells that existed were shallow and polluted, most of them getting dry during the dry season.

There were no public latrines in the village, only 26 compounds out of the 48 in the village had private latrines. Occupants of those compounds without latrines either used their neighbours latrines or went out to the bush. The spread of fly borne and other parasitic diseases are facilitated by such practice.

4. RESOURCES

Being a tripartite funded project all the parties concerned contributed towards it. IDRC put in 44,500 Canadian Dollars, including the cost of one pick-up truck and some of the building materials and well digging equipment. The School of Publid Health provided 44,000 Gambian Dalasis in terms of time given by staff and students on supervisory capacities. The village community did most of the manual work such as cleaning th areas, moulding the blocks, dry digging of the wells and pit latrines etc. It was not easy to translate these efforts into monetary terms but the investigation team agrees on a figure of 15,000 Gambian Dalasis. A significant contribution also came from the Ministry of Water Resources which provided the expertise and equipment to complete the wet digging part of the wells.

4.a. METHODS OF HEALTH EDUCATION USED

Right from the start it was accepted as a precondition to get the local inhabitants who were the target for behavioural change to be deeply involved in every part of the programmes. Two mature, experienced and well respected persons were therefore choosen by the community from the two main ethnic groups to be trained as health educators. Their training consisted mainly of elementary courses in food and nutrition, water and environmental sanitation, first aid, and techniques in field and home visits. They were paid monthly allowance for loss of earnings from their farms because they spent most of their time on health education work, community mobilisation and involvement.

The low literacy rate among the villagers ruled out the use of written materials and posters, the best approach was to have face to face discussions with individuals and groups on choosen topics based on the group dynamics method when everyone spoke freely. Role playing maong the children was also a regular feature.

The trained local health educators used to arrange regular health talks with various groups of the village community. They quickly realised that the message got home quicker among small groups rahter large crowds. Their work schedule, was as follows. On Monday evenings they would visit the village Bantaba "chatting spot at the centre of the village" where men and some of the upcoming adolescents gather to chat and exchange ideas.

On Wednesdays, when most of the women stay at home they make home visits. It has been a culturalhabit for a long time for women in the rural areas to stay at home during those days when the children have their weekly holidays from the religious schools. In most areas Wednesday is observed as a break. But now, this day and age when we have cross cultures requiring children to go to both Arabic and English schools, the practice of having women to stay at home on Wednesday is fading out. Thursday morning activities were always centred around an old well on the outskirt of the village where women gather to do their laundry, and exchange gossips. On Saturday afternoons they turn their attention to an open field south of the village where the youths meet to play or watch games.

The main topic of discussions has alwyas centred around the ways of protecting the wells from sources of contamination, the advantages of using the VIP latrines and the proper disposal of their domestic wastes.

FINDINGS

1. it has been proved once again that when the need for behabioural change is iminent the provision of enabling and motivating factors would facilitate, synergise and accelerate such change.

2. Pre-project data showed that out of the 48 compounds in village only 26 had latrines. The majority of the occupants of 22 compounds without latrines used the bush. After the erection of the public latrines not a single person in the village used the bush again. Another encouraging discovery has been that families take turns to maintain the good standard of cleanliness of the public latrines near them, and also dump their refuse at central points before incinerating them.

2. The villagers quickly realised thta the project wells yielded more wholesome and palatablewater, consequently they are now the only wells used for obtaining drinking water. The prevalence of gastro intestinal diseases has also been reduced drastically.

The availability of ample, wholesome water and the other sanitary structures attracted more people to the village and since the commissioning of the structures the population has grown from 247 to 800 people.

OVERALL PROGRAMME EFFICIENCY

After intervention the project provided five new wells and rehabilitated two old one, each capable of producing more than 5,000 gallons per day. This increased the quentity of water for the village by over 70% and brought the quality to WHO Standard for small rural water supplies. With regards to the ventilated improved pit latrines 70% overall programme effici-ency was also achieved. It is sometimes difficult to measure behavioural change, but the complete and total change over of the village community in favour of the use of the latrines and wells illustrate that this part of the project objectives was fulfilled. Another objective was to desseminate the findings and carry the ideas and technology to other villages. It should be emphasized that wide publicity was given to these areas through meetings with other village communities, publications, workshops and seminars.

In making a general conclusion we can say that the project was as effective as planned. The community through their participation fully accepted the appropriate technology provided, and the quality of life greatly improved.

Rural water supply borehole construction programmes in Africa

M. J. JONES, MSc, DUC, FGS, Acer Consultants Ltd

SYNOPSIS. Drilling programmes for rural water supplies often fall behind schedule and have limited long term success due to continual failure of borehole pumps. This has lead many observers to question the appropriateness of such programmes. Examination of drilling performance over several years shows the technology to be sound although more demanding on transport and operational costs than recognised by project planners and funding agencies. Borehole pump problems largely stem from relatively minor errors in installation which could be eliminated by improvements in the pump construction. The importance of keeping good records on the drilling programmes is emphasised.

INTRODUCTION
1. Successful development of groundwater to meet the increasing demand for safe, clean water has assumed a vital importance in the economic and social development of the rural areas in Africa. While traditional sources, springs and hand dug-wells still provide adequate water supplies for many communities, boreholes and deep well pumps can, and have, increased the available supplies to satisfy extra demands. These developments, however, rely on correct construction techniques, and require reliable and well maintained drilling rigs and pumping equipment.
2. This technology is usually acquired under grant aid or development loan projects. Ethiopia for example (ref. 1) has received considerable assistance in acquiring the necessary techniques and facilities and by 1987, the well records held in the Welo regional offices at Kombolcha of the Water Supply and Sewerage Authority (WSSA) and the Ethiopian Water Works Construction Authority (EWWCA) listed approximately 400 boreholes. Of these, about 80 per cent were productive at the time of construction but during a pre-project survey in 1986, only 50 per cent of all pumps installed were operating. In operation, at the time of the survey, was considered to be due in some cases to over pumping, and in others to a lack of water because of reduced water table levels following years of below average rainfall, and in others due to mechanical failure. As

maintenance work progressed, approximately 70 per cent of the problems encountered with pumps installed in boreholes could be traced to incorrect installation or selection of equipment.

3. With similar reports from projects elsewhere in Africa (ref, 2) observers and planners rightly question whether developing groundwater sources by boreholes and deep well pumps is appropriate. Hydrogeologists however point out that the distribution of rural populations and local groundwater occurrences make boreholes the only feasible water supply option and the purpose of this paper is to show that, with a few reservations, it is an appropriate method.

BOREHOLE DRILLING PROGRAMMES

4. Project planners and drilling rig manufacturers agree that a modern rotary rig operated by a government agency should be expected to complete a borehole in two to six days. This output is seldom achieved. Most government operations would be satisfied if a rotary rig completed two or three boreholes per month.

5. Table 1 shows the performance of aid sponsored drilling programmes operating two new rotary rigs over four years and the same operation using three rigs 10 years later. In 1976 and 1977, drilling performance was slow as both new crews were being trained and the geological conditions were not suitable for the drilling equipment originally supplied. The 1980 data refers to a drilling programme for a Water Master Plan in Tanzania using a local crew and an eight year old government rig (ref. 3).

6. While the rigs seldom achieved two boreholes per month, when the drilling performance is measured against the number of productive days worked, the 1979 and 1989 outputs are within the manufacturers' expectation.

Table 1. Drilling performance based on productive days.

Year	Potential rig days available	Total boreholes constructed	Number of productive days (%)	Productive days per borehole
1976	470	20	362 (77)	18
1977	640	24	435 (68)	18
1978	640	34	365 (57)	11
1979	640	50	314 (49)	6
1989	960	45	269 (28)	6
1980	341	22	132 (28)	6

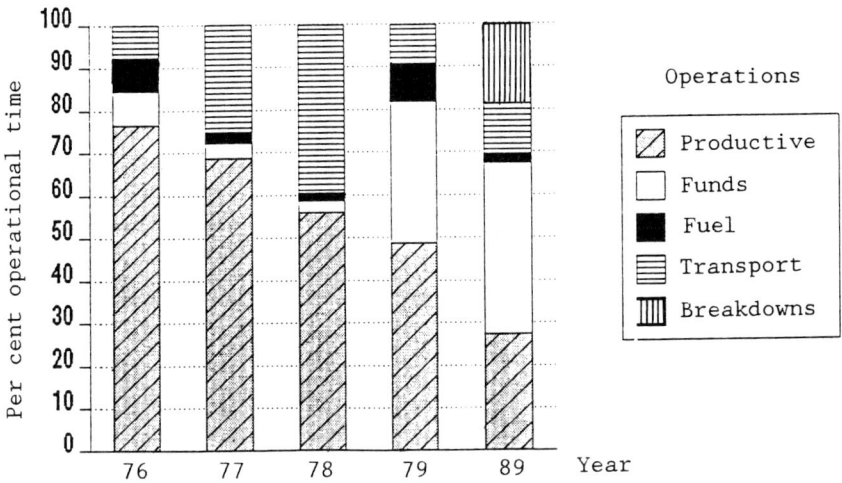

Fig. 1. Comparison of drilling programme productive and non-productive time

7. Fig. 1 shows the drilling programmes in terms of productive and non-productive time. Major loss of time was caused by the lack of transport and money and, to a lesser extent, fuel shortages and mechanical breakdowns. For most of 1976 only one rig was drilling, in 1977 the two rigs were working close together but in 1978, the rigs had increased production and were drilling in different parts of the region. This led to the time lost due to the lack of transport. The donor provided additional vehicles in 1979 but by then there were only limited local funds available. An extreme example of the lack of transport was in East Africa in 1980, where one government drilling agency tried to maintain over 50 rigs in the field with only six support trucks and 12 crew vehicles. In Botswana, rotary drilling using mud circulation can be prohibitively expensive in the semi arid Kalahari areas where the nearest readily available supplies of make-up water may need transporting 100 km or more to the new borehole site.

8. Breakdown time losses were very limited between 1976 and 1979 as the rigs were new, well maintained and supplied with adequate spare parts. By 1989 breakdowns were becoming significant due to the arrival of different types of drilling rigs and carrier vehicles which were supplied with insufficient spare parts. In the Tanzanian example given in Table 1, 40 per cent of productive time was lost due to major breakdowns to the 8 year old rig. 11 per cent was lost while the rig was re-equipped with new drill pipe and tools and 11 per cent was lost waiting for fuel. As the donor agency, Danida met all local costs and crew salaries and provided 4 support trucks, no time was lost on transport and administration.

9. Faced with these constraints project planners and government agencies should review new drilling programmes to ensure adequate local funds and logistical support will be available for each rig. Typically the local recurrent funding requirement would appear to be about 15 to 20 percent of the capital value of the equipment and materials employed. While in many cases this may lead to fewer rigs being deployed in the field, the final number of holes drilled may well increase.

10. If cutting the number of rigs deployed is politically unacceptable an alternative is to use low cost percussion drilling methods that are widely and successfully used in central and southern Africa. (ref. 4).

BOREHOLE PUMPS

11. Experience in borehole rehabilitation and maintenance in Ethiopia found that over seventy percent of the mechanical problems with the pumps could be traced to poor or incorrect installation which often stemmed from the manufacturers' poor design or quality control.

12. Much has been made of hand pump design and testing, often with low unit price and VLOM being the main objectives. To a rural water supply agency the main criteria for a successful hand pump installation programme are ease of installation, and low maintenance requirements. Frequently the local costs involved in installing and maintaining hand pumps considerably exceed the capital cost of the pump. A hand pump design that ensures fool proof installation has considerably greater merit, than a cheaper pump with a problematic installation. Similarly a hand pump where removed can be installed independently of the piston and pump rods or rotor and drive shaft the rising main and cylinder or stator makes for simpler maintenance. The material cost of large diameter rising mains is more than offset by the locally incurred maintenance costs. Other pump manufacturers should look to reducing the large number of loose components that have to be assembled to make up their pumps.

13. Motorised pumps are most often installed in larger rural centres and generally perform well. The manufacturers should pay attention to reports of recurring design faults.

14. Electric submersible pumps are often most appropriate and, if correctly installed, perform well. Manufacturers could reduce the risk of incorrect installations involving mismatching starter controls, cables and pumps by a colour coding of compatible items. In many government stores a considerable number of pumps, motors and starter boxes can be found with illegible or missing part numbers, identification or specification labels. Pump manufacturers should note also that the local market can not be relied upon to supply ancillary items required to install pumps such as pipe clamps and well caps.

15. Points to be established by project planners when considering pump orders are details of pumping heads, borehole capacities and the depth at which the pump will be set. This information can be obtained from the records of earlier boreholes drilled in the area. All too frequently, repeat orders are placed for inappropriate pumps. Often too high a capacity powered pumps are ordered when compared to the average borehole yields achieved. Excess rising main is often ordered with the hand pumps. One regional store was noted as having 10 km of 12mm India MK2 pump rods against a requirement for 800m.

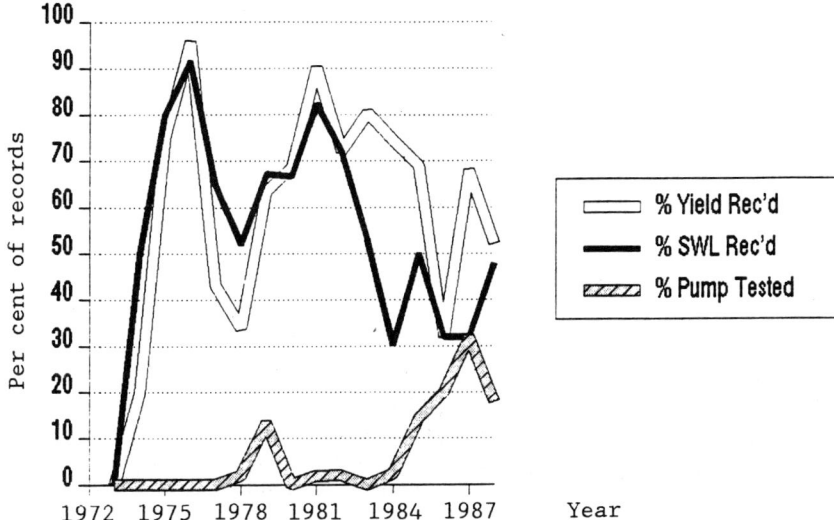

Fig. 2. Per cent recorded groundwater data between 1975 and 1988

BOREHOLE RECORDS

16. The absolute need for complete and accurate record keeping on drilling programmes has been widely stated in a number of countries it is required by law (ref. 5). These records should include the location and owner of the borehole, full construction details and information on the geology and groundwater occurrence, ideally including chemical quality. This information will form the basis for groundwater evaluation, aquifer development, resource management and well rehabilitation and maintenance programmes. Certain donor organisations with the declared aim of rapid development of groundwater by drilling and equipping boreholes have chosen to limit project record keeping to a minimum. The very limited amount of groundwater data collected in one project can be seen in Fig. 2 which shows the percentage of static water level (SWL), yield and pumping test data recorded between 1975 and 1988.

Examination of even these limited records in terms of borehole depths static water levels and yields however provided information on potential pumping depths and yields (ref. 1).

17. Without adequate records, boreholes may become overlooked or lost as they fall out of service due to the lack of maintenance. In these cases a new borehole may be drilled close to an existing but unrecorded borehole that may only require minor rehabilitation to put back in service.

CONCLUSIONS

18. Although groundwater development by boreholes and deep well pumps requires fairly high technology, the main constraints to a successful programme are not the equipment and manpower but the availability of transport for materials and equipment and local funds for salaries, field allowances and fuel. Donor project planners have been slow to recognise this and continue to supply new drilling rigs without regard to these constraints.

19. The position with regards to borehole pumps is still not clear. There are examples of well installed borehole pumps running, almost maintenance free, for 10 or more years. These are the exceptions, the majority of pumps will be subject to frequent breakdowns, many of which can be traced to poor installation which in certain cases, can be traced to design.

Finally to obtain the fully value from a borehole drilling programme, detailed records must be kept given time, in the most extreme cases, given time, these may be the only concrete contribution of a project.

REFERENCES
1.   JONES, M.J. Rural well rehabilitation and maintenance in Welo, Ethiopia. Water Wells, Monitoring, Maintenance, Rehabilitation. International Groundwater Engineering Conference, (Cranfield Institute of Technology), Spon, London 1990.
2.   SUTTON, S.E. and SUTTON, J.S. Rehabilitate or renew? An example in Western Zambia. Water Wells, Monitoring, Maintenance, Rehabilitation. International Groundwater Engineering Conference, (Cranfield Institute of Technology), Spon, London 1990.
3.   CCKK - DANIDA Water Master Plans for Iringa, Ruvuma and Mbeya Regions, Tanzania. Volume 9 : Hydrogeology. CCKK 1982.
4.   SUTTON, S.E. Percussion vs. Rotary - Myths exploded. World Water, November 1986.
5.   WATER RESOURCE DEVELOPMENT CENTRE Large Scale Ground - Water Development. United Nations, New York 1960.

Community wastewater treatment systems using indigenous aquatic/marginal plants

P. C. LAWRENCE, Watson Hawksley Ltd, J. BUTLER, Portsmouth Polytechnic, and U. BURKA, Camphill Village

SYNOPSIS. Western urbanisation, developed over centuries has led to the adoption of policies of centralisation of services and utilities. In wastewater treatment the trend has been towards energy intensive technologies to minimise the land areas required to treat large volumes of sewage. The transfer of such technologies to developing countries in hot climates has often brought many problems; mal-operation; breakdowns; overloading; odours; corrosion. New developments using aquatic plant systems of sewage treatment offer an attractive alternative to communities in developing countries. Effective treatment, community involvement, localised systems, environmental enhancement, simple O&M and product re-use are demonstrated through the work of *Portsmouth Polytechnic* and *The Camphill Village Trust*.

WASTEWATER TRANSPORTATION & TREATMENT

1. Waterborne sewerage systems have become the norm in the West and will continue to spread amongst the developing world as a safe and hygienic way of transporting domestic wastes from the home. The costs of sanitary fittings and reasonable lengths of piping are within the reach of an increasing proportion of the world population and if leading to a localised treatment facility are not disproportionately expensive.

2. The affluent West has been able to afford the luxury of centralising its treatment facilities and has developed some sophisticated techniques to treat ever increasing volumes of sewage on smaller unit land areas. Invariably these techniques involve significant capital expenditure, high energy inputs to provide the oxygen demand of the bacteria which mineralise the sewage, skilled operation and maintenance and availability of spares. Even the affluent West has not maintained its check on pollution control and the UK is currently faced with a heavy capital expenditure programme to meet the EC bathing water standards and North Sea Protection Regulations.

3. In developing countries the concept of centralised waterborne sewerage and treatment systems is questionable. Many poorer countries are unlikely to be able to afford such systems at all. In the oil-rich Middle East a number of problems have been encountered in water borne sewerage and sewage treatment:- *Septicity and Corrosion* first became a major issue in the 1970's. Early measurements undertaken by Watson Hawksley identified pH levels as low as 1 in sewer slimes in the Arabian Gulf and the widespread effects of corrosion of cementitious materials is still being dealt with at enormous cost.
Odours from sewerage systems within cities occur with high temperatures and long retention times. Control measures can be costly and do not treat the problem at source.
Operation and Maintenance of sewers, pumping stations and treatment facilities is often inadequate unless the country can

support a properly managed, adequately trained staff with full M&E spares availability. An extreme case of totally clogged biological filters is illustrated below.

Fig.1 Example of Maloperation of STW, Middle East

4. Even in some of the wealthiest Middle Eastern States there are examples of inadequate maintenance programmes for sewers and pumping stations resulting in continuous discharges through overflows to the sea. At least two Middle Eastern cities are now embarking on very expensive deep tunnelled sewer schemes with the intention of eliminating existing pumping stations and pumping large quantities of sewage to major, remote sewage treatment works. The capital expenditure for such schemes is very high and the long term operational benefits have yet to be demonstrated. With the tendency to re-use effluents from these works in municipal landscaping and beautification schemes, further high costs are incurred in returning the treated effluents to the city areas.

ALTERNATIVE TECHNOLOGY - LOCAL, AQUATIC AND PLANT SYSTEMS

5. The science of using marginal aquatic plants in the purification of wastewater emanates from the work of Kathe Seidel in the early 1960's (ref 1). She identified the particular properties of helophytes such as *Phragmites australis*, the common reed and *Scirpus lacustris*, the true bullrush which play a role in the natural purification and stabilisation of watercourses. Through extensive and complex root systems these plants can variously; transfer oxygen; host a wide range of bacteria; exude substances which can assist in disinfection. These functions are all performed in natural water courses and phragmites can be seen growing in abundance around polluted areas in many climates.

6. The initial work of Seidel involved growing these plants in mineral granular beds fed vertically with wastewaters which supply the plants with the nutrients for growth. The systems act as filter beds hosting bacterial cells whose mineralising activity is governed by the supply of oxygen which, unlike traditional biological filters, is actively augmented by the complex plant root matrices. Many systems have been developed by groups around the world including a recent research programme in the UK monitored by WRc (ref 2). Some of these systems, particularly those which have departed from Seidel's concept of gravel planting media, have developed problems of blockages and short-circuiting but the work of two successful groups is highlighted below.

PORTSMOUTH POLYTECHNIC - GRAVEL BED HYDROPONICS (GBH)

7. GBH systems have been developed over the last five years as inclined, gravel-filled channels lined with impermeable membranes and planted with helophytes. Portsmouth Polytechnic has two large scale pilot schemes, one in the UK and one at Abu Attwa in Egypt (ref 3). A comprehensive monitoring programme has resulted in an extensive data bank which is leading to a better understanding of the chemical and microbiological processes in the systems. The 100m long horizontal flow channels support different bacteria on both the roots and the gravel; ammonifiers (anaerobic) decrease in population; nitrifiers and denitrifiers (aerobic) increase in population along the length of the channels.

8. At Abu Attwa, in Egypt, where trials have been undertaken with settled sewage, average effluent qualities of 20mg/l BOD and 3mg/l Ammonia have been achieved. The mode of feeding the beds (continuous or intermittent) is found to affect the levels of nitrate in the effluent allowing a degree of control over the end use (discharge to watercourse - low nitrate; agricultural re-use - higher nitrate).

CAMPHILL VILLAGE TRUST, Oaklands Park - Gloucestershire

9. Considerable attention is being paid by the water industry and the media to two sewage treatment systems developed for the Oaklands Park Camphill Village in Gloucestershire (ref 4). These systems, which follow Seidel's recommendations for vertical flow beds, are remarkable for a number of reasons:
- they were conceived, built and are operated by the community with no background in wastewater technology.
- their performance (monitored by Severn Trent Water and the NRA) has been consistently high; 98% removal of BOD/SS; nitrified effluent; high bacterial removals - effluent ponds meet EC bathing water standards.
- the systems have been carefully landscaped using a variety of marginal plant species and FLOWFORM cascades. As such they enhance the landscape of the park and represent a village amenity and the concept of sewage treatment as an odorous and unattractive process is dispelled.

Fig.2 Oaklands Park STW - System 2

10. Oaklands Park systems include a separate reed bed for the dewatering and mineralisation of cold digested sludge from the two works. After a year's operation, the build-up of composted sludge averages about 30mm across the bed which is designed on about 5 persons / sq m.

11. Oaklands Park practices the organic agricultural system of *Biodynamics* – a balanced, integrated farming system of animals, crops and woodlands which eliminates the need for artificial chemicals. A principle of biodynamics is that human wastes should not be used in the direct production of human foodstuffs. The use of animal wastes and composts on the food crops avoids short circuiting of the human food chain. Many cultures have religious or philosophical concerns about the re-use and handling of human wastes and in developing countries the nutrients in human sewage wastes can be utilised in woodland development providing timber and the benefits of enhanced micro-climates for other crops or such crops as cotton/flax.

RELEVANCE TO THE DEVELOPING WORLD

12. The Oaklands Park systems were *managed and planned* by a village community resulting in a pride and interest in the end product. The Oaklands Park and Portsmouth Polytechnic systems described above demonstrate how effective treatment of sewage can be achieved both in temperate and hotter climates. The suitability as a *choice of technology* is illustrated by the rapid growth of the plants in Egypt permitting six harvest of the reeds per year – the reeds may be used for roofing, matting and basketry. Experimentation is continuing with downstream re-use for various types of cropping – particularly cotton and fodder. *Maintenance* of the systems is more easily understood by local rural communities than that of mechanised systems facilitating local *education and training*.

13. Rural water supply schemes in developing countries have demonstrated the benefits of community involvement in planning, construction and operation leading to a better understanding of and pride in the systems.

14. The World Health Organisation is favouring Wastewater Stabilization Ponds as a method of sewage treatment in warm climates because of the benefits of helminth removal (ref 5). The incorporation of an aquatic/marginal plant stage in series with ponds is found to reduce significantly the area required. Due consideration to detail and adequate maintenance should minimise the risk of mosquito breeding.

15. Species of aquatic and marginal plants are indigenous throughout the world. These treatment systems are applicable to simple rural communities in the third world. A more localised treatment policy utilising such systems could also be applied to towns and cities, reducing the expense and problems of major sewerage and providing 'green' inner city, amenity areas.

REFERENCES

1. Seidel et al. Contributions to the Re-vitalisation of Wastes. Proc. Nat Conf on Mun. & Ind. sludge Disposal, State of New Jersey, 1978.
2. Boon AG. Report on a Visit by members and staff to Germany to investigate the Root-Zone method for Treatment of Wastewaters, WRc, 1986.
3. Butler et al. Comparison of Chemical and Microbiological Processes in Gravel Bed Hydroponic Systems for Sewage Treatment. Proc Artificial Wetlands Conference WRc/IAWPRC, Cambridge. 1990
4. Burka & Lawrence. A New Community Approach to Wastewater Treatment with Higher Aquatic Plants. Proc Artificial Wetlands Conference, WRC/IAWPRC, Cambridge 1990
5. Report of a Scientific Group. Health Guidelines for the Use of Wastewater in Agriculture and Aquaculture. Technical Report Series 778, WHO, Geneva, 1989

Use of seeds of *Moringa oleifera* and solar radiation for drinking water purification in West Africa

O. ODEYEMI, BSc, MSc, PhD, Obafemi Awolowo University, Nigeria

SYNOPSIS. One of the simplest possible means of providing safe drinking water in rural areas of developing countries is the use of solar radiation for disinfecting bacteriologically contaminated water. The technique consists of exposing the water sample to about 600 W/m^2 of solar intensity for 5 hours in a transparent container. A turbid water must be clarified with ground seeds of Moringa oleifera prior to solar treatment.

PROCEDURE FOR SOLAR DISINFECTION OF DRINKING WATER
1. The process of employing solar energy to disinfect drinking water consists of simply exposing one to two litres of the water sample in a clean transparent container to about 5 hours of intense sunshine (ref. 1). However, in spite of the simplicity of the technique, certain conditions must be met in order to achieve the desired result. For instance, the water sample must be relatively small in volume, clear and nonturbid, and its bacterial load must not be too high. A turbid water may be clarified with a natural coagulant such as seeds of Moringa oleifera by adding two ground seeds to a litre of water. The water must be exposed to at least 600 W/m^2 of sunshine for about 5 hours in West Africa (ref. 2).
2. The efficacy of this method of water disinfection depends on several factors some of which are the following:
   (a) the type and characteristics of the containers e.g. colour, shape, size, wall thickness and transparency to sunlight
   (b) degree of turbidity and volume of water sample
   (c) intensity of sunlight at the time of exposure, which in turn depends on latitude, seasonal variations, cloud cover, effective range of wavelengths of light and time of the day
   (d) the type of pathogen being exposed, the nature and composition of the medium and the presence of growth supporting nutrients (refs 3 and 4).

APPLICATION OF SOLAR WATER DISINFECTION IN WEST AFRICA
3. In Nigeria, stream, pond and well water samples were rid of their coliform bacteria after 5 hours of exposure to sunshine during which the total heterotrophic bacteria density of

the samples were also reduced considerably. One of the important parameters for assessing the bacteriological quality of a faecally contaminated water source is the level of its coliform content, and sometimes its total heterotrophic bacteria density. Hence in as much as these parameters are used for assessing drinking water pollution, it may be assumed that exposure of bacteriologically contaminated stream or well water samples to intense sunshine may render the water safe to drink.

4. In fact some specific etiologic agents of water-borne diseases have been shown to be susceptible to solar-inactivation. For instance, the cells of Vibrio cholerae were completely wiped out in samples of interilized fresh water exposed to the rays of the sun during 4 hours of relatively high insolation. There was no bacterial regrowth after 72 hours of post-disinfection storage, whereas the V. cholerae regrew in the samples kept in darkness in which the bacterial cells appeared to have disappeared after 24 hours of incubation (Table 1). However, when insolation values are low as a result of heavy cloud cover a complete inactivation of V. cholerae may not be possible. It should be noted that cholera is a major water-borne disease which may occur in explosive patterns in susceptible populations, with death rates as high as 75% (ref. 5). Similarly, some other important etiologic agents of water-borne diseases such as Staphylococcus aureus Escherichia coli, Salmonella typhi, Shigella flexneri, Salmonella paratyphi B and Pseudomonas aeruginosa have been shown to be susceptible to solar inactivation in water sample contaminated with the pathogens (ref. 6).

5. The semi-arid region of West Africa lying between latitudes $14^{\circ}N$ and $16^{\circ}N$ is most suitable for solar energy applications. This belt is characterized by very high insolation, more than 90% of which comes as direct radiation because of the limited cloud coverage and rainfall (250 - 500 mm per year). There are about 3,000 hours of sunshine per year in this region (ref. 3). On the other hand, the southern belt of West Africa lying between latitudes $7^{\circ}N$ and $14^{\circ}N$ is only moderately favourable as the high humidity and frequent overcast that characterize this region give rise to scattered and diffuse radiation resulting in approximately 2,500 hours of sunshine per year. On the whole, there is abundant sunshine year round in West Africa to conveniently practise solar decontamination of drinking water in the rural communities lacking treated water supplies.

6. However, a turbid water sample must be purified by adding two ground seeds of Moringa oleifera to one litre of water. The water is then shaken rapidly for one minute followed by slow stirring for five minutes and subsequently allowed to stand for about forty minutes. This coagulant removes most of the suspended organic matter and abut 80% of the total bacteria. The decanted supernatant is then exposed to solar radiation for disinfection.

Table 1. Effect of solar radiation on the bacterial content of samples of sterilized distilled water and sterilized stream water contaminated with <u>Vibrio cholerae</u> and exposed to sunshine in transparent containers (ref. 1).

	Hours of exposure/incubation					
	0	2	4	24	48*	72*
Cell density/ml sterilized distilled water in sunshine	2.6×10^5	1.5×10^3	5×10^2	nd	nd	nd
Water temp., $°C$	29	32	33	30	32	30
Solar intensity, W/m^2	180	395	419	580	382	592
Cell density/ml sterilized distileed water in darkness	3.5×10^5	2.5×10^4	4.3×10^4	nd	nd	nd
Water temp., $°C$	29	30	31	30	29	29
Bacterial No./ml sterilized stream water in sunshine	3.8×10^4	2.3×10^3	8	0	0	0
Water temp., $°C$	30	37	42	32	33	31
Solar intensity, W/m^2	592	886	736	362	397	594
Bacterial No./ml sterilized stream water in darkness	3.9×10^4	0.8×10^3	2.6×10^2	0	3.5×10^2	2.2×10^5
Water temp., $°C$	30	34	33	32	30	31

* Post-incubation hours to determine possible regrowth.

nd = not determined.

Solar radiation was measured with a mechanical Pyranograph, model 3010.

7. It should be mentioned however that the demonstrated feasibility of using solar radiation for drinking water disinfection has remained a laboratory exercise so far. Therefore there is still a need to test the prototype of the technique under actual field conditions in West Africa in order to achieve the following objectives:

(a) to assess the efficacy of this method of water disinfection at the village level
(b) to determine the sociocultural and economic acceptability of the technique
(c) to determine the cost of solar water disinfection at household level and compare to other available options
(d) to assess the possible impacts of the method at family and community levels
(e) to create awareness and to develop, implement and assess introduction strategies for solar water disinfection
(f) to develop a set of recommendations and diffusion materials for further disemination of the technique, based on the outcome of the field studies.

8. A successful diffusion and adoption of this novel low cost technology of water treatment in West Africa will reduce the alarmingly high rates of morbidity and mortality resulting from water-associated diseases in the sub-region. The two billion rural dwellers of the Developing Countries should also benefit from this technology.

REFERENCES
1. ODEYEMI O. An assessment of solar disinfection of drinking water in Nigeria. The United Nations University, Tokyo, Japan, 1987, Report of MRP No. ICA/86/120.
2. ODEYEMI O. Prospects and limitations of using solar energy for water disinfection. Proc. International Workshop on Solar Water Disinfection, Montreal, Canada. UNU/IDRC, Ottawa, Canada, 1988.
3. ACRA A. et al. Solar disinfection of drinking water and oral rehydration solutions: Guidelines for household applications in Developing Countries. UNICEF. Illustrated Publications, S. A. L., Beirut, Lebanon, 1984.
4. ODEYEMI O. Guidelines for the study of solar disinfection of drinking water in developing areas of the world. INRESA Secretariat, Brace Research Institute, ste Anne de Bellevue, Quebec, Canada, 1986, Publication No. U/86/24.
5. WILSON M. E. and MIZER H. E. Microbiology in patient care. Macmillan Publishing Co., Inc., New York, 1974.
6. ODEYEMI O. Use of solar radiation for water disinfection. INRESA Secretariat, Brace Research Institute, Ste Anne de Bellevue, Quebec, Canada, 1986, Publication No. U/86/32.

Importance of software aspects involved in technology transfer

O. PRAKASH, Consortium on Rural Technology, India

SYNOPSIS : Necessity of amalgamation on a priority basis of an implementing agency involved in any technology transfer with the aims and objective of it and the values and norms of the society is required for successful implementation of any programme.

IMPORTANCE OF SOFTWARE ASPECTS INVOLVED IN TECHNOLOGY TRANSFER

1. Constraints in technology transfer: E.F. Sumacher in his famous book **'SMALL IS BEATIFUL'** mentioned in the very beginning "For rich countries they say, the most important task now is education for leissure and for the poor countries the transfer of technology ....". It is true also, because there are many technologies developed by different Research and Development Institutions to encounter various day to day problems of the rural folk, despite all these facts people are still burdened with numerous problems. Most of the Low Cost Appropriate Technologies fail to give anticipated results, when they are put to actual practice. The problematic ifs and buts can be categorised in two broader categories that is Hardware and the Software part of the technology. The hardware part of the technology can fairly and readily be overcome, while the software constraints being related to the factors like communities, its local norms, customs & rituals etc., are beyond easy control.

2. A problematic Case: Under the programme of drinking water supply to rural population Government of India and other national and international agencies involved in this programme decided to opt for the handpump technology on a mass scale. So far the hardware part of the technology is concerned, the India Mark-II & recently developed **VLOM** models had proved its testimony. Despite all its technical superiorities in the hardware, all the agencies are facing numerous problems in the maintenance of installed handpumps. Reasons are many:

Appropriate development for basic needs. Thomas Telford, London, 1991

2.1 Firstly the success of any programme depends mainly upon the response of the beneficiaries. It is being told that there is often a lack of community spirit towards introduced supply systems even to the extent of Vandalism. But it is not true. The same community who are not sharing community spirit to this present technology were cautiously maintaining their community water sources earlier. It was very common only few decades ago when it was a social duty or a part of **ritual** to desilt the ponds, tanks and open wells. They were also very selective in using different type of materials for the construction of drinking water units. These practices even today can be observed in the areas where modern development mechanisms have not yet reached.

2.2 In the desert areas of Rajasthan (a province of India with acute water crisis, rainfall 300mm./year) one will be surprised to know about the construction and maintenance techniques of community rain water harvesting devices. Before entering into the catchment area people took off their shoes and sleeper. One can find some religious symbols warning & marking of the catchment area. Community water sources are held in such esteem that either a temple or any other religious symbol co-exits.

2.3 The old model of handpumps with all its technical shortcomings and lacunas; can still be seen functional even years after its instalation; by the individual households, while the present model of handpumps with all its technical superiorities can be seen disfunctional at the same place; installed for community purposes. It clearly indicates that involvement and interest of beneficiaries is much more vital then technical qualities.

2.4 Association of beneficiaries with earlier technologies is quite obvious because there was some short of attachment or affiliation of the community with the technology. It was the out come of their own efforts and they werewithall about those technologies. But with the new handpump technology their experience is very short and there have been no effective health education on the values of use of pure drinking water. In most of the cases it is found that the community is not approached & consulted in the site selection, installation, repair & maintenance and other such works. All this creats an impression in the mind of the users that the handpump does not belongs to them. It is a property of the Government, so government will take pain to manage it. It is also because of lack of sense of ownership that people remove & even steale parts of the handpumps thus installed.

2.5. Not only the beneficiaries but sometimes even the agencies administrering the project escape responsibilities. It is because of lack of co-ordination in bet-ween the agencies involve in the project. Construction is often in the hand of specialised well drilling team employed by the government or concerned Voluntary Organisation. But completed wells are handed over to any local govt. or semigovernment agencies like Panchayat Unions or Public Health Engineering Department (**PHED**)

2.6. A **two** & three tier systems have been designed by the government for the maintenance of the handpumps. The result have not remained satisfactory because of various reasons, like non availability of spare parts in time, lack of communication in-between members of the team at different levels, transport problems etc.

3. **The Way Out :** Observing the lacunas in the present maintenance system a voluntary group in Rajasthan though of going for a one tier system, depending upon the local skill only. This organisation started providing training in the maintenance techniques of Handpumps to local skilled, semiskilled a even to unskilled people e.g., cycle mechanic, blacksmith carpenter, agriculture labourers, who have knowledge of 3 **R's** etc. These Handpump Mechanics(HPM) had done marvelous and tremendous amount of job, in comparison to their highly educated and well equiped counterparts. It is only because of the achievement of HPMS that they totally replaced the defunct three tier system in Rajasthan (a province of India) "what was unique about the HPMS was the fact they came from such humble modest and poor backgrounds - the very stuff rural India is made of and what they are capable of doing at nominal cost to the government". The studies of the one tier system had brought it in notice that HPMS had not only done their job fantastically but also brought down the maintenance cost to one third than the earlier system i.e., Rs. 200/handpump/year instead of Rs. 500 to 600/handpump/year. The reason behind the success of this one tier system also lies in the fact of its involvement and attachment with the society and trust on the local person, directly accountable to the society.

4. Conclusive Options

4.1. On the basis of the above discussion and the

other related datas on these issues, there is no denying the fact that unlees and until the software constraints/aspects; related to any technology transfer are given due weightage; any such attempt is bound to be freught with fissures and failures, resulting into unnecessary blame on the technology itself.

4.2. The major objective behind any technology transfer happens to be that of providing its maximum benefits to the target community. It can only be achieved when the community accepts it and adores it. The discussion here highlights another fact that unless the values of the society, its norms and cultural practices are considered - a priority we will meet the failure and otherwise in case we happen to involve the community as per their perceptions we can turn failure into a success story.

4.3. And finally the fact and necessity of amalgamation on a priority basis of an implementing agency involved in any of the technology trasfer; with the aims and objectives of the technology trasfer and the values and norms of the society (the target population) is required for successful implementation of any programme.

Reference :
Moving Technology, Vol. 1 No.3 December 1986
Page 9-14.

Rural water supply: infrastructure development

S. E. SUTTON, SWL Consultants, and J. S. SUTTON, Sir Alexander Gibb & Partners Ltd

SYNOPSIS: Resource surveys and system design are just one part of the building up of a rural water supply system. However, if the resultant supplies are to be sustainable, other factors should also be considered to ensure that any scheme is adopted by the recipient communities and is supported by the local infrastructure.

INTRODUCTION
1. NORAD has been funding rural water supply activities in Western Province, Zambia since about 1980. This activity has consisted principally of the construction of boreholes and wells to depths within the range 5m to 100m generally within the fine single sized sands of the Kalahari Formation. Current targets are to ensure an operating and sustainable network of about 1000 rural water supply points by the end of 1990.

2. It has been found in this instance that high levels of technology in construction are necessary to overcome difficult groundwater conditions and have successfully been adopted by local well construction teams (ref.1). This combined with implementation carried out through local agencies and with the approval and involvement of the local political organisation, has led to the evolution of a rural water supply system which is reliable and increasingly self-sufficient.

3. Figure 1 illustrates the general scale of activities from 1980-1989. The project began slowly, constructing hand dug wells in running sands, (ref.2) with an organisation which had minimal contact with local government, Department of Water Affairs, or communities to be served. In 1982 percussion drilling was started and rates of progress increased. However the number of wells in operation did not markedly rise until 1986, and can be attributed to four main changes in approach.

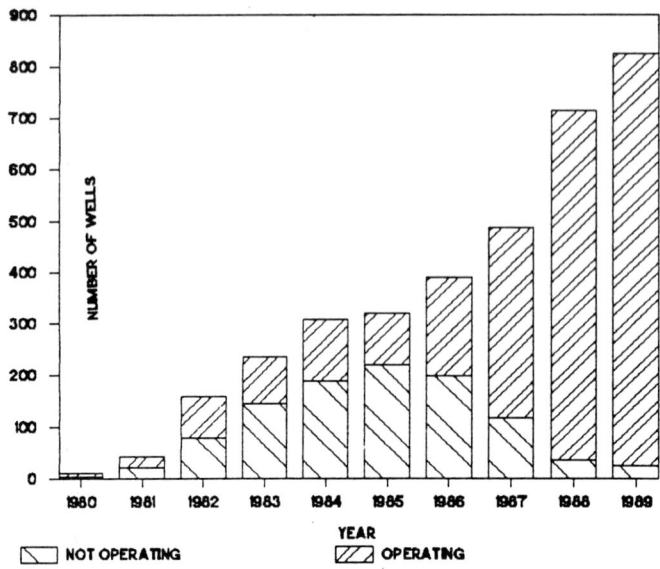

Fig. 1. Well construction and operation: Western Province, Zambia

GENERAL CHANGES
4. These changes were:-
   i. The adoption of construction techniques appropriate to the geological environment.
   ii. The adoption of proven hand-pump technology.
   iii. The adoption of an approach to implementation based on principles of Community Education and Participation (CEP).
   iv. Integration of project activities into the local government structure.

5. The need for the first three changes is self-evident while that for the last is perhaps less obvious. It should be stressed however, that acceptable levels of sustainability require both technological and sociological attitudes to support one another and that much wasted effort can be avoided if due consideration is given to both aspects from the early stages of project initiation.

INTEGRATION
6. Integration into the local government structure was achieved by two principal activities:
   i. Placing the project and its staff and funds within the provincial Department of Water Affairs under the Provincial Water Engineer.
   ii. Establishment of the WASHE (Water, Sanitation and Health Education) structure.

7. The structure of the Department of Water Affairs in Western Province consists of a provincial headquarters in the provincial capital Mongu, with district offices in each of the six District centres of the Province. Implementation of new works has always been the responsibility of the Provincial office. District level activities were previously restricted to operation and maintenance of a small town water supply and revenue collection. Salaries and morale were low. Operationally it was essential to involve District staff in site selection, community training and pump installation procedures to ensure that a nucleus of trained personnel remained in the District on completion of construction activities and to ensure that credit for successful implementation was given to the local office.

8. Integration within this structure required the acceptance of Zambian Government procedures and regulations and recognition of the authority of the Provincial Water Engineer by the donor agency.

9. The WASHE structure is based on close cooperation between government departments, particularly Water Affairs, Health, Education and Agriculture. A provincial committee with representatives of all interested departments and chaired by the Provincial Permanent Secretary acts as a steering committee approving plans, work programmes and budgets, reviewing progress, ensuring interdepartmental cooperation and defining policy and priority areas.

10. Review of day to day implementation is the responsibility of district level committees (DWASHE) chaired by a representative of the District Administration, usually the District Governor or District Executive Secretary and consisting of representatives of interested Government Departments and of the local political structure. The principal functions of the DWASHE are to approve detailed plans and programmes, to ensure involvement of other departments, to resolve disputes and to ensure cooperation from local ward chairmen who are the elected politicians forming the District Council. On completion of new wells, the DWASHE plays an important role as a link between the Department of Water Affairs and the local community, where transport and communications are difficult.

11. Before start of work in a District the DWASHE are given the opportunity to comment on the proposed District plan (already approved at provincial level) and to approve in principal the allocation of resources on a ward by ward basis. This acceptance is essential to ensure the cooperation of local ward chairmen and health assistants in the selection of individual recipient communities and institutions and their subsequent support of them.

12. Selection is usually based on the preparation of a short list for a ward by the Ward Chairman, Health Assistant and other interested officials. As the number of listed sites generally exceeds available resources, selection is then carried out by objective scoring based on population, need, willingness of community to participate etc. On agreement of the final list the process of establishing village water committees and community education and training is set in motion in advance of construction.

13. At community level, the involvement of users in construction, maintenance, and fund raising is now much better accepted as an integral part of rural water supply than it was at the beginning of the Water and Sanitation Decade. The strong development of community participation, including heightened awareness of water supply benefits and responsibilities, has been combined with an increased involvement of many sectors of local government. The resulting infrastructure is evolving into a strong support for the very dispersed rural water supply systems which have been established in Western Province. They provide water to some 200,000 people living in small, isolated communities, which could otherwise not keep such systems running, but which now can boast that more than 90% of wells will now be working at any one time.

CONCLUSION

14. A formal structure has evolved to ensure commitment to water supply development at all stages and in all levels of the political and government and local community structure in Western Province. Such acceptance is essential to ensure maintenance of the institutions necessary to provide sustainability and to support a sense of involvement and responsibility in the local communities. The commitment necessary to operate such structure can only be retained with successful implementation and the adoption of reliable and appropriate technology.

REFERENCES.

1. SUTTON S.E. Rotary vs. percussion - Myths exploded. World Water 1986, Nov.
2. SUTTON S.E. Boreholes or shallow wells for rural water supply in a sand aquifer. Proceedings of the Conference on African Water Technology, Nairobi. World Water 1987.

Financial principles and methods - the WHO handbook

C. TIMBRELL, Coopers & Lybrand Deloitte Associates

SYNOPSIS. This brief paper is intended to summarise the work of the World Health Organisation Working Group on Cost Recovery whose recommendations formulated over the last three years have recently resulted in publication of the preliminary edition of the WHO's "Handbook of Financial Principles and Methods" for application in the water and sanitation sector. The WHO working group has more than eighty members, including senior government officials from many countries, representatives of bilateral and international and technical and financial institutions, consulting firms, public and private water and sanitation agencies and non-governmental organisations active in the field of environmental health.

THE WHO HANDBOOK

1. The handbook is intended to assist all those who are concerned with financing sustainable water supply and sanitation (WSS) systems. The managerial principles and methods which have been selected to inform and assist practitioners and decision-makers are geared towards financial viability and sustainability, not as ends in themselves, but rather as means to ensure attainment of broader public health and environmental objectives.

2. In this context, a major question to be addressed is: "How to improve the effectiveness and efficiency of health development efforts in terms of their impact on the health of entire populations, with emphasis on the most needy?"

3. For the WSS sector, the most common answers available are based on cost containment in design and operation, cross-subsidization, and cost recovery. The purpose of these measures is to ensure overall sustainability, and in so doing avoid service disruptions or lack of WSS facilities, which in developing countries affect primarily the least privileged population groups.

4. These answers are not entirely satisfactory, as the issue of effectiveness of WSS services in terms of their health and environmental impact is not directly addressed, essentially because of insufficient awareness or concern, and lack of practical means to ascertain and measure these benefits. The purpose of the handbook is to facilitate financial management

in the hope that this will contribute to the attainment of health and environmental benefits.

5. The guidance material for the handbook was elaborated gradually, during a series of consultations organized by the Community Water Supply and Sanitation (CWS) Unit of the Environmental Health Division of WHO, and the IRC International Water and Sanitation Center. It was subsequently tested and refined in field activities involving more than twenty countries and a final set of financial management principles evolved. A group of financing agencies then met with representatives of developing countries, WHO and IRC, and agreed that these principles should be compiled in the form of a handbook, which would provide a widely applicable methodology for implementation.

6. While primarily designed as a guide for operation and control, the content of the handbook provides sources and guidance which can also be utilized for training purposes and promoting and creating receptive situations for sound planning. It is addressed to a wide range of planners, project officers, and other professionals (managers, accountants, engineers, health officials, social scientists, etc.), policy makers, advisers, consultants and trainers, of national and external agencies.

7. As concluded by the WHO Working Group on Cost Recovery, sustainability is the most desirable development stage of any WSS system. Efficiency, effectiveness or self-sufficiency are indicators which often deceive planners or discourage promoters, essentially because of their sensitivity to environmental and political change.

8. For WSS systems to be sustainable, all of their costs should be covered. In all countries, cost containment should be an important objective of public utilities, but this is crucial in developing countries, where too many people are still deprived of service. Risk-taking, deficit-spending measures, based on high technology and the assumption that at some future time consumers or government will pay, cannot be afforded and should generally be discouraged.

9. Subsidies, and technical measures to contain WSS costs, are generally country specific and follow multiple rules; they are not treated in any detail in the handbook. The handbook deals principally with methods to determine what the total cost is, and to improve cost recovery through user charges. It does not make any value judgement or recommendation with regard to cost containment measures, except where they are closely related to principles and methods to improve cost recovery.

10. Apart from cost recovery and cost containment, the two basic principles of sound financial management are those of resources coverage and liquidity maintenance. Resources coverage means that at any given time all needs should be covered. Liquidity maintenance means that at any given time all cash needs should be covered. While full resources coverage (including through cash-raising) should be pursued as a matter

of principle, the methods to achieve this objective vary with circumstances: in most developing countries, liquidity maintenance is an essential condition to the attainment of permanent resources coverage, and sustainability.

11. Because of the experience of the last decades, it has become a truism that in WSS inadequate financial management invariably leads to service disruptions and environmental health deterioration. The need was not felt to emphasize throughout the handbook the linkage between public health goals, sustainability objectives, resouces coverage, and detailed financial mechanisms such as cost recovery, cash raising and cost containment. The environmental effects of financial decisions and activities in the water supply and sanitation sector have been documented elsewhere by WHO Working Group on Cost Recovery. The purpose of the handbook is to motivate the reader to adopt some principles, and follow some methods designed to influence these effects.

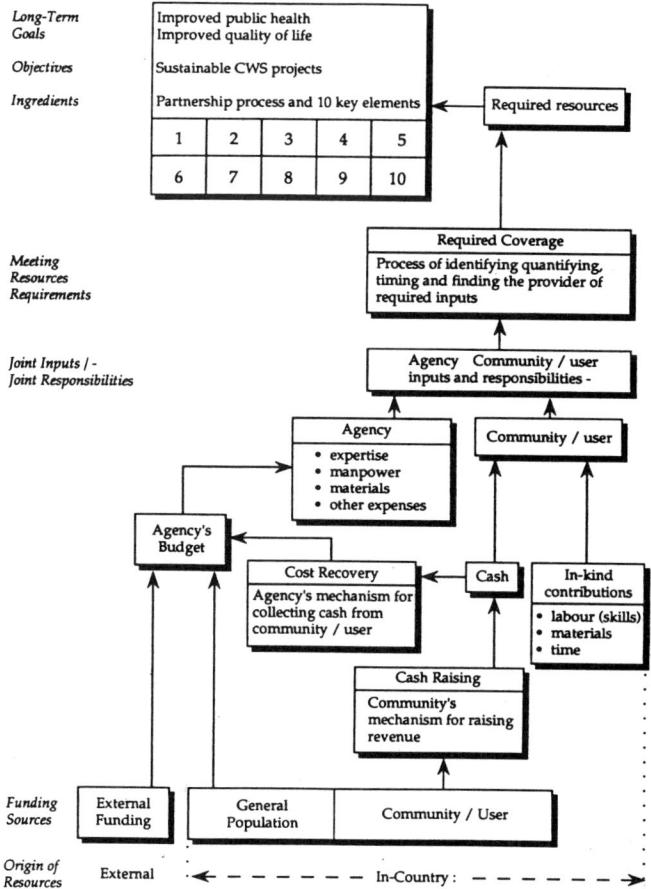

GENERAL MODEL FOR ACHIEVING AND FINANCING SUSTAINABLE WSS

WATER, SANITATION AND FOOD WORKSHOP

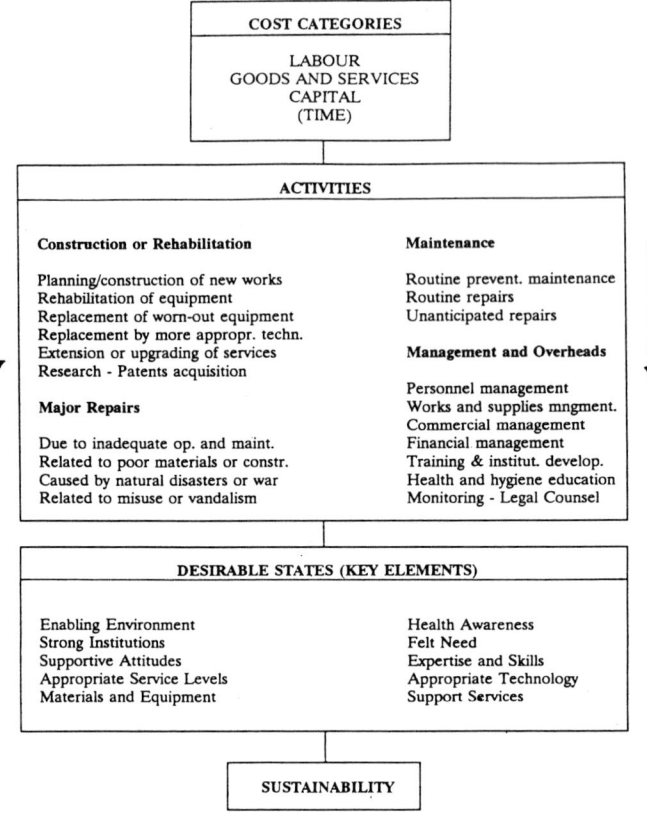

RESOURCES MOBILIZATION FOR SUSTAINABILITY

Key elements

* Enabling Environment

* Health Awareness

* Strong Institutions
  . Community
  . Agency
  . Special interest groups

* Felt Need

* Supportive Attitudes

* Expertise and Skills

* Appropriate Service Level

* Appropriate Technology

* Materials and Equipment

* Support Services
  . Community relations
  . Community support
  . O&M support

These elements relate to the creation and maintenance of conditions that ensure technical, social and financial project success.

THE SUSTAINABILITY OBJECTIVE

The role of education and training in developing countries self-help water supply and sanitation, with particular reference to Sierra Leone

G. WHITESIDE, BSc, MSc, WaterAid

SYNOPSIS. WaterAid works with indigenous local partner groups in the provision of self help water supply and sanitation projects to rural communities. Sustainability of schemes, improved hygiene practices of villagers and the strengthening of local partners are viewed as key objectives which depend crucially on education and training inputs. In this case study, it is argued that project implementation might ideally be seen as series of carefully staged, fully integrated, education and training exercises.

INTRODUCTION
1. The persistent inability of many third world governments to sustain service facilities in recent years has led to a major rethinking on the ways in which rural water supply and sanitation projects are implemented. Today, emphasis is increasingly being placed on maximum community self reliance in the design, implementation and maintenance of schemes. Thus community ownership of schemes and village centred development have become important goals.

SCOPE AND STRATEGIES
2. Agencies such as WaterAid have therefore needed to expand their education and training provisions to embrace not only the improved performance and perceptions of their local partner, but also the knowledge and abilities of key individuals and groups in participating communities.
3. An education and training strategy, fully integrated into the Sierra Leone programme annual cycle, has been developed with inputs targeted group to achieve specific programme related outcomes. This has necessarily meant an emphasis on in-house and local initiatives based not on "off the shelf" academic curricula but on the perceived needs of potential trainees and senior programme staff.
4. The perception of job related tasks as learning opportunities is felt to be a key insight when developing strategy. Analysis of these tasks and establishing appropriate provision at the <u>programme planning stage</u> can lead to implementation being seen as a series of education and training exercises.

METHODOLOGIES

5. Education and training inputs, rather than being formally taught by project staff, have been planned and facilitated so that full emphasis on peer centred participation and learning can occur. Thus, education and training become characterised by participants <u>assuming some responsibility for their own learning</u> - a condition that brings considerable vitality to the learning situation.

EDUCATION

6. As outlined above, the broad remit of self help water and sanitation programmes requires the transformation of many ideas and attitudes held by programme staff and participating communities. This largely depends on appropriate educational inputs.

7. In Sierra Leone, emphasis has been placed on two subject areas. The first - hygiene education - is targeted primarily at communities so that changes in personal hygiene leading to improved health can take place.

8. These sessions have most usually occurred in the village setting and been facilitated by a team of skilled programme communicators. Timing of these inputs to coincide with construction activities is seen as important since, as Laubjerg (ref.1) points out, "behaviour modification can only occur when health education is combined with changes in the physical environment".

9. Since attitudes are most easily formed in the process of interacting with others, group activities and discussions have made up the bulk of hygiene education sessions.

10. The second area relates directly to implementation 'software' issues. These are targeted principally at programme staff and key members of communities to encourage maximum self reliance. Experience has shown that, for staff, this has largely been a matter of helping them refine their working methods based on a knowledge of processes that can lead to community self reliance. Thus, a broad emphasis has been placed on facilitating maximum villager involvement -particularly in decision making- with staff serving principally as guides and advisers.

11. Among skills learned in this context have been communication and adult education techniques which have been used in the education and training of key villagers such as health wardens and maintenance caretakers.

12. If village committees are to make informed decisions on the management of a project then they need to have access to sufficient background knowledge at an early stage in the project cycle. Thus education leading to the strengthening of such key village groups is seen as an important goal. Advice, in this context, has usually been given on topics such as:

   1) Construction stages   2) Health education inputs
   3) Work scheduling   4) Maintenance requirements
   5) Maintenance tariffs   6) Financial management

13. In concluding this section on education it should be noted

that considerable difficulties exist for outsiders who wish to be effective in staff and community education. An in-depth knowledge of local language, culture, customs and perceptions is required if the "pitch" and "level" of education sessions are to be appropriate. Some cross cultural training of expatriate staff is necessary -if only to develop the sensitivity that will allow an appreciation of the complexity of the task.

TRAINING

14. The acquisition of skills and knowledge through training is the principal way in which improved job performance comes about. Methodologies for achieving this have been well documented although very often -particularly in the development context- the selection of trainees, suitability of courses and evaluation of training effectiveness have all given cause for concern (ref. 2).

15. <u>Structured Courses.</u> WaterAid has sought to avoid some of these difficulties by placing a high emphasis on structured in-house activities. Although this implies limited access to specialist knowledge, it is felt that this is more than compensated for by in-depth knowledge of potential trainees, the ability to tailor curricula to meeting real needs and the chance to evaluate training during later visits to trainees in their village work place. In-house training has also shown itself to be highly cost effective.

16. One further, and largely unexpected, outcome of this training has been a spectacular boost in morale. The opportunity to share work experiences, air grievances and socialise has been seen to foster an impressive camaraderie and an identification with programme goals that has a marked effect on overall performance (Table 1).

17. In-house training at a district centre has also been arranged to complement on-the-job training of maintenance caretakers. While the pitch of material has needed to be modified to accommodate background knowledge, similarly beneficial outcomes are thought to have occurred (maintenance surveys suggest a direct correlation between condition of a water supply system and training inputs).

18. <u>On-the-job training.</u> Since this is the time honoured way in which skills are transferred in most developing cocuntries, it is therefore appropriate that construction and maintenance skills be passed on in this way. Site foremen have commonly used this technique to train maintenance caretakers throughout the construction period. Evaluation of learning however has been difficult and necessitated attendance at the more structured district centre course to ensure minimum levels of competance exist before schemes are handed over.

19. Two further training methods used in Sierra Leone are worthy of mention here. These are a) visits to neighbouring country programmes and b) adviser-counterpart relations The numbers involved in both exercises have been relatively small but this belies the fact that each input has been tailored to meet broader programme management objectives for senior staff.

20. <u>Third country visits.</u> In the first situation emphasis was placed on a comparative analysis of water supply and sanitation provisions in a country with a similar socio-economic climate. Although relatively expensive, the need to broaden the perspective of key personal is felt to have justified the costs involved.

21. <u>Adviser-counterpart relations.</u> In their broadest sense, these can be seen as another form of on-the-job training. Here however, a mutual exchange of information and ideas is sought - usually with advisers helping with "technique" and the counterpart offering expert advice on "working context". In Sierra Leone this relationship has existed between WaterAid expatriates (engineers and health coordinators) and senior personnel in the partner organisation with generally productive outcomes.

EVALUATION

22. Evaluation of the effectiveness of education and training as it relates to job performance is notoriously difficult and in a majority of cases the costs of carrying out such an exercise would exceed those of training itself. Thus anecdotal evidence and subjective impressions have often been the only sources of feedback.

23. While this has largely been the case for WaterAid's Sierra Leone programme, course evaluations and overall productivity suggest that education and training inputs have had a marked beneficial effect (Table 1).

Table 1. Programme productivity and coverage 1985-89.

Year	No. Staff	Populations Served		Access to Hygiene Ed.
		Water Supply	Latrines	
1985-86	15	3,500	0	0
1986-87	60	22,000	150	5,000
1987-88*	75	25,000	1,000	10,000
1988-89**	100	28,000	4,500	28,000
1989-90	120	35,000	14,000	35,000

* Introduction of structured in-house training.
** 2nd year of course. Curriculum revised on the basis of observations during the year and further statements of need from participants.

Although difficult, it is important that further indicators be identified to show how education and training influence overall performance. Only then will the allocation of resources reflect the true potential of these inputs to realise long term programme goals.

REFERENCES
1. LAUBJERG K. Training women as health promoters in Tanzania. Waterlines, vol. 4, no. 3. Jan. 1986.
2. HULME D. The effectiveness of British Aid for training. ActionAid, London, 1989, 11-14.

Water quality: the Paqualab concept

N. WORRILL, ELE International

SYNOPSIS. ELE International in collaboration with the University of Surrey, have designed a water quality testing system Paqualab which incorporates all the tests needed to measure drinking water quality according to WHO and EEC guidelines. Its compact, completely portable design and user friendly instrumentation, makes it particularly attractive for testing water quality in developing countries, where the infastructure is often unable to cope with the demands placed upon it. It is currently in use in over 60 countries worldwide, by Ministries of Health, Water and Sewerage Boards, Water Pollution control Boards, WHO, UNICEF and UNHCR.

1. Continous monitoring of drinking water supplies is essential for the preservation of water quality and for the maintenance of adequate and safe water for all communities. However, many countries in the developing world have never had a national water quality monitoring programme, and the significance of this is obvious when one considers that contaminated water supplies are the most common cause of sickness in the world today. (1)

2. Contamination of drinking water can be divided into two major types; that caused by water bo rne infectious agents such as protozoa, bacteria, viruses and worms, and that caused by chemical contamination. In the developing world water borne infections are the most common type of water contamination and infectious diseases such as cholera, typhoid, diarrohea, filiariasis and schistosomiasis infect millions of people annually. Indeed, the scale of the problem

is enormous; the WHO estimated that in the world as a whole, 80% of all sicknesses are attributable to inadequate water supply and sanitation .[1]

3. For many third world countries with no significant infrastructure for monitoring and testing drinking water it is a formidable task to improve the situation, especially on a limited budget. Unlike Europe, where water quality testing is backed up by the latest high-tech, high-cost equipment including central laboratories, many developing countries have a low investment potential, shortage of properly trained staff and few, if any, central testing facilities. Combined with scattered and remote water sources in many areas this has often meant that an effective monitoring programme has been difficult to implement.

4. The Paqualab, originally designed by microbiologists at the University of Surrey, has been developed to meet the very specific problems facing these countries. It is designed to be completely portable, a self-contained water quality testing laboratory, able to monitor drinking water supplies in remote areas where formal monitoring programmes are inadequate or non existent. Of the 60 or so parameters listed in guidelines for drinking water by the World Health Organisation (WHO, 1984) certain tests are agreed to be the most important in the day to day control of water quality and supply. The tests: faecal coliform, total coliform, turbidity, chlorine, conductivity, pH, nitrates, nitrites and ammonia are specifically incorporated into the Paqualab range of equipment and can all be transported in one robust box weighing only 20kg. It is therefore possible to carry out all the major water quality tests to determine whether the water is safe to drink using one completely portable system.

5. Generally speaking, in the developing world, it is widely accepted that the most important aspect of water quality is microbiological safety, and the bacteriological quality of water is often the most common if not the only measure of water quality. At the core of the Paqualab system are dual incubators, which with improved electronics, internal construction, insulation and reliability enable the user to carry out accurate, on the spot, microbiological evaluations

of water quality. Each incubator section takes 25 reusable aluminium petri dishes and samples are prepared using a field sterilizable membrane filtration device included in the kit. The incubators have a wide range of power options and can be used with either 120/240V AC 12 or 24V DC external sources, or the internal rechargeable battery. A range of hand held digital meters to measure the essential physical and chemical parameters of water quality: pH, conductivity, temperature, turbidity and around 22 chemical parameters, including fluorides, nitrates and nitrites complete the system. The modular construction of the Paqualab allows the user to tailor the Paqualab to suit their specific requirements.

6. There are several advantages in using this type of field testing equipment. All the equipment in the Paqualab is reliable, easy to use and requires little training for effective results. Low cost consumable items, offer considerable savings compared with central laboratory charges and, with basic training, field staff can conduct the appropriate tests as well as collect samples, thus making a further saving in both manpower and time. Using the membrane filtration technique for the microbiological assessment of water samples can be analysed and results obtained within 16 hours. This compares favorably with 48/96 hours typical of other methods such as the MPN (most probable number) method. By carrying out the water tests in the field, sample deterioration is also avoided as tests can be carried out on the spot.

7. Paqualabs are already being used sucessfully in rural water improvement programmes in Nigeria, Tanzania, Botswana and Kenya. In Malawi where there is essentially a rural population, Paqualab equipment was chosen to monitor the countries many and diverse water supplies. The portability of the Paqualab was a particular asset as it was possible for field operatives to transport the Paqualab to the remotest water sources using motor cycles. This represented a cost effective means of testing in terms of fuel cost per sample. The long journey times between the central laboratory and some of the sampling sites also necessitated the use of a portable testing kit.

8. Lives are continually endangered by contaminated drinking water and the provision of clean and safe water is one of the cornerstones of economic and social development for any country. The Paqualab system, currently in use in over 60 countries worldwide, is an economic, sustainable method of monitoring water supplies, from piped water schemes to boreholes and dug wells in remote rural areas.

REFERENCES
1. BOURNE, P. In: Falkenmark, M., ed. Rural water supply and Health. Uppsala, Scandinavian Institute of African studies, 1982 p34.

Summary of discussion

I. A. RICHARDSON, Groundwork in Heartlands, and H. M. BYRNE, W. S. Atkins Group

The topics of the workshop papers were diverse and covered both case studies of particular development programmes and research into individual technologies. Unfortunately they did not present a balanced overview of the problems in the sector. The technologies that were presented tended to concentrate on the idiosyncratic rather than the appropriate technologies more likely to be employed on a wide scale. This is not to decry their value when applied in the right circumstances.

The crisis in the water and sanitation sector was identified, but the papers did not present a solution on the same scale as the global problem. Consequently an all-embracing strategy for the future was not reached.

A multidisciplinary approach was considered most important with the engineer contributing to a team that works together. In particular health education was identified as the most important adjunct to any programme addressing itself to improving water supply and sanitation in rural areas. It was suggested that the ICE should promote such an approach.

Several papers and speakers cited the negative impact on local organizations that resulted when external donor agencies implement their projects independently of indigenous institutions. Funding may be available for development over a short period and may then be suddenly withdrawn leaving local agencies unable to continue the project or maintain what has already been built. Despite limitations and difficulties the ICE should recommend to donors that expatriate engineers operate with and through indigenous organizations. Strengthening local organizations should be stated as an objective in aid packages and receive the same priority as the physical objectives. Project finance should include some maintenance provision, e.g. spare parts.

Donors should be encouraged by the ICE to make longer term commitments, and be sufficiently flexible over a longer period of time in order to respond to need and to new directions that may be unearthed only as the programme develops in the field (the NORAD programme in Zambia reported by Sutton and Sutton was started in 1980 and it was not until 1986 that it got going).

WATER, SANITATION AND FOOD WORKSHOP

The workshop looked at training as one of the means of strengthening the indigenous organization and recommended the development of in-house training programmes that would

(a) address directly the specific requirements of the programme and organization
(b) improve morale and increase cohesion among the local staff (see the Paper by Whiteside).

Bespoke in-house training courses were considered to be more cost-effective and reached more people than off-the-peg courses at academic institutions. Similarly academic courses in-country are more cost-effective and likely to be more relevant (but not necessarily) than courses in the First World. The ICE should recommend to the British Council (and others involved in funding education and training) that an increased proportion of resources should be invested in developing training in Third World countries. Post-graduate degrees in the UK taken by Third World nationals should reflect problems encountered in their home countries.

There was opposition to the concept of technology being transferred from the First World to the Third World and it was recommended that more support should be given to advance research and development of appropriate technologies in the countries where they are to be used (e.g. Zimbabwe's Blair Laboratory's work on ventilated improved privies) and to encourage the transfer of technologies between the less developed countries (e.g. the Vonder Rig hand-drilling system developed in Zimbabwe and in use in Kenya and Uganda). This should be backed up by investment in local manufacture (e.g. local production of Tara hand-pumps in Bangladesh).

Community ownership and management of facilities were seen as the only way of sustaining services for the poor. This means that development agencies (local or external) need to participate in the communities' projects rather than communities participate in the agencies' projects. To do this effectively engineers need a range of sociological and management skills which at present do not form part of their training. The workshop recommended broader education for engineers to help them relate more effectively with the communities who may benefit from their involvement, with local counterpart staff, and with co-workers in other disciplines. The ICE might consider demanding proficiency in some of these non-engineering areas as a necessary qualification for professional status.

Self-sufficiency and sustainable food security in Africa is one of the goals of the new decade and it is likely that irrigation will play a significant role in the intensification of agriculture in the region. The Authors describe the potential for increasing the currently cultivated area of shallow ground-water in valley wetlands fourfold and for intensifying production in these areas. The Paper describes the use of a simple, human-powered, rope-washer pump which has proved both popular and durable in the field and can be manufactured at the village level.

The following recommendations were made:

1. A multidisciplinary approach should be promoted.
2. A main objective should be the strengthening of local organizations.
3. Long-term commitments are required from donors.
4. There is a need for more in-house, in-country training.
5. There is a need for investment in research and development in the Third World.
6. Technology transfer between developing countries should be encouraged.
7. Investment should be made in local manufacture of appropriate technologies.
8. Community ownership and management should be promoted.
9. Engineers should be given a broader education.

Technology, development and investment appraisal methods

G. K. BAMBRAH, Rofe Kennard and Lapworth Ltd, Kenya

SYNOPSIS. This paper presents an attempt at modelling the relationship between technological progress, development and the appraisal process based on a detailed analysis of past trends. According to this model, the appraisal process will need to include a global and human context and be a multi-faceted, comprehensive and integrated process allowing for the use of optimum and appropriate technologies if sustainable human development is to be achieved.

TECHNOLOGY AND DEVELOPMENT

1. The problem of survival is addressed by human beings in two ways. They either produce artefacts to modify effects of an hostile environment or they employ spiritual and psychological capacities to adapt their needs to environmental realities surrounding them. Though not to the exclusion of the latter, the former, essentially technological, approach has tended to be the premier survival strategy for the industrial development model (ref. 1).

2. Industrial economies are characterised by a higher long term economic growth rate than pre-industrial economies. The usual explanation for this phenomenon has been to breakdown the growth rate into its components namely, capital accumulation, population growth and technological progress (ref. 2). Kogane (ref. 3) argues that the high value of the technological progress component of economic growth implies that it is related to the development of economic and in turn, non-economic variables and that to observe how these interact, the long term past must be examined.

APPRAISAL/EVALUATION

3. Availability of a variety of resources and a number of ways of converting these into required outputs, makes it necessary to justify the choice of a particular method for the required transformation. The objective of an appraisal exercise is to fulfil this purpose.

4. Figure 1 (ref. 4) shows how a number of appraisal/ evaluation techniques have evolved over the years.

TABLE 1. DEVELOPMENT TECHNOLOGY AND APPRAISAL: PAST TRENDS AND FORECASTING MODEL

| Lifestyle | Source of Change | Past Trend / Forecasted Trend |||
		Developmental	Technology	Appraisal
Primitive	Discovery of Time and Space	Super Natural Beliefs	Indigeneous Evolution	Resource Discovery
Invaders	Increased Mobilisation	Religious and Natural Ideas	Diffusion Through Intermingling	Resource Availability
Explorers	Ability to Manipulate Matter	Human Endowment	Scientific Discovery	Interest Group Lobbying
Empire Formers	Capital Accumulation Colonisation	Material Advancement	Industrial Revolution	Efficiency Feasibility Criteria. CBA+
Independent Nations	Need for Freedom	Economic Development	Trade and Technology Transfer	Innovative CBA+
East/West and North/South Blocks	Inequality Poverty Competition (for Markets)	Socio-Economic Development	Rapid Technological Advance	Technology Assessment EIA++
Inter-Dependent Nations	Crisis of Population Food etc.	Limits to Growth/ Doomsday Models	Sun Rise Technologies	Multi-Faceted E.IA++
Globalisation	Improvement of Human Condition	Sustainable +++ Development	Appropriate +++ and Optimum Technology	Comprehensive +++ Integrated Approaches

CBA+ : Cost Benefit Analysis   EIA++ : Environmental Impact Analysis.   Forecasted Trend: +++

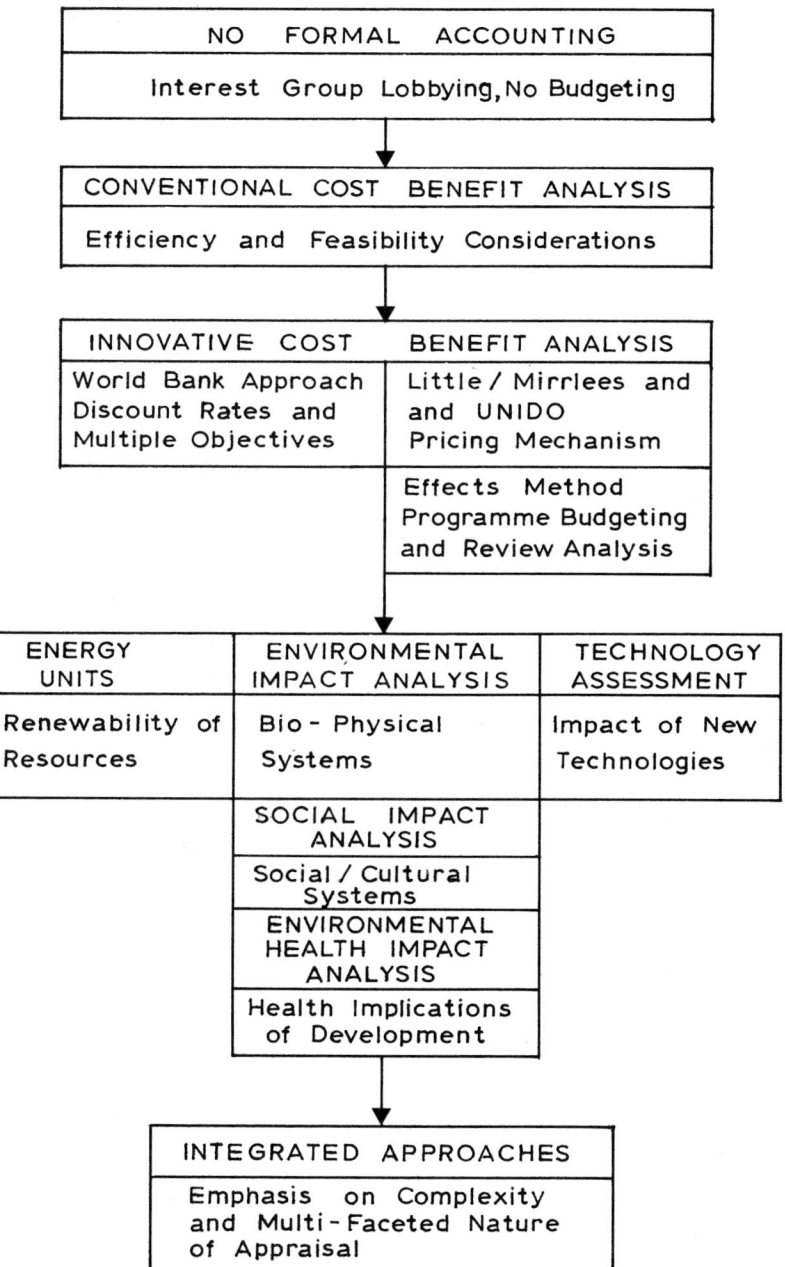

Fig. 1. Evolution of appraisal methods

AN ANALYSIS OF PAST TRENDS

5. Following Kogane's (ref. 3) suggestions, a detailed study was made of the long term past of "development" and "technology" (ref. 4). A general contextual history approach was adopted that emphasized the interpretation as opposed to narration of the histories. This is in keeping with recent trends (ref. 5). A general review was made of the concept of "development" and a case study approach incorporating a comparative study of a developing country (Kenya) and a developed country (Britain) was adopted for the technological part and is contained in previous work by the author (ref 4).

6. On the basis of these studies, Table 1 was evolved (ref. 4). Essentially, Table 1 forms a model of past trends in "development", "technology" and appraisal/evaluation.

7. According to this model present trends indicate that mankind is faced with a crisis of population, food, environment, debt, arms expenditure, resource availability, politics and oil, fuel etc. Most of these being of a global nature and significantly affecting the human condition. In terms of technology it can be seen that it affects all aspects of human life, changing man's ways, his behaviour and even his nature. In the same vein, appraisal/evaluation techniques are tending to become increasingly multi-faceted.

FUTURE CONSIDERATIONS

8. It can be concluded from Table 1 that the key issue today is one of sustainable development, calling for use of optimum and appropriate technologies which will help overcome the current global crisis.

9. Accordingly, it can be concluded that the appraisal process, which has its roots in the decision-making process, should allow for the global and human contexts, be multi-disciplinary, interactive, integrated, comprehensive and flexible and allow for the technological state of a society and the mode of transmission of new technologies to that society to be considered within its framework.

REFERENCES
1. PORTER A. et al. A guidebook for technology assessment and impact analysis, series vol. 4, p. 27-100. Elsevier Holland inc., New York, 1980.
2. TODARO M.P. Economics for a developing world, an introduction to principles, problems and policies for development, p. 108. Longman Group Ltd., U.K., 1982.
3. KOGANE Y. Long waves of economic growth - past and future, Futures, vol. 20, number 5, p. 533. October 1988.
4. BAMBRAH G.K. A systematic approach to appraisal/ evaluation of civil engineering projects with special emphasis on technology, Ph.D thesis, p. 15-94. Loughborough Univeristy of Technology, U.K. 1989.
5. HUGHES T. The seamless web : technology, science etc. Technology and social process, p. 18. Edinburgh Univeristy Press. 1988.

Services for shelter

R. FRANCEYS and A. COTTON, Water Engineering and Development Centre

---

Considering current growth rates in the urban areas of the 'Low and Middle Income Countries', projections for the next twenty years suggest that housing and associated services will be required for an additional 2,690 million people (equivalent to 385 million houses) if housing for all is to be achieved.

According to conventional standards, with household water supply, sewerage, solid waste collection, drainage and surfaced roads, the life cycle cost, that is the total annual cost per household discounted over a twenty year period (TACH) would be in the region of $200 for these services. Sites and services schemes have not significantly reduced this figure.

Considering the financial implications of a conventional solution for services, the total annual income per household for the poorest 40% of the population in the 'Low Income Countries' is approximately $700 (World Development Report, 1989). With affordability normally estimated in the region of 20% for housing and services the total available annual expenditure is $140. A minimum standard 30m^2 house represents a TACH of $100 for housing alone leaving only $40 for services. Income distribution figures indicate that fiscal measures for redistribution of wealth cannot bridge this gap.

Services

Housing and infrastructure standards reflect differing costs, risks and benefits. However, there is confusion between objectives and means; whilst health benefits are often used to justify investments there is little evidence to suggest 'what benefit' accrues from 'what investment'. As time passes and professionals learn by failures ("to engineer is human") there is a tendency to 'ratchet up' standards. That is the standards or bylaws creep up over time. However, this does not necessarily mean that previous 'lower' standards are 'wrong', they simply carry a higher risk in health and safety terms; it should be stressed that any existing 'conventional' standards for all their high cost are not risk free.

INFRASTRUCTURE WORKSHOP

Putting services in their place

Consequently this paper reports on an investigation into alternative means of infrastructure which are believed to meet a minimum acceptable level of provision for environmental health. The study of servicing costs, using data collected during field visits to three cities on separate continents, required the development of a computer spreadsheet to model the significant variables. The model was designed therefore to investigate many different combinations of services at various servicing standards, construction costs, land costs, discount rates, layouts, plot sizes and plot ratios.

It is clear from the study that, as has long been recognised, the servicing costs for 'large' plot sizes is a function of service lengths which is affected therefore by plot ratio. However, using the model, it can now be seen that this is not the case with the small plot sizes of $30m^2$ to $50m^2$ which are becoming more common in Asia and may have to become more common in Africa if the present growth in urban centres continues. At the smaller plot sizes, total service costs are strongly affected by the interactions between services. For example, one interaction which was investigated related the trade off between the use of overhead power lines which required a safety clearance between the lines and any nearby buildings and the use of underground power cables which are more expensive to install but save on land costs. Another example of these interactions is the choice between having unsurfaced earth roads with unlined earth storm drains, compared with the possibility of using a surfaced road with negative camber as the drain itself.

Services spreadsheet

Two standard layouts are investigated in the model. The first is a rectilinear cluster layout with a central area of semi-public land, preferred by planners; the second is a linear street layout with through traffic restricted to define a recognisable community group. Plot sizes may range from $30m^2$ to 500m2 with an option to consider plot ratios of 1:4 and 1:1.
One significant result is that the linear layout produces savings of 20% to 25% over the rectilinear layout in terms of servicing costs. A recommendation to use linear layouts requires increased input from the planners to avoid a featureless grid of straight streets without any identifiable community.

Sanitation

The component of infrastructure which has the potential to produce the most significant saving is sanitation. The choice between water-borne sewerage and on-plot improved latrines has a dramatic effect on costs. Many engineers and planners presume that for high density housing sewerage is the only solution. However improved latrines can work successfully on the smallest plot sizes with 'normal' ground conditions.

The exceptionally high difference in costs of the alternatives results principally from the costs of the water supply and waste water treatment required for the sewerage approach. For sewerage to work there has to be on plot provision of water through a yard tap at the least, in order to flush the toilet. There is an advantage in having sewerage in that the sullage water can also be disposed of through the sewers whereas for latrines alternative methods of sullage disposal have to be provided. However the high cost of transporting sewage to a treatment plant and the subsequent treatment costs lead to significant increases in overall costs as opposed to latrines.

Using one set of data it was discovered that the TACH of a sewerage system will be $64 higher than for an on-plot system. This saving represents a reduction in sanitation costs of 30% to 45%.

Access

After sanitation the next most important area to consider is access width. There are land implications as well as resulting construction and surfacing costs dependent upon the size of the access roads and footpaths. Options range from footpath access only through an intermediate emergency/intermittent vehicle access at low speeds up to conventional five metre wide roads.

Reducing the access width from five metres to a two and a half metre restricted speed access has the potential to give savings of between 8% and 16% of TACH depending upon the approach taken to interacting services. For low income housing where the inhabitants are unlikely to be able to afford motor vehicles in the foreseeable future it is difficult to justify conventional roads; but if it is at all possible limited vehicle access has significant benefits.

This reduction in access width is not believed to be viable at the largest plot sizes of $500m^2$. If land is so low cost that an individual household can be given title to such a large area there is no advantage in saving on land use by restricting access widths.

Drainage

One of the major problems on any low income housing site is inadequate drainage. In financial terms the choice between options is less significant but the cheapest system is to use the road-as-drain approach wherever possible. This saves on landtake because there are no side drains and also saves on drain lining, whilst gaining the maintenance advantages of a surfaced road.

Where sewerage is used for excreta disposal a footpath-as-drain can be utilised down the backs of houses for storm water disposal with the sullage removed in the sewer. The use of a road-as-drain rather than employing lined channels as a drainage system is estimated to give savings of 10% to 20%.

It should be pointed out that because of the interactions between different service options the percentages given cannot be summed to give a total saving.

INFRASTRUCTURE WORKSHOP

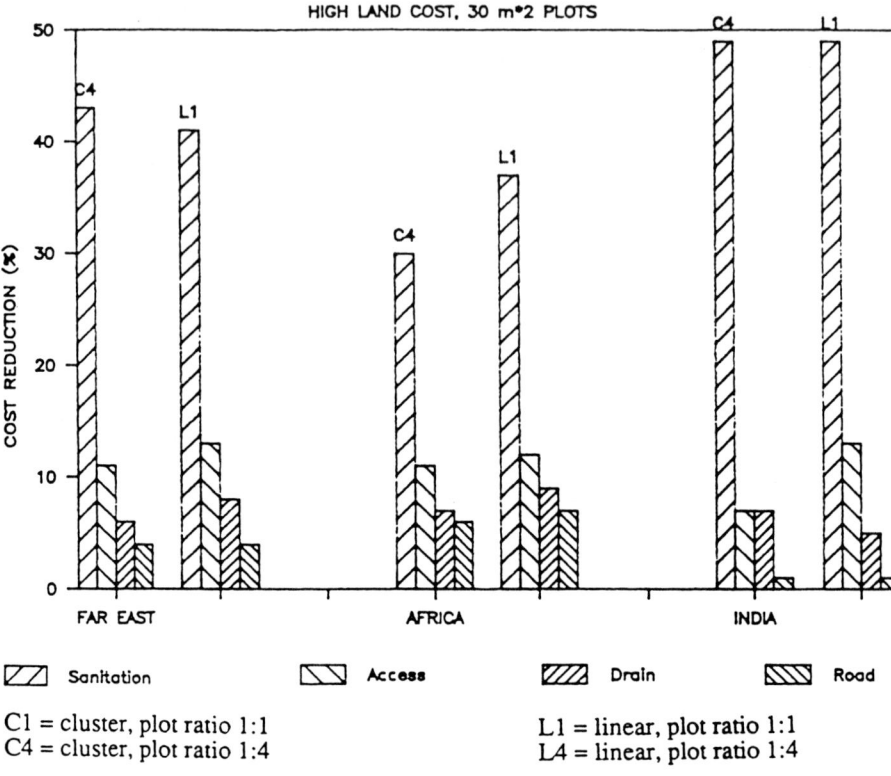

C1 = cluster, plot ratio 1:1
C4 = cluster, plot ratio 1:4
L1 = linear, plot ratio 1:1
L4 = linear, plot ratio 1:4

Potential cost reduction

Conclusion

Careful attention to design of services can bring housing and infrastructure within the affordability range of low income households in the growing cities of the Low Income Countries. Total savings which can be achieved when compared with a conventional sites and services scheme range from $82 to $114 TACH for a high land cost area to $43 to $82 TACH for low land cost area. These figures may not appear significant when seen from a High Income Country perspective. However, when multiplied by the number of households required to be established over the next twenty years and compared with competing demands for scarce resources, that is a saving which should be appropriated.

Acknowledgement

The infrastructure study upon which this paper is based was carried out by Dr Andrew Cotton, Eur Ing Richard Franceys and Lawrence Hedderley on behalf of the Overseas Development Administration (Project No 4404) whose support is gratefully acknowledged.

Low density foundation systems for human resettlement programmes

T. H. HANNA, University of Sheffield

SYNOPSIS. Soft and highly compressible soils with high groundwater tables hinder the construction of economical houses and lightweight buildings, necessitating the use of deep and expensive foundations. Through the use of lightweight materials used for the strip and spread footings the nett applied load can be kept small. Whilst the concept is not new, perhaps this is an appropriate time to consider alternative solutions to soft ground engineering, the primary aim being to prove that the concept is technically sound and feasible.

THE CONCEPT
1. Consider the principle of foundation loading. At depth z the total stress is

$$\sigma_v = \gamma h + (\gamma - \gamma_w)(z - h) \tag{1}$$

and the hydrostatic water pressure is

$$\sigma_w = u = \gamma_w(z - h) \tag{2}$$

where h is the depth to the water table. The gross pressure, q_{gross}, at the base of a strip footing is the total weight of the structural load to the base level of the foundation/total area of the foundation. The nett pressure is

$$q_{nett} = q_{gross} - \sigma_v \tag{3}$$

2. How may q_{nett} be made $<<q_{gross}$? Possible solutions include: (i) basement type structure - difficult below the water table - expensive; (ii) backfill the footing trench with a less dense fill than the soil removed and place a strip footing near the original ground surface; (iii) fill the trench with a very lightweight structural material. Place the strip footing on top and integral with the lightweight structural material; (i) fill the trench with a light-weight watertight box with the footing on top. All

Appropriate development for basic needs. Thomas Telford, London, 1991

proposals rely on the principle of reducing the nett pressure applied to the ground.

3. Consider a strip footing 1m deep, 1.5m wide with the water table at 1m depth. Let the density of the footing backfill be $\gamma_b \ll \gamma$, the bulk density of the soil.

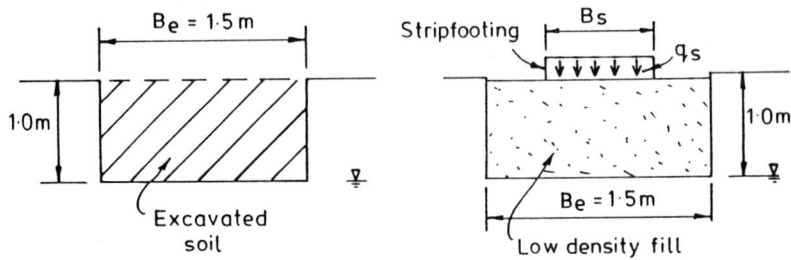

Weight of soil excavated
$= \gamma . B_e . 1$.

Weight of low density fill placed
$= \gamma_b . B_e . 1$.

Fig. 1. Reduction in vertical stress at base of foundation trench due to use of lightweight trench fill

Place the strip footing on top of the backfill at ground level. Let the width of the strip footing be B_s and that of the trench be B_e = 1.5m. The nett additional load to be applied to the strip footing to bring the ground back to its pre-excavation stress state is $B_e(\gamma - \gamma_b)$. Hence the average stress which may be applied at the base of the strip footing, q_s, is

$$q_s = \frac{B_e(\gamma - \gamma_b)}{B_s} \qquad (4)$$

For $B_s = 0.5 B_e$, $\gamma = 1.5$ tonne/m^3

$\frac{\gamma_b}{\gamma}$	0.5	0.4	0.3	0.2	0.1
q_{s_2} tonne/m^2	1.5	1.8	2.1	2.4	2.7

4. From this simple analysis the value of q_s rises with increase in footing depth, D; with increase in the depth h to the water table; with decrease in B_e.

METHOD OF ACHIEVING THE DESIRED SOLUTION

5. The second and third possible solutions are technically and practically sound. Lightweight aggregates which do not absorb water, are inert and can be compacted or lightly cemented could be placed within a lightweight and durable cage, Fig. 2. Load efficiency depends on the relative values of B_s, B_e, D, γ, γ_b. Possible limitations are cost of fill, cost of the basket, placement difficulties and heave of the trench base. A low density structural fill has the advantage of ease of handling and placement. Know-how exists for road embankments and bridge abutments (ref 1) - polystyrene blocks. The load efficiency is controlled by the relative values of the main variables. Limitations appear to be cost, availability, moisture absorption and deterioration. Composite action between the strip footing and the structural fill is possible.

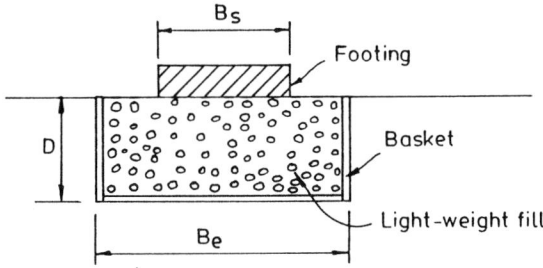

Fig. 2. Proposed method of lightweight trench fill placement

6. From a construction consideration there are no major problems which cannot be solved. Examples include cross-walls, floor slabs, service outlets, uneven loads. There are, however, a number of precautionary measures deemed necessary before such concepts may be applied. These include: (i) the need to understand the origin of the soil and its geological history; (ii) the need to understand ground water flow, particularly consolidation; (iii) the realistic assessment of foundation loads; (iv) the need to understand the significance of additional loading after construction; (v) changes in drainage after construction.

7. To give confidence to the proposed system it is prudent to carry out several field trials and observe settlement behaviour as well as construction difficulties.

8. There are several potential problem areas. These include: (i) soft soils which are under-consolidated. Building on such deposits is unwarranted; (ii) the ability of drains and services to accommodate ground movements; (iii) the effect of heavily loaded parking areas on adjacent buildings; (iv) the influence of surcharges from

storage areas; (v) general drainage of the area causing settlement; (vi) disturbance caused to the soft ground by trench excavation work; (vii) effective methods of coping with uplift and overturning forces; (viii) efficient methods of dealing with the placement in-situ of lightweight fills and lightweight structural materials, eg automation.

GENERAL INFORMATION

9. Little information appears to exist on the practical use of lightweight foundations. Two US Patents (Refs 2 and 3) are known and trade literature exists on the uses of polystyrene blocks in road, embankment and abutment construction over soft soils (Ref 4). The proposal brought forward is a natural extension of the earlier reported work. Very considerable desk studies coupled with field trials and performance data on a wide range of lightweight foundation materials is warranted.

10. Despite these perceived problems requiring practical solution, from a mechanics consideration there does not appear to be any reason why the proposed solution cannot be used. The lightweight trench backfill or the lightweight structural backfill may be reinforced either traditionally or by the use of a range of geotextiles. Uplift forces can be catered for by use of a reinforced pile or pier constructed of lightweight fill. Suspended floors and services may be supported by the lightweight foundation system. Durability could be a problem but by careful selection of the foundation trench fill, for critical areas, this potential problem can be controlled. Modification to buildings would demand careful control. The use of a check list would be required to ensure that any work carried out does not interfere with the functioning of the building.

11. Rotation and/or overturning of the strip footings could occur prior to the placement of the superstructure load. Practical means of overcoming this potential limitation are the use of a series of shear pins driven through the trench fill and into the underlying ground, similar to the "chicken-foot" foundation system. The practical feasibility of these general proposals can only be confirmed by field scale trials complemented by careful desk studies.

REFERENCES

1. Plastic foam in road embankments. Proceedings Norwegian Plastics Conference, Oslo, Norway, 1985.
2. Floating foundation and process therefor. US Patent No 3626 702, Dec 14, 1971, E J Monahan.
3. Novel low pressure back-fill and process therefor. US Patent 3747353 July 24, 1973. E J Monahan.
4. Expanded polystyrene blocks for civil engineering construction works. Vencel Resil Ltd. promotional literature.

Economic transportation influenced by development and environmental issues

A. G. H. McCLINTOCK, McClintock & Skinner Inc., South Africa

SYNOPSIS. The South African Iron and Steel Corporation, Iscor Limited, wish to develop a coal mine in Venda, an independent state in the extreme north east of South Africa. The coal mine would need a private railway of 125 km to link the mine to the Spoornet main railway line. The consultants engineering studies and design were aimed at providing the greatest benefits to Venda where development is essential. The consultants carried out an environmental impact assessment of the proposed railway corridor which resulted in major deviations from the most economically viable alignment.

1. The South African Iron and Steel Corporation Limited, Iscor, have expanded an existing pilot coal mine at Tshikondeni in Venda from 1000 tons per week to 3000 tons per week. The labour force is predominantly Vavenda (the people of Venda), as it is Iscor's policy to assist local development wherever possible. This particular coal field has the highest grade of metallurgical coal in Southern Africa, and when blended with the normal grades of metallurgical coal results in a dramatic improvement to the output of the blast furnaces at the steelworks.

2. The Management of Iscor decided to expand the mine to produce 14 000 tons per week with a possible future maximum of 19 000 tons per week, the benefits to the Vavenda of this decision were many. Local people would be employed during the construction of the coal plant, and over five hundred would be employed on a permanent basis at the Mine. A new town would be built at Masisi to accommodate the mine workers with the associated infrastructure of shops, recreation centres, restaurants, roads and other services creating further employment opportunities. To supply water for the town and the Mine, a dam would be constructed on the Mutale River, and a telephone exchange built to serve the town and the Mine, linking them to Thohoyandou, the capital, and the Southern Africa telephone network.

3. The prospect of having a major coal mine with all the necessary infrastructure, and employment opportunities in an area devoid of work is of major benefit to the population.

4. The main problem, is how to get the coal from the Mine to a station on the Spoornet (the National Railway Authority) main railway line a distance of about 125 km. To investigate this aspect of the project the Management of Iscor Limited appointed McClintock & Skinner Incorporated (M & S), Consulting Engineers, to carry out a feasibility study to determine the most economically viable mode of transport to get the coal from the Mine to a railhead on the Spoornet main line between Louis Trichardt and Messina Stations in the Northern Transvaal.

5. Iscor specified that the study should cover the following transportation systems; road haulage, railway, aerial ropeway, conventional belt conveyor, cable belt conveyor and pipeline. Due to the confidential and sensitive nature of the project the study had to be carried out with maximum security, with the result that it was not possible to undertake the normal research and data collection.

6. After studying twenty eight alternative routes, the alternatives were reduced to the two most viable systems (i) rail transport with high initial capital cost, negligible replacement cost over twenty three years, and low operating and maintenance cost and (ii) road transport with lower initial capital cost, high replacement cost over twenty three years, and high operating and maintenance cost. After Iscor had completed a financial and economic evaluation taking into account the cost of the Mine, town, dam and services, it was decided that a private siding railway should be designed and constructed between the Mine and Huntleigh Siding on the Spoornet main line.

7. As a private siding railway, Iscor would build and pay for the railway, but Spoornet would operate its locomotives and freight wagons over the line, no fare paying passengers would be permitted on the line.

8. The terrain between the Mine and Spoornet main railway line at Huntleigh Siding is one of gently undulating ground with isolated high rocky outcrops, and wide river beds. The possibility of building a railway to other stations was discounted after study of aerial mapping, followed by aerial and road inspections. The only alternative was Mopane Station some 12 kilometres north of Huntleigh Siding which is reasonably well developed with station buildings and staff houses. The main objection to Huntleigh Siding was the lack of services and infrastructure.

9. M & S were then appointed by Iscor to carry out the design, supervision of construction, and project management of the 125 km private railway

siding. Soon after design commenced, Iscor decided that every effort should be made to minimise any adverse environmental impact along the route, and that environmental specialists should be appointed to investigate this aspect of the project.

10. At the specific request of the Venda Government, and with the approval of Iscor, senior staff members of the University of Venda were appointed by M & S in their private capacities to undertake the assessment of the impact of the proposed railway. M & S were instructed to manage this part of the project and to complete the final report. M & S also arranged for the Environmental Evaluation Unit of the University of Cape Town to be appointed to give guidance and assistance to the University of Venda specialists. The aspects studied were: zoology, limnology, socio-economic, botany, agriculture, pedology, ecology, aesthetics, acoustics, health, archaeology, anthropology, history and tourism.

11. Due to time constraints and economic considerations the assessment of the impact of the proposed railway was restricted to a corridor of interest 1000 metres wide, i.e. 500 metres either side of the economic engineering route. Each specialist was asked to report on three major aspects
(i) identification of impact (ii) assessment of significance of impact and (iii) recommended mitigation, and then to prepare a map of sensitive areas identified within the corridor. The current environmental conditions along the entire length of the proposed line were recorded in terms of a three point ranking using a common legend for: (i) relatively undisturbed (ii) disturbed (iii) degraded. The scientists were asked to propose measures to be taken to reduce the negative aspects of the proposed railway and enhance positive aspects.

12. The terrain from the Mine to the South African border is generally open arid shrubland with clumps of Mopane and Baobab trees. The proposed railway would be north of the Soutpansberg Mountain range where temperatures in the range of 40°C to 50°C in the Summer are often experienced with long periods of drought. This is unlike the southern half of Venda which has a more temperate climate, lush vegetation, arable land and high Summer rainfall.

13. There were a number of instances where the proposed railway line would pass through, or close to, local villages. This occurred in most cases because the railway line runs alongside an existing major gravel road. This has the advantage of having only one transportation corridor for both the road and railway line. Should the railway line be deviated too far from this road then the railway servitude would need to be increased in order to accommodate a maintenance road for the railway line thereby creating two corridors instead of one. This would be less desirable, so careful

consideration had to be given to all the costs and benefits before a decision was made to divert the railway line.

14. Iscor accepted, in principle, the findings of the specialists and most of the recommendations made in the environmental report. For example Iscor instructed M & S to find alternative alignments in Venda to avoid Sanari Village, Sagole Spa, Muswodi Village and the Nyala Magnasite Mine. It will be appreciated that having determined the most economic engineering route, any deviation would result in significant cost increases. This is especially the case with Sanari Village and Sagole Spa.

15. Iscor also accepted the scientists' view that the Nwanedi National Park in Venda, and the game, cattle and citrus farms in the South African section of the proposed railway should be avoided if at all possible. From this followed an instruction to M & S to investigate alternative routes to avoid these areas and to find an acceptable socio-political alignment.

16. Unless Europeans have had the opportunity of visiting Southern Africa they will have difficulty in visualising the terrain conditions for areas classified as parks, game and cattle farms, as they are completely different to European standards.

17. M & S found an alternative route which was in essence most of one of the original study routes, which had been rejected because the cost of earthworks were high. Nevertheless Iscor accepted the major deviations of the alternative route with its consequential increase in capital cost. The alternative route was then presented to the specialists who carried out a further environmental assessment on a 1000 metre wide corridor as before. As expected the specialists found the alternative route to be more acceptable, although they still had areas of concern.

18. It was noted that the environmental specialists were specifically concerned about noise pollution affecting the hunting of game and the serenity of the Tshipise Resort which is visited by over one hundred thousand tourists per year.

19. The environmental team acknowledged the effort that Iscor made to mitigate the effects of the proposed private siding railway. The implementation of the recommendations and mitigatory measures proposed by the environmental specialists, for the main issues identified in the transportation corridor in Venda and in the Republic of South Africa, should result in a development that is acceptable to all the affected parties, and with minimal additional stress to the existing ecosystems.

The apparent duality of infrastructure design strategies

K. G. SMITH, University of Liverpool

SYNOPSIS. The paper develops the theme that from an engineering systems viewpoint the difference between the design process of a high profile project and a low technology one should be minimal. Although superficially the solutions may appear to be very different there are often relatively sophisticated engineering science principles applied to make the low technology solution a success.

DESIGN STRATEGY

1. In the limited space available I shall assume familiarity with the established definitions of appropriate technology (refs 1-3). A discussion of the background design philosophy is also available (refs. 4-6).

2. The aim is to show that even when a low technology situation and solution arise there is still a need to consider, from a fundamental engineering science and design strategy point of view, some sophisticated principles. It is a matter of managing the quality assurance of the design process. From various experiences a series of pairs (or duals) of examples has been chosen to help illustrate this. From the casual observers viewpoint the solutions are apparently different. From the engineering fundamentals viewpoint the differences at a strategic or abstract level are minimal. The duality is superficial and we may sometimes be in danger of forgetting that. What is different is the specification of the knowledge base of experiences and the use of in-service feedback to ensure design goals have been achieved.

3. For our purposes a design strategy could be seen as an interaction of the following
   (a) Project and environmental data acquisition
   (b) Defining the criteria for success (goals)
   (c) Reference to the knowledge base of experiences of past projects
   (d) Creative generation of schemes
   (e) Checking and ranking of solutions
   (f) Engineering judgement
   (g) Development and execution of the chosen solution

INFRASTRUCTURE WORKSHOP

(h) In-service feedback from the environment during the years after construction has finished.

4. In the above list by environmental I mean the physical, social, economic and cultural powers that need to be directed for the use, benefit and convenience of mankind. In using the knowledge bases of experience it is the business of engineers to break what Bronowski called the eleventh commandment, "..Those shalt not question" (ref. 7). Recent discussion on the generation of solutions in the structural field has been aired by Burgoyne (ref. 8). Traditional education concentrates on the checking, development and execution phases of the project. There is analysis without questioning the proper bounds of that analysis. No sense of perspective is encouraged.

5. As part of the continuing feedback process we need to affirm a policy of never covering up mistakes. Many have been catalogued in technology for development and survival, "....the inadequacy of many designers was seen for the first time. The point is that the third world situation was only an indicator, a test which showed up certain bad attributes of certain bad designers, but these people are probably still making similar and different mistakes at home (the developed world); appropriate technology is on our doorstep and for that reason alone you should worry." (ref. 5). I am interested in how the strategic design process goes wrong. If the fundamental strategy is right then mistakes will be fewer, especially for novices in a field. I have found appropriate technology examples useful for design teaching for this reason. Some experiences from that and associated research and consultancy areas are now passed on to support my argument.

MASONRY STRUCTURES

6. I had been using slides to explain to students from over twenty countries some fundamentals about design in general and masonry in particular. These had included slides from the Intermediate Technology Development Group (ITDG) in London. The aim was to train them in British practice but I considered a wider perspective useful. Clay bricks featured heavily and I set a tutorial exercise for the construction of a low technology brick water tank. It cannot be done was the cry from the U.K. part-time post-graduates. Only steel or concrete would satisfy them. The cry from some of the overseas ones varied from rage that their country was being partonizingly portrayed in the slides (as they perceived it) to assertions that helping poor people to help themselves was commercially inappropriate. I urged on them to develop a sense of detachment. There is no room for emotion in the practice of engineering. Then I proceeded to show two solutions. One an ITDG slide using semi-circular hand-made clay bricks. Another that I developed from fundamental principles of engineering science relating the needs of stable masonry to arch action and hydrostatic forces. On plan the structure was generally circular, consisting of a series of

jack arches convex inwards to the centre of the circle. At each arch abutment a buttress was provided and aligned radially. It was thicker at the base to accommodate the water pressures. The whole structure was axisymmetric and we proceeded to analyse it in as much detail as any reinforced concrete 'proper' tank. As the analysis progressed, in their eyes this low technology project became an acceptable one as it was subjected to theory. To make this simple structure exist theory had been used. It was superficially simple, but not really so at the strategy level.

7. Space precludes discussion but the same group learned not to confuse the potentially low technology clay brick with the autoclaved calcium silicate one (refs. 9-10).

CONCRETE STRUCTURES

8. Engineers often regard houses as fairly low technology, at least from their structural analysis aspect. That need not be so. However, one I was consulted on resulted in an interesting apparent dual although the examples were separated by a few years. It transpired that the house was in a region where there was an expectation of attack by fire arms. A sacrificial ballistic energy absorbing wall was therefore built around parts of it. A few years later I became aware of some experiments being done in the high technology area of North sea oil production to protect storage tanks in a similar way. The same engineering fundamentals and correct strategy applied to the high and relatively low technology situation.

9. My own research at that time was into earthquake resistant design of concrete structures. Base isolation is a possible option and calculations can be quite absorbing. In the literature I came across a Chinese method of base isolation which did not use expensive bearings but did use the same scientific principles. Here smooth grains of manually sifted and sorted sand are placed at a level similar to the position of a damp proof course in the walls (ref. 11). Another case of a clever theory used simply.

HYDRAULIC MACHINES

10. Another case of coincidence will end these examples. An engineering friend asked me how a particular old ship lift of which he had an illustration may have worked. I retrospectively analysed the situation in its contextual historical low technology situation and made my suggestion. I later found a contemporary reference which validated both the analysis work and strategic fundamentalist approach (ref. 12). Sometime later I saw an illustration of a modern lift using a similar principle being used in a yacht marina. The same fundamental principle was in use in each case, it was just a difference of investment level.

COMPUTERS AND EXPERT SYSTEMS

11. In the above paragraphs the phrase knowledge base has been deliberately used in describing where our experiences are

stored. It is the phrase used in expert systems. An expert system represents expensive skills so the introduction of appropriate expert systems is developing countries could be equated to a capital injection those skills represent. In water engineering this has been reviewed elsewhere (ref. 13). With the correct design strategy the approach could apply to many infra-structuctre projects.

CONCLUSION

12. I do not believe in a pantheon or even a duality of technologies. There is only one at the systems level. The only road is the one we started with Galileo and the others who broke the eleventh commandment. The solution for appropriate development for survival must be a strident call for more technology, not less. We do need more quality in the design of that technology and that will come from a better understanding of design strategy and being alive to what is only an apparent duality between high and low technology situations.

REFERENCES
1. DUNN, P.D. Appropriate technology. Macmillan, 1978.
2. I.C.E. Appropriate technology in Civil Engineering. Conference proceedings. 14-16 April 1980. I.C.E. 1981.
3. PAPENEK, V. Design for the real world. Thames and Hudson 1972.
4. ANONYMOUS. The Consulting Engineer. Northwood Publications, London, 1977-78.
5. SMITH, K.G. The message of appropriate technology, in papers from the conference on engineering management and social responsibility, Danbury Park. Polytechnic of East London, (NELP), 1979.
6. DEBONO, E. Technology today. Routledge and Kegan Paul, 1971.
7. BROWNOWSKI, J. The ascent of man. BBC 1973.
8. BURGOYNE, C.J. Lets teach design: we already teach analysis. The Structural Engineer, London, April 1990.
9. B.R.E. Overseas Building Notes, 154, Feb., 1, 1974. HMSO.
10. S.C.I. Autoclaved calcium silicate building products symposium. Society of Chemical Industry, London 1967.
11. SMITH, K.G. Ph.D. Thesis. University of London. In preparation.
12. WALFORD, E. Village London. Alderman Press, London 1985.
13. KELSEY, G.R. Expert systems as a preliminary design tool for drinking water supplies in developing countries. Civil Comp. 87, Civil Comp Press, Edinburgh 1987.

The human infrastructure requirements of technicians

E. G. SNAPE, Mid-Warwickshire College

SYNOPSIS. The problems facing technicians in Developing Countries are considered and explanations proposed to account for the fact that they do not always attain the expected level of performance. A possible technician network is to be developed in order to continue the gains in confidence brought about by training courses.

The title page of this conference volume should be carefully studied. The topic is Appropriate Development For Survival and the picture shows a person lifting industrial development from a well in much the same way as thousands of people in the developing world lift their Water For Survival. The implication is that development is there for the taking, all that is needed is an appropriately sized bucket and enough strength [economic resource?] to lift it. That development is like any other commodity and can be just picked up.
The reality is, I would suggest, rather different and that what we ought to focus on is the person doing the lifting. In the long term the major resource of a nation is its human resource. Other resources can generally be bought in when the wealth is available, but it is not easy to buy in a trained and educated workforce. It can be done, and is done, on a project basis. Even where there exists a well qualified pool of staff on which to draw it will often be the case that short term specialists are used to establish new schemes or processes which are subsequently 'localised'. The history of civil engineering is of itinerant specialists from the 'navigators' of the canal age through the crews on every major construction site since then to the professional engineers moving with their high tech solutions of today. Often one or two of the construction crew and technical staff would 'settle down' when a job was completed and remain as its maintenance team.
When my students are shown round the local boreholes by the Water Authority supervisor they are in fact being shown around by the person in charge of the original drilling team. He met and married a local girl and stayed behind to look after the boreholes when the drilling crew moved on.

INFRASTRUCTURE WORKSHOP

In this way experience would be both gained and distributed throughout a country. A technical infrastructure was born.

Technicians, more than most, need and benefit from such an infrastructure. The craftsman carries his skill with him and the professional, through institutional support and education has greater access to travel and peer group support. The technician, the man hauling up the industrial development in the bucket, is often denied these assets. A new scheme or industrial development will usually require an element of training as part of the tender package. Such training will be carefully selected and structured and will be delivered to a high standard. These days the value of such training is not in doubt. And yet experience tells us that often such schemes grind to a halt after a few years because of a lack of 'something'. Sometimes it is a lack of maintenance, sometimes a lack of parts, sometimes it is a lack of experience or know how, sometimes it is simply a lack of information. Always there will be a good reason for the lack of performance but it is basically a lack of infrastructure. Consider a technician here in the UK. It is likely that his [or her] interest in the subject goes back to his early teens following on from a fairly broad and comprehensive education and often, but not always, reinforced by a family background in the subject area. The technician has already acquired knowledge and an understanding about his trade long before any formal education and training takes place. This process is so natural and commonplace that it is often forgotten or discounted. In my own experience with technicians from the UK and from developing countries the former always seem to have a greater background on which to draw [although they are likely to be less motivated in so doing!] My initial reactions when confronted by such discrepancies was to explain it away by a straightforward lack of knowledge. To assume that part of the syllabus had been missed or not properly understood. It is only recently that I have seen an extra dimension to the problem.

For many years when travelling around the UK with technicians from developing countries I have been impressed by their knowledge of, and interest in, the land, the crops and the animals seen grazing. The same route taken with my home based students elicits no response about the countryside at all and if the topic is raised it is soon dropped. That the two experiences are different should not be a surprise because that is the natural experience base of most of the overseas technicians. Their experiences in childhood are very reminiscent of experiences described by people born in the early part of the century. They have grown up and spent their formative years in a predominantly agricultural and rural environment. Their knowledge of technical matters and systems is much more recent and much less comprehensive. Also because it is not part of their core experience they are much less confident in deploying their technical abilities and skills in problem solving situations.

Teacher trainers are well used to the concept of an hierarchy of knowledge, indeed Bloom's Taxonomy of Educational Objectives is a well known lecture topic in all education courses. Its significance in this discussion is in the concept that students can possess knowledge at different levels. A fact can be known as just a fact, it can be understood and used and can be still not part of a person's operational experience. We are aware from our own studies that we can 'know' something in order to pass examinations and yet be quite incapable of using that information or theory in any useful or practical way. It is insufficiently known to become part of a technician's problem solving armoury. For it to become such a part the technician has to operate in an environment where its use and the inter-relationships with other facts are continually reinforced. This is where the lack of infrastructure appears to be most important. My technicians are lacking in the confidence to use the knowledge they already possess. Given time and an environment where collectively they can develop their problem solving skills the confidence grows. This is supported by employers of the technicians who have been through such a developmental experience and has implications for the design of training programmes for staff.

As with any educational experience there is both the product and the process. It is comparatively easy to define an educational need by comparing what is already known with some kind of analysis showing what needs to be known. Once that has been done a syllabus can be drawn up and a course planned to rectify the omissions. Most training schemes operate along such lines and the results are generally satisfactory. The above argument however, would suggest that such an approach, on its own, would be insufficient because all it would provide would be the factual knowledge and not the confidence to deploy that knowledge. In other words we ought to pay much more attention to the process by which the knowledge is acquired and to pay attention to the environment in which it is to be used. It is one thing to train a technician in a skill and ask him to use it in a company or institution alongside many other technicians who have all been through the same course last year and the year before, it is quite a different task to train a technician in a skill and then send him to use it in complete isolation from other staff. The levels of confidence required are orders of magnitude apart. As engineers we are acquainted with the concept of structural members acting together to give a greater strength than their individual sum, this is the human resource equivalent.
We are assuming that individual technicians will perform as well as when they are operating in a self supporting team.

INFRASTRUCTURE WORKSHOP

How can such support be provided?

Clearly there cannot be any great increase in the numbers of technicians so those that are in post will have to continue to act as single stuctural members in the foreseable future. However technicians are people, not steel beams and what is important is the linking of minds and not physical proximity. The concept has arisen of using the core of technicians who have benefitted from the British Council training programme and who have therefore already got a common bond and common experience to develop a continuing educational process. To enable, through an exchange of ideas, solutions, problems, etc, the educational process to continue long after the formal experience has finished. As we all know the simple act of writing a report often clarifies in our own minds the nature of the events on which we are reporting. Such a conduit will enable technicians to undergo that process but within a community of which they were once part. That is to say that as individuals they have a relaxed relationship with the reporting and recording system. In time they will in fact own the system and will be able to develop it in whatever way they think can best serve their particular needs. In the short term it should provide some of the support which will enable each technician to operate that little bit better than when left on his own. The initial steps towards setting up such a network are taking place now. By the time of the conference it may be possible to report on the responses to this initiative.

The application of appropriate technology for rural development in Thailand

M. SRINARAWAT, Public Works Department, Bangkok, and
K. J. MILLBAND, T. P. O'Sullivan & Partners

SYNOPSIS. In support of a rapid expansion of the Thai economy, considerable investment has been made in recent years in urban and industrial development. However, the vast majority of the population live in the rural areas and depend on agriculture for their livelihood. This paper describes a rural development project designed to redress the investment imbalance and through the use of appropriate technology, improve the infrastructure and create additional employment opportunities in the rural areas.

BACKGROUND

1. Thailand has a population of some 56 million of which 83% live in the rural areas. For 70% of the population agriculture is their principal means of support. Agricultural activity is seasonal, being concentrated in the monsoon months of June through October and wages are low resulting in the migration of large numbers to the cities. The Royal Thai Government, concerned at the widening gap between the relatively well off urban minority and the rural majority, embarked on a longterm programme of rural development.

2. A pilot project implemented in 1984/85 demonstrated to government that rural roads in Thailand could be built economically to acceptable standards with a mix of village labour and locally manufactured equipment and tools. Using the experience gained from the pilot project, the Public Works Department with central government support, drew up guidelines and an initial work programme for a Labour Based Construction Project (LBCP).

DEVELOPMENT GOALS

3. The broad goals set by government for the LBCP are:
   - To stimulate the socio-economic development of the rural areas through the provision of improved infrastructure.
   - To create productive employment opportunities in the rural areas and hence reduce poverty and urban migration.

4. Four specific objectives were recognised as crucial for the realisation and sustainability of these goals:

(a) strengthening the Public Works Department's technical and administrative capability in implementing efficient labour based road construction and maintenance programmes on a large scale;
(b) improving the management and technical efficiency of labour-based road construction and maintenance operations.
(c) maximising the socio-economic impact of construction;
(d) promoting a positive attitude towards labour-based construction methods among engineers and administrators.

5. The LBCP was effectively launched in 1987 on an expanding programme of labour-based road construction in the north of the country. Attention has since been focussed on implementing solutions designed to achieve the key objectives.

SOLUTIONS ADOPTED
Institutional strengthening

6. Government recognised the interdependance of institutional, managerial and technical capability in undertaking the project. A sub-unit was set-up within the Rural Roads Department of the PWD and given a budget and specific responsibility for policy direction and execution.

7. Limited technical assistance was deemed necessary to obtain direct access to international experience of labour-based construction, and to help with planning, organisation and training. Two kinds of inputs were commissioned under UNDP provisions and financing:
(a) 30.5 man months by international consultants under the auspices of the ILO;
(b) some 150 man months by national consultants.
These inputs were to be provided over the initial 18 months and 30 months of the project respectively.

8. Additional strengthening measures comprised:
- streamlining administrative systems to ensure the release of budget funds prior to the start of the construction season, and timely payment of the labour force (crucial for efficient labour-based operations).
- the introduction of improved planning and programming measures using systemised feedback from the construction sites to support budget requests and to optimise the use of available resources.
- the provision of comprehensive formal and on-thejob training programmes for management and field supervisory staff.

Organisational and technical aspects

9. In setting technical standards for the work, a balance has been struck between construction standards and equipment usage on the one hand and maintenance requirements and labour inputs on the other. The prime objective of LBCP is to construct acceptable roads. If labour employment was made the main consideration without regard to the economic or engineering consequences, labour-based construction would have

been brought into disrepute to the longer term detriment of the project.

10. In general the roads serve to connect villages to the national highway system. They comprise a 6 metre wide pavement of 150mm laterite with conventional low cost earthworks and drainage. However, within village boundaries, the laterite is replaced by a 150mm bamboo reinforced concrete slab. Whilst having a higher initial cost (laterite US$12,000/km, concrete slab US$40,000/km), the slab has a lower maintenance requirement and avoids the dust hazard.

11. Village labour is hired for bush clearing; earthworks, drainage and borrow pit excavation; loading and spreading; concreting and culvert installation. Labour operations follow the well documented principles established by the ILO with one exception. The Thai is communal by nature; while the conventional approach to large scale labour organisation is activity-based, the use of fixed gangs of 20-25 workers covering all activities has been found more appropriate for Thailand.

12. Good quality tools and equipment are manufactured in Thailand. A range of hand tools have been developed based on local agricultural implements and designed to improve worker performance. The single axle tractor is a popular form of motor power for farmers and is often owned by the village. Simple towed equipment comprising rollers, graders, water bowsers and tippers have been designed for use with this tractor for which a hire charge is paid.

13. Maintenance is accorded a high priority both for protecting the investment made in the roads and as a means of longterm employment. Various methods are under review including the lengthman system, the deployment of mobile gangs and the setting-up of small village contractors. A pilot project has been established to conduct trials and undertake technical and economic evaluations.

Socio-economic improvements

14. Three broad solutions are being pursued to maximise the socio-economic impact of the project:
  (a) identifying selection criteria and producing a simple method of road selection to ensure that those schemes with the greatest development potential are accorded the highest priority;
  (b) applying the expertise gained on roads to other rural construction sectors (findings to date indicate a potential for small scale irrigation works and a demonstration project is to be set-up);
  (c) developing longterm income-generating activities through self-employment programmes which motivate, organise and train the construction workers to collectively use their expertise and invest a proportion of their earnings.

15. Item (c) is particularly important for sustainability of the project goals. At present the best potential would

appear to be the formation of village contractors to carry out routine road maintenance. All solutions under this heading require the commitment and co-operation of a number of government agencies for their success.

Promoting awareness

16. An important requirement for the longterm success of the project is an awareness and acceptance of labour-based construction within the establishment. The need for acceptable technical standards has been noted in para 10. It is also necessary to avoid promoting labour-based methods as a separate entity. Labour usage should be viewed as one of a number of solutions available to the engineer.

17. To this end, special units have not been established in the field and construction is being implemented through the Provincial Engineers' existing organisations. In addition, it is proposed to introduce labour-based construction into University curricula. This will not be achieved quickly but as a step in this direction, the universities are being actively involved in project work through research and training assignments.

PROGRESS TO DATE

18. The project has expanded rapidly with a five fold increase in budget for rural roads. At the end of the 1989 construction season, some 345kms had been built covering 27 provinces at a cost of US$7.3 million. 12,000 village labourers were employed during 1989; the 1990 construction budget alone amounts to US$6.8 million.

19. While this expansion has demonstrated the commitment of government and a neutralisation of bias favouring equipment based construction methods, resources have been concentrated on short term construction activity to the detriment of the sustainable elements of the project. Nevertheless, a new optimism is perceivable in the villages. This is directly attributable to the visible benefits of the improved roads and the increase in earnings.

20. Good roads have been built speedily and economically using construction methods which directly benefit the rural communities which they serve. The organisation is in place for this to continue. Effort must now be concentrated on ensuring the sustainability of these benefits through the development and institutionalisation of training programmes, the extension of labour-based methods to other infrastructure and, particularly, maintenance.

21. If the longterm goals of government are to be realised, alternative sources of productive investment and employment in the villages must be vigorously pursued. Whatever the final outcome, it is clear that the use of appropriate technology has a major part to play in the strengthening of the rural economy in Thailand.

Summary of discussion

G. A. EDMONDS, International Labour Office, Geneva

From the outset the group agreed that it wished to prepare recommendations that were both realistic and coherent. Equally, the recommendations are intended to relate to the mandate and the responsibility of the ICE. A large minority of the ICE's members live and/or work in developing countries.

The group felt that there were three possible ways in which the ICE could help developing countries promote the more effective use of technology for survival.

(a) by providing information on technological alternatives to all members
(b) by providing advice and guidance to governments and other institutions on the technological alternatives available
(c) by promoting and testing alternative technologies (this might be difficult for the ICE but it was felt that it was an important activity which would enhance the reputation of the ICE).

To be able to achieve anything the group felt that there would have to be a focal point for the activities that could be undertaken. It was agreed that this would be the Appropriate Development Panel, which was set up as a direct result of a previous ICE conference. It would therefore be logical for it to be the focal point of the activities arising out of this Conference.

RECOMMENDATIONS
One way for the Appropriate Development Panel to structure recommendations would be to carry out a review of its work over the past ten years, highlighting its successes and failures and then leading on to a programme of future work. This programme should have clearly defined objectives and outputs relating to those objectives.

In developing recommendations it was felt that the Panel should take the following specific points into consideration.

1. The need to support the establishment or strengthening of professional bodies in developing countries. These

bodies, like the ICE, could promote the role of the engineer, advise on the most appropriate technological development path to follow and provide a forum for discussion on professional engineering matters, including the role of technology in development.
2. The need for better information flow. A great deal of information exists on technological alternatives. Equally, several institutions around the world are carrying out research into technological alternatives. Unfortunately a lot of this information remains locked within a small group of institutions and individuals. The ICE could play a role in making this information more widely available. Also, the Institution may be able to produce a simple brochure on technological alternatives and promote the transfer of knowledge by the linking of institutions in the north and the south. The idea of networking was consistently raised as having proved effective in other areas.
3. Training programmes should always be undertaken with two specific points in mind: that training should be country-specific or, more generally, related to the environment where the work is to be carried out, and that the long-term requirement is to institutionalize the training in the specific country. The latter objective should be considered right from the start of any assessment of training needs.
4. It is vital for the long-term acceptability of a more rational choice of technology that the use of local resources forms part of the engineer's curriculae. The ICE could take the lead in promoting this awareness. In addition, the development of a data base on alternative technologies would provide the substance for the development of course material related to the use of local resources.
5. The Panel could initiate work on the development and/or modification of standards appropriate to the needs of developing countries. This is particularly important in relation to the introduction of new technologies for which there are no recognized standards. It also relates to the certification of training related to new and alternative technologies.
6. In relation to appraisal and evaluation there is a need to promote the concept of the integration of the soft and hard aspects of technology.
7. It was also suggested that UK members of the ICE could do a great deal to assist colleagues in the developing countries and the ICE might try to put this on a more formal footing.

There was also a very specific proposal made regarding the testing out on a pilot basis of various alternative techniques. This would be done at the village level in sub-Saharan Africa. It was suggested that this proposal would be most effectively dealt with by the Project Management Forum.

It was felt important that action should be taken by the ICE on these recommendations as a lack of response at this stage would strain the credibility of the participants in their belief that the ICE was a learned body capable of making an impact in an area of significant importance.

Discussion on workshop summaries

BRIGADIER J.N.S. DRAKE, Institution of Civil Engineers
Membership of the ICE can be obtained without a degree, as Incorporated Engineer or Technician and through the mature candidate route.

The ICE is promoting a strategy of a high profile for civil engineers and the profession. This is to encourage proper recognition and recruitment of high quality people into the profession.

The training of civil engineers is regulated by the ICE. However, there is a requirement for experienced employers to help in the training of those working for them. Every engineer should approach problems with an open mind and be ready to make appropriate choices of technology, techniques, materials and so on. Each engineer has a responsibility for others, as well as the ICE.

The ICE is requiring increasing accountability of its committees and panels. This will include the assessment of priorities against available resources, the setting of specific targets and the monitoring of performance. It will complement the future work-load created by the proposals for future activity made by the Appropriate Development Panel.

The content of courses is customer-led. If appropriate technology is required in education or training courses the customer should make appropriate recommendations for change.

P. GUTHRIE, Scott Wilson Kirkpatrick & Partners
I disagree with the view that the introduction of choice of technology into degree courses would be difficult to sell because it would be impossible to tell which engineers on the courses would use it. Many elements of any educational degree are never used by a graduate but that does not make them less valuable.

Until choice of technology is introduced as a serious part of degree courses at leading universities in the UK it will not be accepted in the UK by the profession, the funding agencies and implementing authorities.

WORKSHOP SUMMARIES

DR M. SRINARAWAT, Public Works Department, Thailand
Thailand is engaged on an expanding programme of rural infrastructure using labour-based techniques. A major constraint to the programme is the negative attitude of Thai engineers to labour-based work which stems to a large extent from the education system. Engineering education in Thailand is based on a high-tech approach from a narrow base. As the Thai system (and the systems of most developing countries) is based on the European or American system, this suggests that changes are needed in engineering education in both the developed and developing worlds. Also the dissemination of information on the use of appropriate technology needs to be improved considerably.

J. GOULD, International Rainwater Catchment Systems Association
Thailand is one of the few countries in the developing world to have come anywhere near achieving the targets of the International Drinking Water Supply and Sanitation Decade for rural water supply provision. This has been achieved largely through the Thai jar programme which has resulted in the construction of about 10 million 1-2 m3 ferrocement roof tanks since the early 1980s. This example is one of a number of achievements in the field of appropriate technology implemented predominantly by indigenous engineers in Thailand. The opportunity exists in the near future for the expertise which exists in Thailand to be used to assist in the widespread implementation of appropriate technologies in neighbouring countries in Indo-China where the need is considerable. More emphasis needs to be put on technology transfer between developing countries; the developed world could assist in providing the resources for this.

T. ARMSTRONG, Binnie & Partners
The paring down of consultants' time inputs into projects which may be to the detriment of a holistic, multidisciplinary approach is largely because of the high cost of consultancies from industrialized countries. The growing gap in relative wealth between industrialized and less developed countries is exacerbating this. I suggest that there is an enhanced need for partnerships between consultancies from developed countries and indigenously-based groups. This would promote a more local perspective on projects and programmes, support local consultant capacity and skills, tend to expend consultancy earnings more in the countries concerned and may possibly be cheaper. Some UK consultants already undertake such partnerships.

DR J. M. JEWSBURY, Liverpool Associates in Tropical Health
Most communities in developing countries have well-established (sometimes semi-formal) means of organizing health care (in the broadest sense). These systems include decision-making and education-duplicating (or worse).

DISCUSSION

Ignoring these existing systems is very bad practice and likely to be counter-productive. There is much experience in health education to show that the best - sometimes the only - way to achieve any progress is through the village health committee, even if that progress appears to be slow.

PROFESSOR K. G. KIDAN, Independent consultant
My experience is that scholars in developing countries lack the depth and sensitiveness of their surroundings. Syllabuses should be designed to match the problems existing in those countries and should not be copied directly from experience elsewhere. Training should take place within those countries and only selected individuals with good know-how and the ability to innovate should be sent abroad. Research and development should be encouraged.

Any project should be labour-intensive; developing countries are not in the euphoria of computer-oriented methods and high-technology. Transfer of technology must be combined with local skills and promote the use of local materials.

This Conference has made a good start to solving problems in developing countries. Future conferences should have greater involvement from people in those countries.

I. A. RICHARDSON, Groundwork in Heartlands
I agree with Mr Guthrie's view on the content of degree courses and would add that, unless the choice of technology is introduced into the education of engineers, the profession risks failing to address the needs of most citizens of developing countries. This omission contributes in part to the problems of disseminating information on appropriate technologies as mentioned by Dr Srinarawat.

Given the complexity of social factors and the frequent simplicity of technical details, the engineering institutions need to decide whether their aims and objectives are compatible with providing the right professional expertise to enable a poor community to benefit from and sustain, say, a primary water supply and basic sanitation facility. People will need a wide knowledge of suitable technologies to make the appropriate choices and this will have to be combined with a high level of social awareness, communication skills and sensitivity to enable the professional to work in adequate partnership with the community.

It is therefore as important to educate engineers inappropriate working methods as in technology choices if they are to contribute effectively in the process of sustainable development in developing countries.

It is evident that in the poorest, remotest areas of many countries non-engineers (e.g. health workers) are taking the lead in the provision of clean water supplies and basic sanitation. They are doing so in response to desperate need, often without sufficient technical training or support, in the absence of any engineering-led initiative.

WORKSHOP SUMMARIES

This is partly due to the prejudice in favour of a high-tech approach which attracts engineers to towns or to prestigious projects. The same prejudice is prevalent among many qualified engineers from both sides of the north-south divide. This relates to the status attached to their work, and that in turn depends very much on what is or is not perceived to be of value. At the risk of over-simplifying the situation, I believe that most engineers value their work in terms of its technical merit, its complexity and the size of the project, before its contribution to the alleviation of human suffering. It could be argued that engineers are merely reflecting the values of modern western society as a whole. Given that this is likely to be absorbed by people from developing countries undergoing a western education, there is good reason to advocate more training and education opportunities in the countries concerned combined with more appropriate syllabuses.

Several countries are moving towards this approach and finding it a more cost-effective way of training local professionals to fill the huge gap in skills. Ironically a disproportionate number of the grants and scholarships funded by donor countries are available only for students studying in the west. Institutions in developing countries require greater support and acceptance from the developed countries before this is likely to change. The danger is that the qualifications of students in developing countries may not be accepted internationally. High-cost consultancies from the industrialized countries will continue to undermine their position and the more local perspective described by Mr Armstrong will be lost.

The challenge facing engineers in developed countries at the end of the twentieth century is very different from that facing their colleagues in the developing countries. Philanthropy and engineering were once close bedfellows, as the contribution of civil engineering to public health in Britain in the past century bears testament. Out of necessity development philosophy has moved on, the paternalism of the professional Victorian is no longer acceptable, nor is the technical chauvinism that often accompanied it. Instead the call is for a partnership of mutual respect between professionals and the benefiting community, combined with the ability to find and develop innovative solutions under severe economic constraints.

If engineers are to make a contribution they must do so within this framework. Their training and personalities must provide more appropriate skills and knowledge. Their professional institutions must recognize, afford status and promote those qualities. I believe the professional bodies should encourage governments and donors to spend on more appropriate, long-term development programmes aimed at the neediest communities and develop an international training policy that will specifically meet the requirements of developing countries in the twenty-first century.

Open forum

P. C. BARLOW, Binnie & Partners
The point that the people in LDC are not always asked what their requirements are for development can be highlighted by the example of a successful infrastructure project carried out in India. Visiting government officials from India, the UK and other countries were shown what can be done. A nearby town was also visited to show what the place was like before it had been developed. The headman was heard to say in Hindi, 'Why don't you stop interfering and leave us alone?'

It has been suggested that engineers should move into the field of politics in an attempt to influence governments. In my experience the actions and effects of non-government organizations like Oxfam tend to be more successful at getting to the root of a problem than those of those organizations that work directly for donor and recipient governments. This does not mean that politics and people can be divorced from one another: indeed they are the same.

DR P. WASS, Intermediate Technology Development Group
I should like to put forward some proposals for tackling some of the constraints on the application of appropriate technology on a much wider scale.

(a) The status of appropriate technology approaches to solving the problems of the urban and rural poor through salaries, price incentives and so on should be improved.
(b) Funding agencies should ensure that appropriate technology is specifically addressed in programmes and projects, e.g. by writing this into TORS for projects and allocating funds to research and development.
(c) The economic analysis of investment proposals should be broadened, e.g. environmental economics should look at issues of sustainability and the external factors influencing and being influenced by the proposed investment.
(d) There should be a greater spread of appropriate technology information to engineers through networks and newsletters, taking ODI networks and publications as a model (e.g. in agricultural administration,

OPEN FORUM

pastoralization and irrigation). Intermediate Technology Publications might be able to assist in this.

DR R. E. SOWDEN, The British Council
Professional bodies in the UK might encourage local professional bodies to offer prestigious awards to engineers responsible for successful appropriate development projects, and might even consider contributing towards the costs. This is done in India.

P. LAZENBY, Engineering & Power Development Consultants
Such long-term programmes for the development of intermediate technology and training as were dealt with in the workshops do not recognize the fact that present development projects are not keeping pace with the demand generated by an increase in population.
   Rather than concentrating on the appropriate nature of technology I suggest that the Institution of Civil Engineers should direct its efforts towards finding mechanisms which will evaluate the implementation of sustainable projects.

P. GUTHRIE, Scott Wilson Kirkpatrick & Partners
In 1981 the UK water industry set up a charity called WaterAid in response to the UN Water Decade. It has proved to be a highly successful operation both in raising money from water users and the water authorities, and in implementing community-based projects. WaterAid could be used as a model for a similar organization in the provision of power to the poor in developing countries. PowerAid, as it could be called, could be established by the new companies in the UK electricity industry.

DR M. R. STARR, Sir William Halcrow & Partners
The technology exists, but the main reason why it is not being applied is the long time - perhaps even generations - it takes to build up the critical mass when change can take off in rural areas of developing countries. It takes at least five years for pilot plants, another five for demonstration plants and another five for pre-commercial/ small-scale local production. Then enough people (governments, funding agencies and the general public) know enough to say, 'Let's go ahead' - the technology has reached critical mass and the explosion begins.

A. REED, Oxfam
The major issues of population growth, international debt and conflict cannot be addressed satisfactorily by a conference such as this. However, the technologies appropriate to the lesser issues can be addressed, and the more tools there are the better. The larger problems will be solved at other levels and Oxfam attempts to address these by putting more of its resources into social organization and campaigning than into technical projects. If this Conference could send a

signal to such countries as Angola, Mozambique and Ethiopia saying, 'We have the technology - please stop fighting among yourselves so that you can use it' this would be a major contribution to one of the root hindrances to development.

W. M. HOUSEGO-WOOLGAR, Senior Architectural and Planning Adviser, Overseas Development Administration

The problem with food shortage is not the inability or lack of capacity to produce the food - where people have the resources and cash available to buy food farmers will quickly produce it to meet that demand. The solution to the scarcity of food is to create greater economic activity and employment in the developing world to ensure that funds are available to encourage farmers to produce more food.

Emphasis has been given to rural technological projects. Everyone should be aware that in the next thirty years, two-thirds of the increase of the population of the developing world is going to be in the urban areas. It is in the urban areas where the vast numbers of population and the economic prosperity in the developing countries are going to be. Already 30-40% of the population in the developing world that live in the urban areas are producing 60% of the GNP. It can therefore be concluded that there will be millions of people in the urban areas who will require services: water, waste disposal, transportation, electricity and so on.

There is going to be an immense need for the skills of civil and mechanical engineers.

The technology needed to provide these services exists. Why is it that the solutions and the need for these services do not come together? The reason must be the lack of expectation of the population, i.e. it is not until people see what is possible that they come to expect services: when someone sees that his neighbour has piped water or a plot allocated to him, only then does he realize that these items are within his grasp. His expectations are raised and he calls for and is prepared to pay for or demand these services. The solutions to meeting the needs of the poor in the developing world are not more conferences or research, but an awareness of what is possible. One way to do this is through pilot projects.

With the mass expansion of population in the urban areas, one can see an immense growth in the need for mechanical and civil engineering skills. As more services become available, so expectations will rise and demand will increase. The current shortage of these skills is a deterrent to the economic and social development of the developing countries. More projects are required to provide the services and develop these urban skills.

Closing address

PROFESSOR R. SEVERN, University of Bristol

The splendid title of this Conference - Appropriate development for survival - reminds me of an American professor of mathematics - Tom Lehrer - who achieved some fame as a singer. One of his songs was, 'We'll all go together when we go, We'll be suffused in an incandescent glow'. He was referring to the nuclear holocaust as he saw it, but the thought is equally relevant to this Conference, which concerns the survival of everyone, not just those in the developing countries.

We are now in the International Natural Hazard Reduction Decade which was launched through the United Nations. The Institution of Civil Engineers has taken the initial lead through its former President, Alastair Patterson, in bringing together Professor M. W. Thring and the Institutions of Mechanical, Civil and Electrical Engineers into the Hazards Forum. In parallel the Royal Society and the Fellowship of Engineering are acting as the United Nations' focus, but the Institution of Civil Engineers has widened the activity to include man-made as well as natural hazards, and these are not generally well distinguished. Many so-called natural hazards (e.g. flooding and even earthquakes in some instances) are man-made.

The Institution of Civil Engineers has corresponding members in about 40 countries. One has to be careful not to encroach on national preserves, but the Institution is very willing, through the corresponding members, to help the local institutions to develop and to promote whatever kind of technology they wish. I myself have recently been to Turkey to help the local institutions of engineering there to implement their own activities.

The key problem is to change the minds of people. There are many problems, including that of population, and that is linked with religion. In the absence of a change of mind in the matter of population and some basic beliefs technology will not cope.

It is not so much technical education that is needed but the more basic kinds of education and awareness that 'we will all go together when we go'. As well as the population problem and the differing attitudes to religion there is also a cultural problem as to the proper division of labour. All three aspects are linked in many countries. What it is proper for the skilled person to do and the link between the professional and non-professional are key aspects. The inability to link professionals and non-professionals causes failure and disaster. I have visited several earthquake disaster areas where that matter is obviously the most important of all. The ability to link advanced technology to the workplace is not easy to achieve because of the basic culture of the countries concerned.

Waste is a word that I do not like because what is one man's waste is another man's resource. It seems to me that recycling is of the utmost importance.

Water is another key issue linked with politics and culture. I addressed the University of Bristol twenty years ago on the subject of dams and their consequences, with particular reference to the Central Africa Federation. I pointed out that the Kariba Dam had held the Federation together, that the Indus Valley project had prevented a war between Pakistan and India, and that the Aswan Dam had caused a war between Egypt and other countries, including the UK.

Another important point is that of afforestation. In Ankara, Turkey, on a site owned by the Middle East Technical University, 30 million trees were planted over 20 years on a 50 000 ha site and this has changed the climate there.